The Fall of
Baghdad

JON LEE ANDERSON

First published in the United States of America in 2004 by The Penguin Press
First published in Great Britain in 2005 by Little, Brown
This paperback edition published in 2006 by Abacus
Reprinted 2006

A CIP catalogue record for this book
is available from the British Library.

ISBN 0 349 11878 7

Printed and bound in Great Britain by
Clays Ltd, St Ives plc

Abacus
An imprint of
Little, Brown Book Group
Brettenham House
Lancaster Place
London WC2E 7EN

A member of the Hachette Livre Group of Companies

www.littlebrown.co.uk

To Erica, Bella, Rosie, and Máximo

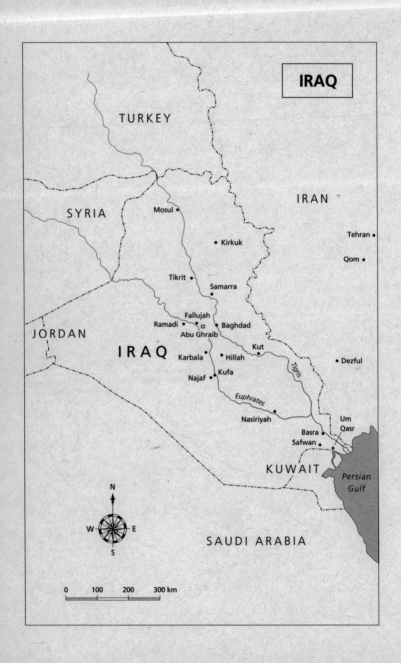

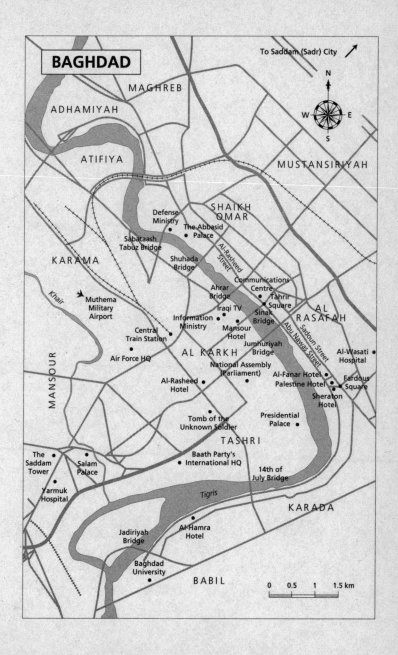

BAGHDAD

To Saddam (Sadr) City

N
W E
S

MAGHREB

ADHAMIYAH

ATIFIYA

MUSTANSIRIYAH

KARAMA

SHAIKH OMAR

Defense Ministry

The Abbasid Palace

Sabataash Tabuz Bridge

Shuhada Bridge

Al-Rasheed Street

Communications Centre

Ahrar Bridge

Iraqi TV

Tahrir Square

Muthema Military Airport

Khair

AL RASAFAH

Information Ministry

Sinak Bridge

Central Train Station

Mansour Hotel

Jumhuriyah Bridge

Abu Nawas Street

Sadoun Street

Air Force HQ

AL KARKH

National Assembly (Parliament)

Al-Wasati Hospital

Al-Rasheed Hotel

Al-Fanar Hotel
Palestine Hotel

Fardous Square

MANSOUR

Sheraton Hotel

Tomb of the Unknown Soldier

Presidential Palace

TASHRI

The Saddam Tower

Salam Palace

Baath Party's International HQ

14th of July Bridge

Yarmuk Hospital

Tigris

KARADA

Jadiriyah Bridge

Al-Hamra Hotel

Baghdad University

BABIL

0   0.5   1   1.5 km

Preface to the Paperback Edition

On the second anniversary of the fall of Baghdad, April 9, 2005, a large crowd of Shiite demonstrators gathered in the plaza where Saddam's statue had been pulled down by American troops two years earlier, and chanted: "No to America! No to Saddam! Yes to Islam!" It wasn't a new sign of the times, though. Only a few days into the American occupation of Iraq, angry demonstrators had gathered in the same spot to chant exactly the same slogan. At the time, the display of public outrage had seemed unprovoked and unwarranted, and most onlookers dismissed the protestors as a marginal group of malcontents. It was certainly bewildering to the young American troops on the scene, who still thought of themselves as the liberators of the Iraqi people.

It has taken time, and a great deal of bloodshed, to alter those early perceptions of America's role in Iraq—and those of its chief ally, Great Britain, as well. As things turned out, the violence did not end with Saddam's fall, but intensified to an almost unimaginable degree. To many, the gruesome scale of the carnage in the ongoing war has become a wall of white noise, its unending cruelties simply too much to grasp or absorb. Some cite the extremism of Iraq's insurgency as validation of the Anglo-American invasion—whatever the original motivation—and for a continued military presence in Iraq. Others believe the exact opposite, that Western intervention is what engendered hostilities in the first place, and that the only solution is a prompt withdrawal of British and American troops. But whatever their views, there must be few Americans and Britons living today who do not understand that, whatever it was meant to bring about, the invasion of Iraq has not yet ushered in a better life for Iraqis, nor, for that matter, for anyone else.

Instead, just as George W. Bush eventually declared it to be, Iraq has become the "central battleground" in the global War on Terror, a place where Islamist extremists from around the world have flocked to seek their martyrdom, joining forces with Iraqis who believe themselves to be fighting a war of resistance against foreign invaders. By late September 2005, with no end to the conflict in sight, over 1,900 Americans, 96 Britons, hundreds of people of other nationalities, and untold thousands of Iraqis had died in the fighting; many more had been wounded or crippled for life. But mounting casualties are not the only consequence of the Iraq misadventure. Iraq has also become a place where, as previously occurred in Vietnam and Kenya respectively, a new generation of Americans and Britons has been forced to confront the evidence of its own capacity for sadism—as shown by the photographed sexual torture and humiliation of Iraqi prisoners at Abu Ghraib prison, and in the periodic court martials for murders and other abuses committed in Iraq.

Iraq will one day emerge from the catastrophe that has enveloped it, although not without a great deal more of pain and suffering. In January 2005, the country held its first true elections in many decades. Several million Iraqis cast their votes despite threats of retaliation from the insurgents, and by doing so appeared to have lain the tenuous groundwork for a new, participatory civil society, in which Iraqis themselves—not tyrants, nor foreign powers—will decide their futures. At some point, too, no doubt, the United States and Great Britain will begin to withdraw their soldiers from Iraq. Once that happens, it will be easier to judge whether the Iraq invasion was a success, or—as it has seemed thus far—a calamitous failure.

This book is not about the current political situation in Iraq, however, nor is it an attempt to predict its future. History will continue to unfold in Iraq, and like all histories, Iraq's will have new and unexpected turns in the future. This is instead a personal eyewitness account of a particular time and place, a history of what I saw in Baghdad during the final years of Saddam Hussein's dictatorship; what happened there before, during and after the war that toppled Saddam in 2003, through the chaotic and troubled first year of the U.S. and British-led occupation. It is the story of what happened when Baghdad fell.

Preface

I first traveled to Iraq because of the phenomenon of Saddam Hussein. In a sense Saddam inhabited a mythological realm, like a throwback to Herod's day, when warrior kings reigned as semidivine creatures, malevolent and munificent all at once, capable of the greatest cruelties as well as the most extravagant gestures of patronage. There he was, at the dawn of the twenty-first century, a head of state who was indisputably a war criminal, an international fugitive who lived a clandestine life in his own nation and who survived in power thanks to—not in spite of—the terror he inspired in his people. Anything that could be said of Saddam had become, somehow, believable.

I wanted to witness Saddam's tyranny and to understand what made it work. I was also drawn by a feeling of certainty that there would inevitably be a new war between the United States and Iraq. It was something that had been preordained, I believed, since the Gulf War, when Iraq's army was defeated and yet Saddam had been allowed to remain in power. By the time George W. Bush was sworn into office in January 2001, it was clear that the UN sanctions regime that had held Saddam in check for the past decade had run its course and that a new means of dealing with him had to be found. As we now know, Bush had already decided that the best thing to do was to go to war and to get rid of Saddam Hussein.

This book is my account of that war, about what led up to it and what has happened in Iraq since it occurred. Iraq's story is still an unfolding one, of course, and now it has also become an American story. By invading and occupying Iraq, the United States has fused its destiny with Iraq's for the foreseeable future. What shape the relationship will take and how long it will last are things none of us can yet know, but so far it has been an unhappy encounter.

Most of all, this book is about a handful of people I came to know in the ancient city of Baghdad during one of the most tumultuous and decisive periods in its long history. When I first got to know them, they were inhabitants of Saddam's Iraq, and most had survived by collaborating in one way or another with the regime. The perverse beauty of Saddam's special brand of tyranny was that Iraqis were obliged to be participants in the very system that oppressed them. Most assuaged their consciences by telling themselves that they had no other alternative because they had families to support and to protect, and because the only other option was prison, exile, or perhaps death. A few of the Iraqis I came to know followed the latter path. For all of them, the drastic changes brought by the war and the fall of Saddam meant an abrupt end to the lives they had known until then. For some it represented a new beginning, but for others it was the end of the road. Their stories are here. In the ongoing trauma of post-Saddam Iraq, a new country is emerging, and each day brings with it new endings and new beginnings, and not just for Iraqis but for Americans too.

ONE

Nasser al-Sadoun lived in a secluded limestone villa on the outskirts of the Jordanian capital of Amman with his wife, Tamara, their two German shepherds, and a Sri Lankan maid named Daphne. From their house, they enjoyed a sweeping westerly view over a panorama of rolling stony hills dotted with scrub pines and olive trees. Just beyond the last of these hills, the land falls away into the deep cleft of the Great Rift Valley, where the river Jordan and the Dead Sea straddle the present-day border with Israel. When I first visited him, a few months before the Iraq War began, in early November 2002, Nasser proudly showed me around his living room, which was festooned with old muskets, swords, battleaxes, and other family heirlooms. He pointed out two of his most prized possessions, a pair of spiked bronze helmets that dated from the seventh-century Islamic wars that ensued after the Prophet Muhammad's proclamation of the birth of Islam in A.D. 610. On a sideboard stood a personal photograph of Iraq's ill-fated last king, Faisal II, shirtless, smiling, on water skis, taken not long before he was murdered along with most of his family in the revolution of 1958. On the walls hung framed portraits of other illustrious ancestors—sheikhs and pashas and royal guard commanders, all bearded, all wearing dashing robes with daggers—from the late nineteenth and early twentieth centuries, when Iraq was still called Mesopotamia.

Nasser, a handsome, silver-haired man in his late sixties, is a descendant of a legendary Sunni Muslim clan that once possessed its own sheikh-dom, called the Muntafiq, which had ruled over most of southern Iraq for four centuries. One of his great-uncles had served as prime minister of Iraq four times in the early twentieth century, and his Dagestani-born grandfather had been the commander of the king's army. Nasser is also a direct descendant—thirty-sixth in a direct line—of the Prophet Muhammad. He pointed out, teasingly, that the late King Hussein of Jordan, a distant relative of his, "was only forty-third." Nasser displayed a kind of rueful good humor about his family's decline and fall, attributing it to a woeful penchant for making bad choices: "We used to rule over an area in the south of Iraq that was larger than England and Wales put together. But we made one mistake, which was to side with the Turks against the British, and so we lost our land, our powers, and our land was distributed to other tribes. . . . One of my grandfathers took Kuwait, stayed a few days, and left again, saying: "It's not worth staying here." That was a few years before they discovered oil." Nasser chuckled and threw up his hands in a fatalistic way, with no trace of bitterness.

During Saddam Hussein's rise to power in the early seventies, Nasser and his wife, Tamara Daghestani, who is also his first cousin, moved to Jordan at the invitation of Crown Prince Hassan, and they never returned. Tamara became pregnant and gave birth to a son, and Nasser, an engineer who in Baghdad had helped run the central power station, Al-Doura, found employment with Jordan's electricity board and later as an adviser to the Arab Potash Company, where he worked until he retired, a few years before I met him. Nasser remained active, however, serving on the company's board of directors, and he still drove a company Mercedes. He was not rich, but he was comfortable, and he seemed quite content with his life. Once a year he and Tamara visited London to see friends and relatives who lived there, and

Nasser indulged himself buying old, out-of-print books about Iraq at London's rare book dealers.

I had just come back from a trip to Iraq, and I told Nasser about my visit. I had covered Saddam's so-called loyalty referendum, in which millions of Iraqis had been herded to polling stations around the country and told to sign either yes or no on ballot papers approving Saddam for another seven-year term in office. I had spent voting day in Saddam's hometown of Tikrit, where I witnessed groups of men dancing and chanting, "Yes, yes, yes to Saddam!" and then slashing their thumbs with razor blades in order to cast their yes votes in blood. I asked one of the polling officials what he thought the yes percentage would be. "All," he replied confidently. "Why?" I asked him. "Because the people are in love with Saddam Hussein," he explained. "Saddam Hussein is our spirit, our hearts, and the air we breathe. If the air goes, we will all die."

That same evening the polling results were ecstatically announced by Saddam's information minister: The dictator had received a resounding 100 percent yes vote. A day or two later Saddam expressed his gratitude to the Iraqi people for their loyalty by ordering the immediate release of all the prisoners held in the country's jails, except those accused of spying for the United States or the "Zionist entity," Israel. I had rushed out to Abu Ghraib, Iraq's largest and most notorious prison, near the city of Fallujah, and watched as thousands of bewildered inmates, some of whom had been held for many years, stumbled out of the horrid place into a melee of shouting, weeping people searching frantically for their relatives.

When I arrived, the prison gates were still shut, and a few prison officials stood around outside, still apparently unsure what they were supposed to do. A huge painting of an unsmiling Saddam Hussein wearing a fedora and firing off a rifle with one hand adorned a great concrete billboard at the main entrance. Within minutes, however, large numbers of Iraqi civilians, relatives of prisoners, began gathering on the road outside the entrance. Within an hour there were many hundreds of them. Most were yelling excitedly and jumping up and down and chanting praises to Saddam Hussein. A woman with white hair explained in fluent English that her husband was inside. He had served six months of a thirty-year sentence, she said, but she refused to say what he had been charged with. What were her feelings toward Saddam? "We love him, because he knows how to forgive the mistakes of his people," she replied, and moved away, looking worried. Behind her, the crowd was chanting, "Saddam, Saddam, we give our lives and blood for you," their fists pumping in the air. Some men were beating on drums. As I watched, a huge flatbed truck moved slowly past the throng on the road. On the flatbed lay a long cylindrical tube coated in green military paint, about the size of a Scud missile. No one seemed to notice. A man emerged from an administrative building and introduced himself to reporters as a judge, the chairman of the "prisoner release committee." Someone asked about the threat to society posed by such large numbers of released criminals, and he replied: "The state is like a father and will deal with this problem." Nearby, a man in a dishdasha robe began shooting a Kalashnikov repeatedly into the air.

Then the mob of relatives overcame the prison guards who had been trying to keep control at the gates and swept through into Abu Ghraib. I was carried along by the force of the crowd. Inside I could see the cellblocks in the distance, several hundred yards away across a vast empty space of rubbishy desert covered with mounds of earth and open holes. The relatives tore across this space, heading in different directions, everyone yelling and chanting. Seagulls wheeled around in the sky above. A repulsive stench hung in the air. I joined a group heading for a building directly across from the main gates of the prison. As I drew nearer, the stench intensified. Here and there were prisoners, wearing dishdashas and looking gaunt, bearing bundles of clothing, trudging out toward the gates. Some were accompanied by healthy-looking people who must have been their relatives, many of whom were weeping and kissing and embracing them. One man came past me carrying a wasted-looking young man, perhaps his brother, who looked to be near death. A couple of old men came past, looking completely lost and disoriented, dragging their belongings on the ground behind them by ropes.

At the end of the great dirt space, the crowd I was in came to a large wall with an arched tunnel-like driveway, and we moved through it to the other side. I found myself in a rectangle of filthy desert surrounded by walls and caged entrances leading to cellblocks on all sides. To one side, I saw the source of the stench. It was a gigantic mound of garbage. It was, I calculated, about the size of a very large family house and looked as though it had been piling up for years. The odor it gave off was stomach-churning.

The scene inside was one of complete anarchy. Men and boys ran across the yard, climbing onto cellblock roofs, tearing aside loops of razor wire to gain access, all the while yelling at the top of their lungs. Confused groups of men and women ran back and forth, and a few guards also ran around waving and yelling in Arabic. It was difficult to know whether the men on the rooftops were prisoners or relatives. I caught glimpses of some prisoners staring out from the bars of upper stories of the cellblocks. Human shit clung like caked mud to the razor wire that was looped outside their barred windows. As I stood watching, Giovanna Botteri, an attractive blond reporter for RAI 3 television, came up to me. She was wearing skintight white Armani jeans and a white shirt. Her cameraman was caught up in the mob, she told me, and she was getting felt up by the men. She asked me to help her. A plainclothes Iraqi agent of some sort approached; clearly agitated about Giovanna's presence, he told me to get her out of there. Groups of young men had quickly gathered around us, like wolves, commenting and laughing and pointing at Giovanna excitedly. She hooked one hand into the belt at the back of my trousers, and we began to move through the mob, as the agent moved protectively ahead of us, pointing to openings in the throng and shouting at the men around us. Now and then some of the men moved in, and I could feel Giovanna flinch, or yell, as they grabbed her. At one point she quipped, "I don't think it was a good day to wear Armani."

We found ourselves back near the tunnel-like opening in the wall. It was blocked by a mob of men. The helpful plainclothes agent had vanished. There were some guards there, beating men back to clear the driveway, and they began to scatter. When we approached, one of the guards began pushing me. I pushed him back and yelled at him, and he pushed me again. A pickup truck appeared with a couple of soldiers on the back, and I forced my way onto it, with Giovanna still attached. The pickup accelerated and braked crazily into the tunnel. On the other side of the wall, one of the soldiers forced us off. A minute or two later, after more scuffling, we emerged from the mob and back out into the great open space, where hundreds of prisoners were moving toward the open gates of the entrance. We joined them.

In Baghdad, a couple of days later, a crowd of Iraqis who said they were the relatives of missing prisoners gathered in front of the Information Ministry, where the Foreign Press Office was located. They had made their way through Baghdad's streets shouting praises of Saddam, but when they came within earshot of journalists, they made it clear that they were upset their relatives had not appeared when the others were freed. Such a protest was an unprecedented event in Saddam's Iraq. Before journalists were able to interview anyone, however, the officials at the ministry mustered guards with guns to disperse the group. The next day guards were posted around the ministry, and the ministry's senior officials were all in a foul mood. They were especially furious with CNN, which had transmitted a live broadcast of the protest. Within days the network's bureau chief, Jane Arraf, was ordered out of the country.

A night or two later, in an interview with Saddam's deputy prime minister, Tariq Aziz, I questioned the wisdom of suddenly releasing so many prisoners, including thousands of common criminals, onto Iraq's streets. In between puffs on a Cuban cigar, Aziz replied smoothly: "The families of those prisoners had demonstrated their loyalty to the president, you see, and so we had to reciprocate their faithfulness. The president has asked their families to correct these men, and I am sure many of them will support him and fight for him. A president like Saddam Hussein would not release tens of thousands of prisoners if he felt threatened by them. If we were afraid of the prisoners, we could surround the prison with tanks and massacre everyone. But we didn't. We believe in God. We are like Jesus Christ, who pardoned the people who crucified him."

The stage-managed dramas taking place in Iraq occurred as the American and British buildup to war was gathering pace; I had left Baghdad wondering what to make of it all. After hearing my stories, Nasser al-Sadoun chuckled and told me that I had nothing to feel perplexed about. The episodes I had witnessed, he said, were merely the latest of many similar acts of political theater put on by Saddam to demonstrate to the world that he was a popular leader, while reinforcing his control at home, and that was that. As for what Iraqis truly felt about things, he said, it was impossible to know as long as Saddam remained in power. Everyone was simply too afraid to speak his mind.

Nasser predicted that an American-led war on Iraq was inevitable and that Saddam would lose, but he warned: "The Americans themselves should not take things into their hands, you know, because the Iraqis cannot stand foreigners. Something to know about Iraqis is that you can win them over fast and you also lose them very fast. Individually they are very nice people, but you cannot know what they will do as a group. If the Americans come, they should not stay and try to run the Iraqis and decide things for them. They should put in any government they can find, and then they should leave."

Nasser told the story of how his own great-uncle, Abdul Mohsen al-Sadoun, who had been one of Iraq's early prime ministers, had committed suicide in 1929 because of his inability to secure fuller sovereignty from the British, who had retained neo-colonial treaty powers in Iraq after granting independence in 1920. "He'd been promised full independence by Great Britain," Nasser told me, "but when this didn't happen, he was accused of betrayal in the parliament. So he went home and killed himself. You see, the thing about Iraqis is they are very proud of their responsibilities, but if there is someone else in charge, they don't care about anything. So put the Iraqis in charge."

Over the coming months Nasser's words of warning stayed with me, festering away like a seer's prophecy. The war had indeed come to seem increasingly inevitable, and to judge from the remarks being made by U.S. officials, so did some kind of postwar military occupation of Iraq. As an American who had come of age during the traumatic years of the Vietnam War and the "never again" psychology that followed it, I regarded the prospect of an uninvited U.S. military force invading and then occupying a foreign country as extremely disquieting.

Like anyone else who had visited Iraq in the era of Saddam Hussein, I knew it to be a house of horrors. Saddam's regime was without a doubt the most terrifying tyranny I had ever seen up close. The only real evidence I had of its crimes was what I had read in books and newspaper accounts and human rights reports, but there was also the eloquently deadly pall of silence I had found inside Iraq, where no one ever dared say anything against Saddam. Such a silence, I understood, could come only from an extraordinary degree of fear. On a handful of occasions I had been given fleeting glimpses of people's true feelings.

Once, when I was walking on my own around Baghdad's thieves' bazaar, where old curios and coins and contraband CDs were sold, a young vendor in his mid-twenties called me into his tiny shop and invited me to sit down and have some tea with him. After waving away several curious onlookers, he asked me where I was from, and when I told him the United States, he brightened and gave me a thumbs-up sign. "America is good!" he said. Then, noticing that I was wearing a wristwatch with the face of Che Guevara on it, he asked curiously: "Che Guevara was in conflict with the United States, wasn't he? Doesn't wearing that get you into trouble with the American authorities?" I told the shopkeeper that in the United States such a thing was not a crime. If I wanted to, I said, I could go around saying that Saddam was good and that Clinton was bad, and the police could do nothing to me. His eyes widened in surprise, and then, with a broad smile, he quipped: "So, the American system is the same as Iraq's!" He wiggled his eyebrows theatrically. "Here in Iraq—" He stopped speaking, held out his arms with his wrists together, as if handcuffed, then flailed one arm in a violent beating motion. Bending over and placing his mouth close to my ear, he whispered: "Mukhabarat"—Iraq's all-pervasive intelligence service—and sat back in his chair.

I said, a little lamely: "*Inshallah,* if God wills, things will change."

"No," he replied softly. "Maybe in America things change, but not in the Middle East. Nothing ever changes in the Middle East."

I couldn't argue with the young shopkeeper's cynicism. Within his lifetime, nothing had changed, not in Iraq anyway. In spite of Iraq's dauntingly old pedigree as "the cradle of human civilization," and in spite—some would say because—of its immense oil wealth and strategic location as the Middle East's ultimate buffer state, its people had never known democracy. In 1932, when the colonial British withdrew from the fractious territory they had seized sixteen years earlier from the Ottoman Turks, who had ruled it for the previous four centuries, they left behind a handpicked Hashemite monarchy to look after their interests, which included a controlling role in the fledgling Iraqi oil industry. But in 1958 Iraq's royal family was butchered in an anti-Western revolution spearheaded by nationalist Iraqi officers. In 1968 the regime they installed was in turn violently overthrown by the Arab Baath Socialist Party, the Iraqi offshoot of the ultranationalist pan-Arabist Baath Party that had been founded in Syria in the 1940s. Thirty-one-year-old Saddam Hussein al-Tikriti, a veteran Baathist conspirator with one aborted magnicide attempt to his credit, became Iraq's vice president, serving under his cousin Hassan al-Bakr. Saddam soon became Iraq's real strongman, however, and in 1979 he dispensed with his cousin altogether and assumed power for himself. Immediately afterward Saddam launched a bloody purge of his potential foes within the Baath Party, and he had held a firm grip on power ever since, showing himself to be one of the world's wiliest and most ruthless political survivors. In that time Saddam had also refashioned Iraq to suit his own whims, and the results were downright stupefying.

Baghdad is an unrelievedly earth-colored city, its drab vistas broken only by the occasional peacock blue and golden domes of mosques, which glisten prettily in the sun, and by the dusty stands of eucalyptus and date palms that seem to grow everywhere, cushioning the skyline with a feathery gray-green fringe. Otherwise, there are few soft edges to Baghdad; most of it is a harshly modernist geometry of brown squares, rectangles, and concrete spires. During the seventies and eighties, in a modernization campaign reminiscent of Ceauşescu's in Romania,

Saddam had some of the city's oldest neighborhoods—ancient mud and stone buildings with arched wooden doors and windows and hanging balconies—torn down and replaced by uniform blocks of buildings in a style that is described in Baghdad as New Islamic. It is a form of architecture characterized by a preponderance of stylized archways, columns, and minarets, all of it hewn out of unpainted slab concrete or else, more felicitously, dressed up with fascias of ivory-colored limestone.

Coursing between concreted banks, the gray-green waters of the Tigris River flow southward through the heart of Baghdad in a great meandering loop. On the river's east bank lies the commercial heart of the city, with its frenetic souks and bazaars, while to the west spreads a vast complex of parklands, government buildings, presidential palaces, and several of the great public monuments Saddam erected over the years. These are places built on an epic, almost pharaonic scale, and many have a vindictively necromantic spirit to them, because most of them consecrate death in one form or another. The first time I saw Baghdad, I was struck by the thought that if Saddam were somehow reincarnated as an American and given free rein in Washington, D.C., the graves of Arlington Cemetery would probably have been exhumed and transplanted to the Mall and the trees there chopped down to make way for wide new roads to hold military parades; then a three-mile stretch of the Potomac River, say, from Ronald Reagan National Airport to Georgetown, would be sealed off with security fences and guarded by men with guns with orders to shoot any intruders on sight. Finally, the Washington Monument would be rechristened as the Glorious Victory over Vietnam, and the ground at its base artfully littered with thousands of bronzed coolie hats for visitors to stamp on.

Saddam's Tomb of the Unknown Soldier was a man-made knoll of sculpted concrete crowned by a half-open lid that looked like a flying saucer but was intended to resemble a soldier's helmet. At night, the tomb was illuminated by hundreds of fluorescent strip lights showing the white, red, and green colors of the Iraqi national flag and was visible for miles around. Hanging suspended in a chamber underneath the great helmet was a coffin containing an anonymous Iraqi soldier's body, and below it was a subterranean gallery where visitors could view dead soldiers' uniforms and an arsenal of arms used by Iraqi warriors over the centuries, ranging from maces and swords used by seventh-century Islamic crusaders to the brace of automatic weapons fired by Saddam Hussein in his failed attempt to kill Prime Minister Abdul Karim Qassem in 1959.

Across a stretch of parkland from the tomb was Saddam's so-called Hands of Victory Pavilion, a mile-long marching ground that was guarded at both ends by identical sets of giant human arms made of bronze, based on a cast made of Saddam's own extremities. The arms held swords that were crossed overhead to form triumphal archways. From each of these massive arms hung large nets that were filled with hundreds of authentic Iranian soldiers' helmets, many of them perforated by bullets. Others had been set into the surface of the road itself, shiny metal bulges, which gleamed in the sunlight and were meant to be driven over and trodden upon.

One of Saddam's more recent creations, completed after the Gulf War, was the Triumph Leader Museum. It was located under Baghdad's new clock tower, a samovar-shaped structure that rose in a high spire from parklands near the Hands of Victory. Inside the hollow clock tower, a pendulum, inexplicably decorated with four gilded Kalashnikovs, swung slowly back and forth over a floor of inlaid marble. Around the base of the chamber, seven large galleries housed the eclectic collection of gifts received by Saddam from friends, admirers, and foreign heads of state over the years. When I visited the museum for the first time, in 2000, the exhibit included a pair of decorative riding spurs that, according to the museum labels, were a 1986 gift from Ronald Reagan; a collection of guayabera shirts from Fidel Castro; a pair of massive ivory elephant tusks from the former Chadian dictator Hissène Habré; a diamond- and ruby-encrusted gold Patek Philippe watch from the sultan of Bahrain; and ceremonial swords from Jacques Chirac and Vladimir Zhirinovsky. There were also a pair of gold-plated grenades and a matching .45 automatic pistol from Muammar Qaddafi and a gorgeous double-barreled shotgun and sniper scope from the chief of Russia's intelligence service.

A special attraction, which the curator excitedly pointed out for me, was an old, long-barreled flintlock that he told me had been used to kill "the famous British spy Leachman." Colonel Gerard Leachman was a British military intelligence officer, a colleague of T. E. Lawrence's and Gertrude Bell's. Leachman was shot in the back and killed by a sheikh's son during the 1920 anticolonial revolt by Iraqi tribesmen. The killer's family had kept the murder weapon for many years, the curator told me, but had given it to Saddam as a gift not long before. From the curator's reverential tone, I surmised that the weapon held a certain pride of place in Saddam's gift collection. My personal favorite, however, was a weeping porcelain elephant, of the kind one sees in rural American gift shops. Next to it was a handwritten note in English to Saddam, dated 1997, and signed by someone named Ruth Lee Roy, which read, "This is a crying elephant, but we want you to be happy."

In the gallery called Um al-Marik (Mother of All Battles)— Saddam's moniker for the Gulf War—hung a wall-mounted electronic map of the Middle East. When it was lit up, red flashes pinpointed all of the places hit by Iraq's Scud missiles during the Gulf War, and the score was tallied below. As the curator obligingly pointed out to me, according to Saddam's tally, fifty missiles had landed on allied forces in Saudi Arabia, while forty-three more had landed in Israel. Nearby, in a glass cabinet, several letters of loyalty from Iraqis to Saddam were displayed.

Each of the letters had been written in the author's own blood. In gold-leaf lettering, etched into the marble wall of the final gallery, named Al-Abid after one of Iraq's ballistic missiles, a quotation from Saddam was translated into English: "The clock chimes away for time to keep record of men and women, some leaving behind the mark of great and lofty souls, while others leave naught but the remains of worm-eaten bones. . . . As for martyrs, they are alive in the Heavens, ever immortal in the presence of God. No heritage is worthier or more sublime than theirs."

In such ways Saddam had been building his legacy, quite literally out of bricks and mortar. This had been going on for many years, but since the Gulf War he had embarked on a palace-building obsession of truly gargantuan proportions. During the 1990s he had built dozens of them, all over the country. Without a doubt, these palaces were the most surreal aspect of life in Iraq, because they were everywhere, and invariably enormous, but people didn't acknowledge them. As was required of all foreign journalists, when I arrived in Baghdad in 2000, I was assigned a Ministry of Information "guide" and interpreter, who thereafter accompanied me virtually everywhere I went. My guide was a thirty-year-old Kurd, Salaar Mustafa, a thin, intelligent, chain-smoking man with an English-language degree from Baghdad University. Salaar was voluble about most things but always fell silent whenever we drove past one of Saddam's palaces, as was often, and usually feigned deafness when I asked him what the buildings were. If I insisted, he would reply briskly: "A guest-house."

Iraqis carefully adhered to a set of rules regarding what could or couldn't be said about the president and his family. Some of the rules were self-imposed, but others were official. Verbally insulting the president, for example, was a crime that carried the death sentence. This kind of punishment understandably had a dampening effect on discussion of nearly everything to do with Saddam, and his palaces were unanimously understood to be a taboo topic. In practice, what this meant was that the palaces had become, as in the old fable about the emperor's clothes, places you saw but pretended not to see, and which you certainly didn't talk about, at least not in loud voices or to people you didn't completely trust.

The exteriors of Saddam's palaces were immense and forbidding and, like his monuments, had the effect of making ordinary mortals seem antlike in their insignificance. Most of them were protected by high cement walls, made of identical plaques engraved with his initials in Arabic script, and were guarded from intrusion by soldiers in sandbagged machine-gun nests, massive sentry towers, and blockaded entrances. One of the Baghdad palaces was crowned by a vast limestone dome, beneath which stone parapets jutted out in a horizontal star design. Perched at the points of each star were four identical gilded bronze busts of Saddam himself, staring out vigilantly over the city beyond and wearing what appeared to be winged helmets, but were actually, I learned, representations of Jerusalem's Dome of the Rock mosque. In the main Republican Palace complex, where there were several more palaces, one was similarly guarded by several towering busts of Saddam, but these effigies were faced inward, their backs turned to the outside world.

One day, when I was the lone visitor to a fish restaurant on the east bank of the Tigris, opposite the Republican Palace complex, the owner silently motioned me over to the rear door of his establishment. Opening it wide, he pointed to a high chain-link fence that ran just behind the building, separating it from the edge of the riverbank. He pointed across the fence to the other side of the river, where I was able to make out the minarets and cupolas of several large palaces. "All of this is Saddam's," he explained, with a wide wave that took in the river and both of its banks. He informed me that the presidential complex stretched for several miles and that nobody was permitted anywhere near the river on either side. I noticed that his rear garden was neglected and overgrown, and I asked if he ever walked over to the perimeter fence, which stood about twenty feet away. He raised his eyebrows in a look of disbelief and exclaimed: "No! Never!" In a quick and impromptu pantomime, he acted out a scene in which he forced a man roughly to his knees and then shot him in the back of the head. Then, dramatically, he turned and slammed shut the door that opened onto the rear garden and ushered me back to the front of the restaurant. Afterward, driving farther along the riverside drive, I could see that, indeed, for a couple of miles the strip of park that lay between the road and the river opposite Saddam's estate was unkempt and devoid of people. In one place a public sculpture depicting several maidens dancing in a circle was almost swallowed up by a thicket of tall yellow weeds. Several of the maidens were missing arms, and one was decapitated.

Another day, when I was with my guide, Salaar, visiting an art gallery across town, I noticed several towering construction cranes jutting into the sky nearby. They were positioned around a gigantic unfinished concrete structure with several domes. I recognized it as one of the sites of Saddam's new mosques. He was building two mosques, and together they would represent his greatest construction project ever. The larger of the two mosques was supposed to become the Middle East's biggest, second only to the Great Mosque of Mecca, when it was completed, while the other one would be the biggest in Iraq. The building I was looking at was the smaller of the two, going up on the site of Baghdad's former racetrack, which Saddam had razed a few years earlier. When I asked Salaar if I could take a photograph of the site, he told me no. It was against the rules. No one, he said, could photograph the mosque until it was completed—or even discuss it, for that matter. "Please don't insist," he begged me.

Incredulous, I said: "You mean you and I can both see it, but we have to pretend it's not there?" Salaar nodded vigorously, and from the tense expression on his face I could see that he was perfectly serious.

A decade after Iraq's Gulf War defeat, in the period referred to officially as the Era of Saddam Hussein, Saddam himself had become invisible as a public figure, seen by his people only on nightly television, depicted meeting with the members of his Revolutionary Command Council in anonymous, windowless rooms or greeting well-wishers in one of his palaces. He made almost no public appearances, and when he did, they were never announced beforehand. He simply appeared and then vanished again—like the visitation of a divinity. At the same time Saddam was everywhere. On the avenue leading into Baghdad from Saddam International Airport a sign greeted visitors: WELCOME TO THE CAPITAL OF ARAB SADDAM. There was a Saddam River, Saddam Dam, and a Saddam City. His visage adorned the faces of wristwatches, radios, and wall clocks. On the facades of every public building, inside every shop and every home I visited, hung portraits of Saddam. Throughout the country there were thousands of larger-than-life depictions of Saddam, painted on huge billboards; vast oil canvases, inlaid in glazed mosaic tiles set onto concrete plaques; in granite, bronze, and gilded busts and statues. He was seen standing, right arm raised aloft in commandment; praying piously; mounted, sword raised, on prancing stallions. He was smiling, frowning, shooting off guns, smoking cigars, wearing a black leather greatcoat and matching trilby; in military uniforms and in Arab robes, in three-piece Western suits, even, oddly, in Alpine climbing gear. In some renditions, Saddam was thin, or imposingly muscular, while in others, he was obese, his face pouchy and double-chinned. He was seen wearing the robes of justice and balancing the scales in his hands, holding court like a biblical patriarch as men, women, and children swooned in his presence; in doctor's whites; dandling small children fondly on his knee; standing with bloodied sword over a mutilated serpent, its tail transmogrified into a U.S. cruise missile. On one building, eight identical smiling Saddams were set together in a cultish repetition not unlike Warhol's *Marilyn Diptych*.

Iraq's art czar was Mokhaled Mukhtar, a middle-aged man with an Einsteinesque frizz of hair who, he told me proudly in 2000, put in twelve-hour days as the director of the Saddam Arts Center, a large gray concrete building done in the New Islamic style and part of a large complex of similar buildings erected in the heart of Old Baghdad. I counted six different portraits of Saddam in Mukhtar's large, art-filled office. He informed me that as the official patron of Iraqi artists, he thought of his job as a labor of true love and that in his task, he enjoyed the full support of President Saddam Hussein. "Upon assuming power, the president said that artists are like politicians; both help nurture and promote society," said Mukhtar. "If a society does not have artists, you cannot have wise politicians. So art in Iraq has flourished because of the direct support of the president." When I asked him about the plethora of public art dedicated to Saddam, Mukhtar explained that Iraq's artists liked to paint the president because he was "the national symbol." As a child, said Mukhtar, he had painted pictures of other heroes of his imagination—he named Burt Lancaster and Clark Gable—but now Saddam had replaced them. "Today this same love and imagination have expanded to the point where they allow us to express our love for the president."

Mukhtar began to list some of Saddam's achievements, which he seemed to think were nothing short of miraculous. For instance, he told me, when he was a young boy growing up in the northern province of Nineveh, there had been only two secondary schools, but now there were two hundred. At that time, he went on, Iraq's population had been small, only seven million people. "But now we are twenty-two million, even after twenty years of killing! How can anyone explain that? Is there any one person who symbolizes this?" Mukhtar pointed to an easel standing near his desk. On it was a painting of Saddam's face set against an intricate backdrop of ancient Sumerian cuneiform symbols. It was, he told me, one of his own paintings. "If you'd been here before the revolution, you would be as proud of Saddam as I am now."

A few nights later, I visited the home of an Iraqi painter, Kassim Mussin Hassan. His living room was decorated with his own art, mostly oils of prancing Arab stallions and scarfed women carrying earthen jugs of water or paddling boats in the southern marshes. He explained that his style was from the "realist school" of Iraqi art. Hassan showed me a ream of photographs of his other works, including one of a vast canvas of a fat Saddam in robes. It was his greatest work. Hassan said that the painting was eighteen feet long by twelve feet wide and that he had been commissioned to paint it by the Baath Party headquarters in a western Iraqi town. It had taken him three weeks to complete. He had painted it on the flat roof of his house, and when he finished, it was lowered with a crane from his roof onto a truck. Noticing a framed photograph of Hassan standing with Saddam, who was beaming and had one hand on his shoulder, I asked him about the encounter. He explained that he had been summoned to meet Saddam after he had sent him one of his paintings—of a woman cutting reeds in the marshes with a stallion in the background—for Saddam's fifty-ninth birthday, in 1996. "Saddam called me by my name," said Hassan. "And he told me that he had been following my career. I was face-to-face with him, and I had the urge to embrace him, but I couldn't. He has very strong eyes. You feel that there are many Iraqis in his eyes, that his eyes hold the struggle for the Arab homeland in them, and that he is farsighted and can read what you think.

He exudes self-confidence, and this makes you feel strong too, just like him."

For most Iraqis, Saddam was an all-seeing, all-knowing, and all-powerful eminence who lived in their midst but existed beyond their ken. Like the subjects of a wrathful god, they paid him homage to invoke his attention, his compassion, and his mercy. An Iraqi writer, choosing his words carefully, advised me to look to ancient Mesopotamia as a means of understanding the cult of Saddam. "People who come from the West, where the reality is today and tomorrow, and the past is irrelevant or hardly exists, are wrong to perceive Iraq in the same measure. Here past has created the present and continues to be a part of it. Here the first gods with human faces were created. There were gods for water, for agriculture, and so on. I think of them as Saddam's ministers. There was a link between heaven and earth in these gods, and they set off the tradition of treating kings as gods. Divinity lies in the intermingling of heaven and earth. It may be a way to explain what you are seeing in Iraq."

As the ruins of Ur, Nineveh, and Babylon bear witness, Iraq has a very old culture indeed, and an archaeological history dating back some ten thousand years. Iraq was the seat of the Sumerians and Assyrians as well as the Abbasid dynasty and, long before them all, of humankind's first organized settlements. The ancient Iraqis were the creators of the wheel; of the world's earliest-known handwriting, the cuneiform alphabet; of its first written epic, *Gilgamesh;* and of its first recorded code of laws, in which Hammurabi's concept of an "eye for an eye" was set down for eternity. Alexander the Great died in Iraq, as did Prophet Muhammad's son-in-law Imam Ali and Ali's son Husein of Shia devotion, and it was the birthplace of Nebuchadnezzar, of Salahuddin the Conqueror, and of the biblical Jewish patriarch Abraham. It seemed a cruel irony that after such a history, the Iraqis had ended up with Saddam Hussein.

Only Saddam's most self-confident apparatchiks dared talk openly about him, and even they found it difficult to deny his brutality categorically. They spoke euphemistically about how he was "tough," or "strong," while offering up fawning endorsements of his tyranny as the ideal form of tough-love regime required by Iraqis. "Iraq needs a strong ruler," my minder, Salaar, once told me. "This country is like a wild horse, and it needs a tough trainer. Even if he has made some mistakes, it's better to have someone strong like Saddam than someone who is weak."

I soon learned that Salaar's comment was an approved aphorism among the regime's flunkies. "The Iraqi people love Saddam Hussein," Tariq Aziz assured me in an interview on my first visit. "Saddam Hussein is tough when toughness is needed and kind when kindness is needed. He jokes, he listens to you; this is important for a leader." Aziz shared what he said were the secrets of Saddam's survival in power. "The Iraqi people have, since Babylon, toppled the leaders they didn't like, and they have done it in this century. Saddam Hussein has been the leader of Iraq for thirty-two years, and the people know him. They endure all of the difficult circumstances because they love and support their leader. Some say it is because he has a Republican Guard and a Mukhabarat, but history tells us that it would be these same people who would topple him."

Aziz delicately skirted the issue of Saddam's frequent purges of his security forces and intelligence services, as well as the fact that all the most sensitive senior commands were occupied by his blood relatives, but he went on to recount, rather enthusiastically, a litany of the insider conspiracies, assassinations, and military coups d'état in Iraq's history. When he had finished, he asked me, perkily: "So, how can this man keep everything intact if he doesn't have the support of his guards and army? Because he is not boxed into power, he travels, he presides over the government, and the people like him for that. You know, over half of all Iraqis are Shia Muslims, and for years, Iran told them to topple

Saddam, and they regarded that as an insult. And I'm sure they feel the same way about the Americans' telling the Iraqis to topple their president. And Saddam is also popular as an Arab leader to Muslims and to people throughout the third world; it doesn't matter if he's not popular in Chicago and the Côte d'Azur! Did you know that hundreds of Nigerians have named their children Saddam, and they don't even know what it means?" Aziz paused dramatically and leaned toward me. "I'll tell you, it means 'heroism.'" Later, out of curiosity, I looked up the meaning of Saddam myself; according to most of the references I examined, the name translates as "He who confronts." Fair enough.

Other Iraqis offered up personal stories to illustrate Saddam's capacity for mercy. I was treated to one such account by Behjet Shakir, who had been secretary-general of Iraq's Baath Party back in the late fifties, when Saddam was still just a young party militant. A white-haired man of seventy-two, Shakir was living in peaceful retirement when I met him in August 2000. He lived with his family in an apartment in Mansour, a good neighborhood of Baghdad, but he clearly had very little money. His apartment was sparsely furnished, and its walls were unpainted and dirty. An old black-and-white television sat in a corner. I asked Shakir what Saddam had been like in the old days. Shakir complied, telling me that in addition to Saddam's "bravery and determination," he had been an avid reader of books of history and politics. "He was always wanting to expand his knowledge," said Shakir. He recalled an occasion when he and Tariq Aziz had been sitting around discussing psychology, and Saddam, who had been listening in, asked them to recommend some books for him on the topic. Shakir lent him some books on collective psychology. "A few days later," Shakir said, in a marveling tone, "Saddam was arguing with us as if he were a professor of psychology!" I asked Shakir if he thought Saddam had changed since those early days. He said that Saddam hadn't changed at all, except that perhaps that he was "even wiser."

Shakir added: "It is important to mention that he is very strict and tough when he wants to implement justice. But when he does, I can see a tear in his eye, because of the human drama."

I asked Shakir what he meant by that, and he proceeded to tell me a tangled tale about how, years before, during one of Saddam's purges, a friend who was suspected of treason had taken refuge in his house and how this had become known to the Mukhabarat, the secret police. It had posed a terrible dilemma for him, Shakir recalled, because he didn't want to betray his friend, in whose innocence he believed, by forcing him to leave his house, but he didn't want his Baath Party standing, or his patriotism, placed in jeopardy either. So he went to see Saddam and told him of his predicament. After hearing Shakir out, Saddam had reassured him by telling him that as long as his friend chose to remain in his house, he would not send in the Mukhabarat to capture him. But if he gave himself up, Saddam promised, he would not be tortured. Eventually, Shakir said, his friend had "voluntarily" left his home and given himself up, and later, after his innocence had been proved, he had been released. The episode had ended happily and, for Shakir, represented solid evidence of Saddam's humanity.

In the end, after speaking with dozens of Iraqis over several weeks, I concluded that if there was a common denominator to all of them, it was that they seemed utterly terrified of Saddam Hussein and of the horrible fate that might befall them if they spoke out of turn. An Iraqi man highly placed in Saddam's entourage, who was contacted on my behalf through an intermediary, toyed for several days with the idea of speaking to me. But he eventually declined and sent word back that he had decided not to because he was afraid that if he did, he might "fall down some stairs." I came away harboring no doubts whatsoever about Saddam's megalomaniacal despotism or his great cruelty.

Like most people, I also believed that Saddam probably still did possess some hidden chemical and biological weapons and that if he felt threatened, he was perfectly capable of using them, just as he had in the past. I also knew that the UN sanctions regime imposed on Iraq after the Gulf War had crumbled significantly and that without an effective means by the international community to contain him in the future, Saddam would probably try to reassert himself militarily. In the interview I'd had with Tariq Aziz in 2000, the deputy prime minister had told me unrepentantly that he didn't think Iraq's invasion of Kuwait had been a mistake and hinted that it could well happen again. "We should've done it in the seventies or the eighties," he quipped. "It would've been easier." He laughed. "We are not idiots, you know. We did not want to take over Kuwait; we wanted to create a situation that was better for us and better for them. . . . We didn't want the Kuwaitis' oil; we have so much of it we're sick of it! We wanted more shoreline." Aziz acknowledged that Iraq had formally recognized Kuwait's sovereignty after the Gulf War, under duress, but said he did not see this as a permanent situation. "We will honor the commitment we made when we signed the UN cease-fire resolution, which was imposed on us, but the next generation may erase it. It was a big mistake for Kuwait to do this. But we'll honor our commitments, if they do."

As for Iraq's differences with the United States, Aziz was preeningly self-assured. "We are ready to get into substantive dialogue to improve our relations with the United States," he said. "But the United States is afraid to get into a substantive dialogue with us. Because if they argue that we have weapons of mass destruction, we have evidence to show that this is exaggerated." Aziz paused to smile as I pondered his use of the word *exaggerated,* instead of *untrue.* Aziz seemed to be implying that Iraq still had caches of dangerous weapons. "Are we a threat?" he continued rhetorically. "This too can be resolved by sitting down and resolving things with dialogue and by talking things through." It was time, said Aziz, for the United States to get back on board and restore its relations with Iraq. Everybody else was. The situation had changed in the last ten years, and now it was the United States, not Iraq, that was isolated. "The sanctions," he concluded triumphantly, "are gradually collapsing."

This was the kind of hubris coming out of Baghdad prior to the attacks on September 11. After the U.S. War on Terror had begun, and with it, the renewed pressure for Iraq to come clean on its weapons of mass destruction, Tariq Aziz's tone changed. He and every other senior Iraqi government figure now vehemently denied that Iraq had any such weaponry left and scornfully repudiated all allegations to the contrary. But whatever the truth about Saddam's illegal weapons, I was unconvinced by the Bush administration's newfound arguments that Saddam was somehow linked to Al Qaeda or that urgent military action against his regime was justified as part of the War on Terror. I also believed that the moral capital for action by the West against Saddam had long since been squandered. I still recalled the deep sense of shame that I had felt, as an American, when, after Iraq's defeat in the Gulf War in 1991, the first President Bush had done nothing to halt Saddam's slaughter of tens of thousands of Shiites in reprisal for their popular uprising against him. If there had ever been a moment when humanitarian intervention in Iraq was justified, that was it. Or for that matter, a couple of years earlier, when Saddam was known to be gassing the Kurds.

In the intervening years, American policy toward Iraq had lapsed into one of aggressive containment, with U.S. and British warplanes flying daily sorties, and sometimes bombing targets, over the two no-fly zones established in the north and south of the country. In that time there had been virtually no benign Western influence in Iraq that was visible, and the vacuum had been filled by Saddam's unrelenting propaganda machine. On August 8, 2000, for instance, the twelfth anniversary of the end of the Iran-Iraq War, Saddam appeared on Iraqi television to remind his subjects of their "great victory" over "those who wished our people ill and our nation harm, backed by international Zionism, imperialism and the wicked Jews in the occupied land." Saddam then turned his ire on Saudi Arabia and the other gulf states providing bases to the U.S. and British warplanes patrolling the no-fly zones. "The planes of the aggressors take off from their land and territorial waters to bomb the citadel of the Arabs and the cradle of Abraham and to destroy the property of the Iraqis and to kill them all—men, women and children. Is there any other way than this to describe treachery and disgrace? May evil befall them, for evil indeed are the deeds they do!"

As I had learned, Saddam's utterances instantly became official doctrine, and were echoed at every level of society by his Baath Party ideologues. One of those ideologues was Nasra al-Sadoun. She was a woman in her late fifties with short-cropped hair, the editor in chief of the state-run English-language *Iraq Daily,* a poorly translated rag of a thing with a little box on its title banner that contained words of wisdom from Saddam. One of the more popular aphorisms, which I saw reprinted many times in the lead-up to the war, was something Saddam had said on August 8, 2000: "Don't provoke a snake before you make up your mind and muster up the ability to cut its head. It will be of no use to say that you have not started the attack if it attacks you by surprise. Make the necessary preparations required in each individual case and trust in God."

When I visited Nasra al-Sadoun on my first trip to Iraq, she subjected me to a forty-minute tirade about the effects of the UN sanctions, which she blamed on the United States and Great Britain. "One million Iraqi children have died!" she shouted. "What kind of people are the Americans? Are we Red Indians to be slaughtered? This is genocide! Not even Hitler did that! I think it must be because we are not considered human beings. I'm sure that if a million cats or dogs died in the U.S., it would be a huge uproar, but no one cares about us, because we are Iraqis! It is a crime, simply put, a genocide, an American genocide." She concluded bitterly: "You know, I have learned to hate the term *democracy,* because what the U.S. says it is doing by bombing us and killing our children is to bring us democracy and human rights. If this is their idea of democracy, we don't want it! The Americans may have more planes and missiles than we do, but we are an advanced people. In fact, we are a more civilized people than the Americans."

Listening to Nasra al-Sadoun rant was disheartening, because it made me realize that an entire generation of young Iraqis knew virtually nothing about the West beyond what they heard from ideologues like her or from Saddam himself, or were taught in his schools—and it was all pretty much the same thing. On the eve of Saddam's referendum, I visited one of Baghdad's more genteel high schools, the Al-Mansour Preparatory School for Boys, where I was graciously received by its director, Mr. Jawad. He ushered me into his office, which had a huge photograph of Saddam covering the entire wall behind his desk. The effect was distinctly Orwellian. After Mr. Jawad had called in a couple of his teachers who spoke good English, I asked them about the teaching of modern history at the school. One of them, Professor Shamzedin, reacted defensively to my line of inquiry, saying: "Don't ever think that we teach our students to despise the West. We know that the people of the Western countries are humane, and we try to teach our students to be humane too." I asked him to tell me how he taught the history of the Gulf War—the Mother of All Battles—as it was officially referred to, and Iraq's relationship with the United States. Shamzedin was uneasy. He said: "It's not included in our textbooks, which are changed only every thirty years. But we do teach such subjects in the sixth and last year of high school. It begins when Kuwait and other gulf countries began to try to control our oil via this and other conspiracies and our leader warned them not to do such things, but the Kuwaiti authorities continued in their aggressive planning, and you know what came afterward. We explain the facts."

Professor Shamzedin looked over to his colleague, Professor Marouf, for help. He spoke up, saying: "We all know that—it's quite clear to all people—that the American administration is against Arab people in general and Iraq in particular. We all know that because of the UN embargo, one million Iraqi children have died. We don't feel it necessary to remind our people of the facts. We all know these things. We all know that the American people have no ability to change what their administration does. This is why we don't hate the American people. We all hate wars. Iraqis don't like war. But if America attacks Iraq, what should the Iraqi people do? Definitely we will defend ourselves."

Whatever their true feelings were, the professors had delivered the proper Baath Party version of history, and under the circumstances, I expected nothing different from them. I also understood that this was the history that Iraq's schoolchildren had been taught for years, without much recourse to an alternative version. It seemed to me that at the very least, the United States had a lot of public relations work to do with Iraqis if it intended to occupy their country and get away with it. Even away from Saddam's minions, the sentiment I found most prevalent among Iraqis I met was a weary cynicism toward the United States and about life in general.

A few days after Saddam's prisoner amnesty, I secured permission to travel to Basra, in the south of Iraq. Basra lay within the southern no-fly zone, thirty miles from the border with Kuwait, and its atmosphere was something like that of a frontline city. British and American warplanes had bombed the radar installations at the Basra airport a few days before my arrival, and on my first morning in town, an air-raid siren sounded, honking rhythmically throughout the city for several minutes. The siren was ignored by everyone, however, and no jets appeared overhead. My official minder and interpreter for the trip, Ahmed, explained that the sirens went off whenever Iraqi airspace was penetrated. We traveled around with a Mukhabarat agent who had been assigned to escort us everywhere we went. He was a dark-skinned, muscular Bedouin man who told me, in his few words of English, to call him Lion. We had found a local driver who spoke English, a thin, sharp-eyed man named Abu Hikmet. He had once worked for an Austrian company with offices in Basra, but he now drove a taxi for a living.

I had requested permission to visit a number of places around Basra, but as we set off in Abu Hikmet's car, Ahmed informed me that we were first going to visit a local hospital. I had already been through this ritual once before, in Baghdad, and did not raise a fuss. Visits to hospitals to see children dying of cancer and leukemia and to be lectured by doctors who blamed their illnesses on radiation from the depleted-uranium-tipped rockets and tank shells used by the U.S. military in the Gulf War had become obligatory for journalists visiting Iraq. At the spanking-clean Saddam Teaching Hospital, we were received by its director, Dr. Jawad el-Ali, a tiny, soft-spoken man who spoke fluent English with a British accent. He explained that he had studied oncology for four years in the United Kingdom, at Charing Cross Hospital and the Royal Northern. He had become a member of the Royal College of Physicians of London, Glasgow, and Edinburgh and returned to Basra in 1984. As I had anticipated, Dr. Jawad spoke to me about the increased cancer levels among his patients at the hospital. "We have a bad situation." He began mildly. "We have an increased incidence in cancer. We've compared the years before and after the Aggression," he said, using the official term for the Gulf War. "In 1988 we had 116 cancer patients at this hospital, and in 1998 we had 428."

Dr. Jawad attributed the cancer increase to the 140,000 tons of explosives that he said had been dropped in the vicinity by the Americans and their allies in the Gulf War. I challenged him, asking whether some of the cancer increase might have come from Iraq's use of chemical weapons during its war with Iran. He shot me a sharp look and replied evenly: "I know nothing about that. I believe that there was an American aggression against an Iraqi chemical weapons site, which I think was intentional, although they've said they regretted it. Anyway, most of the cancers, while some may have been caused by chemicals, show radiation sources, indicating depleted uranium."

There was no perceptible tone of triumph in the doctor's voice. He carried on, explaining that he now saw many unusual cancer cases, such as patients with multiple cancers and families with several members afflicted with cancers of different types. This kind of thing, he said, was abnormal and simply had not occurred before the Gulf War. "I have lived in Basra for more than thirty years," said Dr. Jawad. "It used to be quite rare to have cancer patients. Now every doctor here has at least one cancer patient on his operations list." He had noticed a higher rate of cancer among farmers who lived to the west of the city, toward the border with Kuwait, where a great deal of contaminated war matériel had remained behind. He speculated that this might be because the farmers had inhaled fumes or been in contact with the uranium-tipped shells. Why didn't the government conduct a cleanup? I asked him. Dr. Jawad smiled. "Even the U.S. Army could not do it. They'd have to take the top fifty centimeters of soil in a thousand square miles and bury it under a hundred meters of soil. It would take the Iraqi government budget one hundred years to pay for it. The whole area is contaminated with radiation." What he was describing, I remarked, was a kind of low-level nuclear war; was that his view of what the United States had done in Iraq? "Yes," he replied quietly. "And the contamination will continue for billions of years."

Afterward we drove out of town to inspect the area that Dr. Jawad had said had the highest radiation levels. A half hour's drive west of Basra brought us to the scrubby little village of

Safwan, the closed Iraqi border crossing with Kuwait. As we approached it, we passed a heavily sandbagged UN observation post at the roadside, and Lion told me that from there on, toward the frontier, no Iraqi military men were allowed to bear arms. At the entrance to Safwan, there was a painted placard with Arabic script and English lettering that read BALESTINE [*sic*] IS ARABIAN FROM THE SEA FILL [*sic*] THE OCEAN and another with a large portrait of Saddam. Safwan's buildings were neglected, and many still bore the telltale bullet holes and pockmarks of war. Lion told Abu Hikmet to drive in for a hundred meters or so, but as a row of concrete barricades became visible down the road, he made him turn around again.

We drove back up the road past the UN post and turned off onto a track that led to a flat area covered with the sun-blackened carapaces of dead vehicles—cars, tanks, and armored personnel carriers—most of them mutilated and twisted. We got out and walked around, with Lion walking vigilantly ahead and telling us not to step off the track because there was unexploded ordnance everywhere. These blackened shells were all that remained of the many hundreds of vehicles full of fleeing Iraqi soldiers who had been massacred by the American military in 1991 in the incident remembered as the Highway of Death. Flies buzzed incessantly around us. Ignoring Lion's advice, Abu Hikmet stopped and picked up a rocket head that lay on the ground in front of us. Lion barked at him, and he dropped it. He pointed a few feet away to an unexploded shell lying on the ground next to a twisted jeep. "Uranium," he said in English, smiling, a reminder of the conversation we'd had with Dr. Jawad. Lion said something else in Arabic, which Ahmed translated. "He says the radiation level at that tank is one thousand times above normal." Lion walked around, looking at the wreckage, shaking his head and whistling now and again in fascination, but he expressed disappointment on my behalf at the scarcity of war detritus. Through Ahmed, he explained that there had been many, many more vehicles before, but people had been scavenging for scrap, and almost everything had been carted away. Wasn't that dangerous, I asked, considering the supposed uranium contamination? Lion and Ahmed both nodded and shrugged their shoulders.

Heading back up the road to Basra, we stopped at a little roadside hut where some robed men were selling cold Pepsis. One of them was a local farmer named Behlul Salman. He told me that he was forty-nine, originally from Basra, and had moved there after the Gulf War because of the good farming opportunities. "I like it here. The land is cheap, and we grow lots of tomatoes, onions, and watermelons." I was shocked at this. What about the uranium contamination in the area? I asked. Ahmed shrugged, and Lion grinned as if he were embarrassed. What about mines? I asked. "No, no mines," Salman replied. What about danger from the air—Americans strafing or bombing?

"No, no problems," said Salman.

"None of your children are sick?"

"No," said Salman. "All the children are healthy."

I turned to Ahmed and said that there seemed to be some discrepancies between official propaganda and reality. According to everything I had been hearing, I said, this was an area under constant harassment by British and American warplanes; it was heavily mined, full of millions of tons of irradiated war debris, and everyone had cancer. What was the truth? Fidgeting uncomfortably, Ahmed translated. A soldier who was standing nearby listening to our conversation spoke up. He pointed to a large hill in the distance, back over by the Kuwaiti border. "There's a lot of uranium over there," he said, "on that hill," and then added, trying to be helpful, that he had heard scientists say that the tomatoes grown in this area were "full of radiation."

Hearing this, I turned back to Salman, the farmer, and said: "So, what are you doing here?"

He said something, and Abu Hikmet, who spoke some English,

stepped in to translate. "He says even if his children die, he will stay here. He likes it here."

"But tell him that he is growing poison!" I said, exasperated.

Abu Hikmet translated. Everyone nodded. Salman replied: "Well, what can we do? We have to eat. And we'll eat and die. Iraqis like to die!"

Everyone laughed at Salman's joke, which was really not a joke at all, but a poor man's stubborn pride. I shook my head, feeling angry. Abu Hikmet patted me on the shoulder and said, winking cynically: "Don't worry, mister. He will keep growing tomatoes because he wants the money. And then he will die and forget about it."

We drove back to Basra. All the land around was spoiled-looking. Everywhere there were large, pointless-seeming mounds of dirt, piles of rubble, hardscrabble little farms, and the odd military bivouac. Above, the sky was big and blue, but large swatches of it were purplish black, like spreading bruises, coming from the gas burnoff pipes that poked up all over the horizon, shooting out orange fireballs and great scudding clouds of black smoke.

Following my encounter in Jordan with Nasser al-Sadoun in November 2002, I returned to England, where the news was filled with terrifying stories about Saddam's reported chemical and biological weapons caches and the catastrophic consequences if he were to use them. Experts predicted that Saddam would probably deploy such weapons in a war if he thought they would save his regime. Some came up with lurid doomsday scenarios in which a besieged Saddam would use poison gas as a final act of spite, killing himself but taking as many American troops as he could along with him. In Amman a high-ranking former Jordanian intelligence official who knew Saddam personally had fretted to me about the possibility that he might resort to international terrorism with bacteriological weapons. "Weaponized viruses, set off by Iraqi agents in different parts of the world— this is my big fear," he said. "Will he use them before there is a strike against him or when he knows the game is up? We don't know."

Stein Undheim, Norway's chargé d'affaires in Baghdad, a veteran Iraq observer and one of the few Western diplomats still in the country, had told me he felt certain Saddam had chemical weapons and would do everything in his power to avoid giving them up. "Many Iraqi military officers," he said, "are convinced that the only reason the Americans didn't come to Baghdad in the Gulf War was that they possessed chemical weapons. They believe that's what saved them then, and what saved them before, in the war with Iran. And they may believe they can save them again." Undheim confided that he was prepared for all eventualities. In an underground safe room at the embassy, he had stockpiled chemical warfare suits, gas masks, and enough medicines, food, and water for himself and several other members of his staff to survive for several months.

In his book, *The Threatening Storm: The Case for Invading Iraq,* which had been published to a great amount of publicity in September, Kenneth Pollack, a former CIA analyst, went so far as to compare the threat posed by Saddam with that of Adolf Hitler back in the 1940s and wrote: "An invasion of Iraq may not be cost-free, but it is unlikely to be horrific and it is the only sensible course of action left to us. We would do well to remember John Stuart Mill's remark that 'war is an ugly thing, but it is not the ugliest of things.' In our case, the ugliest of things would be to hide our heads in the sand while Saddam Hussein acquires the capability to kill millions of people and hold the economy of the world in the palm of his cruel hand."

Pollack's book closely echoed the thinking of the war planners in Washington and Westminster, and its publication coincided neatly with an intensifying campaign of accusations by the Bush and Blair governments against Saddam. Meanwhile antiwar groups and human rights organizations in Europe and the United States had begun making dire predictions about the huge numbers of civilians—some estimates went as high as a hundred thousand—who would likely die if the war went ahead. But the momentum for war had begun, and it was obvious that there was little that anyone could do to stop it. A British humanitarian relief official told me that Iran's government was expecting up to seven hundred thousand Iraqi refugees to flood across its borders and was establishing emergency camps to receive them. Set against the backdrop of the horrors of 9/11, the Iraq War had begun to acquire the psychological dimensions of an impending apocalypse, in which anything seemed possible.

To the journalists planning to cover the conflict, it seemed wise to be prepared for every contingency. News organizations began buying up supplies of protective gear for their correspondents and dispatching them on "hostile environment" courses. *The New Yorker* magazine sent me a chemical and biological warfare protective suit, a gas mask, ampoules of atropine, syringes, and a bulletproof helmet and jacket with antisniper plates in the front and back. Assuming I could obtain an Iraqi visa, I had resolved to take my chances in Baghdad, rather than be "embedded" with U.S. military troops. Toward the end of November, along with a dozen other reporters working for major U.S. and British media groups, I attended a one-day seminar, "Chemical and Biological Warfare Awareness Training," at Heckfield Place, a manor house located in a wooded, leafy estate in Hampshire, a county about an hour's drive from London. The manor was used by a British security consultancy firm called Centurion Risk Assessment Services, which gave courses in warfare preparedness to journalists, diplomats, and humanitarian aid workers. Our classroom was in a former stable on the grounds of the estate.

An ex–British special forces man with a Cockney accent gave us the lowdown on everything from chemical and germ warfare to the Ebola virus and the bubonic plague. After showing us a short video clip from an anonymous battlefield of the Iran-Iraq War, with images of the contorted bodies of Iranian soldiers who had succumbed to Saddam's poison gas, the instructor said breezily: "Chemical warfare has been around since the days of knights in armor; it's just gotten worse." As the Centurion man prattled on, I chewed over the irony of the fact that he had used Iranian war footage as a visual aid yet had nothing to tell us about what had actually happened there. For all the belated talk in the West about Saddam's illegal weapons of mass destruction, no people had suffered more from those weapons than the Iranians had, during the 1980–1988 war. Long before Saddam's infamous use of poison gas in the Kurdish town of Halabja, in 1988, when five thousand civilians were killed in a single day, his commanders had deployed chemical weapons dozens of times against Iranian troops, killing and maiming countless thousands of them. But in those days Saddam's war crimes had been largely ignored by the Western powers, which feared the spread of Khomeini's influence in the region, and most of them, including Great Britain and the United States, had actually supplied Saddam with the weaponry, intelligence, and technical know-how he relied upon to fight the war.

My notes from the Centurion man's warnings about nerve gas read: "Dangerous symptoms: Nausea, vomiting, piss your pants, defecation, stopping breathing. You're dead, basically." He passed around a vial of bitter almond tincture, and we were told to sniff it. It smelled like marzipan. He explained that it had the same odor as a "blood agent" which might be used in the Iraq War. "If you smell that, you have nine seconds to put your suit on. If you've been exposed, the symptoms are dizziness, fainting, heart palpitations, and shortness of breath." He moved on to "choking agents," which he explained could have various odors, including those of freshly mown hay, garlic, fish, and geraniums. He passed around a bottle of Thai fish paste, another of Lea &

Perrins crushed garlic sauce, and a Body Shop aromatherapy product called Geranium Revival, which we all duly sniffed. I asked the Centurion man how in a war situation we would be able to tell the difference between the scent given off by an actual field of fresh-mown hay and the same smell from a chemical weapon. He stopped and stared at me, as if pondering his reply. Then, with a shrug, he said: "You wouldn't."

After the lecture we were handed protective suits, boots, gloves, and gas masks, shown how to get them on and off quickly, and then made to go on a brisk trot through the forest around the manor house. It was a chilly, drizzly winter day, but inside the suits, it was beastly hot, and all of us returned to the classroom with our gas masks fogged up and our clothing completely drenched from our own sweat. By the end of the day few of us had any confidence that we would be able to survive in what the Centurion man referred to as "a chemical environment," and he had made it fairly clear that he didn't think we would either, but we were each given diplomas, stating that we had passed the course.

TWO

Throughout time, Iraq's destiny has been inextricably bound up with that of Persia—modern-day Iran—its much larger neighbor to the east. The border between the two countries has been demarcated along the old fault lines of history, and it is a territorial, cultural, and political boundary that is more blood-soaked than most. It is not only the final frontier between the Arabic- and the Persian-speaking worlds but a dividing line within Islam itself and one that separates Shiite Muslims from one another. The Shiites are the majority population in both nations, but in Iraq they have been ruled by the Sunnis, their ancient rivals for Islamic supremacy, for most of the past four hundred years.

Saddam's entire time in office was characterized by his murderous obsessiveness about the threatening "Persian enemy" at home and next door. He had launched a war against Iran to prevent the contagion of its Islamic revolution from taking root among Iraq's Shiite majority. Apart from the Kurds, no Iraqi community had been so singled out by Saddam for repression as the Shiites. If, as it now seemed likely, the United States was going to invade Iraq, oust Saddam, and restore the country to democracy, then there was a strong possibility that the Shiites would assume power. I was curious to know more about Iraq's Shiites, who their leaders were and what they wanted for the future. Inside Iraq, it was impossible to know. For some answers, I traveled to Iran, where more than half a million Iraqi Shiites were living as refugees. I arrived on New Year's Day 2003.

I spent the month of January interviewing Iraqi exiles and Iranians about the coming war. Among the Iraqis I spoke to, many of whom had lived in Iran for twenty or more years, I found cautious optimism that Saddam Hussein's long dictatorship might finally be about to end. But most were also distrustful of U.S. motives and feared a last-minute deal between Washington and Saddam that might leave him, or one of his Baath Party cronies, in power.

Among most of the Iranians I met, there was a widespread assumption that Bush's planned invasion of Iraq would lay the stage for an eventual U.S. war against Iran. At the time it was a fair enough deduction to make; ever since President Bush's State of the Union address in 2002, in which Iran was named along with Iraq and North Korea as part of what he called the axis of evil, American policy makers and the media had openly discussed the prospects for "regime change" in Iran.

Amir Mohebian, the editor in chief of the conservative Iranian newspaper *Resalat*, informed me that he was one of the conspiracy theorists. An ex–Revolutionary Guard and a war veteran, Mohebian was one of Iran's foremost religious intellectuals, and his newspaper was regarded as a mouthpiece for Iran's Supreme Leader, Ayatollah Ali Khameini. After I made a formal request through Iran's Ministry of Culture and Islamic Guidance, which oversees the activities of foreign journalists, Mohebian agreed to speak to me. We met in a conference room of the *Resalat* offices. He wore a suit and spoke superb English. Straightaway he launched into an acerbic monologue.

"For right or wrong, the United States and Iran have been confronting one another for twenty-four years now," he said. "Both sides are naturally very concerned about each other's actions in the region. We assume that the Americans have a universal plot, and I think that the heart of this plot lies in the Middle East. Energy resources have a significant position in the future of the world, and both the Middle East and Central Asia have significant resources, and so the U.S. sees this region as the key to its concerns. And Iran is the corridor between these two regions, the Middle East and Central Asia. . . . The main concern of American policy makers is providing economic security for the United States. Therefore we see the U.S. attack on Afghanistan as a means of providing gas and oil; Osama bin Laden and the Taliban were only an excuse for the attack on Afghanistan. With regards to the probable U.S. attack on Iraq, we believe this is aimed at dominating a country that can be a source of cheap energy. The U.S. has put its big feet in the region, with the toes in Afghanistan and the heel in Iraq, and we are somewhere in the middle, in the hollow of the foot, and we expect it to put pressure on us at any moment. We do not really believe all the U.S. talk about democracy and fighting terror.

"We believe a democratic regime in Iraq is a good thing and also in accordance with our own national interests. But we think a democratic Iraq regime based on the will of the majority is not what the U.S. really wants. First of all, because sixty percent of the population is Shia, and so it should have the support of the Shia." Mohebian explained that he had read in the Western media about American fears that a democratic post-Saddam Iraq would be ruled "by mullahs" and was therefore not desirable.

"I believe that a pragmatic politician always acts according to a calculation of benefit and loss," he continued. "So, is it reasonable to think that the United States wants to change the present regime in Iraq to a democracy, which will, because of its Shia majority, have many of the same characteristics as Iran's?"

"Which Iran?" I asked Mohebian in a challenging way. "The Iran of 1980, 1995, or of the present day? Iran's Islamic revolution has changed and is continuing to change today. Which Iran will be their model?"

"What you say is true," Mohebian said airily. "We cannot predict how they will choose their path. Maybe, unlike Iran, they will never let the secular politicians into their religious government, thus not paving the way to the eventual reforms, as we have had here, or maybe they will be less fundamentalist. . . ." Mohebian shrugged, as if to say that the question I had raised was, in any case, not the most important one.

"Look," he said, "Saddam has always been a dangerous enemy of ours. Therefore his elimination would be in our favor. But the presence of the U.S. in the region is not in our interests. So the best thing is that the U.S. topples Saddam Hussein, but that it pays a high price for this, because I think that one who pays a high price to take one step will think carefully before taking another. The U.S. actually paid quite a high price in Afghanistan; that's why Iraq has taken longer for them to get to. . . . But the U.S. has not given much thought to what comes after Saddam Hussein, and toppling Saddam is not just a matter of toppling a person or even a system. Quite a few Iraqis are linked to the system, so they have to be knocked down too, and they are a considerable number. I believe these people are standing in opposition to the Iraqi people, and they realize that if Saddam Hussein goes, they'll die. And apart from the Kurds, the forty percent of the population who are Sunni fear the rise of a Shia state. So Saddam is relying upon the fear of some people of a Shia state and fear of death by others, and these two groups provide him with very strong support. So even if Saddam Hussein agrees to step down, the foundation for a civil war may be laid." Mohebian flashed me a triumphant smile. It was obvious that he relished the scenario he had just described.

As I got up to leave, Mohebian made a final remark. "There is a saying by Machiavelli: 'A democratic system can be easily dominated but it is difficult to hold on to; a dictatorship is difficult to take over but easier to control.' If I were an American politician, I would put another dictator in the place of Saddam Hussein, and I wouldn't change the system as a whole. But I hope the U.S. doesn't have an adviser like me!" He laughed humorlessly.

Amir Mohebian's concerns about having the Americans next door were comprehensible. After more than two decades in power, Ayatollah Khomeini's political heirs had begun, rightly, to feel increasingly vulnerable and insecure about their futures. Khomeini, the first imam, or Supreme Leader, of Iran's Islamic revolution, was replaced upon his death in 1989 by Ayatollah Ali Khameini. He was a dour, bearded, and bespectacled but somehow rather Woody Allenish–looking man, whose ubiquitous visage, along with Khomeini's, stared down from portraits on the walls of every shop and public establishment. Khameini represented the hard-line, unelected clerical faction of Iran's government that had veto power over most of the bills put forward by Ayatollah Muhammad Khatami, Iran's democratically elected president. Khatami, who had won two presidential elections, first in 1997 and again in 2001, both times with landslides, represented the coalition of so-called reformers, who sought to diminish the religious conservatives' unpopular stranglehold over state power and many other aspects of Iranians' everyday lives. So far, however, the conservatives, led by Supreme Leader Khameini, had blocked most of the reform initiatives.

The ongoing power struggle had created an Iranian political system, and a society, that was positively schizoid. For several weeks in late 2002, Tehran was the scene of angry student protests and clashes with police after a death sentence had been handed down on a sociology professor. His crime was to have conducted a poll that revealed that a majority of Iranians were in favor of establishing diplomatic relations with the United States—still officially vilified as "the Great Satan" by the conservatives. After a police crackdown in which many of the student protesters were arrested, the protests had all but petered out by the time I arrived in Tehran, while the condemned professor's fate hung in limbo. Then, in early January, the laws permitting stoning as a punishment for adulterous women were overturned by Iran's parliament, the Majlis. This news was followed a few days later by the announcement that women would henceforth be allowed to serve as police officers. Both these events appeared to be major breakthroughs for the reformers. But barely a week later two of the country's last-remaining independent newspapers were closed down by the clerics after one of them published a cartoon that, it was alleged, appeared to belittle the late Ayatollah Khomeini. Hundreds of religious students in the holy city of Qom had demonstrated angrily after the cartoon appeared.

Iran's population had almost doubled since 1979, when Khomeini swept into power. Over half of Iran's seventy-odd million people were under thirty years old, and most of them couldn't find jobs. Iran's unemployment rate stood at around 30 percent. Not surprisingly, Iranian youths, who were allowed to vote at the age of sixteen, were upset about the status quo and were among President Khatami's strongest supporters. Most of the young people I met in Tehran spoke about the religious hardliners with a mixture of fear, loathing, and scorn. Some leading clerics and their relatives had been granted freewheeling control over a number of bonyads, or Islamic foundations, which engaged in a variety of lucrative and entirely unregulated business enterprises, giving rise to widespread allegations of official corruption. Motioning with his hands to a point somewhere near his ankles, and laughing bitterly at the same time, Ali, an unemployed mechanical engineer in his mid-twenties, told me: "The mullahs have deep pockets, very deep pockets. But the people don't have anything. There are no jobs, no future in Iran, and for young people, no fun. No disco, no dancing, no drinking. I am a Muslim, but why can't I dance and drink and be a Muslim too? I hope that after Iraq, Bush comes to Iran and takes away the mullahs."

Under Iran's sharia laws, alcohol was banned; women were not allowed to sing out loud, ride bicycles, show their hair, or hold hands in public with men; and mixed-sex dancing was strictly prohibited, along with the screening of almost all imported movies. These activities went on behind closed doors, even so, especially among middle- and upper-class Iranians, who enjoyed dancing and parties where contraband alcohol flowed; many also owned clandestine satellite television receivers and watched the latest Hollywood movies on counterfeit DVDs. Meanwhile, there were an estimated two million Iranians who were addicted to opium or heroin. It was an epidemic problem, which, along with a huge rise in AIDS cases, mostly from intravenous drug use, was made possible thanks to a cheap and ready supply of the narcotic from neighboring Afghanistan, which competed with Myanmar to be the world's largest producer of opium and heroin.

One day, in an upscale Tehran neighborhood, Ali and I stopped for lunch in an eatery called Boof (which means "owl" in the Farsi language), a Western-style fast-food franchise with high-tech decor offering pizzas and hamburgers and owned, so I was told, by a son of one of Iran's leading religious figures. As we were eating, an attractive young woman in her late teens or early twenties stumbled in and slumped onto a chair near us. She was wearing a hijab—the mandatory headscarf—but, like a lot of younger women, especially in the wealthier parts of Tehran, wore it back on her head so that some of her hair—in her case, bleached peroxide blond and cut punk short—was showing, and under her black manteau (a three-quarter-length tunic coat that is obligatory, like the hijab, and intended to conceal the curves of a woman's body), she wore trendy jeans and red sneakers.

As Ali and I watched, the girl nodded off, her eyes glazed over. Periodically she came awake again but remained in a trancelike state. Now and then she scratched her face obsessively, slowly. Soon the restaurant's waiters noticed her and hovered nearby, watching and whispering to one another. So were we. Ali shook his head sadly and whispered: "Heroin." After about fifteen minutes the girl suddenly woke up and came to her feet and stumbled out to the street. We followed her outside and watched as she stood, weaving uncertainly, on the curb next to a busy lane of traffic. Feeling concerned about her safety, I asked Ali what would happen to her; would she be arrested if she was spotted by the police? After all, I said, this was the Islamic Republic of Iran. He scoffed at this and said that the police would arrest her, yes, but they would let her go if she paid them off. Somewhat embarrassedly, Ali then began trying to explain to me that the girl was probably selling her body in order to buy drugs. I was incredulous, but as Ali spoke, a car driven by a young man pulled up alongside her, and she climbed in. The man did a U-turn into the oncoming traffic and raced off down the street. "You see?" said Ali, with a resigned look. That evening, when I told another Iranian friend about the scene I had witnessed, he quipped cynically: "Welcome to the Islamic Republic of Iran."

Iran's enormous capital city, Tehran, is splayed across the lower flanks of a dark, jagged ridge of mountains, snowcapped in winter, which form a natural barrier between the metropolis and the Caspian Sea. From its hilly northern suburbs, Tehran tumbles untidily southward and eventually peters out on the edges of a vast chocolate brown desert plain. By and large, Tehran's level of affluence abates in a descending north-south line. The city's rich live higher up, closest to the mountains, in what used to be genteel neighborhoods of walled garden villas, which are now rapidly disappearing in a developers' frenzy that is replacing them with luxury apartment high-rises. The shopping streets of the north are lined with designer boutiques, shiny fast-food joints, and watch and gift shops; in the southern suburbs, jostled by factories, warehouses, and repair workshops, the homes are low-level and dingy, most of them dating back to the mid-twentieth century. The colors of Tehran, overall, are gray and white, in various shades.

Thanks to several million cars and cheap, government-subsidized gasoline, Tehran also has unbelievably bad smog, which obscures the city's mountainous backdrop from view most days. There is virtually no traffic control, and the city's drivers typically hurtle themselves along the expressways at high speeds, straddling the dividing lines and even the shoulders; there are usually five cars abreast on three lanes. Red lights are ignored, and almost no one wears a seat belt. At the restive intersections, people cross at their peril, holding handkerchiefs to their faces or wearing antipollution masks over their mouths and noses. Young boys dart into the scrum to sell newspapers and bouquets of fresh-cut white tuberoses, narcissi, and red roses.

Iranians seem to like flowers very much. All over Tehran, on billboards and the windowless sides of apartment buildings, are great painted murals showing prominent martyrs of the Iran-Iraq War or else of the late Ayatollah Ruhollah Khomeini, looking as godlike and baleful as ever; there are almost always flowers, usually tulips, adorning these canvases: lovingly rendered single bulbs free-floating through celestial heavens and also colorful bouquetlike displays. One billboard shows a young boy of about fourteen, his black headband identifying him as a basij, one of the youthful Iranian suicide volunteers who ran to their deaths by the tens of thousands onto the heavily mined battlefields of the front line during the 1980–1988 war with Iraq (in which as many as 600,000 Iranians, and 250,000 Iraqis, were killed). The boy is shown kneeling, his head propped up against his rifle, from which dangles a small picture of Khomeini. The expression on his face is pure, beatific; his mouth wears a slight smile. Around him spreads an unending field of pretty flowers; it is eternal springtime.

Many of Iran's late basiji—now martyrs, or shaheed—are buried in the vast Behesht-e-Zahra Cemetery (which means

"Paradise of Zahra," after one of the Prophet Muhammad's daughters), down on the plain at Tehran's southern fringes. Not far away, inside its own multidomed shrine, looms the mausoleum of Ayatollah Khomeini. A few days after I arrived in Tehran, I went to the cemetery and wandered among the rows of little gravestones and altars erected by the martyrs' families, ornamented with their photographs, plastic flowers, and little mementos inside glass-fronted boxes standing on pedestals over the graves. A few family groups, but mostly women, were quietly picnicking near the tombs; others collected water in jugs from spigots to wash the graves of their dead fathers, sons, and brothers. Passionately drawn-out verses sung by a muezzin floated through the air, amplified by megaphone. Black-chadored women stopped passersby to offer little sweets or cakes from paper boxes in honor of the Twelfth Imam, or Mahdi, the infant heir of the Eleventh Imam, who died in A.D. 873. The Twelfth Imam vanished but is believed by most of Iran's Muslims, who are predominantly Shiite, to be divinely hidden. They are awaiting his reappearance. The Hidden Imam is expected back on a Friday, along with that other revered prophet Jesus Christ, when, it is believed, together they will save humanity. The day I visited was a Thursday, the eve of the potentially fateful day, and this offering of sweets and cakes was an old Shia custom.

I approached an elderly man who was standing over a tomb with a jug of water, stooping to clean it. His name was Ahmed, he told me. He was seventy years old, a retired repairman for General Electric. I asked him if the tomb belonged to a son of his. He smiled and nodded. It was, he said, that of his second son, who had been a Revolutionary Guard and had been killed at the age of twenty-one, in the war with Iraq. I asked him what he thought his son would be doing if he were alive today. He straightened up, and proudly but with slightly watery eyes said, "If he was alive today and there was a need to defend the motherland, he'd be there, and I would encourage him." I asked

Ahmed what he felt about the prospect of a new war against Iraq, this one led by my country, the United States. "If the war is just going to be between the U.S. and Iraq, then so be it," he replied. "I am sorry for the ordinary people, that's all. Nobody likes war."

One of the parts of Iran most ravaged by war was Khuzistan. The oil-rich southwestern Iranian province shares a border with Iraq to the west and, farther south, a coastline on the Persian Gulf. Its population bore the influence of its proximity to the Arab world: 65 percent of Khuzistanis were ethnic Arabs. The province was also Iran's southern front during the eight-year Iran-Iraq War, and it bore the brunt of Saddam's initial military thrust into Iran; the port city of Khorramshahr, which sits across the Shatt al Arab waterway from the city of Basra, was occupied for eighteen months by Saddam's invasion force. After Saddam's troops were dislodged, Iraq repeatedly pounded Khuzistan's cities with medium-range missiles from across the border. Then, after Saddam's vicious crackdown on the Iraqi intifada, or uprising, in 1991, tens of thousands of Iraqi refugees streamed across the border, where many still remained, at the time of my visit, living in Iranian government-administered refugee camps.

Accompanied by several Iranian security men, I was allowed to visit a couple of the Iraqi refugee camps in the old city of Dezful, about fifty miles from the border. When we arrived in Dezful, a sleepy-looking yellow-brick town, my escorts explained that the city had been hit by 280 missiles during the war with Iraq, mostly nighttime attacks, in which hundreds of Iranian civilians had died. No signs of war damage remained that I could see, but there was a monument on the outskirts that commemorated the town's suffering. It consisted of a huge man's fist, made of bronze, rising out of the ground and crushing a camouflage green missile in its grasp. The missile was very lifelike, and it had "U.S.A." emblazoned on it. I remarked on this and asked my

Iranian escorts to explain the significance of the "U.S.A." on the missile. The men in the car seemed embarrassed by my direct question, unsure of what to say. My translator, an Iranian sociology teacher named Mehrdad, explained that most Iranians blamed the United States for supporting Saddam during the long war. "You know, many Iranians refer to that war as the American War," he added. There was no rancor in Mehrdad's voice. The other men in the car nodded their silent agreement to this explanation.

At a camp just outside Dezful, called Ansar, where about six thousand Iraqis were living, I spoke with a number of refugees from Basra. One was a jovial and chubby man who hobbled as he walked. He told me his name was Ali Nuri and that he was thirty-nine years old. He had been a crane driver in Basra before being forcibly conscripted into Saddam's army during the Iran-Iraq War. That was when he lost one of his legs—he pointed below the table—to a land mine. After the war he had to retire from his crane-driving job, but he had taken part in the Shiite uprising against Saddam's rule following the Gulf War. It had been a necessary thing to do, he said.

"Because we were Shia, we were always blamed for being pro-Iranian, and we could no longer tolerate this," Ali Nuri explained. "You may have heard things about other political parties, but the Baath Party is something else. You had to sign up for it; if I hadn't, my pension would have been cut. During the Iran-Iraq War those who were old enough to go to war received notices to go; if they didn't go, they'd be executed. I had a cousin who was executed because he didn't go to the war. Afterward the military went to his family's house and asked for the price of the bullet they had shot him with. No funeral ceremony was allowed, and the women were not allowed to wear black for mourning. So we took part in the revolution because we were Shia and weren't allowed our rights, and so we had to protest against this. . . . When the Iraqis retreated from Kuwait, they threw down their weapons and just fled, and we thought the Americans were supporting us, so we thought, 'This is it!' and people started celebrating and went and killed Mukhabarat agents, and for eighteen days we were sort of free. Then Saddam's planes and helicopters came. They used some sort of floating bridge and brought their tanks into the city of Basra, and we had to flee. The Iranians tried to stop us from crossing the border, but we were too many, and they let us in."

I asked Ali Nuri how he felt about the way the Americans had behaved. He nodded and said: "During the war with Kuwait we saw the Americans actually bring down Iraqi aircraft, and so we thought we'd at least have that protection, but then Saddam's aircraft came, and no one stopped them. When we saw the Americans enter Iraqi territory, we thought they would help us, but this did not happen. Suddenly they were gone. We just hope that that won't happen this time because we've been living here like refugees for twelve years." Ali Nuri's face bore no hint of reproach, but he asked: "Can anyone give us any guarantee that the Americans will come this time? Because if they come, we'll go and help them." He watched my face, waiting for my reply. I told him that I could give him no guarantees. "*Inshallah* [If God wills]." He laughed good-naturedly.

I asked Ali Nuri if he was serious about joining the war. He grinned. "Well, it would be nice if the Americans did it for us this time. I've already fought once, and look what happened." He gestured toward his artificial leg.

Later, in the adjacent refugee camp of Ashrafi Isfahani, a slumlike home to about thirteen thousand Iraqis, I spoke to a soft-spoken man in his mid-forties, a former cheese maker from Basra. He invited me into his modest two-room house. It was next to an open sewer, and the stench inside was overpowering. Over tea, the cheese maker told me that he was keenly following the news of the latest Iraq crisis. Pointing to a shortwave radio set, one of his few visible possessions, he explained that every morning he got up very early and flipped the dials, listening to broadcasts about Iraq. I asked him what he thought of Saddam Hussein. "He is a criminal, a killer, a person who does not respect the rights of others," he replied. But, he added, that did not mean he was necessarily in favor of a war. "If the U.S. and Britain are planning to overthrow Saddam Hussein and install a democracy, then fine, we are with them. If they come to stay and dominate, and if it's because of oil they are doing this, then no."

Before I took my leave, the cheese maker told me he wanted to say one last thing. "We know from the media that other rulers in the world care about their people," he said. "But this is not the case with Saddam Hussein. There are five million people living outside Iraq as refugees, thousands in prison, and hundreds of thousands who have been killed or executed. If he cared about Iraqis, he'd say to his people: 'Make your choice: Shall I stay or go?' But he doesn't. As an Iraqi I want all the organizations and individuals of the world to put pressure on Saddam Hussein so that the regime will change without war. We have had enough of bloodshed. We just want him and his system to change. As long as Saddam Hussein is there, this is our only hope. We want the foreign organizations to lay the foundations to allow the Iraqi people to participate in their future. We know in Iraq that this cannot be done by force."

After my trip to Khuzistan, I met a group of Iraqi women at a community center in Dawlat Abad, a working-class Iraqi immigrant suburb of south Tehran. The women were among the hundreds of thousands of so-called Persian Iraqis, whom Saddam forcibly deported from Iraq after the start of the Iran-Iraq War. Countless thousands of others had been secretly executed and buried in mass graves. It was an episode that had gone virtually unnoticed in the West but must have been one of the greatest "ethnic cleansings" to have occurred in the world for many years.

Because Saddam was still in power, however, the full extent of his purge remained unknown. I had brought along a young Iraqi man with me as my interpreter.

When we arrived, on a bitterly cold January night, we found a group of six women in black chadors sitting side by side in chairs in the large meeting room of the community center. A gas stove had been lit to heat the room, which was unadorned except for pictures of the two Iranian supreme leaders. My translator and I sat in chairs across the room from the women. The setting was very formal and awkward, and I noticed that my translator was nervous and did not look directly at the women, who themselves seemed very shy. Only two of them met my gaze, and one hid her face entirely from me inside the hood of her chador. One of the women, however, who appeared to be in her mid-forties, with warm, intelligent eyes, seemed completely unafraid of me, and as I spoke, introducing myself and trying to put them at ease, it was clear that she understood what I was saying before it was translated into Arabic. She introduced herself, in Arabic, as Um Asil ("Mother of Asil") and explained that she was a Faily Kurd, a Shiite minority group within the predominantly Sunni Kurdish community. "My father was an Iraqi," she said, in a calm, clear voice. "But his father was born in Iran. We were six girls and five boys."

Um Asil proceeded to tell her story. In 1980, just after the war with Iran began, she explained, Saddam's regime had arrested her and her entire family. After several days in detention, the men of the family had been forcibly separated from their sisters, wives, and children and taken away. Only one of her five brothers had escaped the dragnet because he was in the United States at the time. But the other four all had been taken, one of them with his wife and their month-old child. They had been robbed of all their money and their jewelry. "My husband and the husbands of all my sisters were also detained," Um Asil added. "We had been living in England, where my husband, who was a doctor, had been studying medicine." Her husband had been at the Royal College of Medicine in London, she said, enunciating the name of the hospital in English, where she had joined him for three years. They had only just returned to Baghdad. She smiled. The memory of that time was clearly one she cherished. "One of my sisters' husbands, a lawyer, was of Kuwaiti origin. He and his wife were detained also, and she was pregnant. They accused us of being Iranian and suggested that because we traveled a lot, we were taking money out of the country to help support the Iranian revolution."

Um Asil, her sisters and sisters-in-law, and their children, including her own son of four and her daughter of nine, had been taken to a detention center, where they had been imprisoned for four months. The conditions had obviously been humiliating for her. "They brought prostitutes from other parts of the prison and put them in the same cell with us," she said, lifting her eyebrows slightly. Then, one night, they had been taken out of their cell and placed on buses by soldiers and driven to the border with Iran. When the buses finally stopped, it was very late at night, and they were told by their guards to get out and start walking into the no-man's-land between the two countries. "We were a big group of about six hundred people," Um Asil recalled, shaking her head. "They even sent some lunatics with us whom they had taken out of the madhouse and one badly burned woman from the hospital. We were forced to walk for about three days before we reached a safe place. One woman stepped on a mine. It blew her foot off, and she bled to death. And one night a gang attacked us and raped some of the girls. Some of the girls were taken, and nothing more was heard of them. We had to leave our shoes behind to walk in the desert. Finally, some Iranian military vehicles picked us up. They gave us water. We reached a place where they tended to the children and fed us, and afterward they took us to a refugee camp. Two months later we were released. By then many more of our relatives had arrived, and so we gathered together."

Twenty-three years had gone by since then, but I had the impression that this was the first time that Um Asil had told her story to an outsider. The accounts of her friends, the other women with her, were similarly tragic. For most of them, the border crossing had been particularly harrowing. The thugs who had preyed upon Um Asil's group had apparently operated with impunity for some time along the border. One of the other women was part of a group that had been attacked repeatedly by the same gang over several days. In her case, they had raped and murdered several girls. The survivors had found their bodies afterward, dumped farther along on the trails they took to reach Iran.

After all the women had told their stories, I turned back to Um Asil and asked her whether she or her friends believed any of their men were still alive. "We've heard nothing about our husbands or brothers in all this time," she said in a small voice. "We haven't heard a thing about them." Suddenly looking very tired, she added: "When we think of Saddam and of how he behaves, we lose any hope that they are alive, but we still have our faith in God." It seemed a rote response, which clearly even she did not fully believe, but nonetheless the other women all nodded their heads.

The war weariness of the Iraqi refugees was palpable among their politicians as well. One of the most influential leaders of Iran's Iraqi exile community was Muhammad Bakr al-Hakim, a Shiite ayatollah in his early sixties who headed an organization called the Supreme Council for Islamic Revolution in Iraq (SCIRI). Hakim was a scion of one of Iraq's oldest and most highly regarded clerical families; his father, the late Grand Ayatollah Mohsen al-Hakim, had been the world's highest-ranking Shiite religious authority in his day. In 1980, during Saddam's first bloody crackdown on the radical Islamist Shiites who had begun to oppose him, Hakim fled to Iran, where he founded SCIRI under the tutelage of Khomeini's recently installed Islamic revolution. Over the years since, Hakim's relatives living in Iraq had paid a high blood price for his opposition to Saddam; more than fifty had either been murdered or died of illnesses after being locked away in Iraq's prisons. In Iraq a deathly silence surrounded the Hakim family's horrific story, and even mentioning their name was taboo.

Located on a main street in central Tehran opposite Iran's Ministry of Commerce, SCIRI's headquarters occupied a nondescript four-story concrete building with slanting, perforated steel plates protecting each of its windows. Entering the building was like suddenly crossing a bridge between the Persian and Arab worlds. In the reception area, Arabic, not Farsi, was being spoken, and several uniformed men carrying weapons were standing guard. To the untrained eye, they looked like Iranian soldiers, but they were actually Iraqi mujahideen, members of the Badr Brigade, the military wing of Hakim's movement, which was led by his younger brother, Abdulaziz al-Hakim. The Badr Brigade had fought alongside Iran's troops in the Iran-Iraq War and, after the Gulf War, had participated in the uprising in the south. The Badr Brigade had an estimated ten thousand to fifteen thousand fighters, bivouacked in secret camps along the border, many of them in Khuzistan, which was one of the reasons I was escorted by Iranian security men during my trip to the province—so as to prevent me from seeing them.

On the wall of the entranceway hung a series of framed portraits, showing Hakim's position in the canon of militant Shiite clerics. Going from right to left, the portraits depicted Hakim himself, followed by Iran's supreme leader, Ayatollah Ali Khameini; the late Ayatollah Ruhollah Khomeini, and finally the late Iraqi Shiite cleric Imam Muhammad Bakr al-Sadr, a close ally of Khomeini's and Hakim's own mentor. The outspoken Sadr, who had advocated an Iranian-style Islamic revolution in Iraq, had been captured and secretly executed by Saddam's police in 1980, along with his sister Amina, after Shia guerrillas of his party, al-Dawa, or Islamic Call, had tried to assassinate Tariq Aziz. I was shown upstairs and greeted by a man in his fifties who spoke some English and who told me he was the ayatollah's interpreter. He led me to a waiting room, where we sat and chatted. When I asked his name, he looked taken aback but then, with a furtive smile, said that it was "Muhammad." With a little more prompting, Muhammad told me that he was a former schoolteacher, from Basra, which he had fled twenty years earlier. He had left behind his wife and children, he added, and had not seen them since. Seeing my shocked look, he told me that his was a typical story; many of the Iraqi exiles living in Iran had not seen or even heard from their families in many years. "That's how it is, my friend," he said.

After a few minutes we were summoned by some bodyguards, who searched my bag and then showed us into a drawing room with faux Persian carpets and floral print green couches and chairs arrayed around the walls. The decor consisted of vases filled with plastic flowers and a gilt-framed Koranic quotation in Arabic script. I was shown to a small couch in the corner of the room. In front of me there was a little table on which a microphone had been placed. It was attached by a cable to a recording machine that was being readied by two men who sat at the far end of the room. Muhammad sat down near me, perching on the edge of his seat nervously. Suddenly the door was opened, and in walked the ayatollah. Everyone stood up as Hakim strode across the room and greeted me warmly. Once he had sat down, in the chair nearest to mine, everyone else sat down as well. Hakim was soberly resplendent in a black turban and black manteau over his gray cleric's tunic. He was pale, with large, strong-looking hands, and he had large, expressive eyes.

I asked Hakim for his opinion about the proposed American-led war in Iraq to remove Saddam from power. "The U.S. says it wants to change the regime and to establish a democracy in Iraq," the ayatollah replied, speaking calmly in a deep, strong voice. "But it is not cooperating with the popular forces of Iraq; it wants to impose itself on the Iraqi people. This creates suspicion toward the United States, because there is some ambiguity in its declared policy. Will the Americans stay on in Iraq as occupiers, or will they let the Iraqi people run their own affairs?"

I asked Hakim whether he trusted the Americans in light of what happened in 1991, at the end of the Gulf War. After a short pause, during which he merely smiled and shook his head from side to side, he replied: "After the liberation of Kuwait, the U.S. changed their minds and ended up supporting Saddam. This is still a source of anxiety for Iraqis. But now we see that there is a new American seriousness about the change of regime in Iraq. What we worry about is what comes after the change." He added that he hoped that President Bush would, after all, stick to the promises he had made lately, about restoring Iraq to democracy. Toward that goal, he emphasized, his organization had been working hard to establish a unified front with Iraq's other opposition groups, including Sunni Arabs, Turkomans, and Kurds. He reminded me that at a recent summit conference of Iraqi opposition groups in London, which his brother Abdulaziz had attended, the cornerstones of a pluralistic political system for a post-Saddam Iraq had been agreed upon. Any future government, he said, would have to be composed of all of Iraq's ethnic groups and would "respect Islam."

One of the big unanswered questions about Ayatollah Hakim was whether or not he still hoped for an Iranian-style Islamic revolution in Iraq. I wondered whether his views had moderated over the years, if he had become more pragmatic as a result of the changes he had seen take place in Iran, where the appeal of political Islam had dwindled considerably. I posed this question to Hakim, but his answer was ambiguous. "I have not changed my views," he replied. "They have remained the same. Iran's changes

have nothing to do with us." He went on to say, rather delphically, that SCIRI had, depending on the circumstances, occasionally modified some of its positions in order to reach a necessary
political compromise. "Our relationships with the world were
very limited before the Gulf War," he said. "Since then that has
changed, and we've been able to develop many new relationships. But from the beginning it was never our idea to copy
Iran's revolution."

This seemed like an opportune moment to bring up the sensitive topic of SCIRI's talks with the Bush administration. It was
public knowledge that in August 2002 Hakim had dispatched
his brother, Abdulaziz, to Washington for meetings between the
Bush administration and representatives of Iraq's various opposition groups. (In a separate interview, Abdulaziz had acknowledged to me that SCIRI and Washington were conducting a
continuing "dialogue" aimed at securing some kind of coordina-
tion between the organization's underground network inside
Iraq and U.S. military forces in the event of a war.) Ayatollah al-
Hakim would not be drawn out on this, but he confirmed that
there had been talks between his organization and the U.S. government about "Iraqi affairs."

I asked Hakim how long it had been since he'd been back to
his homeland. "I've been out of Iraq for twenty-two years," he
replied. "I returned briefly in 1991"—during the uprising—
"and now I am hoping to return again." He smiled and paused
for a moment. Then he said: "I left when the regime began killing my family and my relatives. The Iraqi regime has killed fifty
members of my family. Five of them were my brothers, and seven
were my nephews. Only one of my brothers, Abdulaziz, survives.
We were ten brothers. One died in a car accident, one is missing,
and one died of sorrow because the regime killed his sons. The
rest were killed by torture."

Hakim related all this in a neutral voice devoid of any emotion. How, I asked him, was he able to cope with this enormous

degree of personal loss? He smiled and replied: "If one is suffering from pain, but sees that there is more pain than one's own, then one's own pain is lessened. All Iraqis are suffering; this decreases my personal pain. We mainly depend on God. And we believe in a second world afterlife where justice prevails."

Even in Iran, Ayatollah al-Hakim and his brother, Abdulaziz, were prime targets for Saddam's assassins. Both had survived several attempts to kill them. The most recent attack, against Abdulaziz in 2001, had involved several gunmen and occurred in broad daylight in downtown Tehran. Although their offices were in Tehran, the Hakims actually lived under tight security with their families in the holy city of Qom, and they discreetly commuted back and forth between the two cities.

Qom lies seventy-five miles from Tehran across an uninspiring landscape that alternates between bleak desert hills and agricultural flatlands. The city was a drab but not unpleasant low-level sprawl of tree-lined boulevards, arched yellow-brick buildings, winding back streets, and a skyline dominated by blue-tiled mosques. Clerics wearing beards and white or black turbans were more in evidence in Qom than in Tehran, and the city's women unanimously wore the all-encompassing black chador, with only their faces showing. In many ways, Qom was a similar place to the Hakims' hometown, Najaf. Qom was the site of the grandiose shrine to Fatima, the daughter of the Eighth Imam of the Shia faith, and had long been an important religious center. Qom acquired additional prominence after the Iranian revolution, because Ayatollah Khomeini lived there, and over the years since, the city had become a sanctuary for thousands of Iraqi clerics fleeing Saddam's purges. Najaf has even greater spiritual and historic significance than Qom, however, as the burial place of the Prophet Muhammad's son-in-law Imam Ali, whom the Shia believe to have been betrayed as the rightful successor as the keeper of the Muslim faith. Najaf is also the home of the world's largest theological university for Shiite Muslims, the place where Khomeini himself studied as a young man, and to which he returned after being forced into exile by the shah.

I drove to Qom one morning and called at the Al-Mustafa Center for Islamic Research. Eager to hear a clerical perspective that was different from Ayatollah al-Hakim's, I had made arrangements to meet there with Sheikh Ali al-Korani, an Iraqi ayatollah who was the Qom representative of the world's highest living Shiite religious authority, Grand Ayatollah Ali al-Sistani. (Sistani was a septuagenarian who had been living under virtual house arrest for several years at his home in Najaf and, to my knowledge, had rarely spoken in public about anything.)

Sheikh Korani was an amiable, clear-eyed, white-bearded man in his late sixties and, on the day I met him, was wearing a dark green manteau and a white turban. He showed me around the center and into its library, where a dozen or so attentive Shiite scholars pored over Koranic texts. Korani explained that these men were seeking, just as Shiite scholars had been for centuries before them, to become experts in Islamic thought and for new inspiration. Waving around him, Korani explained that the center could be compared with the scholarly research centers of the Christian and Jewish faiths. "We need more comparative studies; academic studies between our religions can bring our faiths together and reduce terrorism," he said expansively. "If bin Laden and his followers would have put their thoughts on the table to discuss things, then the problems we have in the world today would not have come to this. Thoughts are like water: If it flows, it remains clear; if it stays in one place, it becomes like acid."

Sheikh Korani explained some of the difficulties of his role as Sistani's representative. He had not been back to Iraq since the 1970s, after the late Imam Muhammad Bakr al-Sadr (who had been his mentor as well as Ayatollah Hakim's) had been arrested and warned him not to return. He was, he said, condemned to death in Iraq, like a lot of the other Shia clerics living in Iran. "We call ourselves the Shia who are forbidden to visit the holy places." He chortled. "When we call friends there, we never identify ourselves by name on the telephone," he said. "Consultations with Ayatollah Sistani are very difficult. It can take a month or more to get a message through. We're afraid to put him at risk. It was only last year that they allowed him a fax machine. Legally there is no law preventing him from traveling, but he doesn't like to, and it's not known whether Saddam would let him. He is under regular police surveillance."

Korani wouldn't comment on the imminent war against Iraq. "I don't get involved in politics," he said serenely, and he explained that this was a theological position. "Within the Shia faith there are two lines. One, like that of the late Imam Khomeini, holds that we must be political and that the *marj'iya*"—the religious leadership—"has the power of the faquih"—literally, the trusteeship of Islamic jurisprudence. *Wilayat-al-Faquih,* the rule of the Islamic jurist, is the guiding principle of Iran's Islamic revolution. It effectively consecrates political Islam as the law of the land by granting the ruling clerics judicial powers over an elected government. "The second line, which is the majority and which is represented by the Grand Ayatollah Sistani, does not believe that the *marj'iya* should be involved in politics," Korani said. "It should just give advice to people, as the Vatican does, but perhaps with a greater impact."

"Where does Ayatollah Hakim fit in all of this?"

"He is free to do as he sees fit," Korani said. "Among all the ulema, the scholars, we respect his point of view, but that doesn't mean we have to agree or disagree with it. We, the Shia, have always represented the opposition group inside Islam, and many of our clerics have not accepted the governments ruling in the Islamic states. We believe that after the Prophet Muhammad there were twelve imams and that the Twelfth Imam and Jesus Christ will return and make justice in the world."

I asked Korani to explain how his fraternal scenario squared with what seemed like a growing rift between the Judeo-Christian West and the Islamic East. "Of course, between Islam and the West there is a history of quarreling," he replied evenly. "And we think that such a situation, of both good and bad, will always remain in the world until the Twelfth Imam appears, with Jesus. As for the new things that have happened, Osama bin Laden and the Wahhabi movement, as you know, they have violence in their basic precepts, because they regard other Muslims as unbelievers, kafirs, who can be killed. They see those with any small differences from themselves as unbelievers. And you in the West"—he broke off to chuckle—"are dependent on those people! You accepted them when the Ottomans fell, and they became the center of the Islamic world and captured the holy places in Mecca. When you depend on violent people, you see the result." Korani said this in an affectionately chastising way.

"So, what can the West do?"

"It's hard for the Western man to think freely now: The pressure of different groups in the United States, the Jewish lobby . . . You are now involving yourselves with world wars, and afterward you will be very tired. Of course you have the power, you have the armies. You can put all the regimes and the countries under your control, but philosophers and thinkers believe that it's not what you can do, but how you make this thing continue. There is a simpler and cheaper way. One is to solve the question of Palestine. You can solve this! Because if you have friends in these Middle Eastern governments, there would be no terrorism; they would deal with them. If the United States stood justly toward such situations, then its moral power would be stronger than its army's power."

Seeing that Sheikh Korani had warmed to his role of Eastern savant, dispensing oracular wisdom to an unlicked cub of the West, I pressed him again to speak about the issue at hand, the imminent American war against Iraq. He pondered for a moment and then, with a look of twinkly admonishment, he yielded. "We all want, of course, to get rid of Saddam," he said quietly. "But I think the Americans will get into trouble there. They talk about keeping a military governor there for a year or so and building democracy. But I think they will grow weary. Because if you put a military governor in Iraq, they will always be thinking: 'This is an American.' If you manage to make a democratic situation for the Iraqis as soon as possible, with elections and a national government, then good, but don't get involved in the shifting sands of Iraq. So if you do anything in Iraq, do it quickly."

THREE

By early February it was no longer a question of if but when the conflict would begin. A massive airlift of troops and military equipment had been under way for weeks, ferrying tens of thousands of American soldiers to bases in Kuwait and Qatar. Dozens of warships were steaming toward the gulf from U.S. naval ports. A similar, smaller movement of troops and war matériel was taking place simultaneously from Great Britain.

By the middle of the month I had a new Iraqi visa stamped in my passport and was on my way back to Baghdad, determined to stay there for the duration of the war. While I was en route, in Amman, I met one of Jordan's wealthiest entrepreneurs, a man who had made a fortune by supplying food to the allied forces during the Gulf War. He told me that according to his sources, the Americans planned to launch their attack in the third week of March. When I asked him how confident he was about his information, he shot me a secretive smile and said: "The people I talk to, they know."

Baghdad was strangely calm and peaceful. No preparations for war were taking place that I could see. Shops and restaurants were all open for business, and people seemed to be going to work as usual. There were no more policemen than usual on the streets, and no soldiers in sight anywhere. The weather was extremely pleasant, not unlike Southern California in the winter. It was sunny and warm, with a slight breeze, and the skies were clear and blue. I headed for the Hotel Al-Rasheed, Baghdad's main hotel, the place where most foreign journalists stayed. As I was checking in, my usual driver, Sabah al-Taiee, tracked me down. A plump, handsome Shiite man of fifty-two with a pompadour of silver hair and carefully clipped mustache, Sabah had been a driver for Iraqi Airways until the Gulf War, when the fleet was grounded, and then had gone to work at the Al-Rasheed Car Service, which had an office in the lobby. Sabah had been my driver on my first visit to Iraq and again during Saddam's loyalty referendum. He had been expecting me to return and been on the lookout for me.

Each time I came to Baghdad, Sabah seemed to have grown a little fatter, and a little better off. On this occasion, I noticed, he had upgraded his twenty-year-old white Chevy Caprice—the all-time favorite Iraqi automobile—for a gleaming white Mercedes-Benz. It was ten years old but looked brand-new, not least because at every spare moment Sabah fastidiously wiped it down with a chamois cloth and had it washed every day by one of the itinerant boys who loitered around the Information Ministry.

When I quipped that I had doubtless paid for the new car, considering his usurious rates, which had gone from fifty dollars a day in 2000 to seventy-five in 2002 and had now reached one hundred, Sabah laughed good-naturedly but immediately embarked on a litany of denials. He pointed out that he owned only half of the car, reminding me that he had a silent partner, with whom he had to split his earnings, that he had a large family to support, and so forth. Sabah's final argument, which I found hard to disagree with, was that we were more than just a journalist and his driver; we were close friends. As proof of this Sabah had long kept a photograph of us standing together, arm in arm, tucked into the sun visor of his car, which he regularly pulled out to show other people, while kissing it and swearing undying loyalty to me. Over the past couple of years, in between my visits, he had often rung my home telephone to say hello and, usually finding me away and the answering machine switched on, left his habitual greeting: "Hello, hello. Mr. Jon, Mr. Jon. This Sabah in Baghdad. Good-bye."

The bond Sabah had so tenaciously forged between us made it virtually impossible for me to consider using anyone else as my driver in Baghdad. Each time I returned, Sabah made himself more and more indispensable. He usually arranged to sleep in an adjoining room of whatever hotel I was in, at reduced Iraqi-only rates, so as to be near me, and waited on me like a faithful man-servant, not only driving me around but taking and retrieving my laundry, changing my money, bringing me coffee to wake me up first thing in the morning. Whenever we argued about money, which was fairly frequently, he invariably reminded me of his beyond-the-call duties, however self-appointed they were. Sabah spoke his very own pidgin English, and I usually rustled together enough words in Arabic so that we could communicate. He had some idiomatic particularities that I had finally come to comprehend. He spoke of himself in the third person, and *you* meant "I," for instance. So, when Sabah asked me, "You go laundry?" he wasn't asking whether I wanted to go, but whether he should. This kind of thing made for some bewildering conversations, but also a great deal of hilarity.

Sabah was a creature of habit. Every Thursday he went to the same barber, Karim, who had a little two-seater barbershop on one of the nameless side lanes between Sadoun Street, the main downtown shopping boulevard on the eastern side of the Tigris (named after Nasser al-Sadoun's great-uncle, the former Iraqi prime minister) and Abu Nawas, the riverside drive, with its smattering of fish restaurants and art galleries and neglected strip of parkland. Sabah had been going to Karim's for a trim and a shave every Thursday for the past thirty years, and when I was in town, he took me along with him. Karim's neighborhood was a run-down but atmospheric warren of narrow streets lined with

Ottoman-era buildings with hanging balconies and crumbling brickwork that had become tenements shared by several families. In the late afternoons the streets were noisy with children playing, and men sat outside on chairs talking or playing dominoes and drinking arrack. Somehow, the neighborhood had escaped Saddam's bulldozers. It was my favorite part of Baghdad.

Karim was a warmhearted man in his middle fifties, but he looked at least ten years older. He had Coke-bottle glasses that made his eyes look huge, and he was missing some of his front teeth, giving him a wizened look. He had old, dirty hair clippers and scissors and greasy bottles of pomade and hair dye, and he used an equally unhygienic-looking strop razor and horsehair brush for shaves, but his barber chairs were genuine red plush vinyl, with chrome footplates, and they had working levers for Karim to lean them back. Everything about the barbershop looked as though the clock had stopped circa 1970. Sabah told me that Karim was poor and had a potbelly because he liked to drink arrack and spent all his money on that, but I don't know if it was true, because he never took a drink when I was there. Karim was invariably unshaven, which I always found amusing because he was a perfectionist when it came to other people. Just having a shave at Karim's meant spending at least forty minutes there, because he always did three separate, meticulous passes with his razor, and not before exfoliating my face with a length of vibrating twine which he held in his mouth and twiddled with his fingers. It was excruciating to go through, but there was no stopping him. While Karim was torturing me, Sabah usually sent for tea to be brought by a boy from the chaikhana, or teahouse, next door. The tea came strong and black with sugar added, served in little shot glasses on saucers. Sabah, like a lot of Iraqis, drank his by sloshing tea onto the saucer and slurping it up from that.

On a street adjacent to Karim's barbershop there was a beat-up narghile (waterpipe) café, run by a jovial Cairene who was another acquaintance of Sabah's. He had stayed on in Baghdad after the great exodus of Arab guest workers from Iraq following the Gulf War. (During the Iran-Iraq War about four million migrant workers from Egypt, Sudan, and other countries had flocked to Iraq, which was flush with oil money and war loans from the gulf states, to take over the jobs of the Iraqi men serving at the front.) Sabah and I sometimes went to the Cairene's café late at night to puff on a narghile of apple-flavored tobacco and drink glasses of sweet tea.

Sabah's favorite lunch place was the Al-Tabeekh restaurant, just off Sadoun Street. It was there that Sabah first introduced me to quzi sham, a delicious dish of Syrian origin, consisting of a ball-shaped pastry stuffed with saffron, rice and almonds, lamb, chicken, and raisins, and taught me that it was available only on Thursdays because it was a special eve-of-holy-day dish and that it was best not to eat it in hot weather because it lay heavy on the stomach. Al-Tabeekh was cheaper than anywhere else, and the food was good; that was why Sabah took me there, always reminding me that he was saving me lots of money. Invariably, after lunch, we walked across the street so Sabah could have his shoes polished, and he always insisted that I have mine done too, by the same group of shoeshine boys on the curb. And right there he always bought his brand of Korean cigarettes, Mild Pine, from the same sidewalk vendor. Sabah's laundry, the Al-Ghazala, was across town, a clean, efficient family-run place with a vintage Italian dry-cleaning machine near the Baghdad Trade Fair; it was where Sabah had taken his laundry for years and now took mine. Right next to the Al-Ghazala were Sabah's preferred money-changers. They had little shops with placards showing oversize Iraqi dinars with Saddam's face and, incongruously, U.S. Benjamin Franklins; freelance changers stood at the roadside there too, clenching stacks of cash and waving them to tempt passing motorists. If we were passing by, Sabah would often slow his car down to banter with the changers and find out the latest spot rate for U.S. dollars.

Sabah was happy to drive me almost anywhere in Baghdad— unless he thought taking me there would get us into trouble with the authorities—but he didn't like leaving the city and adamantly refused to drive any farther south than Babylon. The year before we first met, he told me, he had driven a Swede to the ruins of Ur, in southern Iraq, and while they had been there, they were rocketed, not once but twice, by an American warplane. When I wanted to go farther afield than Sabah felt comfortable with, he'd arrange to have another driver take me. Sabah made no bones about the fact that he was a survivor; in confidence, he had boasted to me about having dodged the draft during the Iran-Iraq War by paying off some officials, for example. Whenever he made reference to gaming the system, Sabah would widen his eyes, smile, and tap his head, meaning, as I came to learn, that he was no dummy.

Official corruption was a fact of daily life in Iraq; without paying bribes, you could not work. Sabah was a masterful practitioner of the art, and he took great delight in the little perks it brought him. For instance, he always paid a few dinars to the traffic cops who sat permanently on the median strip of the boulevard in front of the Al-Rasheed, just so he could make an illegal U-turn there, to get to the hotel more quickly. He had been doing it for so long that whenever he passed, the cops straightened up and smiled and waved at him. At the Al-Rasheed itself, Sabah behaved like a grandee, regularly dispensing little goodwill wads of Iraqi dinars to the concierges, receptionists, security guards, and porters. This, he explained, kept everyone happy and less likely to cause either of us any trouble.

Early on, Sabah had also shown me the ropes at the Information Ministry, where all journalists were obliged to register and be assigned officially appointed minders to request interviews, secure travel permissions, and obtain visa extensions. With rare exceptions, journalists' visas were for only ten days, and so part of every visit involved scheming and bribing and currying favor with ministry officials in order to obtain extensions. Sabah took great pains to ensure that I never had to pay cash bribes, however, suggesting at the end of my first trip, for instance, that I buy three cases of Pepsi (Iraqis are Pepsi addicts, although the beverage was no longer the real thing but a bootleg Iraqi version) for the head of the Foreign Press Office, and two cases of 7-Up for his deputy, who, he confided, was actually a Mukhabarat agent assigned to oversee the place. Sabah made sure I did not have to hand over these gifts myself, but he personally delivered them to their homes a day or two before I left. This, he explained, was a symbolic gesture, to create a feeling of goodwill, and would help me whenever I wanted to obtain a visa to return to Iraq.

The Information Ministry was an ugly concrete ten-story edifice that had antiaircraft guns on its roof and bristled with satellite dishes and telecommunications antennas. It sat on the western bank of the Tigris next to one of the seven bridges that span the river downtown and was surrounded by about fifty identical apartment buildings that housed government employees and their families. Between the ministry and the river stood the Mansour Hotel, a dark brown concrete hulk of early-eighties vintage that had once been part of the international Melia hotel chain. Like Baghdad's several other big hotels, such as the Palestine Meridien and the Ishtar Sheraton (which poked up together, mushroomlike, across the Tigris and about a mile downriver), the Mansour was careworn and had long ago lost its international franchise, but most Baghdadis still called it the Melia Mansour.

The ministry and its next-door subsidiary, the Iraqi Radio and Television Corporation, formed the propaganda and communication hubs of Saddam's regime. The ministry was where Nasra al-

Sadoun's *Iraq Daily* was published, as well as a torrent of leaflets and pamphlets containing Saddam's speeches and his government's position papers on such topics as "Embargo or Genocide," "American Double Standard Policy," and "American Crimes Against Iraq." The ministry was where most official press conferences were held and where, in a cramped warren of grimy little rooms and cubicles on the ground floor, the Foreign Press Office was located. A number of international press agencies, mostly wire services, had been allowed to rent cubicles and keep staffers there. These tended to be Iraqi or Arab journalists who knew how to operate within the system or else were actual ministry employees who moonlighted as paid fixers for different media organizations. Most such arrangements had come about as the result of a good deal of prior diplomacy and graft. CNN had worked out some special deal for itself years before. It had long been the only U.S. television network permitted to run a permanent bureau in Baghdad and keep a correspondent there.

It was one of the anomalies of Iraqi life that satellite television was forbidden to ordinary Iraqis, while in the press center, BBC and CNN were readily available, and its functionaries constantly monitored their broadcasts, as well as Al Jazeera's, which operated out of its own villa nearby. Most Iraqis had to make do with either of Iraq's two state-run TV channels, which consisted of an ad nauseam diet of potted official news, old black-and-white Egyptian movies, and Saddam reruns. These were bizarre nightly videos, an edited pastiche of clips of Saddam's past appearances, that went on endlessly. They showed him waving to crowds, greeting groups of children, accepting praise or bouquets of flowers from homage payers, overlaid with songs lauding his intelligence, his courage, and so on. After a while it became a kind of white noise. Rather more popular was Youth TV, the channel owned by Saddam's elder son, Uday, which showed pirated Western films, mostly teen slasher flicks and action-suspense movies, and MTV music videos.

At the press office, journalists were assigned "guides" to be their official translators, men whom we referred to as our minders. Most of them, like Salaar, my first minder, were merely Iraqi university graduates who happened to speak one of several foreign languages and could find no better way to earn a living. They were survivors with families to support, and most kept their political views to themselves, but some of them allowed reporters they trusted an occasional hint of their true feelings about things. They had figured out how to perform their official duties while allowing reporters as much leeway as they dared. They were all, however, obliged to keep a close eye on us and file reports about whom we talked to and what we talked about. Their official salaries were a pittance, something like five dollars a month, but we were obliged to pay fifty dollars a day for their services in cash to the ministry. We were also expected to tip them at the end of our trips. At Sabah's suggestion, I paid Salaar a modest forty dollars each week, and he seemed content with this.

Everything changed during Saddam's October 2002 referendum, however, when the regime allowed hundreds of journalists into Iraq to cover the event. Many used the occasion to pre-position themselves for the coming conflict. By this point reporters hoping to cover the war had three possible alternatives. One was to travel into Iraqi Kurdistan via Iran and wait there until the war began. Another was to sign up with the Pentagon as an "embedded" reporter with U.S. troops. The third option, which was the most uncertain, was to try to stay in Baghdad. The problem with this was, it was difficult to get visas in the first place, and then they were valid for only ten days. Since no one knew when the war would begin, it meant constantly finding a ruse to reextend one's visa, and there were no guarantees that this would be possible. During the referendum, major Western news organizations began paying huge bribes to officials at the ministry in the hope that this would guarantee them visas and a secure foothold in Baghdad. They also snapped up many of the minder-translators to be their in-house fixers, paying them a hundred dollars or more a day. Several of the better minders received thousands of dollars paid up front as salary advances.

This Klondike effect meant that by the time I had my Iraqi visa and returned in February 2003, most of the translators were already in someone else's pay, and the ministry's fees for everything had also skyrocketed. The new official daily fee for guides had been set at $100 a day, and the charge for having a satellite phone was $125 per day. The Al-Rasheed had jacked up its rates as well, and it was necessary to pay a bribe to the manager just to get into the hotel in the first place, then another to be moved to the south-facing side of the hotel, which had satphone reception. On the eve of the war, the cost of staying in Baghdad had risen to $450 a day, minimum. Since credit cards were not accepted in Iraq, it had become essential to bring in huge amounts of cash.

Hundreds of journalists were flooding into Baghdad, and a feverish scramble was under way to obtain visa extensions. The word going around was that a major American TV network was paying five thousand dollars in bribes for each of its extensions. The bigger media organizations certainly seemed to have figured something out, because all the large U.S. and European television networks had brought in tons of equipment and sizable crews, and most of the major American, British, European, and Japanese newsmagazines and newspapers had opened provisional bureaus and sent in several correspondents. For everyone else, the question of how to stay in Baghdad remained an unanswered riddle and a source of extreme anxiety.

To make things even more confusing, there had been some recent personnel changes at the Foreign Press Office. A pouchy-faced, passive-aggressive little man in his mid-fifties named Mohsen, a veteran second-tier deputy of the office, had been improbably promoted to director, and the former chief, a Mukhabarat man named Hillal, had vanished. A new man, Khadum, who was rumored to be a senior Mukhabarat officer, had come onto the scene. A feline, athletic fellow who wore smart suits and spoke superb English, Khadum had moved into Mohsen's cubicle with him. Mohsen and Khadum sat at desks facing each other. No one in the ministry seemed to know who was the real boss. When I asked Mohsen who was in charge, he shot a glance across the room at Khadum and, with an ambiguous smile, said quietly: "We both are."

Not surprisingly, a few journalists committed some grievous blunders. In an incident that quickly became a cautionary tale to the rest of us, a Korean television journalist hoping for a visa extension proffered a stack of hundred-dollar bills to the deputy minister of information, Uday al-Taiee. After the Korean handed him the money, al-Taiee had apparently thrown a furious shouting fit, hurled the dollars back at the hapless correspondent, and ordered him thrown out of Iraq immediately. The Korean's mistake, evidently, had been to produce the cash in the presence of al-Taiee's assistant. He had not been wrong to think that al-Taiee would take a bribe, but he had not observed the proper protocol.

A goggle-eyed man of around fifty, al-Taiee had a large office on an upper floor of the ministry and was the ultimate overseer of the foreign press. He worked directly under the minister, Muhammad al-Sahaf, and often appeared seated gravely next to him during press conferences, the very picture of Baathist propriety. In private, al-Taiee was an eloquent and loquacious man who spoke both French and English, but he was given to mood swings, and I always tried to avoid him. He had a habit of delivering long, patronizing lectures to newly arrived British or American journalists about the perfidy of Western democracies, and I had been subjected to one of these harangues in the past. Al-Taiee had spent some years in Paris, where he had supposedly worked under diplomatic cover for Iraq's counterintelligence service, spying on Iraqi dissidents. Whatever the truth, he had returned home an unabashed Francophile. Knowing this about him, the French reporters devoted special attention to al-Taiee, crowding around him warmly when he made his regular evening appearances at the press office. It became commonplace to spot al-Taiee in the evenings being hosted for dinner by French correspondents at one of Baghdad's finer restaurants. He always sat at the head of the table as they arrayed themselves around him in respectful postures, their eyes shining with the rapt gazes of a guru's apprentices.

One of the first things I did in Baghdad that February was to look up Dr. Ala Bashir, an artist and a plastic surgeon whom I had gotten to know quite well on my previous visits to Iraq. Bashir was also very close to Saddam Hussein, and that relationship made him an extremely influential person in Iraq. He greeted me warmly and seemed very pleased to see me. After we had exchanged news, and I had told him my hopes of staying for the war, he asked me about my visa situation. In fact it wasn't good; I told him that my visa would expire within a few days. Bashir immediately called Uday al-Taiee at the Information Ministry. He did this in front of me, in his office, speaking in Arabic. "As it happened," he said later, "they were reviewing your application just as I called. I told them that you were a friend of mine." He laughed. "Anyway, they will put down my name on your application letter as the person recommending you." I never again had a problem renewing my visa, nor was there any suggestion that I had to pay money under the table, as almost everyone did, and I noticed that when the officials took note of Ala Bashir's name on my forms, they seemed impressed. Even Khadum, the mysterious Mukhabarat official, took me aside one day to say: "Ala Bashir says you are his friend. Just come to me if you ever have any problems. If there is anything I can do for you, let me know."

I had first met Ala Bashir in Baghdad in August 2000, when

I was given a letter of introduction to him by Naji Sabri al-Hadithi, whose acquaintance I had made in Vienna when he was Saddam's ambassador to Austria, and who had since become Iraq's foreign minister. Naji Sabri had told me that Bashir was a close friend and confidant of Saddam's and that I could learn more from him than anyone else I might see in Iraq. I had visited Bashir at the Saddam Center for Reconstructive Surgery, which he ran out of Baghdad's old Al-Wasati Hospital, and we had talked about politics and history. He was an unusual-looking man. Most middle-class Baghdadi men his age—he was then sixty-one—are rotund and pale-skinned. Bashir was tall and lithe, and his skin was a walnut brown color. He had a large, beaked nose, and his face was clean-shaven, also unusual among Iraqi men, who generally have thick mustaches. His features, I realized, were remarkably like those of the figures carved on alabaster vases by Sumerian artists five thousand years ago. But the most distinctive thing about Bashir's appearance was his hair, which hung in a long white fringe from the sides and the back of his head, which was otherwise totally bald. Most Iraqi men have neat haircuts or, possibly, if they are young, shaved heads with a little bristle visible—the Uday Hussein look. Iraqi professional men also tend to dress very conservatively, usually in dark suits and ties. But Bashir dressed in a distinctively casual Western style, often wearing a polo shirt and chinos or, when the weather was cooler, a brown corduroy suit, a very un-Iraqi thing to wear. I don't recall ever seeing him wear a tie. Bashir's office in the dilapidated Al-Wasati Hospital was also unusually austere for an Iraqi of his station. Accustomed to finding Saddam's officials ensconced in lavish offices that were chilly with air-conditioning and adorned with art, I had been surprised to find Bashir in a small room with slightly grubby walls painted an institutional lime green, appointed only with a filing cabinet, a chair, and a simple desk. An old air conditioner sat in a hole in the wall, but he kept it switched off. The only decorations in the room were an official portrait of Saddam that hung on one wall and a small bust of Saddam that sat next to the lamp on his desk.

Ala Bashir had a quiet and self-effacing manner, but even so, we had a rather contentious first encounter. I had told him that it was my hope that he, as a friend of the Iraqi leader, could tell me what kind of man Saddam Hussein "really" was. Bashir listened to me without expression and then, after a long pause, began speaking. First of all, he said, I should be prepared for the fact that all that I would hear about Saddam Hussein in Iraq was praise. He explained: "He is our president, and we are within our rights to praise him." Then he informed me that he knew that anything he told me about Saddam would not be reported accurately. When I protested and asked him why he thought so, Bashir explained that he was referring to the Zionist domination of the Western media and its conspiracy to control the world. "I have evidence that you will not be able to tell the truth because when people have tried to in the past, they have been crushed." He related the case of a contemporary French philosopher, whose name he could not recall. "You know the one I mean," he said animatedly, "the one who wrote that the numbers of the Nazi Holocaust had been greatly exaggerated, maybe only two or three thousand dead, not the figures they give, of millions—which is a lot of rubbish. What did they do? They moved against him in the courts, they attacked his books; bookstores were attacked!" Bashir concluded: "I believe Hitler must have done some good things for Germany, but who can say this today? No one can, because of Zionist control of the media."

I began arguing back, but Bashir interrupted me. He said: "Christians and Muslims, you know, we are very much alike; we share the same values, but I don't think the Jews in America want to allow the Christians to think for themselves, independently." He paused for a moment, and asked: "Do you know Eichmann, the one the Jews executed in Israel?" When I replied that I did, he smiled, and said: "Well, Eichmann said that he acted against the Jews because they kept to themselves and did not consider themselves to be Germans. This is a real problem, do you see?" When I replied that, actually, I didn't really see what the problem was, Bashir obliged me with a personal anecdote. The previous year, on a visit to London, he had hailed a taxi and been picked up by a chatty driver who had introduced himself by saying, "I'm a Jew. Where are you from?"

"You see?" exclaimed Bashir. "He didn't say: 'I am English.' He said: 'I am Jewish'! So you can see this still is a big problem." Ala Bashir's point, as far as I could make out, was that just like Adolf Hitler, Saddam had gotten a bad rap, and it was all the fault of the Jews.

"Anyway," he added with vehemence, "Saddam Hussein doesn't care what the West thinks. He thinks as an Iraqi, and he thinks foremost for the country. He doesn't care about elections every four years and all that rubbish. He wants Iraq to be strong, and he is trying to do the best thing for his country. . . . And yes, Saddam is a strongman, and this is maybe why he punishes his enemies and traitors so . . . strongly. Because in our civilization we are like a family, and betrayal is the worst thing you can do. But he is a good friend; a good friend to his friends—that I can tell you. Unless he is betrayed."

In spite of our obvious disagreements on several major issues, Ala Bashir seemed keen to keep talking, and he invited me to come for lunch at his house a few days later. We met once or twice more during my stay and continued to have wide-ranging discussions about art, history, and architecture, as well as Saddam. Bashir knew that I disapproved of many of the things he said, but he seemed to enjoy being provocative and also being argued with. Our meetings were refreshing for me as well, for I soon discovered that Ala Bashir was held in sufficient awe by the Information Ministry that I did not have to see him accompanied by my minder. Afterward I quoted some of Bashir's remarks about Hitler and Saddam in an article I wrote about Iraq, and I sent him the article but never heard back. I imagined that he had not liked it much.

When I returned to Baghdad in October 2002, I had visited Bashir again and asked him what he had thought about the article. He smiled and looked away shyly and said in a soft voice that I had perhaps "overemphasized" his remarks about Hitler, but that it was otherwise "fine." Bashir clearly did not want the issue to stand between us. Once again, he invited me to lunch at his house. Then, one evening, a few days after Saddam's prisoner amnesty and just before I was due to leave Iraq, Bashir telephoned me and asked me to meet him in an art gallery. I was intrigued. I had been trying to locate him for several days without success and thought he had been dodging me. When I arrived at the art gallery, he took me into an empty room hung with art where a large air conditioner wheezed noisily. There, standing very close to me, he asked me what was on my mind. I said I wanted him to decipher the riddle of the events of the previous few days, beginning with Saddam's loyalty referendum, followed by the bizarre spectacle, a day or so later, of former political prisoners emerging from years of confinement in Abu Ghraib, shouting praises of Saddam, and the almost macabre performance by the relatives of the disappeared, protesting in the streets of Baghdad but masking their true intentions by singing odes to the Iraqi leader. Bashir listened closely and then shocked me by saying in a soft, low voice: "You call these things a riddle. I guess that is what they are. But I think you are an intelligent man. So you should not expect to hear the truth about things when you talk to Iraqis. They cannot speak the truth, and I think you know why. There is a great deal of fear among people in Iraq, and for very good reasons." As for the protest by the missing prisoners' relatives, he let me know that the missing men were probably gone for good. "There are many missing people in Iraq. Many.

"There are many people in Iraq who do not agree with this release of prisoners into the streets," he added quietly. "Because they are criminals, they committed crimes, and many of them belong in prison. So in fact, to have released them is a crime, really. Those who decided to release them in fact were criminals." He paused, as if to allow me to absorb the enormity of what he was saying. Then he repeated: "Many people do not agree with this, but they will not tell you that." He paused again, then said: "I will tell you a story that will help you understand." He proceeded to tell me about the time he'd been visiting a hospital in a European country and was surprised to recognize a friend of his from Baghdad. The man walked quickly past him without recognizing him and carried on down the hallway. As Bashir started after him, he noticed that his friend had acquired the peculiar habit of constantly turning around to look over his shoulder. "He looked like he was mad, because he kept looking around, even though no one was there," he explained. When Bashir caught up with his friend, he asked him why he was behaving in that fashion, and the man had said: "That's what they did to me in Baghdad, and now I can't stop thinking there is someone following me."

"That's the way it is here, you see?"

I knew that Bashir had taken a huge risk in saying these things to me, and I acknowledged this by thanking him and steering the conversation back to mundane matters. Before we parted, he gave me a final piece of advice: "Listen closely to the people, and judge for yourself. But remember, the truth is to be found in what they don't say." When I went to see him a day or two later, to say good-bye, I intentionally did so quite formally, in front of several of his colleagues.

Ever since our conversation in the art gallery, however, our relationship had a strong element of complicity to it, and after I returned to Baghdad in February, Bashir and I met every few days, sometimes at his home but usually at his office. He urged me to visit him frequently and behaved anxiously when I didn't show up for several days. If there were other people there—Bashir had many visitors—our conversations were fairly superficial, like those between polite friends, and dealt with topics of current interest, like the looming war. He had me to dinner at his house a few times and also began taking me with him to the home of a friend of his, Samir Khairi Tawfik, who was introduced to me as a senior official at the Foreign Ministry. Samir seemed to enjoy cooking for us and other friends who dropped by. He lived alone in a large house, with stylized crenellations along the edges of its flat roof, like those of a fortress, which was situated next to a mosque on a quiet residential street in the neighborhood of Mansour. Samir was an affable fellow who bore an uncanny resemblance to those Ruritanian nobles and government ministers depicted in Hergé's Tintin books; all he lacked was a monocle. He was tall and corpulent, with a large, bald head that had a fringe of remaining black hair around the sides and a great mustache of the sort that was last in fashion in the West in the 1890s, and he had very large, drooping black eyes.

Bashir himself lived in an unassuming brown stucco Western-style house, built in the 1960s, in the middle-class neighborhood of Al-Jihad in southwestern Baghdad. Two Mercedes and a Hyundai SUV were always parked in the carport. None of them was new, and they seemed never to be driven. Bashir usually traveled in a chauffeur-driven government-issue Toyota Land Cruiser. The curtains of the house were always drawn, and in the dim light the place seemed rather forlorn. Bashir's wife, Amal, also a doctor, and their daughter, Amina, then twenty-three, were in Amman. He explained that he had sent them out of the country a couple of months earlier and told them to stay there until the war was over. He had four children, the first two of which, both boys, had been born in England, where he had worked as a surgeon in the early 1970s, after he received a degree from the Royal College of Surgeons in Edinburgh. His two eldest sons lived in England now, in Sheffield and Nottingham, and another son studied music at a conservatory in Montpellier,

France. There were family pictures on the wall in the living room, among them a recent one of a smiling toddler grandson and, in a discreet corner, a framed portrait of Bashir standing at some public function with Saddam Hussein. It was the only image of Saddam I saw there. Large paintings were hung on most of the walls, and pieces of sculpture dotted the room.

Most of the art in the house had been made by Bashir, who was an eminent painter and sculptor as well as a medical doctor. He had received commissions from Saddam for several large public monuments in Baghdad, including a prominent one, unveiled in 2001, at the memorial to the attack in 1991 on the Amiriya air-raid shelter, where an American bomb killed more than four hundred people, most of them women and children. The shelter, which had been turned into a museum, was the centerpiece of Iraq's officialized sense of victimhood. For the regime, Amiriya was put forward as the Iraqi equivalent of Guernica or even Hiroshima, a historic outrage described in official Iraqi propaganda as "The Worst Criminal Action by the U.S. in the 20th Century." It was a dark chamber with a huge gaping hole in its flat ceiling where the American bunker-busting bombs had struck it, messy with twisted steel rods and bits of masonry. I had been shown around by a doe-eyed female guide who told me how the people in the room had died in the superheated temperature of the blast, how many of them had simply vanished. She showed me what she said was the photo-silhouette of a mother and her baby on one of the walls. She explained that the intense heat of the blast had had a photographic effect as it incinerated some of the human beings in the room. When I looked closely at it, the dark, shadowy image did resemble something like a human form. I was reminded of the Shroud of Turin, the ancient cloth that was believed to bear the imprint of Christ. My tour had ended in front of a row of portraits of the children who had been killed, with the guide asking me rhetorically: "Why did they have to die?"

Bashir's art is rooted in surrealism, of which he is one of Iraq's pioneers and few practitioners, and much of it is symbolically foreboding. Many of his sculptures feature ravens with their beaks open, like maws. His gruesome, Medusa-like bronze of an androgynous human face grimacing in pain at the Amiriya memorial is a terrifying piece. "It represents the outcome of war and hatred," Bashir explained one day. "It is a reminder to everybody that war is bad. The message we should believe is love, because it's about life and reconstruction. We must overcome our hatred, because it leads to destruction." Speaking about his art always tended to put Bashir in a philosophical mood. Our conversations were often punctuated by silences as he lapsed into distracted reveries. At such times he often doodled with a pen and paper, creating little surreal images. After a moment he spoke again: "This war, I am sure, will occur. It's another sign that we are really far from what God wanted us to be. We are not beyond Christ or Moses. They tried to spread love between people, and they were prophets, but they failed."

After our talk that day we drove out to a traffic circle at the western edge of Baghdad, where Bashir's most recent large piece stood. It consisted of two sensuously joined blocks of cut limestone, about thirty feet high, the shape of one resembling by design, Bashir said, a woman's back. As we walked around it, he explained that he had called the piece *The Union,* but that, at the insistence of Saddam's right-hand man and chief bodyguard, General Abed Hamoud, it was now officially called *The Union Between the Leader and His People.* He smiled thinly and shrugged. It didn't really matter what it was called, he said. At least he had managed to avoid putting a statue of Saddam in front of it, which Abed and several other officials close to Saddam had first requested, or, as an alternative, adding a replica of one of Saddam's fists. Bashir said that there was nothing else like his public sculptures in Baghdad because Saddam preferred literal, figurative art. "He says that he doesn't really understand my art, but that he thinks it is art destined for the future generations of Iraq, who will understand it. And he has said this many times to other people in front of me." It sounded as if Saddam was held in some kind of thrall by Ala Bashir and that this feeling was reciprocal.

Bashir didn't speak freely to me about Saddam Hussein very often, but once, when we were alone in his house, he described the terrified sycophants who surrounded the president, his pathological, "worthless" sons—especially Uday, whom Bashir truly despised—and the curious affection Saddam seemed to feel for Bashir. "Even his half brother Barzan"—the former intelligence chief and Saddam's personal banker—"who is a good friend of mine, says I am blessed by God to speak to his brother in the way I do. No one else can or does. Even his own family is afraid of him." But Bashir also said that most of the people he knew, including several high-ranking generals and ministers, wanted a change and would be angry if Bush decided not to invade. "If Saddam stays in power," he said, "it would be a victory for dictatorship, for murder, for torture and bloodshed." He had traveled to many countries in the world, he said, and he had seen some bad places, but none that he knew of was crueler than Iraq. "Some of the things that have been done to people over the years are beyond any description."

By the end of February the Al-Rasheed was packed with journalists from all over the world. It was like the gathering of a large, discordant tribe, and the atmosphere was jittery and expectant. Some well-known media personalities had shown up, including the redoubtable Peter Arnett, who, having left CNN a few years earlier after a scandal arose over his involvement as narrator in a phony story, had bounced back with a new gig. Wearing a baseball cap and sportily dressed, he was being trailed around by a producer and a cameraman, doing a video diary for

MSNBC's *National Geographic Explorer.* Jim Nachtwey, the king of international war photojournalists, in his trademark white shirt and blue jeans, had arrived, as had Jon Swain, the photographer of *The Killing Fields* fame, who unfailingly wore a red-and-white-checkered Kampuchean scarf coiled around his neck. Ross Benson, the correspondent of the British tabloid *Daily Express,* who had a vintage mods-and-rockers coiffure of white hair and burning cigarette fixed permanently in one hand, seemed to have assumed a position in the hotel lobby and restaurant, for I always saw him in either of the two places. Benson was always impeccably dressed in a tailored blue blazer with gold buttons and expensive leather loafers. Finally, there was the unmistakable figure of John Fisher Burns, the veteran two-time Pulitzer Prize–winning *New York Times* reporter, who, at six foot two and with his tousled crown of silver hair, towered over everyone.

It was, to say the least, something of a circus atmosphere. One morning, in the breakfast room of the Al-Rasheed, I spotted Ramsey Clark, and we spoke briefly. He was vague about what he was doing in Baghdad, but I assumed it had something to do with Saddam, with whom he had been friendly in the past. I recalled seeing an autographed copy of Clark's 1992 book *The Fire This Time: U.S. War Crimes in the Gulf* on display at Saddam's Triumph Leader Museum. I had spoken with Clark a few years earlier, in his capacity as a lawyer for the murderous Charles Taylor of Liberia. Since then he had embraced many more unpopular causes, such as Slobodan Milošević, to whom he had paid homage during the 1998 NATO air campaign. Clark had also provided legal counsel for a follower of Osama bin Laden's who was implicated in the terrorist bombings of the U.S. embassies in Kenya and Tanzania. Most recently, I'd heard, Clark had signed up as the defense lawyer for one of the Rwandan Hutu leaders accused of genocide. Within a few days of our encounter at the Al-Rasheed, the reason for Clark's visit became clear, as the news broke that he had helped Dan Rather obtain an interview with

Saddam, the first granted by the dictator to a Western journalist in many years.

The war attracted many other colorful personalities to Baghdad as well. One of the more eccentric characters was a hyperactive Russian photographer who always wore a green paratrooper's outfit, as if he were prepared for war at any moment. Most of us gave him a wide berth on the assumption that when the war did begin, he would be the first among us to die, shot by Saddam's people under the entirely reasonable misapprehension that he was an enemy soldier. There was also a large contingent of Korean feminists, a delegation of African-American and Arab-American clerics from the United States on a "multiracial interfaith peace pilgrimage," and a group of Green Party activists from Turkey.

Yevgeny Primakov, the former Russian prime minister and KGB chief, also came through town on a last-ditch peace mission and, having failed, quickly left again. He and Dan Rather and the reigning Miss Germany, Alexandra Vodjanikova, crossed paths at the Al-Rasheed. With her publicity agent in tow, the nineteen-year-old beauty queen was in Baghdad to fulfill a wish she had expressed at her coronation: to discuss peace with Saddam Hussein. The lovely Vodjanikova never got to see him, but on her last night in town she was invited to dinner by Saddam's famously priapic and psychotic elder son, Uday. The next morning Miss Germany left without saying a word to the press corps.

The most engaging group by far, however, was the so-called human shields, who arrived in Baghdad in a caravan that included a London taxicab and a couple of rickety red double-decker buses, having taken three weeks to make the journey from London through Europe and Turkey. They had been warmly received by the apparatchiks of the Baath Party's international propaganda arm, the Committee of Friendship and Solidarity with the Peoples, which had installed them in a small hotel, the Al-Andalus, next to the Palestine, with all their expenses paid.

They were an eclectic bunch and included Americans, Belgians, South Africans, Germans, and Australians; pierced faces and dreadlocks were in abundance. One of their more prominent members was a tall young man with spiky blond hair named Gordon Sloan, who was famous for having participated in the Australian version of *Big Brother.* He had been filmed naked in the shower during one of the episodes, evidently, and was subsequently known as Donkey Boy. Another shield, Godfrey Meynell, a retired British civil servant, wept often and recited the poetry of Kipling and Gerard Manley Hopkins. He had served as an officer in the British colonial service in Aden—now the nation of Yemen—back in the 1960s, but had since turned to pacifism. His wife back in Derbyshire, he explained, was a vicar with the Church of England and was praying daily for him and for peace in Iraq.

Donkey Boy and the other shields were under the nominal leadership of a charismatic Californian in his thirties named Ken O'Keefe, who had organized the group in London. O'Keefe was covered with tattoos, including a blue teardrop on his cheek and some arcane Sanskrit writing on his neck. He explained that the tattoos were his way of showing people that he was not part of "the mainstream" and added: "Despite the fact that my appearance might marginalize my message, I've been able to win a lot of people over. Two months ago this was just an idea, and now it's grown. Not as fast as I'd hoped. I wanted ten thousand human shields, but it's a start, and it's time to act now, for better or worse."

O'Keefe made much of the fact that he had been a U.S. Marine and served in the Gulf War, although, as it turned out, he'd been put in the brig and kept in Kuwait during the action, after leading a protest about the lack of air-conditioning aboard the ship that had brought him to the gulf. I asked O'Keefe what had caused his volte-face in life. "In those days I was brainwashed," O'Keefe explained. "Hell, you read a few Chomsky books, and you get a pretty clear picture of U.S. foreign policy." O'Keefe said he believed the 9/11 attacks had been carried out by the CIA so as to justify Bush's doctrine of preemptive war under the guise of the War on Terror. "The U.S. needs bogeymen," he said. "First it's Osama bin Laden, now it's Saddam, and who's next? Look, George W. Bush is a member of the Skull and Bones Society, right? His father and grandfather were too. If you look at the membership, you'll see that these people are the elite, they meet in secret, and I don't think it's to discuss the Super Bowl. I think they're setting the agenda, putting their puppets in place. That's not democracy at all!" Bush had to be stopped, he said, before he provoked World War III.

I asked O'Keefe how he felt about risking his life to defend someone like Saddam. Surely there were many other, worthier causes in the world, ones that might elicit more sympathy? "This war must be stopped," he replied, a little uncomfortably. "It would be so much better if the Saddam issue wasn't a factor, but it is, so what can I do? Stop doing what I'm doing?" Brightening, O'Keefe remarked that he had in fact been thinking ahead to the question of other causes and was pondering moving on to Palestine from Baghdad. "There, it's black and white, and there's no Saddam factor."

When we met, it had been a week or so since O'Keefe and his retinue had arrived, and the Iraqis were already pressuring them to leave their hotel and go to their "deployment sites." These were potential bombing targets, which had been selected for them, mostly power stations and oil refineries located around Baghdad. The shields had expected to be placed in schools and hospitals, however, and there was some argument over this imposition, but the Iraqis were adamant. This peremptory attitude of Saddam's officials discomfited and alarmed many of the shields, but most of them relented. I went along to one of their first deployments, at the Al-Doura oil refinery on the banks of the Tigris, the place where Nasser al-Sadoun used to work back in the early 1970s. The grim expressions I saw on many shields' faces told me they were just beginning to realize that they were, after all, in Saddam's Iraq and that a war was really coming. It seemed likely that it was only a matter of time before many of them lost heart altogether and pulled out. As he laid out his sleeping bag on a military cot in a room that had been outfitted for his group of shields, Godfrey Meynell, the vicar's husband, quoted some verses of Kipling and broke down in tears.

When O'Keefe, who had remained behind at the Al-Andalus Hotel, brought up the possibility of traveling on to Palestine, I wondered how long he intended to stay in Baghdad. I asked him his plans. "I plan to stay as long as there are people who stay whom I've motivated to come here," he replied, a little evasively. O'Keefe had a lot of things on his mind, not least of which was a gorgeous blond woman, who was said to be the former Miss Norway, whom I once passed in the foyer of the Al-Rasheed as she did a kind of catwalk for the benefit of some TV crews. As the days passed, the rumor mill had it that O'Keefe and Donkey Boy were at odds over Miss Norway's favors and that Donkey Boy was waging a mutinous struggle for the leadership of the shields.

A different group of peace activists were lodged next door to the shields, in the Al-Fanar Hotel, which looks out onto Abu Nawas, the beat-up corniche that runs along the east bank of the Tigris opposite the Republican Palace complex. They included twenty or so Americans from Voices in the Wilderness, a group that had sent many delegations to Iraq over the years to protest against UN sanctions and U.S. policy toward Iraq. It was led by a former high school teacher from Chicago named Kathy Kelly, a thin woman with piercing blue eyes and long gray hair. She had the habit of wearing girlish sundresses and buckle shoes, which gave her a certain Pippi Longstocking quality. Kelly was a former Catholic lay worker, an ardent pacifist whose antiwar

activism had begun during the Vietnam War. She was later involved in the antinuclear campaign and the U.S. sanctuary
movement for Central American war refugees during the Reagan
years. Since the first Gulf War, Kelly had spent much of her time
lobbying against the Iraq sanctions, and her activities, which had
been welcomed by Saddam's regime, had made her something of
a celebrity in Iraq. She was very popular with the Baathist
nomenklatura. They had often cited Kathy Kelly to me as an example of a "good American," who understood that the draconian
sanctions imposed on Iraq were killing Iraqi babies, and so forth,
making the argument that this was the only real problem that
existed in Iraq. Because of this, I had formed a rather jaundiced
opinion of Kelly and imagined her to be a female equivalent of
Ramsey Clark, well intentioned but morally blind, one of those
Americans with a pathological belief in the ultimate evil of the
U.S. government, someone willing to defend any cause just to
oppose the United States' policies.

When I first met Kelly in Baghdad in October 2002, however, I'd found her to be both articulate and thoughtful. "I never
thought we'd see this move by the U.S. towards what looks like
empire," she confessed. "It worries me that many people in the
United States may be willing to go along with war for the sake
of 'preserving the American way of life,' which President Bush
has said is 'nonnegotiable.' It seems that people's abilities to
think rationally have been eroded; it seems that fear of an attack
like 9/11 seems to have been the factor. . . ." Kelly said she believed that Bush's linkage of Iraq to the War on Terror was
merely an excuse; the real motivations for the Iraq War were, she
believed, the commercial interests of U.S. oil companies and the
defense establishment. "I don't think the U.S. necessarily wants
regime change so much as they want someone, I don't know
who, to come in on a white horse. I suspect they just want Saddam Hussein and his coterie out but will leave the rest in power.
The U.S. is mainly interested in Iraq's oil production, so they'll

need the existing Baathist structure to man the revitalization of the oil industry and to beef up production."

When I suggested to Kelly that her activities had made her a useful tool for Saddam, she defended herself calmly. "I don't support the current regime," she replied. "I've always acknowledged that there's palpable fear here and that human rights aren't respected. Yes, I'm a useful dupe in some ways, but at least they hear the truth from people, and when I come here, I ask people like Tariq Aziz, 'What about the political prisoners?' and 'Why do you teach your schoolchildren to hate Israelis?' By and large, there are no people coming here and saying things like this to figures in power. Sure, they deserve more than a high school religion teacher, but no one else is doing it!" She laughed bitterly. "And why, as a pacifist, would I ever say that warfare, with all its tragic consequences, should be used to accomplish change here?"

Another guest of the Al-Fanar Hotel was Patrick Dillon, an Irish-American from New York City in his early fifties. Patrick was on his own in Baghdad, and he cut an extremely distinctive figure. He was very pale-skinned, and he always wore black clothing. His head was shaved, and he had a tattoo of the crosshairs of a rifle on the back of his skull. Patrick had come to Iraq because he was against the war, but he was not a human shield, nor was he a journalist. He was a one-off. He told me he was trying to make a documentary, shooting video on his little Handycam. It was to be titled *Raining Planes*. He had no formal backing for the film. He had earned the money to come to Iraq by selling certificates he made up himself and had sold to friends and neighbors. He gave me one of them. It was a big mock dollar bill, which said "War Bond," and inside one of the leafy cameos in the center there was a photo of Iraqi children marching with guns. In the other, an American soldier was holding what looked like a rocket or missile. At the bottom it read *On s'engage et puis on voit* ("Jump in and then figure it out"— Napoleon's battle advice).

Patrick explained that the conceptual model for his movie was *Le Petit Soldat,* Jean-Luc Godard's second film, which was made in 1960, during the last years of the Algerian war for independence from France. The narrator of Godard's film is a deserter from the French army who works for a right-wing terrorist organization and has come to Geneva to assassinate an important commentator for the Arab side of things. The movie is full of moral and narrative ambiguities and has some nasty scenes of torture. Patrick told me that when he was a young man, he had served as a soldier in Vietnam. It was an experience that he said had marked him for life. He confessed that he had been obsessed with war and killing ever since. "I was killed in Vietnam and I came home with three million dead bodies sewn inside me, and I've spent the last twenty-five years trying to get the flame—of love, innocence, and all those other highfalutin notions of a psyche that is well ordered—rekindled. Now I'm here trying to civilize myself, to break my addiction to war, which was mainlined into me in Vietnam." Since Vietnam, Patrick had spent time in Northern Ireland, Somalia, and Kosovo, sometimes as a filmmaker and sometimes as a relief worker. "I love death," he blurted out. "I know it's wrong, but I do. Don't you? Isn't that why you're here?"

Patrick was carrying a copy of Joseph Conrad's *Heart of Darkness.* He explained that he was rereading it for the umpteenth time, and he read aloud the passage from which the title is derived: "The reaches opened before us and closed behind, as if the forest had stepped leisurely across the water to bar the way for our return. We penetrated deeper and deeper into the heart of darkness. It was very quiet there." His voice was reverent, and he repeated the passage, then turned to me: "Doesn't that just fucking say it all? The heart of darkness. That's where we are, right here, right now, in fucking Baghdad." Patrick said that as soon as he'd finished reading the book he would give it to me.

A couple of days later, while I was out, Patrick left me his copy of *Heart of Darkness* at the Al-Rasheed. There was a note for me and a marker tucked between two of the pages. It was a section that dealt with Marlow's attempt to comprehend Kurtz's demons: "The thing was to know what he belonged to, how many powers of darkness claimed him for their own. That was the reflection that made you creepy all over."

In his note, Patrick had written: "Jon: Kurtz is yours. Beware! There is a notion that if one isn't crying hysterically or laughing one's balls off when laying down the words, then it had better be done again, deeper. I've been shooting my eyeballs out, the underworld of sewage streets and feral packs of night children who remind me of me, and always on the verge of tears because of what Curtis 'Bombs Away' Le May invented in Japan, evolved in the valleys of N. Korea and perfected in Vietnam, the firebomb, which is about to erase whatever is left of Iraqi life as it was known and lived and celebrated for what, four or five thousand years? But what's one or two or a hundred cultures or ethnicities tossed into the dustbin of history, among friends, right? If they can't compete, if they aren't viable, fuck 'em, right? Right?

"Anyway, I've moved my bed away from the balcony sliding doors and taped the great panes of glass in cross-shaped patterns but I'll be damned if I can find any earplugs. What kind of a dump is this, hey? I hope you're lowering yourself deeper and deeper into this heart of darkness and crying and laughing and writing your heart out. Patrick."

When I stopped by the Al-Fanar to thank Patrick for his copy of *Heart of Darkness,* he informed me that he had begun rereading Orwell's *1984,* another of his favorite books. He took me up to his room, saying he wanted to show me something. I noticed that his room was very orderly, almost Zen-like in its tidiness. Everything was fastidiously in its place, and the room was spotlessly clean. On a little night table he had arranged what he called a collage, a collection of items he'd found around Baghdad: some snapshots, a hypodermic, a child's legless and armless doll, a couple of animal bones, a shoe, and, lining the table all around the edge, like a frame, Pepsi bottle caps. He explained that he makes these kinds of collages wherever he goes. Of his Iraqi collage, he declared: "This is to show the world that there was once life here, and they even drank the drinks of the empire." On the wall above his bed, directly in the center, he had taped a piece of white paper on which, in black Magic Marker, he had written the following: "'All the other stuff, the love, the democracy, is sort of by-play. The essential American soul is hard, isolate, stoic, and a killer.' D. H. Lawrence."

I liked Patrick, but I worried about him. It was not a concern I acted upon; he was a grown man and experienced in ways of the world. But his search had a wounded innocence to it. He reminded me of the character played by Christopher Walken in Michael Cimino's film *The Deer Hunter,* whose pysche is damaged by his ordeals as a POW in Vietnam, and who afterward succumbs to a fatal attraction with death, playing Russian roulette for money in Saigon's back alleys until he blows his brains out. Patrick was a man who felt things too deeply. In our conversations, he veered between manic exuberance and grief, and he frequently broke down in tears. He could not hold his tongue, and his appearance attracted more attention than seemed wise, under the circumstances. Sooner or later, I feared, Patrick would run into trouble in Baghdad. I often saw him as I drove around the streets near the Al-Fanar. He would be striding purposefully along the sidewalk, and he was always alone.

During the first few weeks of March, as the Bush and Blair governments furiously lobbied for a new UN Security Council resolution in favor of war, over the strenuous opposition of France, Germany, and Russia, everyone I knew in Baghdad began shopping for emergency supplies of food and bottled water. Those who could afford them bought generators and fuel as well.

A great race also began among the journalists at the Al-Rasheed to rent rooms at other hotels as backup options. There was a widespread assumption that the Al-Rasheed would either be targeted by U.S. air strikes or be caught up in the thick of the battle for Baghdad when it finally came. The logic for this was derived from the state-owned hotel's strategic location in the midst of many government ministries and its close proximity to the Republican Palace complex. There was also a long-standing belief that Saddam had some kind of secret tunnel network beneath the city that connected to the Al-Rasheed, and that he had used its underground air-raid shelter during the Gulf War as a command bunker. Because of this, everyone assumed that the Americans were likely to have placed the Al-Rasheed at the top of their priority list of buildings to secure in Baghdad. Many people also speculated that once the war began, the western part of the city, where the Al-Rasheed was situated, might be quickly cut off from the east and become an island, especially if the bridges over the Tigris were blown up. Therefore it would be wise to have rooms in several different hotels around the city as a fail-safe contingency. Led by CNN, which booked several of the upper floors of the Palestine Hotel, which overlooked Saddam's palaces from the other side of the Tigris (offering unrestricted views of what was expected to be the prime bombing arena), many other media outfits began snapping up rooms there and in the adjacent Sheraton.

I had always disliked the Al-Rasheed intensely. It was a big, fifteen-story brown cement building erected by Saddam in the late 1980s, and while it was the most comfortable place in town, with a swimming pool and tennis court and large garden—with its own helicopter landing pad—I found it to be a creepy place. It was crawling with plainclothes security people, and every floor had Soviet-style concierges who sat at little desks near the elevator and noted down your comings and goings. You always felt as though you were being watched. In spite of this, I had decided to stay there because many of my friends were there, and because this time around, it seemed a good idea to be around other journalists, to know what was going on. Another advantage of the Al-Rasheed was the new twenty-four-hour Internet café that had opened on the ground floor. It was closely supervised by several men, presumably state security agents, but it was a convenient way to keep up with breaking news and also, with discretion, to send and receive some e-mails. (Ordinary Iraqis were forbidden access to the Internet, although a few months earlier, during Saddam's loyalty referendum, there had been a great fanfare over the opening of Baghdad's first Internet café. It was a very carefully monitored operation, with access to most Western Web sites blocked, and all e-mail went through the government-operated Uruklink service provider. It was a given that e-mail traffic was closely scrutinized.)

Communications were a tricky business. Every journalist who had brought in a satellite telephone had been told that it could be used only at the Information Ministry, which was now a swarm of chaotic activity and which was where all the TV organizations had their satellite dishes and did their live feeds, but most of us tried to avoid the place if we could, if only to avoid questions about the validity of our visas. Those of us who had bribed our way into south-facing rooms at the Al-Rasheed, which gave us access to the Indian Ocean Inmarsat satellite, began to use our satphones clandestinely from there. This is how I usually sent and received e-mail, via my laptop computer, since I didn't trust the Internet café downstairs. There was a real risk in doing this because we had been warned that if we were caught, we could be expelled from the country. There were several scares when the Information Ministry dispatched officials over to the Al-Rasheed to catch transgressors, but so many of its apparatchiks were in the pay of journalists that one of us was usually tipped off beforehand. To be on the safe side, I began carrying my satphone and laptop with me in a small shoulder bag whenever I left the Al-Rasheed, and stored it in the trunk of Sabah's car.

When the great hotel room frenzy began, I decided to play it safe and began prowling around town with Sabah, inspecting hotels. I teamed up in this quest with Paul McGeough, an exuberant, bearded Irish-Australian in his late forties who was the international writer at large for the *Sydney Morning Herald.* Paul had covered the Gulf War in 1991 and had returned to Iraq many times since. He was a natural-born reporter with an unerring eye for a good story and had an unquenchable taste for adventure. He had spent the summer of 2001 on his own traveling around Taliban-held Afghanistan, was in New York City on September 11, and a couple of weeks later had made it back to Afghanistan to cover the war against the Taliban. We had met in Baghdad during Saddam's loyalty referendum and had remained in touch with each other. Paul lived in New York City, and before coming out, he had graciously offered to bring me the flak jacket and helmet that *The New Yorker* had bought for my protection. In return, I had picked up his prescription of atropine and syringes at a London pharmacy. When he arrived in Baghdad, it was apparent that Paul had come prepared for all eventualities. In addition to his own flak jacket, helmet, and chem-bio warfare suit, he had a full medicine box, several wearable headlamps, a camelpak (a back-carried water container with a handy drinking tube), a multibladed Leatherman, and several large cardboard boxes filled with meals ready to eat, or MREs, bought from the same company that supplies them to the U.S. military. Paul confided that he had also brought in the astronomical sum of forty thousand U.S. dollars in cash, which he kept secreted on various parts of his body. Seeing my shock, Paul advised me that money was the real key to surviving in Baghdad during a war, as he knew from past experience. (I soon realized that he was right. I had come in with fifteen thousand dollars, which at the time had seemed like an extravagant sum of money. But after only two weeks in Baghdad, half of it was already gone.)

Together, Paul and Sabah and I inspected a dozen or so hotels around town. Looking at each of them with an eye to our future security, we crossed many off the list because they seemed too isolated or vulnerable to attack. One place Sabah led us to turned out to be a kind of love motel, and the staff there consisted of shifty-eyed, unsmiling men who did not inspire trust. We inquired at the Palestine, but amazingly all its rooms had already been taken. In the end, I opted to rent a riverfront room in my old favorite hotel, the family-run Al-Safeer, a small, friendly hotel in the same neighborhood as Karim's barbershop. The Al-Safeer sits on Abu Nawas Street about a half mile down from the Al-Fanar, where Patrick Dillon was staying.

Paul, meanwhile, rented a two-bedroom suite in the Al-Hamra, a residential hotel several miles away, in the quiet residential neighborhood of Jadiriyah. After the Palestine, the Al-Hamra had become the next favorite place in Baghdad to have a room and was quickly filling up. As at the Al-Rasheed, it was necessary to pay a hundred-dollar bribe to the Al-Hamra manager just to obtain a room. I had my doubts about the place. It was located uncomfortably close to the Jadiriyah palace complex owned by Saddam's family, and it was also just a couple of blocks away from a large bomb shelter connected to a bunkerlike villa that was said to be used by Saddam's son Uday. Even so, Paul and I both felt immensely relieved to have these two contingency options, and we agreed to share our rooms should a move to either hotel suddenly seem wise. Over the coming days, as we bought provisions, we laid in stocks of food and water in both places, as well as at the Al-Rasheed.

A few journalists were still trickling into Baghdad. Some of the newcomers were reporters who had been unable to obtain press visas for various reasons and had come in under false pretenses as human shields. Among them were two friends of mine, Matthew McAllester, a Scottish reporter for *Newsday,* and his Palestinian-Peruvian-Spanish photographer, Moises Saman.

They were trying to keep a low profile and bide their time until the war began and were keeping away from the other shields as well as from the Al-Rasheed Hotel, with all of its minders and spies. They had booked a duplex suite at the Al-Hamra. Matthew, who had an unerring sense of occasion, sent me a discreet message that he had brought in some good vodka and a set of proper martini glasses and that he was hosting a small dinner party. I went with Heathcliff O'Malley, a British friend who was also staying in the Al-Rasheed. Heathcliff was a photographer for the *Daily Telegraph,* and we had traveled together in Afghanistan for several months during the war against the Taliban in 2001. Janine di Giovanni, a war reporter for the *Times* of London and *Vanity Fair,* and Anne Garrels, the veteran NPR correspondent, were also on hand. Anne and I had become acquainted many years before in El Salvador, during the civil war there, and we had met again in Baghdad a few months earlier. The filmmaker Saira Shah and her cameraman, James Miller, who had produced the award-winning Afghanistan documentary *Beneath the Veil,* had come as well. During the evening it emerged that Saira and James, who had only just arrived in Baghdad, had decided not to stay on for the war. They said they planned to go to Gaza, to do a film about Palestinian children caught up in the intifada. (Two months later came the tragic news that James had been killed while he and Saira were filming in Gaza. He was shot dead by an Israeli soldier, apparently on purpose.)

Matt and Moises's tenth-floor suite at the Al-Hamra had a large balcony with panoramic views of the city and many of the large palaces and government buildings that, everyone assumed, would be prime bombing targets. Our get-together that night was enjoyable but strange, dominated by black humor and shoptalk about emergency escape plans and the comparative qualities of our biological and chemical warfare suits. As determined as we were to have a good evening, just as we might anywhere else, as friends, to have some drinks and eat some good food (prepared by Moises, an excellent chef), the fact of the matter was that we were gathered in Baghdad to witness a war, and the war was imminent, but none of us knew exactly what was going to happen. We all expected a bloody showdown in Baghdad, however, and as we looked out at the nocturnal skyline, we speculated endlessly about which part of town would be the safest to be in when the time came. It was an eerie sensation, rather like what it must feel like to climb up onto a tall ship's crow's nest and look out over a calm sea just before a hurricane strikes.

All of us were becoming acutely aware of just how vulnerable and exposed we were in Baghdad, living as we were under close government supervision in a handful of hotels. Very few of us could count upon the Iraqis we knew to hide us in their homes; the risks of reprisal were simply too great for them, apart from anything else, and most of us had already discounted this option. We all feared the possibility that Saddam might take us hostage, as he had done with some Westerners during the Gulf War. Such worries were rampant among the press corps and grew in intensity every day, because it was increasingly obvious there was no way to guarantee our own safety. Realizing this, some people had already begun to pull out. One morning, in the Al-Rasheed, I overheard a tense conversation between a British television producer and his reporter, a woman in her thirties. He was telling her that he was going to leave Baghdad, because he had a young family, and he urged her to leave too. "You're going to have a difficult time of it if you replace me with another family man," he warned. She argued with him and accused him of leaving her in the lurch. He was unmoved and repeated his intention to leave the next day.

Sabah didn't want to believe the war was coming. He said he was convinced that there would be some last-minute deal that would allow both Saddam and George W. Bush to save face and back away from the brink. When I argued with him about this, Sabah laughed and shook his head and said, unconvincingly:

"You'll see." I got the feeling that it wasn't so much that Sabah really believed what he said as that he didn't want to confront the truth. He announced that his eldest son, Diyah, was getting married. He was throwing a wedding party for him, and he wanted me to come. The party was held in a large hall, where the bride and groom sat on a kind of throne-altar while a band played music and some of the male relatives danced together. The other tables were packed with women and children. After taking me to greet the couple, who sat frozen in place, smiling, Sabah seated me at my own table like an honored guest and brought me refreshments and several male relatives to come and sit with me. Sabah was dressed in a white blazer and white shoes, and he strode about grandly like a master of ceremonies, barking out instructions to a man whom he had hired to videotape the event. Laughing manically, he pulled out bunches of Iraqi dinars from his pockets to hurl, like worthless confetti, over the dancers' heads.

I fell into conversation with Ayad, one of Sabah's nephews, an architect in his early thirties. Our conversation turned inevitably to the prospect of war. He told me that he was very concerned about it, although as I could see with my own eyes, he said, pointing to his happy relatives, most people were trying to ignore it. Leaning closer, he whispered: "Please understand. We are not afraid of the Americans. What we are afraid of is this regime"—he pointed to the ceiling—"because of what it might do if the Americans don't come and finish things quickly." He explained that people were terrified of a reign of terror like the one that had followed the Gulf War in 1991, if there was to be a prolonged siege of the city or if the Americans pulled back before toppling Saddam. The army and the Mukhabarat, he explained, had increased their presence in civilian neighborhoods of Baghdad. Everyone he knew, he said, was planning to stay in his home until whatever happened was over. No one wanted to take any chances.

*

The Ministry of Information had assigned me a minder. His name was Khalid, and he was a listless young man with café au lait skin, a thin mustache, and a thief's watchful eyes. I didn't like or trust Khalid, and neither did Sabah, but there was nothing we could do about it. Salaar Mustafa, the quick-witted Kurd who had been my first minder in Iraq, and whom I liked a great deal, was unfortunately out-of-bounds. He had risen meteorically within the press office to become its de facto deputy director and was already on the *Los Angeles Times'* payroll. It was a pity. Over time I had come to recognize that there was much more to Salaar than met the eye. In public, he always comported himself like a tail-wagging Baathist drudge, but on a few occasions, in small ways, he had let me know that he had an independent mind. After Saddam's loyalty referendum, for instance, Salaar had come up to me and said, in a quiet deadpan: "Jon, did you hear the wonderful news? The president has received a hundred percent of the vote! Some people say it may even be more than that." Only Salaar's twinkling dark eyes betrayed his sarcasm.

Khalid was a different sort of person altogether. He was humorless and did not engage in small talk or waste time on pleasantries. I sensed in him an innate antipathy toward me as a Westerner, which was unusual in Iraq, where almost everyone was warm and friendly. At any rate, I was stuck with him, and to keep up appearances and stay on his good side, I allowed him to set up some interviews for me with people he thought I should see. On the top of his list was Muhammad Mothaffer al-Adhami, a Baathist Party deputy and the dean of political science at Baghdad University. According to Khalid, Adhami was an extremely intelligent man, someone I should meet.

We went to see Adhami in his office in a modernist block on the landscaped grounds of the main Baghdad University campus. Adhami was a stout man in his late fifties with Brylcreemed dyed black hair and a carefully tended face, which was plucked clean of hair except for his gleaming mustache. He wore a black suit and carried himself with great self-importance. A young bodyguard showed us into his office. Adhami briefly stood up to shake my hand before sitting down again behind his desk. Several portraits of Saddam were positioned around the room. I did what was expected of me and asked Adhami his opinions about the imminent American war against Iraq. "I believe the political situation is against the American war plans for Iraq," said Adhami, obligingly. "I know they may be able to come here and destroy some of our bases of life, occupy some of our towns, but it will be difficult for them to keep this going. They bombed us for forty-three days in 1991, and when they saw the Republican Guards, they asked for a cease-fire. In 1998 they bombed us for five days, but not one person moved against the government, which is what they were counting on. In 1920, the British were here, using the exact same language as the Americans today, saying they were saving us from the Ottomans. This caused a revolt against them. And in the end they were defeated and forced to give Iraq its independence. Mr. Anderson, the Iraqis like foreigners, but they don't like to be governed by them. I don't know what will happen, but in the long run, they will lose. In the end the Iraqis always unite in the face of foreign aggression. . . . I am hoping that there is still some way for the Americans to find some face-saving measure to stand down from this war."

Adhami went on in this vein for some time, giving his view that the Americans were primarily after Iraq's oil as part of an all-out bid for global conquest, and that the Israelis were the masterminds of this plan, which also involved the expulsion of the Palestinians from the territories occupied by Israel. "By controlling the oil of Iraq, the Americans will control all the world, including Europe and Japan"—which rely heavily on Iraq's oil—"and by occupying Iraq, America will link Iraq to the territory they've already occupied in Afghanistan." Adhami claimed to feel sanguine about Iraq's odds in the coming war. "Iraqis are already living in a state of war, and they know what it means. As for death, you know, we are Muslims, and Muslims believe that there is a date for death that has been fixed by God, and man cannot change it. . . . In the cities, I think we are prepared for war, and the tribes in the countryside are also organized. The Americans don't want to lose soldiers, and they don't want to fight in the cities. The government has doubled our food rations, and we have water; we are ready for a siege. I don't think it will be a short war; I think it will be a long war. The Americans can bomb us, but in the end they will have to occupy the land, but as I have said, this will not be easy."

I found Adhami's patronizing self-regard so galling that I couldn't restrain myself from baiting him. Surely, I remarked, he realized that this war was going to be different from the previous altercations. There was talk coming out of Washington that Iraq would be hit by thousands of cruise missiles in what was being described as a "shock and awe" bombing campaign. Wasn't he a little worried about that? "Cruise missiles, what are they?" Adhami snorted derisively, and waved a manicured hand as if shooing away some mildly irritating insect. "We know these cruise missiles. We are not afraid of them." He laughed heavily. "In 1991 they had more than half a million soldiers. Now they only have one hundred and fifty thousand. Are they really going to occupy this country, do you think?" Adhami drew his voice into a falsetto, as if ridiculing the very thought of it. He added portentously: "I know Saddam Hussein, I know him very well, and I know he will fight until the last minute of the war. I too am prepared to die, because I am not prepared to accept American occupiers in my country."

While I was still trying to grapple with the unlikely image of this lardy functionary fighting valiantly in the streets of Baghdad with a Kalashnikov, Adhami crowed: "Iraq is a democratic country. We have a parliament with delegates in all the towns and villages. There is Internet. It is a free country. People can express their views. As for the single presidential system we have, this is an Arab tradition, the same as it is in Egypt, Yemen, Syria, and Jordan. And as in the old days of the Caliphate, the people do not like to have their president criticized. . . . What's the difference between Syria and Iraq? Between Jordan and Iraq? Why is only Iraq considered a dictatorship?"

As puerile as they were, Adhami's opinions were a faithful reflection of the prevailing posture among Saddam's senior loyalists. It was difficult to find anyone in Baghdad who would veer from this line, with a couple of notable exceptions. One of the very few Iraqis who had ever dared question Saddam's policies and lived to tell about it was Wamidh Omar Nadhmi. A prominent political scientist and a university lecturer at Adhami's faculty, Wamidh was from an old, established Baghdad family, and he lived in a large, rather run-down home on the banks of the Tigris, in the exclusive neighborhood of Adhamiyah. Wamidh was a vestigial survivor of the old Baath Party, before Saddam hijacked it, purged it, and converted it into a political vehicle for his personalized dictatorship. He had stayed on in Iraq in the vain hope that Saddam would eventually open up the political system. He clung to a cherished vision of the days when being a Baathist meant being anticolonial, pan-Arabist, and secularly reformist—a progressive—in a backward region emerging from colonial rule but still dominated by British-appointed monarchs, tribal sheikhs, and Muslim imams. I had met with Wamidh several times over the past few years and had found him to be a measured man, someone of avid intellectual curiosity, but still very isolated by his circumstances. He always grilled me about Western publications he had heard of but not yet gotten his hands on, and whenever I could, I brought him recent copies of American and British magazines with articles about the Middle East in them.

The first time I visited Wamidh, in the summer of 2000, and in the company of Salaar, it was after nightfall, and we sat on his riverside terrace in pitch-darkness because of a power cut in his neighborhood. The banks of the river below us were luxuriant with reeds, and from a nearby mosque came the wail of a muezzin's voice, calling the faithful to prayer. Now and then the smallest of breezes came off the river. Except for the occasional speedboat that came zipping past, the scene felt almost biblical. Wamidh, a tall, jowly man in his sixties, was dressed comfortably in a white dishdasha robe and sandals. In the summers, because of the intense heat, he explained, he spent most of his evenings out on his terrace, where it was cooler, and sometimes even slept there. Wamidh had earned his doctorate in political science at St. Andrews University in England and described himself as one of the very few Iraqis with his level of education who had stayed on in Iraq after the Gulf War. He confessed that it had not been an easy thing to do. There were many difficulties, mostly economic ones. "But," he explained, nodding to the river, "I am from here, from the Tigris."

On that occasion, Wamidh talked about the long standoff between Iraq and the United States. "I believe, and I have said so openly in the past, that Iraq's invasion of Kuwait was a huge error," he remarked. He recalled how before the Gulf War took place, when Iraq's troops were still occupying Kuwait and the crisis was building, he had been summoned to speak before a presidential advisory council. Saddam's advisers had asked to hear his opinions about the situation. He told them that he thought the invasion of Kuwait was a mistake and that Iraq's troops should withdraw as soon as possible. "What I actually said was, 'Better today than tomorrow, and better tomorrow than the day after.'" No reprisals were taken against him for speaking his mind, Wamidh hastened to add, nor had any actions been taken against him since. I asked him why he thought this was so. He replied thoughtfully: "They know that I am an academic, and that I am critical, yes, but that I am not a political conspirator, and the fact that I have chosen to remain in Iraq means that I have some feelings of loyalty and patriotism."

Choosing his words with great care, Wamidh added that in his opinion Saddam should publicly accept that his invasion of Kuwait had been "an error." If he did this, said Wamidh, he believed that the fence-mending could begin between Iraq and the West. "What is more," he added, "I think the Iraqi people would accept this and think more of him for it. I know of very few Iraqis who don't think the invasion of Kuwait was what started all these problems. But he refuses to say so." Wamidh guessed that Saddam's recalcitrance was due to his deeply ingrained rural values, which hold that toughness is a virtue and that the worst fate that can befall a man is to lose face. "For this man, to have watched everything he built be destroyed—and in some cases with his own acquiescence—must have hurt him terribly in private. But because of his culture, he cannot show this."

To all intents and purposes, Wamidh Nadhmi was a token domestic critic who was allowed to remain alive because he was a fervent Iraqi nationalist, and because he provided a semblance of measured criticism that was a good thing to display to visiting journalists. Wamidh reminded me of some of the *disidentes legales* I had met in Cuba, people who were unofficially tolerated because their criticism was reformist rather than counterrevolutionary, and with whom foreign journalists were allowed to speak without fear of being deported. The difference in Iraq, of course, was that he was alone; there was virtually no one else like him.

Now, in late February, in the unwelcome company of Khalid, I returned to see Wamidh. I watched him sizing up Khalid during the habitual courteous preliminaries, as he showed us to seats in his living room, as we asked after each other's health, and as he offered us tea, and so forth. Wamidh seemed to understand that Khalid was not trustworthy. Once he began speaking, he deftly avoided the issue of who would win the war, leaving it clear enough by omission that he believed Saddam would be overthrown. Wamidh said that his worries were about the aftermath of the war. He predicted that there would be serious social divisions among Iraq's various ethnic groups, leading to civil strife and terrorism, and he feared Islamic fundamentalism would take root and spread in Iraq. "I don't know why the Americans are insisting on having their own military administration," he added, looking genuinely perplexed. "I can't imagine seeing Western troops walking in the streets of Baghdad. I can't imagine this being accepted by Iraqi people, and I think if there is, we will see a growing resistance to them in the future. Remember how the Iraqis revolted against the British in 1920. At the same time, today Iraqi people are tired, and you'll hear them be more concerned about their economic problems than politics. . . . But the other problem is the Iraqi people's perception of the Americans and the English. You see, they are seen somehow to be enemies of Iraq, to have shown a certain ruthlessness toward Iraq. If the post-Saddam era was under the so-called blue helmets of the UN, soldiers of countries other than the U.S. and UK, it would be, I think, somehow more acceptable for Iraqis. I don't envy any American general his task; he's going to be walking a very thin rope."

The Arab revolt of 1920 seemed to be on the minds of every older Iraqi I spoke to. Hearing Adhami speak of it had not moved me, located as it was within his hemorrhagic flow of bluster and conspiracy theory. But Wamidh Nadhmi's invocation of Iraqis' resistance to Britain's colonial presence as his point of reference for the near future struck a chord. His concerns closely echoed Nasser al-Sadoun's, and, for that matter, those of the Shiite exiles I had met in Iran. Whatever else they disagreed on, they were unanimous in their conviction that Iraqis would not view a foreign occupation kindly. I knew that when it came to Iraq, the thoughts of most Americans did not extend much beyond Saddam Hussein. Iraqis were seen almost exclusively as hapless victims of his tyranny, or else, as conniving participants in it, but either way, they were essentially faceless. The pre-Saddam Iraqi past was perceived, by and large, through an uncertain filter of half-digested history and romantic Hollywood imagery, which consisted of Lawrence of Arabia, Sinbad the Sailor, the biblical Tower of Babel, and *The Thief of Baghdad,* starring Douglas Fairbanks, with its Ali Babas and harems, flying carpets, and veiled belly dancers.

There was a reason for the American ignorance about Iraq's history. Apart from U.S. oil interests, the country had always been part of the British sphere of influence; there was little in the way of shared history before Saddam came on the scene. Iraq had attracted archaeologists and travelers of the intrepid Edwardian sort, like Wilfred Thesiger and Freya Stark, but they too had been British. Iraq had never been an American tourist destination. A few historians and academics had written books about Britain's early-twentieth-century colonial experiences in Mesopotamia, but knowledge of the period was not widespread in the United States. I wondered whether Washington's war planners had studied the history and taken some of its lessons into account. Somehow, I doubted it.

FOUR

The March 6 issue of the *Iraq Daily* carried an editorial with the headline THE U.S. ARMY GENERALS DREAM OF THE BRITISH VANISHED EMPIRE. Addressing himself to Colin Powell and Donald Rumsfeld, the editorialist, one Jassim Obeid Jabbar, referred to Britain's calamitous past experiences in Iraq and predicted that the Americans would share a similar fate: "We have prepared for you a nice and comfortable grave next to your inferior Stanley Maude," the British general who captured Baghdad from the Ottomans in 1917 and died there while attempting to impose some kind of order on Mesopotamia's many tribes and clans of Sunnis, Shiites, Kurds, Jews, Christians, Assyrians, and Turkomans. The editorial concluded: "We advise you to take additional lessons in mathematics, politics and art of war. This is because in your calculations you have ignored the political, economic and military consequences of war. I believe we did not spare anything to say except an Iraqi proverb: 'Could the perfumery renovate what age had corrupted?'"

Sir Stanley Maude was the British general sent to dislodge the Ottoman Turks from Iraq during the First World War. When he arrived in March 1916, the Turks had the upper hand. The British-led Mesopotamian Expeditionary Force had begun well but became bogged down. Landing by sea on the Persian Gulf, British forces had first invaded Iraq in 1914 and quickly seized the southern city of Basra. Moving north, they came to within 18 miles of Baghdad. At the ruins of Ctesiphon, seat of the ancient Sassanian empire, the Turks met them in strength, and after a bloody battle the British were forced to fall back to Kut, a squalid garrison town on the Tigris 120 miles southeast of Baghdad. There, on December 3, 1915, they were encircled by the Turks and their Arab allies. In April 1916, after a sixteen-month siege, during which nearly ten thousand British and Indian soldiers died, most from dysentery and typhoid, the British surrendered. Twenty-three thousand more troops died trying to rescue the trapped soldiers. The siege of Kut had been the longest and bloodiest in the history of the British Empire, and the garrison's capitulation one of the empire's greatest ignominies. Although the tragedy was eclipsed by the terrible carnage taking place in France and the disaster of Gallipoli, "Kut" touched off an outpouring of anger and shame in Britain because of the perception that the War Office had largely abandoned these men to their fates. In July 1917, in his poem "Mesopotamia," Rudyard Kipling gave expression to the lingering public bitterness over the affair.

> *They shall not return to us, the resolute, the young,*
> *The eager and whole-hearted whom we gave:*
> *But the men who left them thriftily to die in their own dung,*
> *Shall they come with years and honour to the grave?*

The defeated British were not treated graciously by their Turkish captors. Of the thirteen thousand soldiers who surrendered at Kut, more than half died of disease, hunger, heatstroke, and abuse during the next two years, as they were led across the country toward Turkey, on foot, in a kind of death march. Many were forced to work along the way as slave laborers on the Baghdad–Basra railway line, and those who reached Turkey were put to work in salt mines. They were given especially pitiless treatment from the people of Tikrit, the sun-baked Tigris river town a hundred miles north of Baghdad that had been the birth-place of Salahuddin the Conqueror and that would see the birth of a new native son, Saddam Hussein, in twenty years' time.

Eleven months after the fall of Kut, Maude's troops finally overcame the Turks, and in March 1917 they triumphantly entered Baghdad. Maude issued a lofty proclamation to Iraqis, with no apparent irony intended, announcing their liberation from "the tyranny of strangers," meaning the Ottoman Turks. Maude's conquest ushered in three decades of proconsular British colonial rule in Iraq, but he did not live to see any of it. He died a few months after his arrival in Baghdad, at the age of fifty-three, of cholera.

Years later, in his remarkable memoir, *Seven Pillars of Wisdom*, T. E. Lawrence sourly summed up the British war in Mesopotamia as an unnecessary disaster brought about by a combination of hubris and shortsightedness. At the time Lawrence had been a young member of an emergent cabal within the British foreign policy establishment that advocated an alliance with nationalist Arabs in the Ottoman dominions as the best way to undermine the Turks. "The conditions were ideal for an Arab movement," he wrote. He pointed out that an Arab independence movement had already begun in Mesopotamia and that there was widespread disloyalty among the Arab troops in the Turkish army. With proper handling, their leaders could have been won over to the British side. It was the same with the tribes in the south, which, Lawrence insisted, "would have turned our way if they had seen signs of grace in the British." But the Mesopotamian mission was handed over to the British government of India, which rejected any alliances or deals with Arabs. Lawrence wrote:

> *Unfortunately Britain was then bursting with confidence in an easy and early victory; the smashing of Turkey was called a*

promenade. By brute force it marched then into Basra. The en-
emy troops in Irak were nearly all Arabs in the unenviable
predicament of having to fight on behalf of their secular oppres-
sors against a people long envisaged as liberators, but who had
obstinately refused to play the part. As may be imagined, they
fought very badly. Our forces won battle after battle till we
came to think an Indian army better than a Turkish army.
There followed our rash advance to Ctesiphon, where we met
native Turkish troops whose full heart was in the game, and
were abruptly checked. We fell back, dazed; and the long mis-
ery of Kut began.

On the same day, March 6, that the gloating editorial about
Maude appeared in the *Iraq Daily,* a turab swept through Baghdad. The turab is an ill wind that makes the air clammy and full
of dust, and this one signaled the beginning of spring, with the
long, hot Iraqi summer soon to follow. The sky turned a lumi-
nescent, murky brown, and plastic bags and other refuse blew
about. Sabah became dour and sluggish and complained of a
headache and fever. He wanted to go to the hammam, the Turkish baths, to relax, he said, but it was women-only day. Sabah
cursed and complained about this, so we stopped at a pharmacy,
where he bought some Panadol painkillers and took several. After a while they had their effect, and he calmed down, but he became even more lethargic and wore a dreary expression. The
minder, Khalid, was also behaving more listlessly than usual,
but he grudgingly assented to escort me to the graveyard where
General Maude was buried.

   The North Gate War Cemetery is one of a half dozen British
cemeteries in Iraq. It is located in the old Bab Al-Mouatham
neighborhood, on the western edge of central Baghdad. The
graveyard is a dusty oblong of around fifteen acres, studded with
regimental rows of tombstones, and open space dotted with the
odd plinth and funereal obelisk. The graveyard was bisected

down the middle by a row of forlorn-looking date palms. Facing it, across a busy street, stood the Turkish Embassy, and a couple of houses farther down, the Saddam Center for Fine Arts, its walls colorfully painted with 1970s-style murals. The other side of the cemetery is bounded by a wall that separates it from the yellow-brick ramparts of a tobacco factory. At the end farthest away from the front gate, the boundary gives way to a no-man's-land of garbage and rubble, where a single leafless sapling stood, its branches festooned with yellow, blue, green, and black plastic bags.

Several laborers were working on a new guardhouse when we arrived, and one of them unlocked the gate and let us in. He pointed to an imposing domed stone mausoleum at the center of the cemetery and said: "That is where most of the visitors go." We walked toward it, along the way passing an obelisk inscribed with the message, in English and Sanskrit, "God is One—His is the Victory: In Memory of the brave Hindus and Sikhs who sacrificed their lives in the Great War for their King and their Country." Etched into a large limestone plinth nearby were the words "Their Name Liveth for Evermore." The wind blew, the dust swirled, and the branches of the date palms rustled and sounded like rain. Pigeons fluttered around, alighting on headstones. Some of the headstones had broken off and lay toppled and neglected. Those still standing were etched with Christian crosses and the insignias of the dead men's regiments: an elephant and palm for the Ceylon Sanitary Section, a castle standard for the Essex Regiment, and a stag's head for the Seaforth Highlanders. On the headstone for 201775 Private S. Brown of the Dorsetshire Regiment, who died on September 28, 1917, at the age of twenty-five, were carved the words "Peace, Perfect Peace." Many of the graves were anonymous and inscribed with the same message: "Four Soldiers of the Great War —Known unto God."

The domed mausoleum was Sir Stanley Maude's. The epitaph on his casket read "He Fought a Good Fight and Kept the

Faith." A marble plaque listing his military rank and achievements was covered with pencil graffito markings in Arabic, the names of some Iraqi boys. Khalid read out some of them for me: "Jassim, Muhammad, and Shakir . . ."

Wandering back out of the cemetery, we passed another obelisk, erected "In Memory of the Turkish Soldiers who fell during the Great War." I pointed this out to Khalid. He looked nonplussed. I explained that the British had honored their dead enemies with the obelisk. He smirked. "So, the British have honor!" He walked away, and as he did, he called back: "Maybe they will do the same for us, after they have killed us. Thank you very much!"

I caught up with Khalid. Seizing our moment of privacy, I asked him how he would vote if he were offered two simple choices. The first choice was to stand with Saddam and face the war threatened by the Americans and the British; the second was to prevent war by voting for Saddam to leave power. How would he choose? Khalid thought a moment, and replied: "I think the former one." I asked him why. He said: "Because war or no war, what they want is the same: to control Iraq. Even if Saddam resigns, the result will be the same. The Americans will come, or if not them, then their spies."

As we drove away from the cemetery, Khalid asked me when I believed the Americans would attack. He said he believed that they would do it on March 14, the Shia day of mourning that commemorates the martyrdom of the Prophet's grandson, Imam Husein, at the Battle of Karbala in the year 680. "I think they will do this on purpose, as an insult to Muslims," he said accusingly. When I told Khalid that I thought the American war planners had other things to consider—the weather, military strategy, political and diplomatic negotiations—he looked unconvinced.

A few minutes later Khalid announced that he wanted to visit his family in Karbala, which is a couple of hours' drive south of

Baghdad. He would be back the next morning, he promised, muttering enigmatically about making some arrangements for them before the war came. After Khalid left, Sabah warned me that he was unlikely to return, and he did not. The next morning Khalid telephoned me from Karbala to say his father had suddenly taken ill and was in the hospital—"there is sugar in his blood or something"—and that he would not be returning to Baghdad for a few days. He advised me to find a new minder.

The turab had brought with it a palpable downturn in people's spirits. It wasn't only Sabah and Khalid who seemed affected; nearly every Iraqi I spoke to that day appeared to have concluded that war was, after all, inevitable. It was, I suppose, simply no longer possible for them to ignore all the signals. The turab meant that summer was on its way, and everyone knew that this meant the war would happen very soon. The Americans and British had made it very clear that they did not want their troops to fight in the hot Iraqi summer. A couple of nights earlier allied warplanes had struck Basra's air defenses more heavily than usual, reportedly killing and wounding a number of civilians. Although both the U.S. and British governments claimed their warplanes were merely conducting routine patrols of Iraq's southern no-fly zone and had merely responded to hostile fire, as they had many times before over the years, the timing and intensity of the raid were lost on no one. The Russians, with the most sizable contingent of foreign diplomats, evacuated most of their remaining embassy staff, and the Japanese announced that they were departing the next morning. The few UN weapons inspectors still in the country were rumored to be on standby, ready to leave the country within two hours. Pretty much everyone else, except for about three hundred Western journalists, was already gone. As expected, some of the human shields had either been expelled (among them their ostensible leader,

Ken O'Keefe) or else succumbed to nerves and squabbling and begun to withdraw.

That evening I received a dinner invitation from Farouk Salloum, an Iraqi poet who was regarded very highly by Saddam Hussein. As with Ala Bashir, Farouk was a friend of Naji Sabri, the foreign minister, and once again it was Sabri who had introduced me to him. We had met on both of my previous trips to Baghdad and talked about Iraqi culture and about Saddam Hussein. A husky, good-looking man in his mid-fifties, Farouk was from Saddam's hometown of Tikrit. He was warm and affable, and I had instinctively liked him. On our first encounter, Farouk had been in an ebullient mood after spending the previous evening with Saddam. Farouk and a group of other poets had been summoned by the dictator to one of his palaces, where he had asked them to come up with the words for a new Iraqi national anthem. The gathering had been televised.

I had watched the spectacle on the TV in my room at the Al-Rasheed and been transfixed. The poets were seated together around a huge conference table, which curved around the edges of a reflecting pool, at the far end of which, wearing an ivory-white tailored suit and dark shirt and smoking a long cigar, Saddam lounged alone in a thronelike chair, with lots of free space on either side of him. Immediately behind him, a uniformed bodyguard stood vigilantly, arms folded behind his back, scrutinizing everyone in the room. It looked uncannily like one of those scenes in the James Bond movies in which the archvillain meets with his nervous minions. Saddam's presence was both hypnotic and terrifying. His hazel eyes were cold and penetrating, and he used them to great effect, sometimes concealing them for long moments behind their heavy lids, then suddenly reopening them and predatorily examining one or another of the poets' faces, as if trying to read their souls.

In a voice that was surprisingly reedy, Saddam informed the poets that the new anthem should exalt, among other things, "soldiers in the battlefields, the steadfast fighters of the air defenses," and "the Iraqi people's spirit of resistance and martyrdom shown during the Mother of All Battles." Afterward the poets stood up one by one and recited declamatory odes of lyrical praise to him. When they were done, Saddam said that he would leave for a while to give them some time to write down their inspirations. As Saddam rose, everyone else leaped to his feet. A half dozen uniformed guards instantly materialized and surrounded him protectively as he strode out of the room. The camera stayed on the poets, who began feverishly scribbling on pieces of paper. Sometime later Saddam returned in the same manner as he had made his exit.

For the next couple of hours, as the poets recited their new verses out loud, Saddam sat, ear cocked, alternately staring at the ceiling or into the middle distance, and smoked three more of his cigars (presumably the custom-made Cuban Cohibas that Fidel Castro was said to send him regularly), which he drew from a special box placed next to him on the table. Puffing away, Saddam acknowledged each poet's contribution with a short nod of the head, a grunt, or a muttered thank-you. He gallantly heaped special praise on the only female poet there, speaking to her in a cloying, flirtatious voice. She beamed with visible pride and looked nervous. Most of the poems, as before, had included praise of Saddam, as in repeated emotional declamations of "O Saddam!" Finally, the meeting had ended with Saddam telling the poets that he would examine what they had written and then choose one or more of them for Iraq's new anthem.

Farouk told me that the meeting with Saddam had been very exciting, but it had not been his first encounter. Saddam was in the habit of summoning him and a few others to private soirees, to talk about poetry and culture. "He is a villager, from a poor family, but he is aware of and interested in culture," Farouk explained loyally. Sometimes, he added, Saddam produced the architectural drawings for his grand palaces and other public buildings and asked his guests for their opinions. It seemed, to judge from Farouk's tone, that this was a great honor. Farouk emphasized that Saddam had not forsaken his humble origins. "He is a nature lover. I know that he sometimes goes for a few days to fish, to clear his mind, and to drive sheep through the desert, like he used to do as a boy." I found this hard to believe and told Farouk so. He insisted it was true. "I know he does this," he said solemnly.

I asked Farouk what it had been like to grow up in Saddam's hometown. Obligingly, he said that as a boy he had heard many tales of Saddam's youthful bravery. One of the more famous stories he remembered was about how Saddam used to walk every day to school from his home in the village of Owja, a few miles distant from Tikrit. In those days the countryside had been wild and lonely, inhabited by ferocious wolves, and to walk through it as he had done was a very dangerous thing. But Saddam had been unafraid and kept the wolves at bay by singing defiant songs as he walked, and this had instilled others with feelings of courage as well. This story had inspired Farouk so much, he told me, that he had written a special poem in the style of a razaq, a traditional Iraqi lyric designed to give heart to warriors in battle. Translating roughly, Farouk recited: "He who is among the wolves, whose words turn into poison, which frightens his enemies."

When I returned to Iraq in 2002, Farouk had retained his hail-fellow-well-met outward demeanor, but I noticed that his eyes were sad. He had also gained weight and spoke in a rambling, disconnected way, as if he couldn't keep his mind focused. He mentioned that he had just been on a trip to Cairo and had indulged himself in the city's bookstores, returning home with "fifty kilos of books." His eyes shone; he was obviously delighted with his acquisitions. But the exposure to Cairo's cultural bounties also seemed to have made Farouk realize just how desolate intellectual life was in Baghdad. He read me aloud a passage from an editorial he had just written for one of Iraq's official newspapers. He had titled it "The Culture of Change," he said, and in it, he rebuked the United States for abandoning Iraq's intellectuals to lives of barren isolation by cutting them off from contacts with the West through sanctions. "The United States wants us to be more modern, more flexible," Farouk translated aloud, "but the U.S. has not given us any chances for many years to have intellectual, civic, or artistic contacts between Iraqis and Americans. The United States says no to negotiations with Saddam Hussein, but we can do it ourselves, people to people."

I couldn't really see what Farouk was getting at, and I wondered if I was missing something, if perhaps his words weren't also intended as a camouflaged criticism of Saddam's tyranny. The kinds of contacts he was proposing struck me as fanciful, even irrelevant, given the increasing likelihood of war. I asked him about this. Farouk paused for a moment, then said: "I am afraid for my children, and my sister's children. I look at the old people, and I think about what will happen to them. I look at their faces. So although I think the B-52 bombers will come here and destroy, I think we have a chance between Iraqis and American civil society, through humanity, for peace and understanding."

Flashing me a smile, Farouk added: "You know something? I once wrote an editorial called 'I Confess I Like the Americans,' but I also wrote that I wished more Americans had access to free information and that only a tiny number of them can tell the truth." This assertion struck me as totally bizarre, considering the fact that Iraq was one of the most restrictive societies on earth. As if reading my thoughts, Farouk added: "You know, it's not true what people say, that we are out-of-date, isolated, or ignorant. The Iraqis' hunger for knowledge means that we want the most information possible." That was why, he explained, he had loaded up on books in Cairo. His point seemed to be that not just Iraqis but Americans would benefit from more knowledge of each other, especially if, as seemed likely, the Americans went through with their plans to invade and occupy Iraq. He said: "You know, it is not easy to make the changes in Iraq that are being talked about a thousand times a day. The Islamic fundamentalists will rise up; so will nationalism, and even tribalism. You will draw out the Wahhabites from among the Sunnis and the ultraconservative elements from the Shias. I've read the diaries of some of the nineteenth-century European travelers to this region, and I have realized that the Iraqis are still the same people as they were then. We are conservative, with tribal values of social dignity and a strong sense of patriotism."

I left Farouk's office still feeling perplexed about what exactly he had been trying to tell me. There had been some mixed messages. But underlying everything else, it seemed that he clearly understood that the war was coming, and that with it, Saddam's regime would end. I concluded, tentatively, that his plea for cultural interaction with the Americans was intended as both a warning to them about the problems they faced in Iraq and, in his pointed reference to "liking" Americans, a carefully worded message of friendliness. Perhaps it was Farouk's way of casting ahead to secure a place for himself in Iraq's post-Saddam future.

On the evening of March 6, when I arrived at his house for the dinner party, Farouk greeted me effusively, with kisses on both cheeks. He seemed a little drunk, and I noticed that he had gained even more weight over the past few months. Euphorically, Farouk led me by the hand to meet his other guests, and when he did so, he joked to them that I might be an "American spy." There were about a dozen guests, including a Palestinian man and a couple of men and women from a Scandinavian NGO of liberal Christian orientation; one of the men wore a clerical collar. Farouk had organized the gathering with a resolutely Iraqi theme. He played a lute, a beautifully crafted instrument that he said was made by the most celebrated lute maker in Basra, and he sang two songs, a sad one about love, made famous by the late Egyptian singer Um Kalthum, and a composition of his own, which sounded like a poem. The words were in Arabic, and he explained to me that the song was about lost love and a deceitful woman. The Palestinian guest whispered to me that Farouk's lute playing, which I had thought quite lovely, was "terrible," although he sang well.

We drank arrack, the Iraqi national liquor, a kind of anisette. Farouk prepared the dinner himself on a barbecue in his garden. The main course was masgouf, Tigris River fish split open and grilled on hot coals. The fish is toasted until the skin is a golden brown and is then removed from the fire. It is white and tender underneath, and the flesh is eaten with the fingers. It tastes something like river trout, but with an earthier edge to it, like catfish. While Farouk was cooking the fish, three of which had been placed on their sides around his coal fire, built on a steel drum perched on legs in his front garden, he called us over to watch and told us how the dish of masgouf could be traced back to ancient Sumeria. Standing next to me, one of my fellow guests, a grizzled Dane with long experience in Iraq, commented: "I am looking at this and thinking of Iraq's long history and how much of the culture survives today. When they get here, I can't help but think that the Americans are going to be like the New Barbarians."

Throughout the evening, with a passion that seemed increasingly desperate, Farouk insisted that we join him in toasts with glasses of arrack to art, music, love, peace, and friendship. The living room was filled with a superb collection of Iraqi modern art, along with several framed photographs of Farouk with Saddam Hussein. Pointing to his own sizable girth, he quipped that Saddam had recently advised him to lose twenty-eight kilos. He raised his glass and drank a toast to this: "To dieting!" At one point he asked some of the guests to follow him into the garden to see his new well, dug, like many others in Baghdad recently, in preparation for the war. He showed us a pile of dried date palm fronds he had begun storing for fuel and jerricans of gas, for his generator in the garden. "I have everything ready, you see?" Looking up at the moonless night sky, he said, "And I will be able to stand here and watch the cruise missiles going by, on their way to their targets, just like I did in 1991." Speaking about the bombing of Baghdad that had preceded the first Gulf War, Farouk said that he had spent his time getting drunk on arrack and going a bit crazy, so crazy—he laughed—that as he stood in his garden, watching the missiles streak through the sky, he had urged them on toward their targets. He pantomimed himself, weaving on his feet and motioning up to the dark sky, saying: "Go on, hit your targets." The joke was on himself, but there was a bitterness in the way he told the story.

Farouk laughed again, manically, and darted off to see to his other guests. Evidently believing them to be pious folk, he spoke to the Scandinavians about how he sometimes sang lullabies from the Koran to his young daughter to get her to sleep and about the shared values he perceived between Islam and Christianity. He spoke with a fervor that bordered on the embarrassing; they nodded earnestly in response, but said little. Later one of the Scandinavians, the one wearing a clerical collar, came up to me and asked quietly: "So, what do you think is going to happen?" I told him I thought there would soon be war. In early March, in Iraq, this was the only meaning his question could have. He nodded. "Yes, I think so too." He then added that although it might sound strange, coming from him, he wasn't sure that the outcome would be as bad as many people feared. His charity had also worked in Afghanistan, he explained, before, during, and after the American bombing campaign against the Taliban. Contrary to his fears and those of others who had been against that war, he had seen that the bombing had been conducted with great precision. There had been very few civilian casualties. Afterward, when he asked his local staffers their opinions about the bombing, they had told him that it had been the right thing to do. "It was a learning experience for many of us," he told me. He did have one criticism of the American involvement in Afghanistan, he said, which was their lack of follow-through after the war. He thought they had been far too reluctant to extend their influence and, by extension, that of the Karzai government throughout the country. A great deal of civil reconstruction was needed there, and they were very slow about getting projects moving. He then spoke about the high level of fear of Saddam he had detected among Iraqis. "It is pretty clear they want change," he murmured.

At around midnight Farouk announced that he would, with regret, have to bring the party to an end. He was leaving the very next evening on a trip to Madrid. It was a business trip, he explained. He had been invited as part of his government duties. As well as being a poet, Farouk was a senior functionary of Iraq's Ministry of Culture. The first time we'd met, he'd been the director of Iraqi cinema and television, and now he was the director of music and dance. Before he left, Farouk explained, he first had to see off his wife—a beautiful, weary-looking younger woman, a former prima ballerina, who had sat quietly smiling throughout most of the evening—and their daughter. They were getting on a plane to Syria. He didn't explain why, but as we left his house, one of my companions told me that Farouk's wife's family had recently rented a house in Damascus and was awaiting her arrival. Like many other high-ranking Baathist government officials, Farouk was evacuating his family before the war started. "I don't think *he'll* be coming back either," my companion said. As we drove off, Farouk was standing at the gate of his driveway, weaving slightly, and calling out, "Light a candle for us. Light a candle for peace, and for the children of Iraq."

That night, in the United States, President Bush went on national television to announce that war with Iraq was very close.

The next morning I asked Sabah to drive me to the Triumph Leader Museum, where Saddam's large collection of gifts was displayed. I wanted to have another look at the gun that was said to have been used in 1920 to assassinate the famous British officer Colonel Gerard Evelyn Leachman. Like his colleague T. E. Lawrence, Leachman had become famous for his exploits in the desert, living among the Arabs and performing feats of endurance and daring. During the early stages of the Turkish encirclement of Kut, Leachman, who had been covering the flanks of the retreating troops and was outside the town, broke through Turkish lines to rescue some of his servants who were trapped in the village, including a young Indian boy, Hassan, who had become his constant companion. Leachman led a breakout with a few thousand cavalry troops. Leachman and Lawrence met during the siege, when Lawrence arrived on a secret mission to secure safe passage for the besieged garrison from the Turks in exchange for a bribe of two million pounds. Leachman led Lawrence to the rendezvous with the Turkish commander, but the offer was airily rejected by Enver Pasha, the Ottoman war minister. Lawrence left the country for Egypt, and a short time later the Kut garrison surrendered.

Lawrence went on to become a much more celebrated figure than Leachman, largely because of the American journalist Lowell Thomas's razzmatazz presentation of his story, and because Lawrence was a gifted writer who lived to write his memoirs. Leachman, on the other hand, was publicity-shy, a military man of action who rarely wrote anything down, but he was also a heroic figure in his own way, and news of his murder had both inspired the Arab tribes to revolt and horrified the British public, which was already having misgivings about the occupation of the Middle East. Leachman had come to Mesopotamia—or Mespot, as the British called it in those days—in 1907, after serving in the Boer War, in which he was wounded, and then in India. He spent a short time in the cosmopolitan society of

Westerners in the cities of Basra and Baghdad, but he made his reputation moving among the tribes of the Euphrates. He wore traditional Arab garments and rode horses and camels on long trips across desolate, unmapped landscapes, reporting back on the intrigues among tribal chieftains during the last days of the Ottoman Empire.

In the spring of 1910 Leachman was on a spying mission in the desert when he visited the war camp of Nasser al-Sadoun's great-grandfather Ibn Sadoun Pasha, the leader of the powerful Muntafiq clan, which had ruled a huge swatch of southern Mesopotamia for four centuries. When I was in Amman, Nasser al-Sadoun had regaled me with the story of this encounter. At the time the Sadouns were in the midst of a territorial war with rival desert clans, including the Sauds, the future rulers of Saudi Arabia. Most of the tribes were in loose alliance with the Turks but were already being courted by the British as they probed the nether regions of the Ottoman Empire in their own bid for influence. Leachman traveled back and forth across the battle lines between the warring tribes and had met the young prince Saud and his regent uncle before making his way to Sadoun Pasha's camp. The old chieftain had just fought off a raid by an eight-thousand-man army sent by the Sauds and their allies from Kuwait, and on Leachman's journey the British colonel crossed an area of desert littered with human bodies being eaten by hyenas and vultures. He was greeted graciously by Sadoun Pasha, who told him about the battle and informed him that he was expecting a second attack. He invited Leachman to accompany him and his three-thousand-man army, made up of subservient clans, each bearing its own battle standard, on a march through the desert to meet the enemy. When the battle did not come, the army returned to base, and after a flamboyant parade of allegiance to Sadoun Pasha by his assembled warriors, all of them wearing white and carrying swords and rifles, Leachman said good-bye. He later described Sadoun Pasha in unusually effusive language, calling him "a fine old man . . . so courteous, very rich, a splendid soldier, and a cordial enemy of the Turks."

It was the last significant British encounter with the last of the great leaders of the Muntafiq of Mesopotamia. Less than a year later Sadoun Pasha was betrayed by his enemies and captured by the Turks, who imprisoned him in Aleppo, Syria, where he died soon afterward, ostensibly of a heart attack. The British believed he was poisoned. With Sadoun Pasha's death, the power of the Muntafiq declined quickly, as the clan split into two feuding groups and lost its long-standing alliances and ultimately its hegemony over the south. In one of the greatest ironies of the family's story, Sadoun Pasha's son, Ajaimi, who emerged to take his father's mantle, sided with the Ottoman Turks—notwithstanding his father's death at their hands—against the British in the war that began just a few years later. Ajaimi's ill-considered decision not only deprived the British of a potentially invaluable ally, but ultimately cost the Sadouns their dynasty. During the war, Leachman fought several bloody battles with Ajaimi al-Sadoun, who was a constant irritant to the British until he was chased off.

Leachman was a severe man, and by the time of the armistice, in 1918, he had survived many savage battles and many attempts on his life. After the war he was ruthless in putting down Arab uprisings. The British used aerial bombardments as a cost-efficient method of controlling the resentful tribes, and Leachman was especially feared for his ideas about quelling disorder. Not long before his death, he advocated "wholesale slaughter" of unruly tribesmen as the ideal solution. (In this regard, Leachman differed little from Winston Churchill, the British war minister, or T. E. Lawrence, for that matter; both men advocated the use of poison gas to suppress the rebels.) As the Iraqi nationalist rebellion began in March 1920, a fellow officer, H. St. John Philby, the Arabist (and father of the future British traitor Kim Philby), accompanied Leachman on a punishment raid against the

Dulaimi tribe, which was in open revolt. "Six officers had been killed in the ten days before his arrival," wrote Philby. "The Arab culprits were 'doing the peaceful cultivator stunt' when he arrived. They, the 'cultivators,' were not pleased to see him. He quickly put them to the sword. With a party of troops and loyal Arabs he burnt ten miles of huts, drove in the cattle, destroyed everything in sight and wiped out the few Arabs who were courageous enough to resist."

On August 12, 1920, in the midst of spreading unrest, Leachman drove west from Baghdad toward the town of Fallujah, about forty miles away, to meet with Sheikh Dhari, a leader of the Zoba tribe, whose people had thus far not participated in the Arab rebellion. Exactly why they met or what happened that day is unclear, but the British tended to believe that Leachman had been set up, shot in the back in a cowardly fashion by a sheikh's son. After hearing the news, Gertrude Bell, the political secretary of the British high commissioner in Baghdad, wrote in a letter to her father: "The worst news is that Col. Leachman has been ambushed and killed. . . . He was holding the whole Euphrates up to Anak single handed by means of the tribes, troops having all been withdrawn, and we don't know what will happen in those regions. . . ."

Leachman's assassination was a watershed moment in the anti-British revolt. The killing of such a prominent figure gave heart to the insurgents, and the rebellion quickly spread throughout much of the country. In another letter home, dated September 5, Gertrude Bell wrote: "We are now in the middle of a full-blown Jihad." Like her colleague, T. E. Lawrence, Bell had long been an ardent champion of Arab independence. In the three years that had gone by since her arrival in Baghdad in April 1917, shortly after its fall to Maude's forces, Bell, a fluent Arabic speaker, had tried to assuage the rising frustrations of the Iraqi nationalists while unsuccessfully lobbying on their behalf. When the revolt began, she was unsurprised. "When one considers it," she wrote at the time, "it's very comprehensible that the thinking people should revolt at an organization of the universe which could produce anything so destructive as the First World War. . . . The credit of European civilization is gone. Over and over again people have said to me that it has been a shock and a surprise to them to see Europe relapse into barbarism. I had no reply—what else can you call the war? How can we, who have managed our own affairs so badly, claim to teach others to manage theirs better?"

By the time the revolt was quelled a month later, nearly five hundred British soldiers and as many as ten thousand Iraqis, including many civilians, had been killed. The revolt was a determining factor in the British decision to appoint a Hashemite king, Faisal, as Iraq's titular ruler, which took place a year later. Not surprisingly, the British and Iraqi versions of the events of 1920 differ widely, beginning with the circumstances of Leachman's murder. In modern-day Iraq, the man who killed Leachman is invariably referred to as Sheikh Dhari and remembered as a hero and a patriot.

On March 7, 2003, when Sabah took me back to the museum to see the weapon again, I found that many of the display cases were empty. The gun that had killed Leachman was nowhere to be found. When I asked a guard about it, a female curator was summoned to speak to me. First, she asked me where I was from. When I told her that I was from the United States, she uttered the following rhyme in broken English: "Welcome, USA, go away." I asked her about the gun. She explained that it had been removed for safekeeping because of the expected American attack on Iraq. "The gun is very special, you see. All the special items have been taken to a safe place." She walked away. Another curator, a man, seeing my disappointment, approached me and told me he would fetch the gun. He vanished down some stairs. A few minutes later he returned with several uniformed guards, carrying a long-barreled bolt-action rifle. It was, the curator explained, a Czech Brno rifle made under license in Persia in 1902, specially designed for long-distance precision marksmanship. He pointed out some Farsi script on the barrel and its numbered sight for calibrating distance. "This," he said, smiling, "is the rifle that killed Colonel Leachman." I was allowed to admire it for a few minutes, and the gun was taken away again.

Sheikh Dhari's descendants live in the village of Khandhari, named after the sheikh's clan, about thirty-five miles west of Baghdad. On the same day as my visit to the Triumph Leader Museum, I set off for Khandhari with a new government minder in tow, a chubby, diffident young man named Muslim. We found the Khandhari mosque, a yellow-brick building with an ornately tiled turquoise, yellow, and green minaret. It stood directly across the road from the high walls of the dreaded Abu Ghraib prison, with its huge portrait of Saddam wearing black gangster garb placed next to the main gate. It was the first time I had been back since the day of the mass release of prisoners in October, five months earlier. Officially, Abu Ghraib had been totally emptied of inmates, but I had heard rumors that it was secretly up and running again.

The family of Leachman's killers were at noon prayers in the mosque when we arrived. When the worshipers emerged, I was introduced to a trio of three old men with clipped beards in traditional robes and checked headscarfs, Sheikh Dhari's grandsons. I explained that I had come to hear their story of the killing of Leachman. They invited me to come to their nearby compound, a couple of low buildings surrounded by date palms, just off the main road, and led me into their diwaniyah, a long, rectangular meeting room, its walls lined with cheaply tapestried sofas, chairs, and little tea tables.

After motioning for me to sit down, the three elders, Sheikh Muther Khameez al-Dhari, age seventy-one, Sheikh Abdul

Wahab Khameez al-Dhari, seventy-two, and Sheikh Taher Khameez al-Dhari, seventy-five, pulled up chairs around mine. The first to speak was Sheikh Muther, a hefty, mostly toothless man, who began belting out his version of events in a truculent tone of voice. Almost immediately he was interrupted by his brothers, who clearly disagreed with him. After their outburst, Muther shouted something at them and carried on talking. The eldest brother, Sheikh Taher, a distinguished-looking man with clipped fingernails and a fine gold-embroidered robe and a decorated walking stick, stared at his brother stonily and said nothing. Sheikh Abdul Wahab turned away from Muther and rolled his eyes in open sarcasm. This proved too much for Muther, who stomped out of the room angrily, but returned a few moments later. Abdul Wahab then took the floor but was soon interrupted again by Muther. All this was going on in Arabic, and Muslim, my minder, found it quite beyond his abilities to translate, but I heard the name Leachman mentioned a lot. Muslim wrote down what they said in Arabic and occasionally asked them questions, but I could see that he looked totally bewildered. At one point he told me: "They are old men, and each has his story. I will explain later." The bickering continued. Finally, wordlessly and with a great display of dignity, Sheikh Taher removed himself, walking ostentatiously away to sit with his relatives down the room. A dozen or so more men, sons and nephews and grandsons of the old sheikhs, had gathered to listen, and as their elders quarreled, they smiled and shook their heads. One of them tried to approach a couple of times to calm things down but was unsuccessful and finally retreated entirely. He looked at me sympathetically and raised his eyebrows as if to say, "They're impossible."

Finally, one of the younger relatives approached and sat down next to me. He spoke English. He said his name was Abdul Razaq, and asked me whether I was a Christian or a Jew. When I told him that I was of Christian origin, he smiled with relief and said: "I am glad. I don't like Jews." He then pointed to an old black-and-white photograph hanging on the wall near one of the obligatory Saddam Hussein portraits. It was a portrait of Sheikh Dhari, he explained. On closer inspection, I saw that the face had been touched up crudely with paint, and the result was the image of an angelically faced man, rather like the old-fashioned renderings of Joseph in illustrated Bible stories for children. Sheikh Dhari's hands were folded pacifically on his knees. Like his grandsons, he was bearded and wore a robe and headscarf.

Suddenly the oral history was over, and at the sheikhs' insistence I was shown into an adjacent room, where a huge lunch of rice, red beans, grilled chicken, and salad had been served on a tablecloth laid out on the floor. During lunch I asked Muslim to give me the essentials of what had been said. In his quaint English, he explained: "My dear, they say Sheikh Dhari was the master of the plan to kill Leachman, and he slew him with his sword after some relatives had shot and wounded him in the leg. Then he escaped to Turkey. Revolt spread all over the Iraqi governorates. The British put a price on Sheikh Dhari's head. He fell sick and was brought back to Baghdad by a spy in the pay of the British. In the hospital, an English doctor gave him a poison injection, and he died. That was in 1928."

Later, back in the diwaniyah, over tea, Sheikh Muther began declaiming again. This seemed to be his customary manner of speaking. Muslim translated. "Leachman was trying to make war between the people in Iraq in order to get what he wanted," Muther declared. He seemed to be trying to draw a parallel between Leachman and the present day. "Tell America not to attack!" he suddenly yelled at me. "I am a warrior just like Sheikh Dhari was, and I will defend my country bravely." He broke into a chuckle and, grinning toothlessly, grabbed me in an affectionate embrace. Once our clinch was broken, I asked Muther if he thought there would be war, after all. He replied circumspectly: "I don't know. That depends on the leadership of Iraq." Could the Americans draw any lessons from the past British experience? Before Muther could answer, Abdul Razaq, the man who had asked me whether I was a Jew, spoke up: "We learned many lessons on how to defend ourselves from any kind of occupation. The Americans and British cannot occupy Iraq. Nobody can occupy Iraq."

For several minutes Abdul Razaq grilled me about America's political system. All the men in the room listened attentively as he translated my explanations. He began by saying that the Iraqi people had heard America was a democracy and that most of the people opposed its war plans for Iraq. He asked: "How is it, then, that President Bush can go ahead with his war? Is this a democracy?" I tried to explain how it was that although many Americans might well oppose the war, the president had special powers as the commander in chief. Abdul Razaq listened and grinned and shook his head. With a mixture of scorn and triumph, he exclaimed: "And you call this a democracy?" I countered by asking him if he, as an Iraqi, was able to change Saddam's mind on anything of importance. He smiled and arched his eyebrows but said nothing. I said that American democracy was real, in the sense that if afterward people didn't approve of what Bush had done, they could vote him out of office. To this, Abdul Razaq retorted: "Yes, but by then it will be too late for Iraq, won't it?"

Abdul Razaq invited me to go with him and see the spot where his ancestor had killed Leachman. It lay just the other side of the Khandhari mosque, across the road from a travelers' rest stop of brown concrete buildings built in the traditional style with crenellated parapets, fronted by a chaos of sidewalk vendors and chaikhanas and kebab houses. It was all very dirty and dusty and easy to imagine as an old caravanserai, or way station for travelers passing through on camels and horse carts, which is what it had been in Leachman's day. Beyond the buildings lay the open countryside, a spreading patchwork of fields of new green alfalfa, irrigation ditches, and small farms.

Abdul Razaq pointed to an old yellow-brick compound, an Ottoman-era building with arched windows and a single door-way. It was set back from the road amid a stand of eucalyptus trees and a warren of mud hovels. He explained that it had been the Turkish police station, and at the time of Leachman it had been requisitioned by the British. A family was living there now. Leading me to the doorway, he called through, and we were let in by a young man and a couple of small children. A central passageway led past a couple of dark, vaulted chambers to a central courtyard paved with stones. Beyond lay a kind of open stable block, where a large white goose wandered around. In a corner were the black charcoal remains of a cook fire and, next to it, a pile of dried-out date palm fronds used for kindling. A single oil barrel contained water. The family that occupied the place was obviously poor. Abdul Razaq and our host led me up some stone stairs at the side of the courtyard to the flat roof, where, at the front of the building, there was a small room with an arched door and windows covered with chicken wire. Abdul Razaq opened the door; inside there were a couple of bags of cotton sacking coated with pigeon droppings. A few pigeons fluttered around. "This used to be Leachman's office," he said. "Now it is an office for birds."

Before we left the house, Abdul Razaq stopped me at the great front door. He opened it and pointed to the stone floor where we stood. "This is where Leachman was killed, right here." As he told it, Leachman had summoned Sheikh Dhari to a meeting in the police station, and Sheikh Dhari had summoned his clansmen to come and wait outside. They were to open fire on Leachman when Sheikh Dhari gave them the signal, and that is exactly what happened. Abdul Razaq pointed outside to an old tree that stood about a hundred feet away, near the edge of the main road. "From there, on a signal from Sheikh Dhari, Leachman was shot and wounded in the legs by one of his relatives, Salman. He then drew his sword and killed Leachman." I expressed my incredulity that Salman could possibly have shot accurately from such a distance, with Sheikh Dari standing right next to Leachman, inside the doorway of a police station full of British soldiers. Abdul Razaq merely smiled and reassured me that it was possible, because that was what had occurred. "Remember, Iraqis are very good warriors."

I asked Abdul Razaq what happened next. "The rest of the English were killed, and Sheikh Dhari and the others all galloped away on horses." A new argument ensued, this time between Abdul Razaq and a cousin of his, over whether the other Englishmen had been killed, as he had said, or merely captured, which is what his cousin believed. There was more arguing over whether Sheikh Dari had fled to Turkey, as the old sheikhs had said, or to Saudi Arabia. They were still arguing back and forth about this as Muslim and I took our leave.

The Dhari family's rendition of events, I discovered, was remarkably similar to the version offered up in a 1983 film, a British-Iraqi coproduction titled *Clash of Loyalties.* Muslim found a rare videotape copy of the movie for me to watch. In the film, a dissipated-looking Oliver Reed plays Leachman as a drunken, cold-hearted cynic who, on the eve of his death, tells Gertrude Bell: "Killing is something I do well." In Leachman's death scene, Reed is first shot and then struck across the back by Sheikh Dhari's sword, then flops around repeatedly like a hooked trout before finally lying still. It must be one of the most badly acted death scenes in cinematic history. Sheikh Dhari is the tragic hero of the film: He gallops romantically off into exile after his daring feat and then, years later, an aged and sick man, is lured back via trickery to Iraq, where he is captured and imprisoned by the British. In one of the culminating scenes, Sheikh Dhari's death sentence is commuted to life imprisonment by a British judge because of his advanced years and ill health. Next, a British doctor is seen injecting a substance into the arm of the sleeping Sheikh Dhari, which has the effect of ending his life moments later. The closing scene shows a crowd of thousands of angry, chanting Iraqi mourners following Sheikh Dhari's casket down the colonnaded streets of old Baghdad. Sitting inside a gleaming black Rolls-Royce from behind the secure gates of the British Legation, several British diplomats look on smugly. The final image shows spouting oil wells, and then flames fill the screen, and the credits roll.

In actuality, Leachman's body lay where it fell for several hours until one of his lieutenants arrived in an armored car to retrieve it. Because of the unrest, the lieutenant hastily buried Leachman that same day in an unmarked grave in Fallujah's British war cemetery. Six months later the body was disinterred and taken by military convoy to Baghdad. On March 1, 1921, after a solemn funeral service and a procession through the streets, Leachman was reburied with full military honors in the same Baghdad cemetery as Sir Stanley Maude. The *Baghdad Times* reported: "A very large number of people followed the coffin to its last resting-place in the North Gate Cemetery, and the spectacle presented as the long line of mourners wound their way to the burial place to the solemn strains to a slow march was moving in the extreme." Almost precisely eighty-four years after that day, I returned to the North Gate War Cemetery to hunt for Leachman's grave, but I couldn't find it.

As the war loomed closer, it became virtually impossible for journalists to travel outside Baghdad. Most requests to do so were being rejected out of hand by the officials at the Information Ministry. Citing my interest in the British military fiasco at Kut as an excuse, however, Muslim managed to obtain permission for us to visit the British cemetery there. I also had an ulterior motive: to see if there were any defensive preparations taking place outside the capital. In Baghdad there was no such activity that I could see, and the pretense of normality seemed increasingly bizarre.

On March 7, while I had been in Khandhari, the British foreign secretary, Jack Straw, asked the UN to impose a deadline of March 17 for Saddam to demonstrate "full, unconditional, immediate and active cooperation" with its demands for disarmament—or face a military invasion. France had continued to filibuster, however, and said it would veto any such resolution. After further lobbying at the UN, the United States and Britain had agreed to come up with a list of specific demands for Iraq's compliance before a vote on the issue. Their demands were to be made public on March 10. That morning Sabah, Muslim, and I drove to Kut.

The road from Baghdad to Kut cuts through a flat landscape of churned-up, trash-strewn brown earth and an industrial belt of scrubby factories that eventually merges into green fields of alfalfa and small farms and stands of date palms. All along the road, I saw hundreds of newly bulldozed snipers' nests and sandbagged foxholes. They were fragile, rather pointless-looking defenses; a single shot from a tank would obliterate any one of them. Not much else in the way of military preparation seemed to be going on. Just outside the large concrete arches and the military inspection post that served as the gateway to Kut, we passed an army barracks where uniformed men who seemed to be recruits were being rallied at the roadside, but there was a desultory look to their activity.

Kut is an ugly, down-at-the-heels town of a few hundred thousand people. Donkey carts carrying jerricans and fresh alfalfa bobbed along on the streets. The turab had abated, and it was a clear spring morning. We drove to the governor's compound, where Muslim officiously told me to wait for him as he went inside to obtain permission for our visit to the British cemetery. As I waited in the street outside, I could hear children playing in a nearby schoolyard. Birds flitted about busily in the bushes and trees. A friendly young uniformed sentry came up, and in his few words of English, welcomed me to Kut, which he proclaimed to be a "very beautiful city." He said that his name was Abdul, and we shook hands. He beckoned me over to a large bush in the median strip outside the governorate building and picked up some leaves and held them up for me to smell. It was a sweet-smelling plant, which he called *yas*. Abdul made a beatific expression. He seemed not to know, or, if he did, to care, that I was an American. The nearby primary school emptied of young boys, and they gamboled noisily down the road past us. A few hopped playfully in and out of several freshly dug trenches in the median strip and trotted on.

After an hour Muslim emerged from the governorate building with some senior-looking officials. One of them, wearing a military uniform, introduced himself and ceremoniously welcomed me to Iraq "in the name of Saddam Hussein" and told us to follow his pickup to the British cemetery. We drove in a big loop around the town, past a stadium where soldiers were digging more dugouts in the median strip of a boulevard, and into a scrubby older market area of the city, where the brick houses were tiny and badly built, and raw sewage ran down the streets. We drove down a narrow lane where rag merchants had laid out their bundles, and parked in front of some grimy bicycle repair shops. Black Shia mourning flags emblazoned with Koranic script hung from a few of the balconies. The British cemetery lay directly opposite in a sunken square of land that was squeezed by tenements on either side. A fence ran along the street in front of it, but the front gate was open, and I could see that the whole place was strewn with garbage, and about half of it was hidden behind a tall thicket of weeds. An inscription next to the front gate read "Kut War Cemetery, 1914–1918." As I stared in dismay, the man who had guided us from the governor's office explained, through Muslim, that the poor state of the graveyard was the result of the UN sanctions and the lack of diplomatic relations with Great Britain. "The men who used to look after it, and who received salaries from the British, have gone," he said apologetically. "That is the reason it looks like this."

We clambered down to the cemetery grounds, over a huge pile of stinking rubbish. Women peering out a window giggled and chattered. Some young boys sat on a wall, dangling their feet and staring at us. The stench of excrement was strong; in one spot the skin of a freshly slaughtered goat buzzed with flies. Some of the ground was blackened from a recent fire. There was a dead tree with bicycle inner tubes caught in its branches. An unmarked obelisk at the center was splattered with black and yellow paint, and broken-off headstones lay everywhere. Those still standing and legible showed that most of the men who were buried here, English privates with surnames like Martin, Nicholls, Newton, and Rogers, had been killed at the height of the siege of Kut, between January and April 1916.

When I was done poking around, I chatted with the officer from the governor's office. When I mentioned that ten thousand soldiers had died in Kut, he smiled. "And if the Americans invade, you will see many of them killed at the borders with Iraq," he said. "We are here, living in our homes, and America says it will come here, and so we will defend ourselves and our country with courage, the same as people anywhere." Then, in a rather earnest way, he asked: "Why can't Americans convince Bush not to make war?" I smiled and shrugged my shoulders. I had had this conversation with Iraqis before, especially in the last few days, and found it pointless. My explanations of the way politics worked in America were unfathomable to them, and because they were incapable of answering my questions about their political system with any honesty, our exchanges were barren. To be polite, I asked the officer his name. He told me, with some reluctance, that it was Hassan al-Wazaty. When I asked him his rank, he laughed and demurred: "No rank. I am just one of the people of Iraq. We are all like soldiers now."

That same evening, back in Baghdad, I visited Ala Bashir's friend Samir Khairi at his office in the Foreign Ministry. I was anxious to know what had happened in the UN that day, and I figured he would know what was going on behind the scenes. Samir was as warm and jolly as ever as he ushered me in to sit down, but he was very distracted. His phone rang constantly, and his desk was awash in papers. He had a TV set switched on to CNN World News. Samir's eyes wandered constantly over to the screen, and he compulsively turned up and down the volume on his remote control to hear what was being said. He apologized and explained that the U.S. and British list of demands was to be made public at any moment, and this had him on tenterhooks. Even so, he added, whatever happened in the UN Security Council, he expected the war to begin very soon. The unofficial word was that if the United States didn't get the nine votes it needed to authorize war, it would unilaterally begin bombing Iraq at midnight the following night. If it did get the votes, said Samir, the scuttlebutt was that the United States would give Iraq until March 17 to comply with its conditions and then begin bombing. Either way, the war was going to happen. He told me that he expected both the Foreign Ministry and the nearby Ministry of Information to be bombed. "The Americans won't want the truth to be told about what damage they are causing," Samir said. He said this matter-of-factly and then chuckled merrily. His voice was totally devoid of the usual tone of outrage I was accustomed to hearing from Baathists.

I found Samir a fascinating character, but very difficult to read. Since he was a friend of Ala Bashir's, I assumed that he too had a hidden side and possibly even harbored similar feelings about Saddam and his regime. If he did, Samir had not yet revealed himself. As I got up to leave, I told Samir that I would be seeing Ala Bashir later in the evening. He exclaimed: "Good! Tell him I want both of you to come to my house this week for dinner. You must come! I will have shrimp from the gulf. It is the best in the world. You will see." He laughed again in his ebullient way and saw me out.

Afterward I went to Ala Bashir's home. He was expecting me and suggested that we go out to dinner together. We went to a Western-style steak restaurant in Mansour, an upscale part of town. The food was awful, but the place was practically deserted, and we were able to talk freely. Over dinner I relayed what Samir had told me. He nodded. The war was very close now, he agreed. He advised me not to be in the Al-Rasheed if I could help it when the bombing started. He didn't think it was safe, he said, and he warned me that all its rooms were probably bugged. I told him that this was something I had long assumed but had learned to live with. I explained that I had teamed up with another journalist and that we had rented rooms in the Al-Safeer and the Al-Hamra, just in case, to have as alternatives. He said that he didn't think the Al-Hamra was safe either, because there was "something"—he didn't say what—"nearby." He told me that he didn't think the Al-Safeer would be good either. He pointed out that it lay directly across the river from the Republican Palace, which would be one of the main bombing targets. Bashir proposed that I visit him at the hospital early the next morning. He would send me off with his secretary, who was a trustworthy man, to inspect a couple of hotels near his hospital. If I stayed in one of them, he said, it would be close enough for me to walk to his hospital. Once the war started, he said, he would probably not go home but remain at the hospital. For that matter, he added, I was welcome to come stay with him at the hospital when the bombing began.

I told Bashir that I had seen many newly dug trenches and foxholes along the road to Kut. He laughed cynically when he heard this and shook his head. "This is just to keep the people busy doing things," he said. It was obvious they did not intend to defend anything but Baghdad itself, which itself seemed a foolhardy strategy. "If everything else is gone, then why fight for

Baghdad? What is the point in that?" I asked him why he believed Saddam planned only to defend Baghdad. He said that
this was the obvious conclusion to the military movements of the
past few days. The Republican Guard and Special Republican
Guard, he said, had been pulled back to Baghdad from their positions in the south and the north of Iraq and were being dis-
persed throughout Baghdad in civilian neighborhoods. "What is
even worse, they have begun putting antiaircraft batteries on the
roofs of hospitals," he added. He'd been told that they were going to do this at his hospital as well. Bashir shook his head angrily. He was very upset about this, he explained, because the
only possible explanation for placing troops in civilian areas and
putting antiaircraft guns on hospital roofs was to provoke the
maximum number of civilian casualties.

Bashir fell silent for a moment and then confessed that he felt
very confused about the situation. Except for the discreet movement of troops and guns he had described, there was little else
going on that he could see. "I can't understand this," he exclaimed quietly. "There are no really serious preparations going
on." Moreover, he added, in the upper echelons of government
and among the presidential guards, where he had contacts,
everyone was behaving as though nothing were going to happen.
At the ministries, and even at his hospital, which had received
orders to be on an emergency footing, he said, the mood was still
not one of dire urgency. "I just don't understand what is going
on," he repeated, looking bewildered. "Either this means they
are just stupid, and have no real idea of what is coming, or else
Saddam Hussein is planning something to save the situation at
the last minute. But since the only thing he can do is resign—
and this he will never do—I don't know what he could possibly
have in mind."

I remarked that the strangely passive behavior he was noticing
among the people within the regime was the same I was wit-
nessing in ordinary Iraqis. Did he have any explanation for it?

Bashir replied: "The whole country, and even Baath Party members, are weary and apathetic, as if they don't care what is coming and are resigned to whatever happens. You have to remember that every Iraqi has had someone in his family in prison, either here or in Iran, as a prisoner of war. Or else someone in his family has been killed in war or by the regime." Bashir cocked his head toward the street, where his driver, a friendly, lanky man in his thirties who seemed utterly devoted to Bashir, was waiting for us. "You know my driver, Jihad? He was eight years in Iran as a prisoner of war. He tells me he now wishes that he had never returned." Bashir gave one of his small enigmatic smiles. "This repression has made everyone passive. The regime is aware of this, and this is why it is placing its forces among the population, as a coercive measure."

I commented that I found it terribly sad that Iraqis were unable to express their true feelings at such a crucial moment in their history. The obvious thing for them to do if they wanted to avert war, I suggested, was to demonstrate in public and say: "Mr. President, we love you very much, but please resign your office for the sake of the nation."

Ala Bashir nodded. "That's true. And it's the one thing they cannot do, because they know they would be killed."

FIVE

I missed my appointment the next day with Ala Bashir, but I went to see him the following morning at his hospital. It was March 12. When we were seated in his office, he informed me that he had received a phone call before dawn that same morning from a relative of his in California. "He told me I should go visit my wife because she will be operated on in seven to ten days and that it would be best if I arranged to travel in five or six days, maximum, from now." It took me a moment or two, but I realized that Bashir was relaying a coded message about the date the war was going to begin. Just in case I hadn't caught on, Bashir remarked, in a low voice: "My wife is in perfect health."

I was very surprised that Bashir was speaking to me so unguardedly in his office. I guessed that he had reason to know it wasn't bugged. It was consistent with the growing trend toward openness in our relationship. Every time we had met since my return, he had spoken more and more freely. New revelations spilled out constantly, such as the existence of this relative of his, whom I had never heard of before. Bashir explained that his cousin, an older man named Faleh, had emigrated many years earlier to the United States and became a U.S. citizen. He was a well-connected energy expert, he added, who had held public posts under both Ronald Reagan and the first President Bush and was an energy adviser to the current Bush administration.

He remarked that his cousin's call was unusual, and he had concluded two things from it: that the U.S. attack on Iraq was going to be delayed for seven to ten days and, because his cousin had urged him to leave the country, that the attack was going to be more severe than he had been expecting. As usual, Bashir spoke in a calm, untroubled voice, and his face was entirely neutral. He was a master at hiding his emotions.

I asked Bashir what he planned to do. Could he leave Iraq? He smiled. "Well, this is very difficult. I don't see how it is possible. I would have to ask permission from the president personally, and I don't think at this point it would look good. He would think it was very strange." We sat in silence for a long moment.

"Are you worried?" I asked.

He smiled again. "Well, this was the first time my cousin has urged me to leave the country. And because of his connections, I guess he knows what he is talking about." He shrugged. He was stuck; there was nothing he could do.

We talked about safety in the upcoming days. He urged me, as before, to go with his secretary to see a couple of nearby hotels that he thought were safer than the Hamra, the Safeer, or the Al-Rasheed. "That way, when the bombing starts, you can come be with us in the hospital," he said. Though he had mentioned this before, this time I understood that Bashir was advising me, in his circumspect way, that I would be safest with him at the hospital and that I should be as near as possible when the war began. I agreed to check out the hotels he recommended. "Good," he said, looking relieved, and called for his secretary. As we waited, Bashir asked me if, before I left, I wanted to see the model of the latest monument he had created for Saddam Hussein. He happened to have the model in another room of the hospital, he explained, because some engineers were coming to take photographs of it. They would then feed these images into a computer program to make the engineering plans for its construction. "If it is built, and the plans are for that to begin very soon," he said, "it will be Iraq's tallest monument. It will stand forty meters high and thirty-two meters long."

He explained that five years earlier Saddam Hussein had asked him to create a monument that summed up all his achievements as Iraq's ruler, including everything he'd built and also his military victories. It was not the kind of invitation Bashir could refuse, but he had let a lot of time go by before tackling the job. He'd made a few sketches, but that was it. Whenever the president saw him, he had asked him, with increasing impatience: "How is it going? When can I see the model?" Bashir had always begged off by using his doctor's duties as an excuse and by saying that the monument was a very important and difficult task, because he wanted to create something that would last "for the ages." Finally, about six months ago, the president had said to him: "Why haven't you done this? It has been too long." Bashir understood then that Saddam was upset with him and that he could not put it off any longer. He told him he would have it ready in two to three months. And so he had concentrated on it. When he was done, he had taken the model to Saddam, who was very pleased with it. Bashir smiled proudly as he mentioned this.

"He really liked it, and you know, it is a good monument, I think. It shows his achievement, really. Everything about it is a true reflection of his period of leadership. You'll see what I mean. Especially the wars." He added that the name he'd originally given to it was the *Epic of Iraq,* after the *Epic of Gilgamesh,* but that the president had changed the name to the *Epic of Saddam.* Bashir caught my eye and smiled meaningfully. He mentioned that there had also been some talk, as with his sculpture *The Union,* about putting Saddam's statue or portrait in front of it, but he'd circumvented this by inscribing some of Saddam's words of wisdom on the monument and by incorporating within it a likeness of one of Saddam's arms and fists as well. At that moment his secretary arrived. Bashir gave him some instructions in Arabic and then turned back to me and apologized, explaining that he wouldn't be able to accompany me; he had some patients to attend to. But he reminded me that we had a dinner date that night with his friend Samir Khairi. As his secretary led me away to see the model, Bashir said: "I think you'll like it."

The model was very large, perhaps six feet long and eight feet high. It sat on a thick slab of plywood that had been set on the floor in the middle of a nearby staff room. Several doctors and nurses on their breaks sat in chairs arranged around the walls. They were staring silently at the thing and watching as two men, the architectural engineers Bashir had spoken of, took careful photographs of the model from every angle. The model was made of plaster of paris and painted bronze. It was monstrous, quite unlike anything I had ever seen. The main body of the piece was a sloping boatlike structure, rather like an ark. Set along the top of this were dozens of sculpted figures of soldiers, who were depicted marching and in battle. They were made of wax and painted gold. Down the sides of the piece were etched renderings of ordinary Iraqi life, of people farming, fishing, tilling, scenes reminiscent of the old Sumerian tableaux, but also the sketchy outlines of smokestacks and factories, which I took to symbolize oil refineries—modernity. Below these, as if crushed underneath the whole thing, were vanquished soldiers, people bowed in pain and defeat. These, explained Bashir's secretary, represented Iranians. The front of the boatlike body of the piece extended into a great twisting dragon's neck, with gaping jaws, and there was a huge lance stabbing into one of its eyes. The lance rose upward like a battle standard (this, I realized, was the part of the monument that would extend forty meters into the sky), and at the top were sculpted words in Arabic script that read *"Allahu Akbar,"* God Is Great. The lance was gripped midshaft by an enormous fist, part of a man's muscular forearm that grew out of the back of the piece from the field of soldiers and reached out over the front of it, essentially killing the dragon that it was a part of.

Bashir's creation was stupefyingly grotesque. I assumed that he had intentionally invested his piece with a subversive message about the self-annihilating nature of Saddam's dictatorship. If so, he had achieved his aim magnificently. No one could view this thing without a feeling of horror. But I could also see why Saddam loved it. It demonstrated the utter totality of his power and conjoined him symbolically with the entire sweep of Mesopotamian history. If this were ever created, I thought, it would indeed be the ultimate Saddam Hussein monument. I whistled and cooed in what I hoped seemed like an appropriate degree of admiration for the benefit of Bashir's secretary, whose political sympathies I did not know, but whose awestruck expression told me he thought it was a splendid piece. "It's beautiful, no?" he asked me.

"It's amazing," I said.

He nodded, looking very proud. In a year or so, he declared excitedly, I might be able to see the thing in real life, placed in its intended location in the public gardens opposite the Al-Rasheed Hotel. I scrutinized his face for some hint of sarcasm or doubt, but saw nothing.

Bashir's secretary and I left the hospital together to go check out the hotels Ala Bashir had suggested. The first place, the Cedar, was right next door to a derelict building that I envisioned as a perfect sniper's position in the event of street fighting. It was also, I noticed, a mere two blocks away from the Iraqi Air Defense Ministry, which always had many armed security men around it, and which I assumed was a prime bombing target. The next hotel we inspected had a police station right around the corner from it. I didn't feel comfortable about either place. I told Bashir's secretary that I wanted to think about it for a day or two before I made my choice. Privately, my gut was still telling me that when the time came, I wanted to be in the small, friendly Al-Safeer on Abu Nawas Street.

When I had taken my room there, the two brothers who

owned the hotel had asked me to come sit and talk with them. They called one of their waiters to bring us Turkish coffee. After making sure all their employees were out of earshot, they began speaking in very low voices. They wanted to know what they should do when the war began. They explained that they lived with their families in Jadiriyah, in the same neighborhood as the Al-Hamra hotel farther downriver. But they also had houses outside Baghdad, in the countryside. Where would their families be safest? What did I think? What kinds of bombs would the Americans use? They hunched over to listen to what I would say. They clearly believed that I had some knowledge that they did not have access to. I told them that if their neighborhood was one of those where Saddam's military forces had positioned themselves, their families could be at risk from aerial bombardment or street fighting. They looked at each other as I said this but did not say anything. I said I could not judge the safety of their homes in the countryside, since I was not privy to the American invasion plans. A great deal depended on the routes they used to approach Baghdad. I asked whether either of them would stay on at the hotel; they said they had not yet decided. I suggested that at the very least they should tape up the windows along the front of their hotel, to prevent the glass from shattering from the explosions. They said they would do this. They told me that whatever happened, they wanted me to feel at home at the Al-Safeer, that I should consider it my home. They informed me that there was a bomb shelter in the basement that I could use, and if there was anything they could do for me, I needed only to ask. One of the brothers was called away to deal with some problem at the reception desk. As he walked away, the other brother watched him go and then bent over toward me and hissed furtively: "What I want is for this to be over, but quickly." I got the impression that he did not entirely trust his brother.

I had stored a large cache of water and some food in my bolt-hole at the Al-Safeer, and every few days I added to the stock. I had bought a generator and two hundred liters of fuel in case Baghdad's electricity was blown. Sabah kept the generator and some of the fuel at his home in the north of the city and the rest of the fuel at a vacant house in the neighborhood of Mansour, across the river. The house belonged to a Jordanian entrepreneur whom Sabah drove around when he was in town. Sabah kept an eye on the house for him, and he knew the caretaker, who had agreed to let us use it as a safe house if we needed to. By now Sabah seemed to have accepted the inevitability of the war, although he spoke little about it. Instead he had thrown himself into seeing to the details of my war preparations. He loved nothing more than to go off on shopping missions and haggling for things. I had also given him extra money to buy stocks of food and water for his own sizable family, and by my allowing him to keep the generator at his home until I needed it, he knew his family would have an electricity supply as well. I had also brought in an extra chemical and biological warfare protective suit for Sabah's use, but when I showed it to him, he had shrugged in disdain and pointed out that I had not brought him a flak jacket. This was true. It had been a genuine oversight on my part. He laughed off my apologies, however, saying that God would protect him, and that if he didn't, then that was God's choice.

One day a week or so earlier, something unexpected had occurred that bound Sabah and me closer together than ever. We had been out driving with Khalid, the minder, before he left us, looking for the British cemetery in Baghdad. In Adhamiyah, an old Sunni neighborhood in northwestern Baghdad, we had stopped at a café where Khalid said he needed to use the telephone. While he was inside, Sabah and I sat outside at a table to wait for him. All of a sudden Sabah began breathing heavily, wiping his eyes and heaving with some kind of strong emotion. Alarmed, I asked him what was wrong. Between involuntary sobs that he tried to stifle, frantically wiping away the tears that were rolling down his cheeks while looking around to make sure Khalid wasn't returning, Sabah explained that it was the birthday of his youngest brother, Taher, who had disappeared while serving as a soldier at the front during the Iran-Iraq War, twenty-one years earlier. The family had never been given a confirmation of his death, or any explanation for his disappearance, he explained, but Sabah had reason to believe, because of the cold and unhelpful attitude of the authorities during their inquiries, that Taher had not died in the war but had run afoul of Saddam. Every year on this day, Sabah said, his aged mother fell apart, heartbroken, because she did not know Taher's fate. It was very hard for the whole family, he said. Then he cracked again. "Where is he?" he keened in a disconsolate whisper, as I tried to comfort him. "If he is dead, fine, but let us know," Sabah said, speaking to no one in particular. "Sad-dam," he hissed slowly, through gritted teeth, as though uttering the most loathsome name he knew. He closed his eyes and muttered a few other words in Arabic, which I did not understand. Then he took a deep breath and composed himself. He sat up straight and quickly wiped his eyes to remove any traces of his tears. He begged me not to mention what had happened, or what he had told me, to anyone. A moment later, none the wiser, Khalid reappeared.

A few days later, as we stood together and looked out over the Tigris, Sabah turned to me and said: "If God wills, Bush will bomb Saddam into the river. But not the people. Just Saddam. And Tikrit. If God wills, Tikrit will be flattened." He spit and called Tikritis camels' offspring and a series of other pithy epithets in Arabic. It also became a ritual, whenever we passed one of Saddam's palaces, for Sabah to pretend to be Saddam's wife, Sajida, in the throes of copulation with him. In a mockery of the main slogan of Saddam's loyalty referendum, he would moan, over and over again, in an orgasmically rising falsetto voice: "*Na'am, na'am, na'am* [yes, yes, yes]!"

*

Among the journalists in Baghdad there was an atmosphere of mounting anxiety. It had become a ritual to ask one another: "Are you staying or going?" Many reporters were coming under pressure from their families and their bosses back home to leave. Ever since President Bush had advised journalists during a March 7 press conference to leave Iraq, the pressure had increased. Several American and British newspapers and television networks had begun telling their correspondents in Baghdad to be ready to depart. Some were warned that their insurance coverage would be revoked if they disobeyed; others were told they would be fired. I came under no such pressure, but in the United States the editors in chief of the major media corporations were in discussions with the Pentagon, and on March 12 I received an e-mail message from *The New Yorker*. I was told that U.S. government officials were warning media organizations that their correspondents were possible targets of assassination or kidnapping by Saddam's regime for use as human shields—and also that the Al-Rasheed Hotel was likely to be a bombing target. My editors were naturally worried by this and asked me to remain in daily contact with them and also to accept their final decision about what I should ultimately do. I agreed to this but told them about the precautions I had taken and also that I was skeptical about the Pentagon's warnings.

"Many of us here in Baghdad," I wrote in my reply, "have the impression that the Pentagon has been engaging in a certain amount of scaremongering, so as to clear the decks of press. They tend to go first to the networks, it seems, which also seem to be the most susceptible to this kind of thing, and from there it burns through the press corps like a brush fire. Not necessarily for purposes of censorship, but just to have the way clear—i.e., it's probably a real fly in the ointment to have to worry about not hitting journalists when you want to bomb a city. In 1990–1991 they bombed Baghdad forty-three days, and there were cruise missiles, I hear, that were programmed to do loop-the-loops around this building. One missile, however, did go awry and struck the base of the hotel, killing several hotel employees. In 1998, during the four days of strikes of Desert Fox, there were journalists here, and the hotel was not hit. Would the Pentagon risk killing as many as two hundred (estimated current population) of the world's media by targeting the Al-Rasheed—not to mention the scores of civilian hotel employees who work here? I think not.

"I have a couple of allies who are part of the nomenklatura. One of them is a senior member of the Foreign Ministry; the other is the doctor I mentioned in an e-mail a week or so ago. I think they are becoming concerned about having a Western ally for their own sakes, down the road, which may be why we have become so chummy of late, but however pragmatic a relationship, it is still some kind of lifeline.

"As for targeting the press through terrorism or taking us hostage, etc. . . . , these are things we all have thought about, and I suppose there is a small chance this could happen, but it doesn't seem likely. First of all, there's been a distinct buzz here around the apparatchiks in the Ministry of Information that they want the press on hand this time, to document what they believe are going to be civilian casualties and thus try to influence world opinion against the war once it has begun. They seem not to ap-prehend the Pentagon's determination to strike hard and fast and neuralgically and get it over quickly. This mitigates in our favor, obviously.

"I take some comfort as well in the realization that there are, after all, five million people living in Baghdad, and I am just one more among them. Yes, I am a Westerner, and yes, I stand out, but nothing about the mood of the people on the streets makes me feel afraid of them. There is not any sense of hostility toward Westerners, despite the threat of hostilities. There is rather a pal-pable sense of apathy mixed with understandable uncertainty. I don't think many Iraqis are going to lift a finger to defend this regime once the Americans start moving, as long as they move quickly and decisively and show they intend to go the whole way."

This was not sheer bravado on my part. I was, privately, extremely worried about the kinds of threats being raised by the Pentagon, but like the other reporters who were hoping to stay on in Baghdad, I had calculated, not without doubts, that when the war began, the chaos would be so great that I would somehow be able to slip out of sight and remain undetected by Saddam's henchmen. This was to prove a complete delusion, but I did not know it yet.

That night Ala Bashir and I went to Samir Khairi's home for dinner. There were a few other guests, mostly well-to-do Iraqi men who were friends of Samir's. They never introduced themselves or said what they did, but they seemed pleased to have me there. While Samir grilled gulf shrimp on a portable charcoal grill in the kitchen, the rest of us sat in the living room drinking Lebanese arrack, eating warm pistachios, cashews, and almonds, and watching his television set, which had a satellite receiver. I presumed that he was authorized to have one because of his official position. As in his office, Samir had the TV switched on permanently, and whenever he came in to join us from the kitchen, he would pick up the remote control of the TV and flip channels, following the news on CNN, Iraqi state TV, and Al Jazeera. Nobody else seemed to care what they watched. Samir always turned up the volume very loud, and whenever he left the room, Bashir grabbed the remote and turned it down again. This went on throughout the evening and in fact was a kind of friendly game they played whenever we visited. At one point Samir found *My Best Friend's Wedding* playing on a satellite movie channel and stood watching it for several minutes. He laughed delightedly at a scene where Cameron Diaz sings badly in a karaoke bar. When the scene was over, he went back into the kitchen.

As we ate, Samir began flipping channels again, and found another movie, *Six Days, Seven Nights,* starring Harrison Ford and Anne Heche as two mismatched people who crash-land on a desert island in the South Pacific. The movie was subtitled in Arabic, and at Bashir's request Samir kept the sound turned down, but it was pretty easy to follow. Ford and Heche feuded and fought and then, predictably, fell in love. It was a very silly film. Samir and his friends were transfixed. Ala Bashir sat impassively next to me, saying very little. He normally didn't watch TV, he remarked. "Most of it seems to be rubbish," he said. But I noticed that he too seemed rather caught up in the movie. I commented that it seemed a little strange to be sitting in Baghdad watching a Hollywood film a few days before the American attack. Samir and his friends nodded vigorously and laughed, then turned back to the television set.

Samir was interrupted by a phone call from his boss, Naji Sabri al-Hadithi, the foreign minister, who wanted to talk with him about an eleventh-hour invitation by Saddam's government to the UN officials Hans Blix and Mohamed ElBaradei to return to Baghdad to discuss Iraq's offer of "accelerated cooperation" on the issue of disarmament. The foreign minister was obviously giving Samir urgent instructions, which he scribbled down on a piece of paper while saying officiously, "*Na'am, na'am,*" over and over again. Any new initiative seemed utterly hopeless at this point, since the UN Security Council remained deadlocked over a new resolution, and the previous day Donald Rumsfeld had made remarks to the effect that the United States was ready to attack Iraq on its own. When Samir got off the phone, he turned to me and shrugged, as if to say he knew that it was already too late to stop the war, but he had his official duties to perform. "What else can we do?" he said.

As Bashir and I took our leave, Samir confided that the UN in Baghdad had been pared down to a skeleton staff of twelve people who were ready to depart within two hours' notice. He asked me solicitously about my intentions. I told him that I was planning to try to stay for the war, and that I was in the Al-Rasheed but, like almost everyone else I knew, planned to move to another hotel soon. I mentioned the rumors about the Al-Rasheed's being a bombing target and told him that quite a few journalists had begun moving across to the Palestine, on the eastern bank of the Tigris. Samir listened and nodded. He said he had also heard the rumors about the Al-Rasheed and said he believed they were credible. "Check out tomorrow," he advised.

Samir's telephone call from Naji Sabri intrigued me. For me, Sabri was one of the most confounding personalities of Saddam's regime. En route to Baghdad for the first time, I had stopped in Vienna to meet him. As one of Iraq's few senior officials with a reputation for moderation and openness, Sabri had seemed a valuable person to get to know. At the time he was Iraq's ambassador to Austria, as well as its representative to OPEC and the International Atomic Energy Commission, both of which were headquartered in Vienna. Sabri turned out to be charming and cultured, and he had graciously given me letters of introduction to Ala Bashir, Farouk Salloum, and several other key people in Baghdad. But after becoming Iraq's foreign minister in 2001, he seemed to have undergone a radical transformation, at least in his public demeanor. He had taken to wearing a military uniform and behaved very arrogantly in his public appearances, often making statements that were crude and belligerent toward the West. I had repeatedly been refused permission to see him.

On my first night in Vienna, back in 2000, Sabri had invited me to dinner at his official residence and sent his teenage son to drive me there. Guards let us through the gates of a cavernous villa in a leafy area of Vienna's hilly northern suburbs, where Sabri received me warmly. He was dressed casually and fingered a tasseled set of amber worry beads. The formal receiving rooms of his residence were covered with old-fashioned wallpaper and furnished with baroque settees, Persian carpets, and large framed photographs of Saddam Hussein. In one of the pictures, Saddam was smiling and had both hands clasped on Sabri's shoulders. Sabri was beaming happily. Dinner turned out to be an elaborate meal of exquisite Iraqi dishes laid out in the vast dining room, but it was attended only by me, Sabri, and his son. There was a television set showing CNN World News, which was kept switched on in a far corner. Sabri kept one eye on the TV throughout the meal. Afterward Sabri's son excused himself, and the ambassador took me out to the unlit rear garden of the villa.

As we sat drinking coffee in the dark, Sabri spoke nostalgically about his time spent in London during the 1970s running Iraq's information office there, naming some of the journalists and writers he had gotten to know. He mentioned that he had helped the British writer Gavin Young on the journey he had made through the southern marshlands of Iraq, which he later wrote about in his book *Return to the Marshes,* and that he had also once met the venerable explorer Wilfred Thesiger. Sabri spoke with what seemed like genuine sadness about the deterioration in relations between the West and Iraq since those days, and he gamely offered a low-key defense of his government, citing Iraq's secularism, its free health care and education system, and its defense of women's rights. Saddam Hussein's regime, he conceded, was "not democratic in the sense of the West," but, he added, "I don't think it is fair to measure Iraq with the same yardstick that is applied to countries with democracies that are four hundred years old."

The next morning Sabri invited me over to the Iraqi Embassy. It was a splendid old mansion, which overlooked a large public park in downtown Vienna. In the foyer downstairs, at the foot of a sweeping staircase, was a huge, rather crudely painted map of Iraq and the surrounding nations of the Middle East dominated by the Iraqi national emblem, a spread-winged eagle. As far as I

could make out, Kuwait was depicted as being part of Iraq's territory, and Israel—"the Zionist entity," in Iraq's official argot—
was labeled "Palestine." Sabri gestured me up the stairway and
took me on a private tour of the upstairs rooms, a maze of empty
salons and ballrooms with huge windows. The mansion was
damp and neglected, and it echoed with silence. Sabri explained
that the building had once belonged to a Hapsburg prince, and
he regretted that it had been allowed to fall apart, but he blamed
this on Iraq's shortage of money—because of the UN sanctions—to pay for its upkeep. Sabri said, somewhat wistfully, that
he often came upstairs on his own and walked around, trying to
imagine the grand social events that must have gone on in the
old rooms. Sabri struck me as a most unlikely figure to be a
diplomat. That he had willingly placed himself at the service of
Saddam Hussein seemed unfathomable to me, but not as unfathomable as his transformation since then.

Now, after the dinner at Samir Khairi's, I asked Ala Bashir
about the changes I had observed in Sabri's personality. I mentioned a rumor I'd heard that some years earlier one of Sabri's
brothers had been executed on Saddam's orders. If this were true,
I said, it made Sabri's relationship with Saddam completely incomprehensible to me. Bashir confirmed the rumor about the execution of Sabri's brother, attributing it vaguely to "a Baath
Party problem," and suggested that Sabri's recent behavior was
an attempt to show Saddam there were no hard feelings.

"This might be Naji's way of showing Saddam that his loyalty
to him is greater than anything he might feel over the murder of
his brother," Bashir speculated. Why Sabri had continued to
serve Saddam in the first place, Bashir did not know, but he
pointed out that a lot of Iraq's senior officials were virtual
hostages and suggested that this might be the case with Sabri. It
was a long-standing custom, he pointed out, that whenever Saddam's top officials traveled abroad, their families were forced to
stay behind in Iraq, to forestall defections.

Bashir began musing about the oddities of human behavior and brought up the subject of telepathy. He mentioned how, a couple of years earlier, a mentally unbalanced patient of his had come into his clinic and stabbed him in his left arm and his chest. Less than an hour later Bashir's sister, who knew nothing of the incident, had come to him, explaining that their elderly mother had insisted she go to see him because she had had a vision that something had happened to his chest. "This is an inexplicable phenomenon," he concluded, "but it is an example of what the human mind is capable of."

Then, almost casually, Bashir divulged that Saddam Hussein was also very interested in supernatural powers and that several years earlier he had set up a secret government department for "gifted people, people with special powers." They included a young boy from Kirkuk who had been discovered by his schoolteachers to have the ability to see through walls. Bashir had met the boy himself, he said. The boy and his family had been brought to live in a special compound in Baghdad, but after a couple of years the boy's powers had mysteriously diminished and had finally vanished altogether. There were a number of other people with special powers, Bashir added, all of whom Saddam had brought to Baghdad. After meeting him, they were placed in the special compound, where they lived isolated lives, under supervision, as part of his secret department.

"One of them is a woman whom he regularly consults, along with several other people," said Bashir. "This particular woman has some kind of telepathic power." He explained that Saddam used the woman to good effect after his son-in-law General Hussein Kamal, who was in charge of Iraq's weapons programs, defected to Jordan in 1995. Kamal was debriefed by the CIA and gave UN weapons inspectors a large number of secret documents detailing many of Iraq's most carefully guarded state secrets, such as the existence of Saddam's nuclear bomb procurement program. "She began to concentrate her powers on making him

return to Iraq," explained Bashir. "And Kamal did so, inexplicably, after seven months in exile. Saddam sent his sons, Qusay and
Uday, as is known, to kill him." Bashir told me that he had seen
Saddam after the shoot-out in Baghdad on February 23, 1996, in
which Hussein Kamal, his brother Saddam (who was married to
another of Saddam's daughters and who had defected with him),
and several other members of their family were killed in the attack led by his sons. The Kamal brothers had some weapons and
had held out for several hours, but in the end they were killed
along with everyone else in the house. Several of Saddam's guards
had been wounded in the gunfight and been brought to Bashir's
hospital, he explained, and Saddam had come to the hospital to
see them. Saddam told him: "I have no idea of what it was that
led Hussein Kamal to leave Iraq and to betray us, and I have no
understanding of what led him to return." Bashir explained,
"This is what he said. But I knew about the telepathic woman,
and I believe that this is the only explanation for why Hussein
Kamal would have been so crazy as to come back."

As Bashir talked about Naji Sabri and Hussein Kamal and
their strange, compulsive loyalties to Saddam Hussein, I pondered his own relationship with the Iraqi dictator. There was still
a great deal he had not told me. Why had he stayed in Iraq? How
had he allowed himself to become the trusted confidant and personal doctor to one of the world's most violent rulers? It didn't
seem the right moment to ask him these questions, so I decided
to hold my tongue.

On the morning of March 15, a progovernment rally was held
at the main road intersection in Mansour in western Baghdad. A large tribune had been set up at one side of the junction,
behind which there was a large, freshly painted mural featuring
Saddam, white peace doves, flowers, an AWACS plane, and a soldier on a horse. People streamed past along the road in organized

groups, shouting slogans in favor of Saddam and against Bush, Blair, and the war. One placard read, in English, BLAIR IS BUSH'S TAIL. Soldiers in camouflaged uniforms—the first I had seen on the streets of Baghdad—sat on pickups that were armed with mounted machine guns, and I noticed several snipers on the rooftops. Plainclothes security men seemed to be everywhere. Groups of women, teachers, students, and rustic tribesmen, the latter wearing robes and brandishing old muskets and swords, came marching past to the beat of drums. Each group had its own cheerleader, I noticed, who rallied his followers. They broke into chants and dances as they approached the tribune and then settled back into a more desultory pace once they passed it. A truckload of ululating village women in black abayas came rolling past. On the tribune some Baathist officials sat behind a crowd rouser in a double-breasted suit who held a microphone to his mouth and kept up a shouted commentary, pausing to praise the patriotism of each group of citizens as it hove into sight. A woman who identified herself as a schoolteacher walked up to me and sermonized: "Don't help Bush implement Sharon's plan to control the Middle East and take our oil!" She added: "We can't live without a strong leader," before marching off again. A large group of men from a martyrs' brigade gathered in armed formation. They wore all-white tunics that covered their faces and showed only their eyes. They said they were ready to die for Saddam.

The warm spell that had come with the first turab broke the next day, March 16. The weather was cool, and the skies over Baghdad were opaque. Something else was different too. Baghdad's surreal air of detachment from the coming war had ended. Suddenly, everyone was tense and frantically busy; there were policemen and soldiers everywhere on the streets and huge traffic queues at the gas stations. Crowds of people were buying food and water supplies in the shops. The night before, Iraqi state television had announced that the country was now on a war footing. Iraq had been divided into four military zones. Each zone had a different commander, who had been handpicked by Saddam. Qusay, Saddam's younger son, who commanded the Special Republican Guard, was placed in charge of Baghdad and the family's hometown of Tikrit, and his loathsome cousin Ali Hassan al-Majid, known as "Chemical Ali," who had led both the murderous Anfal campaign against the Kurds in the late 1980s and the slaughter of the Shiites in 1991, was named commander of southern Iraq.

Everyone was monitoring the news from abroad that day. In the afternoon, at a summit in the Azores Islands, George Bush, Tony Blair, and the Spanish and Portuguese prime ministers, José María Aznar and José Durão Barroso, issued a joint ultimatum to the United Nations. Unless the UN took action within the next twenty-four hours to secure Iraq's compliance with its disarmament demands, they declared, the United States and Great Britain would attack Iraq in a matter of days. In a television interview, Colin Powell advised journalists and humanitarian workers in Iraq to leave the country.

During the day the trickle of Western journalists leaving Baghdad turned into a full-scale exodus. The American evacuation was led by NBC and ABC television. People gathered to watch them in the lobby of the Al-Rasheed as they paid their bills, loaded up their cars, and left on the road for Jordan. Sabah called me over to the cashier's desk, where several huge bags full of Iraqi dinars were piled up, like mailbags in a post office. His voice filled with wonder, he informed me that the money was for NBC's hotel bill alone and contained several million dinars. Some reporters posed for photographs with their immense stacks of cash. (Until a few weeks earlier the largest Iraqi notes in circulation had been 250 dinars, worth about ten cents; mercifully, the Iraqi government had begun to issue 10,000-dinar notes, worth about four dollars.)

In the afternoon I stopped by to see Patrick Dillon at his

hotel. He was feeling exhilarated about the imminent war, he said. He was also excited because he had found some wonderful subjects for his film: a group of child violinists who were learning to play Sibelius and an Iraqi man who had returned from London, where he had been living for thirty years, and taken on the Sisyphean task of restoring a boat owned by his father. The boat had sunk in the Tigris during the bombing of Baghdad by the Americans in 1991. The man had raised it from the depths and was painstakingly working on it. "The trick to the film is to come back after the bombing and see which of them has survived," Dillon explained. "That's the story. Will any of us survive? Will you survive? Have you thought about that?" He laughed.

That evening I was dining with a few friends at Nabil, a newly opened restaurant in Mansour, when the manager sidled up to me at my table and in a friendly way asked me if I was a journalist. When I told him that I was, he remarked, in a leading way, that Iraq was probably a good place for news. I nodded. He asked if I knew anything "new"—for instance, when the war would begin. I replied that I didn't know, but it seemed as though it would be very soon. I commented on the atmosphere of imminent war. He nodded and said that everyone he knew had been out that day, buying fuel and water and food for his family, enough for one month's supply. "Will it take long, do you think?" he asked. I told him I didn't know, but that I had heard the Americans wanted to wage a war that was as short as possible. He nodded again, smiling. He asked: "Seventy-two hours?"

I said: "Maybe."

He said, whispering: "*Inshallah.*" Leaning close, he added: "I hope so. I hope it is quick. Everything in Iraq is no good. We want to change this. *Inshallah.*"

He asked me to draw the curtains on the window by our table and then called over a half-naked young woman, a belly dancer, who proceeded to jiggle and gyrate beside us for a few minutes.

She was heavily made up and behaved a lot like a stripper in the West, performing her intimate act only feet away from us, but never making eye contact. When she was done, she vanished wordlessly. It was all very strange. During her performance, a couple of waiters stayed by the front door to keep an eye on the street, in case any policemen showed up. Afterward, one of them explained that belly dancing was forbidden by the government.

At about four the next morning, Monday, March 17, Ala Bashir received another phone call from his cousin Faleh in the United States. Faleh informed him that the bombing would begin late on Wednesday night, the nineteenth, or during the wee hours of Thursday, but not before. He told him that President Bush would advise Saddam Hussein to leave the country with his family within that time frame or face war. Bashir told me about the call that evening, at the end of a long and very tense day in Baghdad.

The day had begun with the news that the United States and Great Britain had abandoned their efforts to secure a new UN resolution authorizing war. It had been announced that at 8:00 PM eastern standard time that evening in Washington, D.C., President Bush would make a national television broadcast in which, it was assumed, he would reveal his timetable for the war. The last remaining UN inspectors and diplomats in Baghdad were expected to leave the next morning. An Air France jet was said to be coming to fly out all the remaining French citizens in Iraq.

On all the roads leading out of Baghdad, cars and trucks, loaded up with belongings and crammed with families and live-stock, were on the move. People had begun to flee the city. Sabah informed me that his three closest neighbors, all Shiites like him, had locked up their houses and gone to Karbala, two hours' drive to the south. They had asked him to look after their houses for them while they were away. All day long many more journalists left Baghdad. Most had been ordered out by their employers, but for some the decision to leave was spurred by the appearance at the Information Ministry of a large number of security agents who were said to work for Saddam's son Qusay Hussein. When I heard the rumors, I went over to the ministry to see what was going on. What I saw there gave me a bad feeling. There were thuggish-looking men in civilian clothes stationed everywhere, inside and outside the building. The normal minders were scuttling about nervously, saying little and avoiding eye contact. The ministry appeared to have been taken over by the newcomers.

Many familiar faces, like my hapless interpreter Muslim, had simply disappeared. I kept a low profile and did not stay long. The anxieties of journalists mounted further after ministry officials furtively warned they could no longer guarantee their safety. Several were urged to leave as quickly as possible. These warnings seemed to be a direct allusion to everyone's worst fear, that of being taken hostage. At some point in the day Uday al-Taiee, the choleric deputy minister, now strutting about in a military uniform, announced that henceforth all the journalists in Baghdad would be restricted to three hotels. The choices, he declared, were the Al-Rasheed, the Palestine, and the Mansour, which was right next door to the ministry.

By evening most of the remaining American, British, and Canadian journalists in town had paid their bills and driven away for the Jordanian border in a succession of convoys. Among them was my friend Heathcliff O'Malley, the photographer, whose newspaper, the *Daily Telegraph,* had ordered him and its correspondent, David Blair, out of the country. Heathcliff was very upset about leaving; our good-bye was quite wrenching. As they drove off, I had a fleeting image of myself standing on the deck of the *Titanic,* watching as the lifeboats pulled away.

The pullout by the press corps had an immediate stock-market-panic effect on the prices for transport. As of noon, the normal $200 fare for the ten-hour road journey to Amman had leaped to $500, and by late afternoon it was up to $700. The Al-Rasheed was emptying out fast, and it was an increasingly lonely place. Given all the warnings about it, my Australian friend Paul McGeough and I decided that it was probably time to move hotels. The Al-Hamra, we now knew, was off-limits, and we dismissed the Mansour out of hand as being too close to the Information Ministry. Almost everyone we knew had moved into the Palestine, which was gloomy and dilapidated, but which now, on balance, seemed a good place at least to have a room, if only to be near our colleagues. While Paul went to the Al-Hamra to pay his bill and move his provisions that were stashed there, I went over to the Palestine to see if any rooms had become available. In the lobby, bedlam reigned, with human shields and journalists and Iraqi drivers and minders and secret policemen all milling confusedly about. The going rate for the Palestine's unkempt rooms was $70 a night. I was told there were no rooms left officially, but that I could have one for a $250 bribe. I angrily refused the offer.

Next, I revisited the Al-Safeer. I thought perhaps there might still be some way to slip under the wire and stay there, in spite of the new orders. But when I arrived, the desk clerks, whom I knew, apologetically informed me that they had received orders not to allow any journalists to stay. I paid my bill for the room that I had never used and arranged for my provisions to be loaded into Sabah's car.

In a single day the illusion that most of us had been harboring for weeks—that we could somehow evade official detection and make ourselves "safe" when the war came—had been shattered. As I left the Safeer for the last time, I understood that I was no longer in charge of my own destiny, if I ever had been. If anyone was, it was Saddam's son Qusay. On his orders, it seemed, we were being herded into hotels that had been preselected for us, and we had no choice in the matter. I felt very vulnerable and anxious, and I realized that it was the first time in Iraq that I had felt fear of the kind that most of its citizens had lived with for years.

I went to see Patrick at his hotel, which was ten or so blocks away from the Safeer, down Abu Nawas Street. He commented on the accelerating pace of things, the tension in the air. He was wide-eyed, brimming with nervous energy. He had been out filming the man restoring his boat, he told me, and was hoping to shoot a sequence with the violinist children the next day and invited me to go with him. We spoke a little about *Heart of Darkness,* and I noted how struck I had been by the importance he attached to the moral dilemmas raised in the book. He shot me a sharp look and nodded in acknowledgment. Breathing heavily, he gave vent to an emotional flow of words: "I'm grappling with my own Marlow and Kurtz, you know? I've got them both in me, you know?" He pounded his chest with both hands. "It's why I came here, to be at the heart of this killing, this great murder that's coming, because I don't think if you've got it in you, this killing attraction, that you can go away from it. I want to be in the center of it all, the death, the killing, so that I can settle it once and for all. Am I Marlow, or am I Kurtz? Who's it gonna be?"

Late in the day, I visited Ala Bashir at the hospital, and he told me about his cousin's latest telephone call. As I informed him of the strange activity at the Information Ministry and the large-scale evacuation of the foreign press, Bashir listened attentively. I asked him if he thought it was possible the regime might be thinking of using us as human shields. He didn't think it was likely, he said, because the regime had not done it before to journalists, not even during the Gulf War. I pointed out that this war had a very different goal in mind, and so the regime could well take off the gloves. He nodded and expressed his concern that I remain safe. I told him that I was under pressure from *The New Yorker* to leave Iraq for safety reasons. I didn't want to leave, but

I didn't want to make a silly mistake either. I asked him to help me by finding out what he could about the regime's intentions toward the Western journalists. He promised to make some discreet inquiries overnight about the goings-on at the Information Ministry. He told me to come see him at eleven the next morning, and he would tell me whether he thought it was safe or not for me to stay in Baghdad.

We talked about his cousin's phone call and what he had said about Bush's intended ultimatum, which wouldn't be broadcast until after we were asleep, at 4:00 AM Baghdad time. "Of course Saddam will not go," said Bashir flatly. We exchanged views about whether the war would be short or prolonged. I suggested that it depended partly on how Saddam chose to make his stand: whether, as many feared, he planned to draw the Americans into a siege in Baghdad, with lots of civilian casualties, in the hope of raising an international outcry that would bring a halt to the war, or whether the Americans could isolate Saddam and his inner circle quickly and avoid big battles. Bashir said he thought the latter scenario was possible and intimated that he knew more about this than he had previously let on. "I know that there are many people, including high-level military people and party members," he said, "who are not willing to fight for him. What can they gain from it? They know what the consequences will be."

Bashir asked what I had thought of his model for the *Epic of Saddam* monument. I told him, diplomatically, that I had found it quite extraordinary and very illustrative of Saddam's time in power. He seemed pleased by this and smiled. "Of course this will never be built. I know this," he said softly. I agreed that it seemed unlikely.

When I awoke the next morning, Tuesday, March 18, I heard the news that Ala Bashir's cousin had anticipated: President Bush had given Saddam and his family forty-eight hours to leave the country or face war—as he put it—"at a time of our choosing." By 8:00 AM in Baghdad, the countdown was already four hours old. Later in the day, when Saddam's defiant rejection of the demand was broadcast, war became imminent.

Meanwhile, our hotel predicament appeared to have been resolved when a Canadian friend of Paul McGeough's offered him the keys to his room at the Palestine. His newspaper had ordered him out, and he was leaving that morning. While Paul and Sabah packed up all our belongings at the Al-Rasheed and moved them over to the Palestine, I rushed over to the Al-Wasati Hospital for my appointment with Ala Bashir.

During the drive, I saw large numbers of armed men on the streets, and I noticed new sandbagged ambush positions and foxholes at road intersections and in vacant lots. I wondered if they had been prepared during the night. A couple of days earlier I had begun noticing men digging the odd trench here and there, but without any great urgency. Now there seemed to be defensive preparations under way everywhere. Most civilians seemed to be carrying on as before, however, adhering to their daily routines and wearing impassive, neutral expressions. Some shops serving spicy lamb and chicken shawarma and a few teahouses were still open, and many of the little general stores were still doing business.

Ala Bashir greeted me calmly. When we were alone in his office, he made a wry quip about how his cousin seemed to have "good sources of information." More seriously, he said he'd spoken to Samir Khairi, and they'd agreed that the best thing was for me to leave, on the grounds that I'd simply be safer. As he put it, "Some of the people around the president might become aggressive toward Americans and Westerners." But it also seemed that he didn't really want me to go, because he urged me again to go to one of the hotels near his hospital. I told him I didn't like their location. We discussed my other alternatives. I explained that I was still on tenterhooks with my editors about whether I was going to stay. I expected a decision sometime that day. I told him that I was provisionally moving to the Palestine, where most of my friends and colleagues were, and which, in fact, was only five minutes away by car from the hospital. He said that he didn't like the Palestine and told me that for some reason it was even more full of security people than the Al-Rasheed and also had more electronic bugging devices. He reiterated his invitation to stay with him at the hospital once things began. I thanked him and said that if it seemed the right thing to do, I would. Privately, I wondered whether this would even be possible, given the stricter controls on my movements. We agreed that I would call him later in the day to let him know whether I was leaving or staying.

Before I left the hospital, Bashir told me that the night before, on Radio Monte Carlo, a station widely listened to in the Middle East, it had been reported that Nizar al-Khazraji, a senior Iraqi general who had defected in 1995, had vanished from his home in Denmark the previous day. Khazraji had been under house arrest for several months, under investigation for war crimes. He had been accused of responsibility for the poison gas attacks against the Kurds in 1988, in which thousands of civilians had died. Bashir thought Khazraji's disappearance was a very significant development. He believed that it had been arranged by the Americans. He said that Khazraji, Saddam's former military chief of staff, was a professional officer who had earned his rank the old-fashioned way, through merit, rather than by being "a cousin of Saddam's," and that he therefore had a lot of admirers in the Iraqi armed forces. Bashir clearly thought a great deal of Khazraji himself. He speculated that the news of his disappearance would be seen by military men in Iraq as a coded message from the Americans that Khazraji was with them and that it was time for them to move against Saddam. He believed that some of them might act. "This man's disappearance will hearten those in the Baath Party and the senior ranks of the Iraqi armed forces who currently believe that they can survive only if they stand with Saddam." The next few hours, or days, he said, were crucial. If a coup or assassination attempt against Saddam didn't come before the bombing commenced, it could come during the conflict. Bashir added that during the Gulf War, Khazraji had been wounded in battle in the south of Iraq and that he was the doctor who had operated on him.

Later Sabah and I picked up Patrick at his hotel, and we drove to the home of the violinist children he had talked about. They lived with their parents in a modest but comfortable duplex house on a residential suburban street in southwestern Baghdad. They were gorgeous children with large, expressive eyes, and their father, Majid al-Ghazali, was a strikingly handsome man of forty. He explained that he was a violinist himself, with the Iraqi National Symphony Orchestra. He also had his own chamber music group but earned his real living as a violin teacher at a Baghdad music school for children. He had taught three of his four children to play instruments, he said proudly.

Majid offered to play something himself first. The children were excited. They squeezed together on the couch in the sitting room, whispering and fidgeting like children in a theater, waiting for the performance to begin. Large wooden bureaus had been placed in front of the windows, and the furniture was covered with dropcloths. Majid stood in front of a music stand and played an étude by Jacques-Féréol Mazas, a nineteenth-century composer. It was a sweet, mournful melody, which Majid said was his favorite. Then Hamid, his ten-year-old son, played his own little violin while his father stood next to him, gently directing him with his hand. One of Majid's daughters played a piece for flute, and his eldest child, a twelve-year-old girl, played the piano. Majid apologized about the piano's being out of tune.

He said that the violin strings were not in the best shape either. They were second-rate strings from Turkey and China. "It's impossible to get professional violin strings in Baghdad," he said sadly.

During the family concert Majid's wife, a pretty woman with deep blue eyes, stayed in the kitchen. While Patrick filmed the children playing their instruments, I went in to say hello to her. She was sitting at a table making small face masks with a needle and thread. She put cotton balls and charcoal inside a gauze pouch that would cover the mouth and nose, with little loops of cloth to fasten the masks around the ears. I asked her what they were for, and she smiled shyly. "They are masks, for the smoke, for the children," she said. I asked her if the children knew what was about to happen. She shook her head. "No, they don't, really. They just know there will be a lot of noise and smoke." The children finished playing and wandered into the room. They stood around, watching their mother's activity uncomprehendingly and smiling and staring timidly at me.

Later, in the bunkerlike front room and out of earshot of the children, I asked Majid what his plans were. He wanted to take his family out before the bombing began, to Jordan, he said. He had the right papers to leave, but he had so far been unable to get enough gas for the car journey. He didn't know yet if he would manage it in time; there were huge lines at all the gas stations in town. But he was going to try. He nodded toward his children. "I don't want them to go through this," he said. I asked if he needed any help. He looked embarrassed and shook his head, thanking me for the offer. When we drove away, the whole family was standing outside, and the children were smiling and waving.

As we headed back to central Baghdad, Patrick explained his relationship to his videocamera. "It's a replacement for the gun," he said. "When I joined the army and was handed an M-16, I took to it immediately. The gun was like an extension to my body. I could shoot the asshole off a bearskin rug, man! I don't know why I could, I just could. Maybe it's genetic. Now I still shoot people, but with this." He held up the camera.

At about 4:00 PM I received a phone call from the editor in chief of *The New Yorker,* David Remnick, asking me to leave Iraq as soon as possible. He cited the eleventh-hour decisions by his colleagues at the *Washington Post* and the *New York Times* to pull out their correspondents. Several days earlier I had promised David that I would heed his final word about whether I stayed or not, but had begged for more time, citing the fact that John Burns, the *Times'* correspondent (and the undisputed dean of foreign correspondents, with thirty years' experience in the field and two Pulitzers under his belt for his reporting from Bosnia and Afghanistan), was determined to stay as well. David had reluctantly agreed to wait and see how things shaped up, but now, with the war on its way, and in light of John Burns's evacuation order, he was calling an end to it. I promised that I would leave but said that it was already late in the day and I might not be able to depart until the following morning. The decision made, I felt a strange mixture of relief and despondency.

I told Paul McGeough my news. He had been having similar discussions with his editors, and he agreed to leave with me. Paul called up the car service we knew and asked to have two GMC Suburbans to be ready to take John Burns and both of us to Amman. The fare, we learned, had shot up by more than 100 percent since the previous evening—to thirteen hundred dollars. Then we went to the press center at the Information Ministry, where, if we wished to leave, we first needed to pay our obligatory fees. These amounted to two hundred dollars plus fifty thousand Iraqi dinars—equivalent to another twenty dollars— per day. At the best of times, paying off the press center was an immensely frustrating process that could take several hours.

There was a single cashier there, a man who was missing several teeth and several fingers, who was required to note the serial number of each U.S. bill, and who occasionally became hysterical for no apparent reason. Once this tedious procedure was over, other officials had to be found to sign off on things. Satellite telephones also had to be officially sealed by a man whose sole duty it was to carry out this function.

By the time Paul and I arrived at the press center, it was obvious that there was no way we would be able to leave that evening. The place was in pandemonium, with dozens of reporters trying to leave, minders and translators and security men all jostling around, and tempers flaring. When I managed to push my way to the front of the throng and speak to the cashier, he told me to return the next day. We tracked down John Burns, his photographer, Tyler Hicks, and *Newsweek*'s Melinda Liu. The five of us had been meeting and discussing our options for several days and had agreed to act together. We held a conclave to decide what to do. All of us had been hearing reports that the journalists leaving Iraq since Bush's ultimatum were being arrested at the border. Most of them appeared to be from "coalition" countries—the United States, Great Britain, and Spain—although at least one Norwegian relief worker was said to be among them. I'd had an e-mail from Heathcliff O'Malley, who had reached Amman safely after crossing the border just before Bush's speech, telling me that one of those detained was a mutual friend, Kim Sengupta, of the *Independent*. Melinda had also confirmed the detentions of people working for the NBC and AP television networks. Apparently, the reporters who'd been arrested had been physically searched and found guilty of previously unenforced "currency violations" (i.e., they were carrying too much cash) or were found to be carrying banned handheld Thuraya satphones. After being divested of all their cash, they had been placed under arrest and been brought back under custody to Ramadi, a pro-Saddam town west of Baghdad.

Many of us had smuggled Thurayas into the country but had cached them following Qusay's takeover of the Information Ministry. I had given mine to Sabah to hide at his home, and Paul had concealed his in a ventilation shaft in the service stairwell of the Al-Rasheed. A Thuraya is equipped with a Global Positioning System (GPS), which, in theory, meant that a person with one on the ground in Iraq could pinpoint and send locations of potential bombing targets to the Americans.

With the fates of our colleagues in custody still unknown, the five of us concluded that, given the uncertainties of the open road and the risk that we'd end up in a jail in Ramadi just as the war began, leaving Iraq was no longer a safe option. We agreed to keep the two drivers we had booked on standby and to assess things again in the morning, but we were all fairly certain that our opportunity to leave Iraq had come and gone.

Driving down Abu Nawas, just as the sun was setting, Sabah and I came across a bizarre scene. In the median strip, two men wearing robes were chained to one of the trees there. One was doing his prayers, rising and falling in the fashion of Muslims; the other, a large bearded man, stood up straight like a chained dancing bear. A banner hanging from the tree said NO WAR. Later someone explained to me that the men were Turkish human shields.

That evening, at the Information Ministry, a relaxed-looking Naji Sabri held a press conference. He was in his military uniform, which was a little small for his bulging girth. Sabri repeatedly excoriated President Bush as "an idiot who does not know whether Spain is a kingdom or a republic." He obviously enjoyed saying this, for he repeated it. He said that the only window of opportunity remaining for diplomacy was for the "two despots"—Bush and Blair—to resign. He also described them as "evilmongers," "crazy warmongers," "small, rabid criminals," and "masters of distortion and fabrication." Asked about the mood of Iraq's president, Sabri said: "Saddam Hussein is relaxed and as sure of victory as I am in your presence in this room. He is relying on his deep faith in God and the unlimited potentialities of the Iraqi people."

Later I telephoned Ala Bashir at his home to tell him that it seemed as though I would be staying after all. He sounded pleased. We promised to remain in close contact with each other. Paul and I crammed ourselves into our dirty little room with two single beds on the ninth floor of the Palestine and had a fitful night's sleep.

The next day, Wednesday, March 19, I woke up with a terrific headache. Looking outside the hotel window, I saw that the skies were yellow and thick with dust: another turab. Paul and I decided to return to the Al-Rasheed. John Burns, who had remained there, imperturbable, had made a strong case to us the previous evening that the Americans were unlikely to bomb the hotel. Pointing out the Al-Rasheed's relative luxury and its reinforced outer walls, helipad, and other facilities, he said it was a perfect place for the new U.S. Embassy. After our miserable night's sleep in the Palestine and our inability to get a satellite signal from our room, John's arguments were very persuasive.

Passing the spot on Abu Nawas where the Turkish protesters were chained up, we came across a throng of about fifteen armed Iraqi militiamen in their green uniforms on our side of the street. They were watching the two chained men, who appeared to have just burned something in the road, where there was a large greasy blackened patch. I guessed that it had been an American flag; the burning of the Stars and Stripes was a de rigueur feature of most political demonstrations in Iraq.

Baghdad had become an eerily deserted place. There were very few civilians on the streets, and most of the shops were shuttered, their windows taped with large X's. The traffic on the roads had thinned out considerably, and quite a few vehicles were filled with men in uniform, going here and there in a hurry. Throughout the city, knots of militiamen and soldiers had assembled on street corners. Most of the foxholes and sandbagged dugouts that had begun appearing throughout the capital in the past few days and had sat empty were now manned by men with guns. On Sadoun Street, a normally bustling commercial strip that runs parallel to Abu Nawas, the watch shops and cinemas were battened down, but the garishly painted billboards were still up, advertising *American Pie* and the schlock thriller *Inner Sanctum 2*. Next to one of the cinemas, I saw a bivouac manned entirely by black men, who were unusual to see in Baghdad and whom I took to be Sudanese. Quite a few of them lived in the neighborhood. Like the Egyptians who had come to Iraq as migrant workers in the 1980s and remained, a small colony of Sudanese had stayed behind. Most of them were too poor to go home again. The Sudanese of Baghdad were widely regarded as honest people and good workers, and many were employed as desk clerks or cleaners in Iraq's hotels. The doorman of the Al-Rasheed was from Sudan. He was an immense, perpetually smiling man who dressed in an *Arabian Nights* costume and who lived in a small wooden house on a vacant bit of ground nearby, with his two wives and their many children.

Driving past the Information Ministry, I noticed stonemasons at work, applying finishing touches to some newly built offices on the ground floor. This activity seemed bizarre given the likelihood that the building would be destroyed in the next few days, but I supposed that Saddam Hussein had issued orders for government business to continue as usual, to make everything appear as though his regime was still firmly in control and confident of victory in the coming war.

At the Al-Rasheed, the gardeners were still out watering the lawn and clipping shrubs, and the swimming pool was filled with shimmering water. The hotel seemed gloriously clean and luxurious by comparison with the Palestine, and the staff was extremely pleased to see us back. Salman, the flirtatious desk manager, scolded us for having left in the first place. Paul and I resolved to stay, although we decided to keep the Palestine room as well. We took a suite for ourselves, with adjoining rooms for Sabah and Paul's driver, Muhammad, on the eighth floor and dispatched them to bring over all our belongings and supplies. The suite faced south, where there was good reception for our satellite telephones and a panoramic view of some of the prime bombing targets in Baghdad, including the immense Baath Party headquarters (which had been almost completely rebuilt after it had been destroyed in President Clinton's four-day Desert Fox bombing campaign in 1998), the tall, spindly Saddam Telecommunications Tower, and several of Saddam's grandiose domed palaces. In the course of the day, other journalists, exhausted from all the moving and the anxieties over the approaching war, also began trickling back from the Palestine. By afternoon the lobby of the Al-Rasheed, which had had a funereal appearance just twenty-four hours before, was once again thrumming with activity.

We had found out more about our colleagues who had been detained attempting to leave the country. Most, it seemed, had been released after being jailed overnight in Ramadi and fined by a judge for their alleged offenses. A French photographer friend of mine had to drive to Ramadi, where he bailed out several of his colleagues to the tune of forty thousand dollars. They had returned with him to Baghdad. Others, like the NBC crew, had been allowed to leave the country, but Kim Sengupta had been forced to return to Baghdad. More worryingly, several others who had been reported missing were still unaccounted for. Paul and I had a final conference with Melinda Liu, John Burns, and Tyler Hicks, and we all concluded that it was safer, on the basis of what we knew, to remain in Baghdad. We paid off the cars we had kept on standby. Afterward we all informed our bosses.

I sent e-mails to David Remnick and Sharon DeLano, my editor at *The New Yorker,* explaining the new situation. They replied immediately and positively, saying they understood our decision and offering their full support for whatever my family might need during my absence. No longer faced with the pressure of leaving, I felt immensely relieved and knew that whatever happened, I was in good company. Many people had left, but in addition to Paul and John and Tyler, there remained Jim Nachtwey, a personal friend of many years' standing, and the Russian photographer Yuri Kozyrev, whom I had gotten to know in Afghanistan. Anne Garrels of National Public Radio had stayed as well, as had Anthony Shadid of the *Washington Post,* Tim Judah of the *New York Review of Books,* John Daniszewsky of the *Los Angeles Times,* Robert Collier of the *San Francisco Chronicle,* and Larry Kaplow and Craig Nelson of the Cox News Service. Some days earlier Robert Collier, Craig Nelson, and I had all recognized one another and caught up for the first time in years; we had last seen one another in Central America in the 1980s. A new friend was Patrick Graham, a warm and witty Canadian reporter who happened to be the son of Canada's foreign minister, a fact he tried to keep as quiet as possible. Patrick was writing for the Conrad Black–owned *National Post,* which was having serious financial difficulties; with black humor Patrick quipped that he might well have found himself a war to cover but no one to cover it for. A few days earlier he had introduced me to Sasha Trudeau, the son of the late Canadian prime minister Pierre Trudeau. Sasha was a thin, intense man in his early twenties who was trying to begin a career as a documentary filmmaker. He constantly fingered a string of azure prayer beads. He intended to evade the authorities and live with an Iraqi family during the war, he had confided in a whisper.

Amid all the chaos, it was impossible to do a head count of Americans, but a few days later I learned in an e-mail from Joel Simon, from the Committee to Protect Journalists, that in all, sixteen Americans had remained in Baghdad. The inimitable Ross Benson of the *Daily Express* and a few other Brits and Canadians had stayed as well. They included Jon Swain; the *Guardian* reporters Suzanne Goldenberg and Jonathan Steele, the paper's long-serving international correspondent; Rageh Omar, a young Somali-born BBC presenter; and Lindsey Hilsum of the ITN network. A last-minute arrival was the *Independent*'s Robert Fisk, who showed up after an overland journey through Syria from his home in Beirut. The dean of British Middle East correspondents, Fisk was a fidgety, taciturn man with a blotchy red face, but Saddam's people positively adored him. The Irish-born Fisk was an ardent Arabist whose acerbic viewpoints on Western policies in the Middle East had made him wildly popular throughout the Muslim world. That afternoon Fisk's colleague, the hapless Kim Sengupta, reappeared after his travails at Ramadi, completely penniless after his fleecing and looking weary but behaving stoically despite it all.

The diminutive Peter Arnett was still around as well, huffing self-importantly to anyone within earshot about his single-handed coverage of Baghdad during the Gulf War of 1991. Arnett was regarded as a pariah by most of his Western colleagues, but Asian and Arab television networks clearly considered him something of a celebrity. I often saw him in the hotel lobby giving interviews, his voice booming out portentously. All told, about two hundred journalists representing some thirty nationalities had stayed on, including a large and seemingly disproportionate collection of Spaniards, French, and Greeks. I no longer saw the zany Russian photographer in the paratrooper's uniform and assumed that he had taken the wise decision to remove himself from harm's way.

After his unexplained absence of several days, my minder, Muslim, showed up at the Al-Rasheed. He told me that he had moved his family to a village outside Baghdad, where he thought they would be safer, and he asked me for some money so that he could buy supplies. He was going to join them, he explained, "until the war is over." He asked me if I was staying for the war. I told him I was. He seemed very pleased, somehow comforted by this news, and he shook my hand. I gave him some money and wished him good luck. It was the last time I saw him.

In the afternoon I fell into conversation with Saad, John Burns's newly appointed minder, a man who had been imposed on him by the Information Ministry a few days earlier and who made little pretense about the fact that his duty was to monitor John's activities. John had written highly critical reports about Saddam's regime in the autumn. Unable to get normal press visas, John and Tyler Hicks had returned to Iraq on questionable "peacenik" visas, which they had paid bribes for, and had lain low for several days until Uday al-Taiee, at the Information Ministry, had demanded they show their faces. In their meeting, al-Taiee had told John that he would allow him to stay but expected him to report the truth about the slaughter of civilians that would occur once the Americans started bombing. It was obvious to everyone that John had been placed under special surveillance. In public gatherings, men who appeared to be security agents were always around him, looking attentive. Al-Taiee was given to hailing John in public and then declaring him loudly to be "the most dangerous man in Iraq." Clearly, the intention was to make John feel as uncomfortable and insecure as possible. John took it all with a display of equanimity and good grace, but it was clear that more than any of us in Baghdad, he was on a knife-edge.

John's minder, Saad, was a former military officer in his midfifties. As we sat talking, he adopted a grave expression when he assured me: "America is making a big mistake. It will have to use the atomic bomb to win over Iraq. The people are all ready to fight; everyone is ready to fight. This will be a very long war." I nodded noncommittally, not quite sure how to respond. He went on for some time in this vein, repeating the official Baathist

version of history, which held that the Americans had been defeated in the Gulf War and that the United States, not Iraq, had
sued for peace after being confronted with the terrible fighting
prowess of the Republican Guard. He said this with a straight
face. I didn't know whether Saad actually believed what he said
or if he was simply doing his job.

At around 5:00 PM, the men who ran the Internet center announced that they would be closing earlier than usual, in two
hours' time. As their customers finished at the computers, the
men turned them off, unplugged them, and began packing them
away into cardboard boxes. Out in the lobby, I noticed that all
the floor-to-ceiling windows that looked onto the garden had
been taped up. In the outer foyer, opposite the kilim shop, in the
spot where a salesman dressed as a Bedouin normally lounged on
a carpet in a faux tent and hailed passing guests to sit down and
drink Iraqi coffee with him, the windows were not only taped up
but covered with beautifully woven rugs. It was like walking
through a luxurious Bedouin tent.

About an hour before dusk, Paul and Sabah and I went out for
a drive through almost empty streets. There were very few
civilians out. Security people were everywhere, however, looking
vigilant. Armed soldiers perched at sandbagged dugouts; groups
of alert-looking men in civilian clothes strolled the streets, looking keenly at the occupants of passing cars, and at intersections
the traffic policemen—normally benign, bumpkinish figures in
their old-fashioned buttoned uniforms and spiked helmets, like
those of early-twentieth-century Prussian soldiers—were now
holding assault rifles. On the dirt of one earthen bunker a looping line of whitewashed bricks spelled out the word *victory* in
Arabic. The setting sun, obscured by the yellow dust, was pale
white. It looked like a great peeled kumquat in the sky, and for
a moment I confused it with the moon.

Here and there families were loading refrigerators, butane canisters, and other belongings onto small flatbed trucks, preparing to leave town. At a street corner on the empty shopping street of Mansour, we stopped momentarily to observe a group of men—three generations of the same family, presided over by a taciturn, formally suited grandfather—who were sitting in chairs on the sidewalk playing dominoes outside a shuttered goldsmith's shop. They smiled affably at us but said nothing and continued their game. A sidewalk vendor standing nearby with a colorfully painted cart stocked with some home-made beverage suddenly looked up and yelled out, portentously but without any particular passion: "Iraq! Iraq!" He pointed to the twilight sky. He had a lit cigarette in his mouth, which he puffed without using his hands.

We drove off the commercial strip into some of the residential back streets. Most of Mansour's large, flamboyant houses appeared to be unoccupied. These were the homes of wealthy Iraqis, people with the access to cash and passports that would have allowed them to leave or at least to evacuate their families to safety in Damascus and Amman. A lone servant woman walked down one of the lanes, carrying several loaves of large, round flatbread on her shoulders, her arms making her black abaya robe billow out like a kite. Back out on the main avenue, we stopped at the roadside, where a few people were buying last-minute items from several men and women who stood by little mounds of stacked-up wares: kerosene lamps, cans of Milkyland infant formula from Egypt, instant coffee, Vienna sausages, tins of Lebanese halal chicken meat, and five-liter plastic jugs of soybean oil carrying the logo of the World Food Programme. As I approached her, a Bedouin woman with a tattooed face who was selling flour and oil called out to me, cupped her hands, and raised them heavenward in a beseeching fashion. Two young men at one of the impromptu stalls looked at me in surprise and pointed at the sky. One of them asked in broken English if I was staying in Iraq for the war. I shrugged and nodded, and he smiled and said that he hoped I didn't get killed. We shook hands. I told him that I hoped he didn't get killed either.

I walked back toward the car, where one of the vendors, a robust market lady with two young boys standing by her, stopped me with a challenge in Arabic. I said, "Hello," an anglicism that is part of the Iraqi lexicon and is used, interchangeably, to mean "hello" and "good-bye." Looking vexed, she began yelling something in Arabic, and a man stepped in helpfully to translate what she was saying. Before he could do so, she yelled at him, and he said to me: "She doesn't want me to translate what she is saying." At my insistence, he explained that she had said: "Hello? What is this, hello? This is not a time for hello. The bombs are about to drop! Why are your countries coming to attack us?" I asked the man to point out to her that I might be a Westerner, but that I was in Baghdad, like her, running the same risks as she was. She visibly softened at this and actually smiled. She dropped her loud tone and asked: "So, is there any news? Will there be an attack tonight?" I said yes, it seemed there would be an attack, and urged her to take care of her boys.

Driving on down the avenue, we passed an old man out for a solitary walk, his hands clasped behind him, dangling a string of prayer beads. He appeared to be in deep contemplation. He strolled obliviously past a youth who stood fanning the embers under a flaming spit of meat at a portable shawarma trolley, as if he was expecting customers to arrive at any moment.

When nightfall came, the air turned cool, and on the darkened streets I suddenly felt very conscious of being an American moving around Baghdad on the eve of an American invasion; it was a strange, disquieting feeling. My apprehension deepened when we stopped at a traffic light and the man in the car next to us, a rustic-looking character in a red-and-white-checked kaffiyeh headscarf, pointed a Kalashnikov out the window and, with a sidelong glance at us, began loading the clip. He finished with a single, muscular thrust, and I could hear the metallic click. The gun was now loaded. He shot another quick look at us and then, as the traffic light changed, put the gun away. I told Sabah to slow down, to put some distance between us and the man with the gun. Sabah harrumphed at my nervousness and said: "No problem, Mr. Jon." Smiling, he reached down, and drew a handgun out from the side pocket of his door on the driver's side, and showed it me. "Colt .45," he said proudly. "From USA. Number one."

An hour after sunset I noticed some soldiers out digging an eleventh-hour trench in a median strip of the boulevard that ran past the Al-Rasheed. On the back streets near the Al-Safeer, which now had its ground-floor windows boarded up, all seemed normal: Some children played with one another, and old men sat around in one of the narghile houses, doing nothing in particular. On an unlit section of Abu Nawas, a crowd from the Baathist youth union was holding an impromptu rally in front of the shuttered masgouf restaurants. I stopped to take a look, but there were too many excitable-looking men with guns in their hands. It did not seem wise to be out on the streets any longer, and we returned to the Al-Rasheed, to wait.

SIX

Baghdad was unusually still that night. I stayed up until the small hours in my comfortable new room in the Al-Rasheed, writing and catching up on e-mail correspondence. Before he turned in, at around 1:00 AM, Paul taped up the windows of our rooms with large X's of duct tape and filled our plastic jerricans with water. At 3:30 AM, as President Bush's deadline neared, all I could hear was the noise of an occasional whooshing car and some barking dogs. At 5:00 AM, feeling weary and thinking that perhaps the attack would not begin that night after all, I lay down on my bed to try to sleep. I had just begun to drift off about a half hour later when I heard a big, muted whoomping noise. My bed moved, as if there had been an earthquake rather far away. Then I thought I heard a high-flying jet go past. I leaped up and called to Sabah and Paul. As I did, there were louder, quick sounds, either bombs or antiaircraft fire—I couldn't tell which—and then air-raid sirens. As Paul appeared and then Sabah, there was more firing. Some cars raced by, men shouted, and after a few minutes some more detonations could be heard, and then all around us the clatter of ack-ack fire started up. One very loud bomb landed—a terrific explosion—and then more antiaircraft fire whoomped. At 6:00 AM a light blue dawn broke, and there was silence except for the sound of a single rooster crowing, birds singing, and a muezzin who was calling out,

"*Allahu Akbar,*" over and over. There were no more explosions.

A few minutes later Paul received a phone call from his editor in Sydney advising him that the Australian Foreign Office had just relayed a message that we urgently needed to move out of the Al-Rasheed, because it was "a high-value target," and go to the Palestine, which was "safe."

We tried calling John Burns's room to warn him, then ran down and knocked on his door. There was no reply. After grabbing some of our most indispensable things—our satphones, laptops, money, and a few clothes—we raced down to Sabah's car. We told Muhammad, Paul's driver, to bring the generator, fuel, and the water jerricans in his car. We stopped at the desk to relay the warning to the receptionist there. There were very few other hotel employees, or guests for that matter, in sight. The receptionist seemed not to grasp what we were trying to tell him. He kept repeating, rather dumbly, that it was his job to stay where he was, that his "bosses" would be angry if he left. He pointed out that there was a bomb shelter in the Al-Rasheed where he would be safe. We told him that the Americans had bunker-busting bombs; he wouldn't be protected there. If he heard planes or sirens, we advised, he should go out to the garden. He nodded, looking unconvinced. He asked us about our bill. Exasperated, I told him that we were keeping our rooms for now and not to fret about the bill. We left and drove through empty streets back to the Palestine. I was tense and bleary-eyed from lack of sleep and feeling irrationally furious about having to leave our nice new suite at the Al-Rasheed.

After we had moved back into our miserable little room at the Palestine, I sent Sabah home to see his family, and then, leaving Paul to organize things, I fell into an exhausted sleep. When Sabah returned a couple of hours later and woke me up, I asked him how his family was. He became tearful. He motioned with a hand to indicate the smallest of his grandchildren, and he said, choking up, that they had been terrified by the bombing and had spent the night sitting with their parents, his wife, and his mother in an inner family room, huddled together, with the lights off. Looking skyward and speaking in a low voice, in his broken English, he said, "OK bombing for Saddam, but not Iraqi people. One bomb—finish everything, good."

About a week earlier Sabah had invited me to his home for the first time and introduced me to his wife and many relatives. He lived in a working-class neighborhood but had one of the nicest houses on his street, paid for, he explained, with the money he had made working as CNN's driver during the Gulf War. Like many Iraqis, Sabah had his immediate clan gathered around him. He and his wife and the youngest of their six children lived in one house, and right next door, with an adjoining garden, lived his mother and several of his married sons and brothers, their wives, and his grandchildren, nieces, and nephews. Sabah was not the eldest brother, but he was the most economically successful and essentially supported the entire clan. In all, there were twenty-two people living in the two modest houses. Sabah's two grown sons, Safaar and Diyah, the one whose marriage I had attended, lived together in a house Sabah had rented for them a block away.

I told Sabah he could stay with his family if he wished, but he said no, he wanted to remain with me. His family was well provided for, he explained, and he would look in on them whenever he could. Besides, he said, there were too many small, noisy children there, and they drove him crazy. There was no room for Sabah in the tiny space Paul and I now inhabited and no other free rooms in the Palestine. He said he would see if he could share a room with a friend, another driver, who was lodged at the Palestine, and if not, he would sleep in his car.

Somehow, Patrick Dillon had learned that I hadn't left Baghdad, and while I was asleep, he'd come by the room and pushed a note under the door. It read: "Jon. Albert Camus said 'At 4 AM, everyone in the world is exactly where they are supposed to be.'

I'm thrilled that you are where you are supposed to be. . . ." Paul had finally tracked down John Burns, who, it turned out, had not heard our calls or the knocks on his door because he had stayed up until after dawn, filed a dispatch about the bombing, and then gone to sleep with earplugs in to block out all noise. He and Tyler were moving over to the Palestine, as was everyone else, it seemed. By then the warnings about the Al-Rasheed had been relayed through other sources, including the Pentagon, and been circulated widely. The warnings also named the Mansour Hotel, which was next to the Information Ministry, as being an unwise place to stay, because the ministry was a priority bombing target. In a secret briefing for American media executives, the Pentagon had apparently said that news organizations still operating in Baghdad should advise their correspondents to stay away from the ministry during the next forty-eight hours.

At around noon I drove back over to the Al-Rasheed to retrieve some of my belongings. Once again, the hotel was deserted. I had a hot shower and made some satphone and telephone calls to my family, to reassure them that I was fine. I used my laptop to check the Internet for news from the outside world and learned that the air strikes early that morning had been aimed at "decapitating" the Iraqi leadership and had been directed at one of Saddam's retreats just outside Baghdad. Already, it seemed, American officials and journalists were speculating that Saddam might have been killed in the attacks. For an hour or two I entertained the thought that Saddam might actually be dead. If it was true, I realized, there might be no war after all. I felt tremendously elated about this possibility. On my way back to the Palestine, around midafternoon, I saw that cars were back on the streets, and there were even a few buses running, but almost no people were visible walking around. At 3:15 PM, I heard a few distant bomb explosions, but that was it; there was nothing else.

Walking back into the lobby of the Palestine through the

scrum of milling journalists and minders and Mukhabarat men and human shields who seemed to have taken up permanent positions there, I noticed a knot of people gathered around a TV set. I pushed through and saw that they were watching Saddam, in a rough video image, speaking to the camera. From what I could make out, he was saying things that made it clear that the video had been shot earlier that day, after the air strikes, which meant that he was still alive. As we walked away, I asked Sabah what he thought. He was uncertain. He said it was possible that the man in the video might not have been Saddam but one of his presumed "doubles." Sabah said doubtfully: "He had bigger ears, looked old, and wore glasses. Maybe not Saddam."

Our room in the Palestine overlooked Patrick's smaller hotel, the Al-Fanar, which had become the hotel of Kathy Kelly's peaceniks and sundry souls like Patrick Dillon. Expecting the bombing to resume that night, Paul and I kept watch. Our balcony had a view of a section of the river, several of the bridges that spanned it, and part of the palace complex on the other bank. In the distance we could also make out the Baath Party headquarters, the Al-Rasheed Hotel, and the Information and Foreign Ministries. Farther on we could see the Saddam Telecommunications Tower and the immense domed humps of Saddam's half-built mosque, which always reminded me of a nuclear power station, on the grounds of the former racetrack.

The bombing began again at about 6:30 PM. Suddenly there were three great crashing explosions right across the river from us. Several of the palace buildings and ministries appeared to be hit, but after the initial fireballs, it was difficult to see much. The Planning Ministry, a large ocher-colored building at the edge of the palace complex next to the nearest bridge, appeared to have its lower floors on fire. Here and there flames leaped and flared, and columns of dark smoke rose into the night sky. All the great symbolic edifices of Saddam's dictatorship still appeared to be standing, as was the Al-Rasheed. After the violent roar of the bombs, a hush descended on the city.

I looked down from the balcony to see if I could spot Patrick on his balcony at the Al-Fanar. I couldn't see him, but I saw several other guests, European or American peaceniks, sitting on theirs. One of them, who sat hunched, peering outward, had erected a white flag, which hung limply from a pole over the street. A few doors down, on the sidewalk in front of the entrance to another small hotel, the Al-Rabe Tourism Apartments, a dozen or so people, Iraqis, sat in lawn chairs, like a family group out enjoying the fresh evening air. I saw a few cars driving around, even over the bridges. Dogs barked, and the river looked as calm as olive oil, with just a shimmer of motion on the surface.

A few hours later I received an e-mail message from my editor, Sharon DeLano, in New York, relaying urgent not-for-attribution warnings to the media from Pentagon officials. The message suggested that much heavier and more sustained air strikes were on their way and could begin within hours. "If you want to save your eardrums (in Baghdad)," it said, "stay at least two miles south of 14th of July St. and the railway station, especially near the Al-Azamiyah bridge beginning 2 am Thursday night (Friday Baghdad time) for 48 hours and stay out of the Al-Karamah district for about a week." A little while later, Sharon forwarded another message, which read: "I just received this message from a Pentagon source who's noticed journalists continue going to the Ministry of Information in Baghdad: tell your (Baghdad) team not to get overconfident about being on the streets." I was awestruck: Did this mean everything we did in Baghdad was visible to some kind of all-seeing American Eye in the Sky? Or did the Pentagon already have people on the ground reporting back to it?

I snatched an hour's sleep before Paul woke me up, just before

2:00 AM. A few minutes later someone banged on our door to
warn us that security men had roughed up some cameramen and
photographers who had stolen up to the Palestine's roof. Among
them was Jim Nachtwey, who had had his digital camera thrown
off the roof, eighteen stories above the ground. (Amazingly, he
recovered the camera afterward and found that it still worked.)
This coincided with the news that CNN was being thrown out
of Iraq, effective immediately, in retaliation for broadcasting the
evening's bombings live from the Palestine. Led by CNN, the
networks had been arguing fruitlessly for several days with Uday
al-Taiee for permission to broadcast from the Palestine, citing
the mortal risk of continuing to operate from the Information
Ministry. He had consistently rebuffed them, insisting that the
ministry was the only place from which they were authorized to
work. No doubt he hoped their presence would save his ministry
from devastation. On the heels of the news about CNN, we were
warned that the Mukhabarat was conducting a floor-by-floor
sweep of our hotel for satphones. Fortunately, Sabah was still on
hand. He quickly put both our satphones in a bag and hurried
down the service stairwell to the street, where he stashed the bag
in the trunk of his car. We waited tensely for an hour, and when
no one came, Sabah brought the satphones back up. What remained of the night passed peacefully. At around 4:00 AM, I fell
into a deep sleep and did not awaken for seven hours.

It was a clear, sunny morning. Buses were running in the
streets below, cars went past, and even a donkey cart clattered by.
Smoke still rose from the ruins of one of the buildings across the
river hit the night before. In daylight I could see that it was not
the Planning Ministry that had been bombed but a smaller
building next to it, just inside the palace grounds.

I hadn't been awake very long before Patrick Dillon showed
up at my door. He had his Somali "toothbrush," as he called it—
a stick taken from the branches of a medicinal tree in Africa—
jutting out of one corner of his mouth and was jumping with

energy. Thinking he wouldn't find me in, he'd written me a note, which he handed to me. He told me that the previous day, after the first round of air strikes, he'd been back to see Majid, the violinist, who had not left for Jordan with his family after all. While Patrick was visiting, some police had arrived and questioned both of them for an hour. Patrick didn't understand what it was all about, but I suspected that more than anything else it was Patrick's odd appearance that had attracted the attention. Patrick was in a rush, off to do some filming, he said. I advised him, as I had a couple of times before, to take care and, if possible, to wear a hat to conceal his singular tattoo. We promised to check in with each other later in the day or the next morning.

After he'd gone, I looked at his note. It read: "Jon Lee: This ex-MP military policeman I know was stationed at this firebase up by the DMZ. Every night, just about, during his whole tour, the VC would mortar his arse at precisely 3:30 AM. He said it took him years to learn how to sleep again. Maybe the Pentagon has taken a page or two from Uncle Ho and applied it here. I did sleep like somebody hammered my head with nails and hope you did too, because as my friend Michael reminded me, once the bombing begins again, it could be a very long haul."

Sabah turned up. He was still bleary-eyed, having grabbed only a couple of hours' sleep in his car before going off to see his family. They were still fine, he said. He informed me that everyone he had met with, his friends and relatives and neighbors, was very confused. They all were wondering why the American bombing had been so light. "They are saying: 'Saddam is still here, strong. Where are the Americans? Why haven't they taken Basra, Kirkuk, Mosul?'" If there was no more bombing that night, he said, the city's shopkeepers were planning to return to their stores and reopen them, because they'd been ordered to by the regime. Sabah looked perplexed and troubled. He spoke about the news reports that Iraq had fired a number of missiles into Kuwait, and he shook his head anxiously about this. When I explained the version of events I was hearing—from news reports coming from outside Iraq—of American and British troop advances in the north, south, and west of the country, Sabah said: "Good," but still looked unconvinced. It was obvious that he had heard nothing of these actions. He seemed to rely exclusively on Iraq's official news and street rumors for his information.

Sabah drove me over to the Al-Rasheed again to clear out the last of my belongings from our rooms there and to take another shower. (Electricity was fitful at the Palestine, and there were long periods of time every day with no running water.) John Burns came along as well, and afterward we each called our wives in England on his satphone. It was a very welcome interlude for both of us. We were very conscious of the fact that it might be the last moment of relative tranquillity we would enjoy for some time. We were also keenly aware that we were inside a building that might be turned into dust and rubble within a few hours. It was a beautiful day, very springlike, with clear blue skies, and I noticed that in the garden below there were now flowers in bloom, showing up pink and red amid the dusty green. The gardeners, who had been out there persistently watering and clipping until a day or two earlier, were gone. They had been replaced by huddled teams of security agents. John and I watched for several moments as the men came and went from what looked like a secret passageway in the very thick, fortified perimeter walls that ringed the hotel.

Down in the lobby, two of the cashiers remained on duty, as did some of the assistant managers and lobby security men. Bizarrely, the kilim shop in the foyer had reopened for business. The hotel was empty of guests except for an odd group of French and German journalists whom we found having a meal in the restaurant, and an Italian reporter, who had just arrived in Baghdad and came over to ask us if we thought it was all right to stay in the Al-Rasheed. He explained that he had been turned away from the Palestine for lack of space and had been directed to here. We advised him strongly against it. In the restaurant, the menu had been whittled down to a wartime offering of chicken or lamb tikka. Muneer, my favorite waiter, was there, and he brought me my favorite double Turkish coffee, medium sweet. I passed on to him the warnings we'd received about the hotel's possibly being bombed, and he listened attentively and said in a low voice that he understood; he would be going home for the night.

Before we left, we stopped at reception and talked with Salman, the unctuous manager, who spoke good English. He chastised us in a friendly way: "Why have you all left us? We are frightened being here alone." Leaning forward, he asked: "Is it true what we have heard? That the Americans may bomb us tonight?" We told him that it might well happen and that he should be sure he was outside the hotel after dark. Looking sideways toward one of his bosses, standing some distance away from us out of earshot, he said: "I can't. This is my job. To be here. I am a manager. Look," he said, indicating the telephone panel, where a phone was ringing. "Even now there are phone calls from people looking for guests. Someone has to answer them." We advised Salman nonetheless to try to be outside the building, if at all possible, after nightfall. "I will try." He nodded, looking uncertainly again toward his boss. He asked: "This building is very hard, though, like the Americans." He giggled. "Is it true what I hear that they want to take this place for themselves and stay here?" His face looked hopeful. We told him that we had also heard this rumor. He laughed again and said: "Good. If they come, that's fine for me. Americans, Iraqis, it doesn't matter. So long as the hotel isn't empty. My job is to serve people."

I visited Ala Bashir, whom I had not seen for two days. I found him sitting imperturbably in his little office at the hospital, adhering to his daily work routine. Sunduz, a woman in her thirties with a badly burned face and a wonderful smile, brought us small cups of Turkish coffee, followed a few minutes later by small glasses of sweet tea. Sunduz had been brought to the hospital years earlier as a patient after a terrible fire incident, which had destroyed much of her face. Bashir had given her many skin grafts, he explained, and done just about all he could do for her. Sunduz's family had never returned for her, however, and he had "adopted" her. She lived at the hospital, sleeping in a camp bed in his outer office, and she cleaned and made tea for him and his immediate staff. It was obvious that she was utterly devoted to him.

I noticed that Bashir's computer was gone. He explained that it had been removed for safekeeping. As we spoke about the night's events, he was interrupted by a phone call. He spoke in Arabic for a few minutes and hung up. He turned back to me, sighed, and explained that it was his daughter, Amina, calling from Jordan. "She's been calling me every fifteen minutes, very upset. I keep telling her I am fine, that she's going to spend all her money calling me." He smiled in mock exasperation. The phone rang again. This time it was his wife, who was more relaxed.

Bashir told me that he had heard that the Americans in Kurdistan were moving south with the Kurdish peshmerga militia forces. They were heading toward the oil-rich city of Kirkuk, supposedly. American and British commandos were also said to have entered the western desert and were trying to secure a base there. In the south, meanwhile, they had penetrated some distance inland after seizing the gulf port of Um Qasr and were advancing on Faw, bypassing Basra. With a slight smile, he remarked: "It is interesting to see that they are following the same exact route as the British did when they invaded Iraq in 1914." We were interrupted by another phone call. Afterward he said: "That was a friend who is outside Iraq. He called to say that some B-52s took off from somewhere in Europe about two hours ago." He looked at the clock on his wall. "That means they will be over Iraqi airspace at about eight o'clock tonight, about six hours from now."

There was a knock at the door. A uniformed military officer came in and sat down in the chair next to mine, in front of Bashir's desk. The officer shook my hand and smiled when Bashir introduced us. He spoke to Bashir in Arabic for several minutes, and Bashir then translated for me. "He says that the Americans are lying; Um Qasr has not fallen. He just had a telephone call from his friend, who is an officer there, and he says everything is quiet." The officer spoke some more. "He says it's also not true that they have taken a base in the western desert. In fact, he says, they have taken some British and Americans prisoners, and they will be shown on TV." After a few more minutes of this, the officer left. Bashir turned to me, deadpan, and said in a mild tone of voice: "I don't think what he says is true. The Americans know better than to lie about what they are doing. Why would they claim to have taken Um Qasr only to be disproven, if this were untrue?"

We discussed Saddam's brief appearance on Iraqi television following the first air strikes. "He looked very shaky, I thought," said Bashir. "Perhaps he was very close to the bombing." I asked him whether he thought it was really Saddam or a double, as people were speculating. "It was him, not a double," he assured me. "I know this man. His words, his language, it was all his. Normally he writes all his own speeches and takes time to write the words in very large letters so he doesn't have to use his glasses to read. Obviously he wrote this very quickly, and forgot to write in large letters, and so this is why he had to read from a script, with his glasses. And his beret was not placed on his head in the usual way. It looked like it had been placed carelessly. These are things he normally takes great care about. It was him, but he was not himself."

Bashir was in a contemplative mood and seemed eager for me to stay and chat. He began ruminating about the fall of communism, how he had visited the Soviet Union and China twenty years earlier and how he had come to the conclusion that the systems they had imposed were the worst humankind had created. "It doesn't matter if you feed someone or give him a little flat to live in if he doesn't have his freedom," he said. "This is an essential human need. Without it, life is nothing. It's like how you treat your dog. You give him food and a place to stay, but he's still a dog." He went on to talk about Cuba, which he had visited. He hadn't liked it much, he said. It had reminded him a lot of Iraq. He said he was mystified as to why the United States had allowed Fidel Castro to remain in power for so long. Bashir clearly regarded the United States as an imperial power and was confused by the fact that it had not always behaved as one. We talked about the U.S. policies toward Cuba for some time, but after some minutes, with what seemed like very Iraqi logic, he concluded: "Well, I can only think the U.S. has some reason to keep Fidel there. Nothing else makes sense. But one thing I am certain of: After he dies, Cuba will become part of the United States."

Bashir began to reminisce about the days before Saddam's rule, when many Iraqi professionals of his generation had gone to England and the United States for their university educations. In the early 1970s he had been a medical student at a provincial university in the west of England. It had been a wonderful experience, he said, one of the best times of his life. While he was there, he said, something had happened that, for some reason that he said he could not entirely fathom, had become one of his most enduring memories, something that was always popping back into his consciousness, like a riddle he couldn't solve. He had gone to London to visit the Iraqi Embassy in Queen's Gate Mews to see an embassy official about some paper or permission he needed. "There was a porter who worked there, who had worked there forever. The strange thing was that he was actually an Englishman, a big, tall fellow, who had lived in Iraq. He had been with the embassy for many years. It seems that over the years this had rubbed off on him, because in his behavior he was completely Iraqi. Anyway, when I got to the embassy, I told him who I wanted to see. He told me to sit down and wait. After a long time of waiting, more than an hour and a half, I went and asked him why it was taking so long. He said to me that the official had gone out and that I should come back tomorrow. I became very angry. I asked him: 'Why didn't you tell me he had gone out? I have waited for two hours!' The porter looked at his watch and said: 'Why are you lying? You've only waited for an hour and a half.' I could see there was no use arguing with him. I was so furious that I said I wasn't leaving, that I would stay in the embassy until the official returned. The porter looked at me, and then he went over to the presidential portrait hanging on the wall. He took it off the wall and brought it over. The frame was very loosely attached. He took it off, and then, shoving it under my nose, he said: 'Look.' He lifted the portrait of the president, Abdul Salam Arif. Underneath, I saw the picture of his predecessor, Abdul Karim Qassem. And there were other layers of portraits. I think the last one he showed me was the portrait of King Faisal. It was quite astonishing."

What did he think the porter was trying to tell him? I asked Bashir. He replied: "I think he was trying to show me that Iraq's leaders came and went, and it didn't matter to him, because he was always there. As for me, I was of no consequence at all, just someone passing through." He smiled and peered at me quizzically, eyebrows arched. I deduced that Bashir's story had an allegorical intention and that the point he was making to me was that whatever Iraqis did to change their circumstances and whoever served as their leader was irrelevant, because Iraqis were fated never to be the masters of their own destiny.

Before I left, I asked Bashir if he thought it was safe to continue coming to see him. He said: "Of course. You can always say you need some medicines." He asked me if I had any particular ailment that needed treatment. I told him that I had a bad back, which was true. "Good," he said. "You will need regular treatments from a therapist. I'll make the arrangements. You should probably see him every day." He told me he would call me and tell me when to come.

That night the "shock and awe" bombardment began in earnest. Air-raid sirens started up at 8:15 PM, followed by ack-ack fire and what sounded like ground-to-air missiles. White and red tracers arced up from different points around the city to form a kind of grid in the night sky. The first bombs hit precisely at nine o'clock, and we had a front-row view of the conflagration from our balcony. There were huge blasts, simultaneous concussions with aftershocks that knocked us back on our feet and made us shout involuntarily with the shock. Everyone around me—Paul, John Burns, Tyler and Matt and Moises of *Newsday,* who had crowded onto our balcony because of its vantage point—shouted and gasped in incredulity. One of the main palaces across the river and a big, ugly ziggurat-shaped building some ten stories high were both hit several times and burned robustly. Several other massive explosions whacked the giant Council of Ministers Building, where I had last interviewed Tariq Aziz. There were flames bursting all over the city. In the distance many more bombs landed. It looked as if the Mukhabarat headquarters had been hit. Fireballs were followed by white flashes that lit up the sky. Debris flew through the air from a couple of the blasts as buildings took direct hits. We watched as a cruise missile ripped into the flat roof of the Council of Ministers Building, which was already ablaze, and a great new orange plume of flame rose up.

The bombing extravaganza went on for around thirty minutes:

symphonic crescendos of blasts and noise interspersed by moments of quiet until the next explosions began. With every explosion, car alarms were set off and honked briefly in the streets.

When it was over, I noticed that all the electricity in the city was still on; the palace gardens were illuminated by street lamps, which cast a romantic yellow glow. I could see people—soldiers and civilians—standing and watching in the streets below. A few cars without headlights raced along. A big white dog loped down the center of Abu Nawas Street, followed, some minutes later, by a man on a bicycle, pedaling along in no apparent hurry. An ambulance swept by, followed by a police car. I heard a donkey bray. The night sky, which was a deep blue, was filled with columns of black and gray smoke. The Al-Rasheed was still standing.

The lull lasted forty minutes. At 10:35 PM, we were standing on the balcony when a huge sucking, whooshing metallic sound rushed past seemingly right over our heads, causing us all to duck and fall to the ground. A moment later, when we saw it explode against some building in the distance, we realized it must have been a cruise missile that had flown right past us in the air corridor between the Palestine and the Al-Fanar. Within the next couple of minutes five more missiles slammed into the palaces in front of us, and then a new barrage began. A rain of missiles and bombs struck previously untouched parts of the presidential complex and buildings around the city. I ran to a room on the other side of the hotel to see one of Saddam's palaces burning brightly. Smoke rose from explosions in the distance. The sheer power and scale and precision of the attacks were at once terrible and awe-inspiring and placed us in a state of mind in which almost anything seemed possible. At around 5:00 AM I fell asleep.

SEVEN

When I awoke, on Saturday, March 22, after a four-hour sleep, I found a new note from Patrick Dillon pushed under my door. It read: "Jon: So, I'm out. I got too close to a missile attack site yesterday . . . without knowing it. The peelers reported me, and my sponsor in the Foreign Ministry was forced to pull my visa 'for my safety.'. . . My war's over, Jon. I'm crying right now going over the wall like Chief Broom in Cuckoo's Nest. (And those five missiles directly across from Fanar didn't hurt.) Please keep telling the Truth to Power, and be Marlowe to your own Kurtz, OK? All love, Patrick."

Two days later I received an e-mail message from Patrick. He had reached Amman safely. "Jon Lee: These two gypsy cab riding brothers with a Chevrolet station wagon agreed to make the run for the small fortune of $100. We took off, and for the next 36 hours ducked and dodged U.S. missiles hitting the highway, local militia armed to the teeth and crazed Ali Babas and regional Mukhabarat in Toyotas. My boyos, Ali and his brother Jaffah, were real stand-up guys but too bloody scared of the Yanks to go all the way to the border, so they dropped me off on the highway, and I walked the last 5 klicks nearly shitting myself, past two rather sheepish Iraqi soldiers, a couple of mild-mannered form stampers, and then the last DMZ mile into Jordan on the auld heel-toe express and crying all the way. Am now in Amman, plotting, if it's possible, to come back. . . . Am thinking about you and all my other friends, real worried they'll round you up once the noose tightens, but hope this finds its way to you still in one piece. . . . Su Hermano, Patricio."

I was more relieved than sorry that Patrick was gone. I'd always worried that he was going to get into trouble in Baghdad, and he finally had. From the sound of it, Patrick had been very lucky. Things could easily have gone much worse for him. Now he was safe.

After Friday night's spectacular bombardment, the atmosphere in Baghdad was schizophrenic. Traffic was out on the streets, but there were soldiers everywhere. Saddam's palace complex was littered with the smoking hulks of bombed buildings. I observed that Iraqis did not gather to stare at the damage but cast fleeting, sidelong looks at it. It was as if the palaces were something they were still not supposed to notice. When I asked Sabah, who had spent the night in a friend's hotel room, what he had thought of the bombings, he merely shook his head. I teased him, asking if he was still wondering why the American bombing had been so "light," as he had put it, the previous day. He shot me a wounded look, and I instantly realized that my comment sounded callous and triumphalist; the sheer scale and might of the night's air strikes against the heart of the power of the state must have been deeply humiliating for an Iraqi to bear, whatever his feelings about Saddam Hussein. Sabah demurred; he didn't want to talk about it.

There was something else that was new as well: The Ministry of Information seemed to have moved into the Palestine with us. Uday al-Taiee and his loathsome deputy, Mohsen, had acquired rooms on an upper floor, and I spotted quite a few of the ministry's minions in the lobby. They had set up an information table, with a bulletin board for journalists. Curiously, I noticed, none of them mentioned the night's bombing either. They acted as if it simply hadn't happened until, in the early afternoon, they arranged a bus tour for reporters to see some victims of the bombing raids.

We were taken to Mustansiriyah Medical College, which had received some of Baghdad's first civilian casualties of the war. In the forty-eight hours since the war had begun, a doctor there told me, the hospital had received 107 patients with injuries. Three of them had died. Many of the patients had suffered traumatic injuries from shrapnel, he said; a handful had also suffered burns. Some of them were children, many with piteous wounds, who lay passively in beds, watched over by silent, aggrieved-looking parents. In one crowded ward, a young girl, four or five years old, squeaked in pain on a bed as her parents comforted her. The doctor told me she had been hit in the back by shrapnel. In the bed next to her lay a plump Bedouin woman with ornate tattoos on her face. She held up her bandaged hands to show her injuries. Her fleshy arms were covered with massive bruises. A small boy lay quietly in another bed. He keened spasmodically every few moments. His ankles and heels were bandaged, but I could see his bare toes poking out. They were all torn up and very bloody. His mother, in a black abaya and green headscarf, stood by his bed, saying nothing, holding his hand.

There was a commotion as Iraq's minister of health arrived and marched into the outer lobby. He was wearing a military uniform and a beret, and his face was set in a severe expression. Doctors in white lab coats and nurses began chanting, "Hurrah Saddam," rhythmically, in greeting.

I walked into another ward, where I found a Sky television reporter doing a stand-up to the camera. He had positioned himself in such a way as to show a young wounded boy who lay supine and spread-eagled on a bed behind him. In the next bed, a man in his fifties, a corpulent fellow, had been hit by flying metal in his intestines, and he lay in his bed, shirtless, his chest heaving up and down from his short, violent breaths. His mouth was open, and his eyes were wide and fearful. There was a hose inserted into his stomach. Standing vigilantly by his bed, his wife held one of his hands. She looked terrified too. A doctor whispered to me that he was one of their most critically injured patients, and I came away with the impression that he might not survive.

Suddenly, the Sky reporter began booming out to the camera: "Iraq says these people are the innocent victims of last night's bombing. We've asked to see the sites that were bombed, but so far we've been refused." The reporter did several takes, repeating this phrase loudly four or five times before he was satisfied and moved on.

In the burns unit, a handsome man of about forty had suffered terrible burns on his bottom, groin, and legs. He was naked except for his lower body, which was swathed in white bandages with blood seeping through them. He was positioned on a bed on all fours while two relatives gently sponged his back. I noticed that he was not suspended but was holding himself up on his hands and knees, and he appeared to be in an advanced state of exhaustion. He repeatedly swung his head down and back and forth, in the way that bears do when they are kept in small cages.

I returned to the hospital entrance, where the health minister was speaking to the press, surrounded by doctors and nurses and the relatives of patients. As I made my way back out through the ward, a clutch of hospital cleaning women jumped up and down, singing Saddam's praises, and then giggled when they finished. This was something Iraqis seemed to feel obliged to do whenever there was a public occasion of any sort and whenever there were journalists present. Outside, in the parking lot, a crowd of doctors and nurses and patients' relatives milled around, talking and waiting. One of the men began shouting loudly about his loyalty to Saddam, the perfidy of the Americans and the British, and so forth. As he gained an audience, his voice grew louder and louder, and then, finally, he broke into a kind of rhythmic chant and began jumping up and down in time with his voice, one hand held aloft. Many of the other Iraqis who stood nearby broke into smiles and joined in with him.

Next we were driven over to a grassy spot on the Tigris across from Baghdad University, where three cruise missiles had hit what we were told was a recreational complex. Nestled under a stand of eucalyptus trees were some children's swings and picnic tables and the remains of a little outdoor café. It had been blasted into an incomprehensible mess of shattered trees, bits of Styrofoam, mangled tin sheets, and smashed masonry. A dozen men were lined up on the rubble holding Saddam posters aloft. As we arrived, they began chanting the "O Saddam" song and dance and shouted some insults regarding President Bush. A man who said his name was Ra'ad Abdel Latif Mehdi, the manager of the complex, said that he had been watching TV with his staff at 10:30 the previous night when the missiles struck. "We saw fire from the sky, and we ran away," he said. Fortunately, no one had been killed or wounded. But they had bombed his restaurant and the accounting office, he said. He pointed to thousands of pieces of paper that were strewn all over the lawn. "Those were the accounts," he said. "We don't know why the American and British come all the time for Iraq. This was a tourist place, not military. This is not polite behavior."

I wandered away and climbed up some stairs to the concreted berm of the riverbank to see what I could see. I noticed that we were very close to some of Saddam's palaces. A military man came over, waving his arms in an unfriendly way. He was obviously trying to make me leave. I saw that there were other soldiers staked all along the top of the berm. I balked. The officer made angry motions as if he were about to push me down the stairs. I began retreating. He yelled something peremptory to one of the Information Ministry minders, who quickly ran up and escorted me away as I came down the stairs. I was incensed

and asked him why the soldier had forced me to leave the riverbank. I wasn't some kind of farmyard animal to be shooed away,
I said. He whispered sympathetically: "Very, very sorry. He's
worried because of the other buildings in the area. Important
buildings. You understand what I am saying."

We took a circuitous route back to the Palestine. As we drove
through a neighborhood I didn't recognize, the buses pulled to
the side of the road next to a long trench under a fringe of eucalyptus trees. The trench was full of soldiers who began posing
and brandishing their weapons when they saw the cameras.
About five minutes later a couple of jets flew high overhead and
appeared to launch some missiles, but they landed out of sight,
far away, perhaps on the edges of the city. But the soldiers in the
trench all began to behave crazily. Some scrambled for cover;
others ran around. Everybody shouted and yelled. Our minders
quickly ordered the bus drivers to clear out and to drive us back
to the hotel.

Later on John and Paul and I decided to revisit the Al-
Rasheed and asked Sabah to drive us there. He was upset about
this and argued with me the whole way. He had seen the same
jets we had spotted earlier and was worried they would return
and bomb. When we arrived, he refused to come into the hotel.
Salman, the desk manager, was ecstatic to see us back. We joked
with him about whether or not there might soon be American
GIs swimming in the pool. Because of Sabah's nervousness,
though, we didn't dally but drove on to one of the only restaurants in Baghdad still open for business, Lathikia, in the eastern
residential suburb of Ahrazat.

As we sat waiting for our meal, Uday al-Taiee entered with
a couple of underlings. He sauntered across the restaurant and
sat down at a table near us. He noticed us but did not say hello.
Instead, once he had sat down, he began fulminating in an
extremely loud voice, in English, about "the great crime the
Americans are perpetrating against civilization." His eyes roved

around. Speaking to no one in particular, but obviously for our benefit, he said, "They think this is a picnic, with Pepsi and Coca-Cola, but they will see, we will show them. This will be a slaughter, I tell you! Slaughter!" His delivery was impressive and had a Shakespearean intensity to it. Al-Taiee smiled, as if he were pleased with his own performance. Shifting his gaze onto us, he announced that the Iraqis had "caught" two American pilots. Before any of us could ask whether the pilots would be put on display, a couple of French reporters, a man and a woman, appeared at al-Taiee's table and joined him. He and the woman exchanged kisses on the cheek. Al-Taiee ignored us after that. When he finally got up to leave, I called out to ask him about the pilots. Would they be exhibited to us? Al-Taiee gave me a sidelong look but didn't reply. He put a finger to his lips and then his hands in the air, as if to say he couldn't or wouldn't talk about it, and left.

Driving back to the Palestine, we noticed great billowing spumes of black smoke on the skyline. I told Sabah to drive toward them, but he adamantly refused, saying that we'd get in trouble with the Mukhabarat, and he'd be hauled away. I gave in, and we returned to the hotel. There I bumped into my old minder, Salaar, who had been away in India, where he'd been sent after Saddam's referendum to work at the Iraqi Embassy there. He explained that he had returned to be with his family for the war and was stationed at the Palestine along with everyone else. He informed me that to all intents and purposes the ministry was now going to be based at the hotel. I felt relieved to see Salaar. Although we had never had a heart-to-heart talk, there was something in Salaar's eyes that had always made me like and trust him. When I asked him what he thought about the large contingent of Qusay Hussein's agents that had moved over to the Palestine with us, he looked me full in the eyes, put a hand on my shoulder, and whispered: "Don't worry. We are here with you." When I asked him about the big smoke clouds I'd seen,

Salaar explained that they were not from bombs but from oil fires, set by the regime to disorient the pilots of the American and British warplanes. Back in my room, I could see that there were fires lit all around the city. Some had been set at the edges of Baghdad, but others were blazing only a few hundred meters away. Beginning at 5:25 PM, bombs began to fall outside the city, making noises like distant thunder.

Sabah wandered across the street to the Sheraton to see about a room there for himself at reduced, Iraqi-only rates. He soon returned, looking very pleased with himself, to say that he had secured one and that his new room was much better than ours: It had a nice big bathroom, a big double bed, a sitting area, and a good supply of hot water. He waved an arm at our shabby domain, grinning with scornful delight.

Paul had already converted our room into something resembling a defensive bunker. On our first day there, he had sent Sabah out to buy masking tape. When Sabah returned with several rolls of shocking pink tape, I protested, but he claimed it was the only color he could find. (I doubted this, because I knew Sabah's taste for gaudy colors. During Saddam's loyalty referendum, I had asked him to buy me an ordinary white plastic table and chair to use as my provisional satphone post at the Information Ministry. Sabah had come back smiling contentedly and waving along a laborer he had hired to carry his purchase, a matching table-and-two-chair ensemble done up in an eye-catching lipstick mauve color. In the coming days almost everyone who saw me working at the table stopped to stare at it in wonder, or else to make a wisecrack. When I left Baghdad, I gave it to Sabah to take home to use as garden furniture, which I assumed had been his secret wish in the first place.) Undeterred by the color of Sabah's tape, Paul had used it on every glass surface in the room. The mirrors, the television screen, even the

hotel-issue framed prints of a French impressionist painting and
a drawing of old Baghdad were covered with great pink X's and
crossbars, which looked uncannily like the Union Jack. The sliding glass doors onto the balcony were plastered with a compli-
cated herringbone pattern of X's. "If a bomb hits, you won't get
cut to pieces," Paul said. Next, he had taken apart the two single
beds and placed their bases on their sides in an L shape, to provide a protective bulwark between the balcony and the mat-
tresses, which he laid end to end on the floor, and where we slept
head to toe. Everything in our cramped space was coated in pow-
dery reddish yellow turab dust.

There was little space in the bathroom, because we had stored
our five twenty-liter plastic jerricans there. They were filled with
bathwater in case the electricity went and the water ran out.
Around the room, we had candles and flashlights and headlamps
with fresh batteries, and in the closets, our protective suits and
gas masks for chemical and biological warfare, our atropine in-
jections, Paul's stock of a fortnight's worth of U.S. military-issue
meals ready to eat, and our flak jackets and bulletproof Kevlar
helmets. We had carved out little workstations for ourselves. I
used a narrow desk near the door, while Paul worked at the little
coffee table in another corner. A mess of wires, antennas, and
adapter cables covered most of the available floor space.

In the evening Uday al-Taiee, whom I had begun to refer to as
"Goebbels," held a press conference in the Palestine lobby in
which he announced that if anyone was discovered giving telephone interviews to CNN, which had been forcibly expelled
from the country, he would be thrown out of Iraq. He reminded
everyone that the only place permissible for the use of satphones
was the Information Ministry. "Anyone talks with CNN and
they're out; anyone found with a satphone and they're out," he
declared ominously. Everyone feared that al-Taiee's sermon her-
alded another sweep by the security agents. After the ruckus
with Jim Nachtwey and the other photographers on the rooftop

two nights before, CNN's expulsion, and Patrick Dillon's deportation, we knew he was serious. (A couple of days earlier a reporter from the *Boston Globe* had been made a scapegoat and expelled after he was caught using his satphone at the Al-Rasheed.) For the umpteenth time Paul and I hurriedly concealed our satphones. This time we decided to hide them in the room rather than make Sabah do the run to his car again. Paul opened up one of his large cardboard boxes full of MREs and buried his satphone at the bottom. Then we pried open the baseboard of one of the beds we were using as a blast shield and tore out enough stuffing to make a hole big enough to hide mine there. Afterward we were exhausted, and our nerves were frayed, but we had to stay awake, because both of us urgently needed to use our satphones to communicate with our editors and our families. After a couple of hours we decided to risk taking them out and using them. As soon as we were done, we hid them again. By now we had a message relay system going with several other reporters in nearby rooms and via the hotel telephone with those on different floors, much as prison inmates do in lockdown cells to pass on warnings when the screws are coming and then to give the all-clear. So far we had been lucky, and no security men came to our door that night either.

At a little after 11:00 PM the air-raid sirens began wailing again, and thirty minutes later there were some heavy blasts. From our room, we couldn't see where the bombs had landed. I grabbed a short nap but could not sleep deeply through the unceasing sound of bombs falling in the distance, and I awoke suddenly at 2:00 AM, after several new explosions nearby. Afterward I slept for another couple of hours, until just after dawn.

The skies above Baghdad were suffused with a strange purplish haze. I realized that it was probably from the smoke coming from the oil fires. The Information Ministry sent word that journalists should be ready in an hour to go see "something special." I wondered if it could be the captured American pilots al-Taiee had been crowing about the day before. I heard reports that the American troops invading from the south had reached the city of Najaf, two hours from Baghdad, but also that they were encountering stiff resistance elsewhere, especially in Nasiriyah. Sabah told me that people on the streets were saying that there had been a plane crash southwest of the city and that the pilot, an American, had been captured. He passed on another rumor that forty-five American and British "commandos" had been captured after parachuting in near Ramadi, west of Baghdad, and were being held there. There were, he said, another fifteen Americans being held prisoner in Nasiriyah. As he told me these stories, Sabah smiled and looked rather proud.

The "something special" turned out to be a press conference held in the Information Ministry by the Iraqi vice-president Taha Yassin Ramadan. With the exception of Saddam's halting prerecorded appearance on Iraqi television, no senior official had appeared in public since the bombing had begun. As the bombings had continued on Thursday and Friday, the night of "shock and awe," and then Saturday, many people in Baghdad had begun speculating that Saddam might have been incapacitated. Among the most persistent rumors was that Naji Sabri and Tariq Aziz had been killed.

Ramadan was very short and stout, and his face had a badger's nose and dark, pouchy eyes. He wore the customary beret and crisp uniform of the Baathist leadership, but he looked weary. It struck me as significant that his conference was not being held in the main ministry building, as was usual, but in a smaller, presumably more discreet building next door. A little podium was set up in the foyer, a few feet away from the exit, in front of a portrait of Saddam and an Iraqi flag. Flanked by several bodyguards and with Uday al-Taiee hovering beside him, Ramadan began by saying, in a voice that was as soft as velvet: "The war is proceeding for us in an excellent way. The United States and United Kingdom have based their strategy on the information of traitors." Ramadan was dismissive of the U.S. claims of battlefield advances. "Let them come towards Baghdad. We will not harass them. But if they try to enter any towns along the way, they will face the same problems they are facing in Nasiriyah and Basra." In a reassuring tone of voice, he promised: "Within hours you will see their prisoners on TV." Ramadan said that what was happening reminded him of the Arab Revolt of 1920, "when we taught Abu Naji"—a colloquial term used for the British in those days—"a lesson." At this, Ramadan and all the Iraqis in the crowd smiled and chuckled. "They've said they are roaming in the desert," he added. "We've allowed them to roam in the desert. We hope they come to Baghdad, in order to teach this evil administration a lesson."

Warming to this theme, Ramadan told some stories from the front. "Iraqis have destroyed four tanks of the Americans in Basra and killed a number of their mercenaries," he said. "And the rest flew like rats. And now the militias are surrounding those rats." Elsewhere, in the southern marshlands, "Arab tribesmen and Baath fighters" had captured and killed some American paratroopers, and an enemy drone had been shot down. Ramadan took several minutes to criticize the UN for, as he put it, "doing nothing to stop the aggression." It was the UN's duty, he said, to call a halt to the war "for humanitarian reasons, on behalf of the twenty-six million people of Iraq." He asked Kofi Annan to "stop behaving as if he is a servant of the United States." Ramadan's tone was not plaintive, but his underlying message was. When he stepped off the podium, Ramadan stumbled and fell, but he quickly picked himself up.

Within a few minutes of Ramadan's departure, a commotion began as rumors flew that an American warplane had been shot down and the pilot had parachuted into the Tigris just a block away. I joined a huge crowd of Iraqis running excitedly toward the riverbank. I got there to see several hundred people, mostly men and boys, staring and yelling and pointing excitedly at the river. Hundreds more soon gathered to watch from the sidewalk on the bridge that spanned the river there. Traffic on the bridge slowed down as cars stopped and their drivers got out to join the curious onlookers. The river flowed placidly along. I could see nothing, and each person I spoke to in the crowd had a different story. None was a witness to what had happened, if anything had. Someone told me there had been two planes that had crashed. He pointed to where they had disappeared beneath the water. Another man told me there was one or perhaps two pilots who were hiding somewhere. Someone had seen them swim away. Men and boys were poking the bulrushes along the nearest bank with sticks. A beverage vendor wheeled his cart along the bank to hawk his wares. Very soon the whole scene acquired a carnival atmosphere, as the crowd grew larger and more and more worked up. Before long military men appeared and began racing up and down the river in small motorboats. Some had guns drawn and began shooting bullets into the bulrushes that grew along the riverbank. Men and boys took off their shoes and began searching the reeds in their bare feet. Some hacked at the reeds with machetes. Others began setting fire to the reeds. This went on for several hours. I noticed that the sky was blue again, with a light breeze blowing, though it was still hazy from the oil-fire smoke. To the west of the city, some bombs were dropped by a B-52, but no one at the riverside seemed to notice.

I finally wandered away, feeling fairly certain that the whole episode was a symptom of mass hysteria, that the pilot everyone was looking for was nothing but a phantom. There was something poignant about the people's fervent willingness to believe that they had an enemy pilot almost within their grasp. But their packlike frenzy was frightening too; I had little doubt that if there really was a pilot concealed in the bulrushes, he'd be torn to pieces if they found him. I wondered whether it all had to do with a sense of collective impotence among Iraqis over their fate, which in the last few days seemed to have become the exclusive possession of the foreign pilots who flew high in the skies above, beyond all reach, dropping their bombs at will.

By the time I left, several fires were blazing crisply, blackening the beautiful green reed beds. Egged on by the crowd, the military men were still prowling up and down the river in their boats, searching intently for the enemy hidden in their midst.

That afternoon the mood of the city changed again. A heightened feeling of apprehension seemed to be snapping and sparking in the air. Mukhabarat agents appeared on the streets. They stood at all the major intersections alongside the soldiers and policemen, stopping drivers and demanding their IDs. After passing one of these new checkpoints and heading down a road that led outside the gates of the Republican Palace, we met a group of presidential guards who were scrambling and running around with their weapons pointed, looking fearfully up at the sky. They seemed to take no notice of us at all, but Sabah stepped on the accelerator, just in case.

A minute later Sabah told me he had just seen an American soldier parachuting into the presidential complex. I was dumbfounded by this assertion. When? Was he sure? Yes, Sabah swore. The parachutist was coming down just as we'd passed the palace. Hadn't I seen him? No, I said. I asked him repeatedly if he was sure of what he had seen. Sabah swore over and over again that he had. I was incredulous and told him that I thought he must be going crazy. Why would an American soldier, on his own, parachute into Saddam's palace in broad daylight? Sabah shrugged. He didn't know why, he retorted, but he had seen it. I stared at Sabah's face for a long time, wondering if he was joking. He clearly wasn't. My suggestion that he had invented the story had obviously irritated him. He studiedly avoided my face, staring

straight ahead as he drove. He looked sullen. I decided to drop
the matter for the time being, but I wondered what was going
on. Either Sabah was hallucinating, or he was telling the truth. I
didn't know what to believe.

Back at the Palestine, a large crowd stood watching the TV in
the lobby. It was showing some graphic images, shot by Al
Jazeera, of dead American soldiers, and then, repeated over and
over again, a scene of several captured American soldiers, young
men and women, being questioned by someone off camera. All of
them looked frightened, but I was particularly moved by the
look of uncomprehending terror on the face of a young female
African-American soldier. These images coincided with news reports that confirmed some of what Ramadan had claimed: that
the Americans were bogged down in fighting in several places in
the south and were taking casualties. Reports were also coming
in through the grapevine about journalists being killed in the
north and south of Iraq. A friend of mine, the photographer
Thomas Dworzak, who was in northern Iraq with the Kurdish
forces, e-mailed me to say that the day before a suicide bomber
had blown himself up at a checkpoint, killing Paul Moran, an
Australian cameraman. Several other friends driving up through
the south on their own had been attacked by Iraqi troops and had
gone missing. (All survived and were later rescued by American
troops.) A British television reporter, Terry Lloyd, had been
killed in the south as well, apparently by "friendly fire."

In the midst of all this bad news, a bizarre thing happened. A
French television crew arrived at the front door of the Palestine
in an exceedingly dusty Yukon SUV that was piled high with
gear, having driven that day from Kuwait right through to
Baghdad. Apparently they had not been stopped by anyone.
Iraqis and foreigners alike stood around to gape at the vehicle
and its Kuwaiti plates, wondering what this said about the Iraqi
defenses of Baghdad. Presumably embarrassed by the symbolic
implications, Uday al-Taiee immediately ordered the vehicle's

license plates to be covered over with pieces of cardboard and had the Frenchmen sequestered in a room at the Palestine.

In the evening journalists were summoned to a ground-floor banquet room of the Sheraton to hear Iraq's defense minister, General Sultan Hashim Ahmed, give his account of the war's progress. Sitting on a stage in front of another portrait of Saddam and a big military map of Iraq, Hashim echoed Ramadan's buoyant appraisal. He told us that in the south, for instance, the Americans were having their noses bloodied and had only managed to secure a fragile toehold outside Basra's airport. On all other fronts, he claimed, the invading forces had been dealt heavy blows and been forced to retreat, or else they were surrounded and about to be wiped out. If the Americans and British persisted in their campaign, he vowed to make it painful for them. "We shall fight them in a way that makes us proud, and in a way that makes our children proud of us," he said. "Yes, they may be able to occupy some spot, but at what cost? If they wish to take Baghdad, they'll have to be ready to pay the price."

Afterward, with a display of great magnanimity, Uday al-Taiee announced that henceforth we would be able to use our satphones in our rooms at the Palestine. This was a huge relief and seemed to indicate that the Information Ministry had reasserted its authority over the intelligence apparatus. Suddenly, the atmosphere became less threatening. Now that I was able to take my satphone out of its place of concealment, I installed it on a yellow plastic milk crate on a ledge beneath the parapet of our balcony and propped up its flat, book-shaped antenna with Patrick Dillon's gift copy of *Heart of Darkness,* at the correct angle for the east Atlantic Inmarsat satellite. (People on the other side of the building used the south-facing Indian Ocean satellite.) Because of the seasonal turab winds, which had been blowing every few days, everything was held down with the pink masking tape.

The bombers came again at about 10:30 PM. At least one of

the buildings in the palace complex was hit, causing a large explosion. A few minutes later a ruckus began in Abu Nawas Street. I looked out to see a platoon of Iraqi soldiers running down the street, yelling and pointing into the bushes in the wasteland that lies between the street and the riverfront. Some began shooting their weapons, and then more did so. They looked very confused and panicky. Several of them came running into the grounds of the Palestine and crouched, hiding there for some time. The gunfire continued but moved steadily away. We found out from friends with rooms on the other side of the hotel that the soldiers could be seen searching the riverbank there and shooting into the bulrushes. It seemed that the search for the phantom American pilot continued. At 11:00 PM another very big bomb exploded somewhere in the city, setting off car alarms and rocking the hotel. Afterward, most of the soldiers disappeared. At 3:00 AM the bombers came back.

The next morning, the fifth day of the war, the sky was very dark, and the air had turned cool again. An immense cumulus of black smoke hung ominously over the whole city from the burning oil fires, obscuring the sun.

Sabah arrived at our room later than usual, looking distraught. When I asked him what was wrong, he explained that during the night one of his married daughters, who was three months pregnant, had suffered a miscarriage and lost her unborn child. It had occurred after the big bomb explosion at 11:00 PM. She had gone into shock and began hemorrhaging. At dawn Sabah had taken her to the hospital, where she'd been given a transfusion. He had stayed at her side until he'd been told she was going to be all right. Sabah sighed heavily and wiped his eyes for several minutes, overwrought.

As he did most mornings, Sabah handed me a thermos flask filled with hot Turkish coffee and a stack of warm rice tortillas, freshly made by his wife, whom he referred to as Madame Sabah. It was a routine that had begun in the days prior to the war and had become more vital now that most of the city's restaurants were closed. Madame Sabah's concoctions were brought to us most days by either Safaar or Diyah, her and Sabah's two adult sons. She often sent along a pot or container with a portion of whatever dish she had cooked for the family that day—baked chicken with spicy potatoes, a spinach hot pot, or a lentil and tomato stew. Sabah would reheat these dishes for us on a little Chinese single-burner hot plate I had found in the bazaar before the war, creating a little impromptu kitchen on the floor of the hotel room.

When Tariq Aziz walked into the banquet room of the Sheraton that evening, there was an audible buzz of excitement from the roomful of waiting journalists. We had been assembled there once again without knowing what or whom to expect. The diminutive deputy prime minister, who had the strut and self-assurance of a bantam cock, had not been seen in public since March 19, the eve of the war. Seated at an elevated table covered with a white satin cloth under a huge gilt-framed portrait of Saddam Hussein and wearing a military uniform and a beret, Aziz embarked on an assessment of the events that had led up to the war. He spoke in English, in a calm but fatigued tone of voice. Standing behind him was an unshaved bodyguard wearing a kaffiyeh headscarf. Other guards were arrayed around the ballroom, eyeing the audience. Aziz made the argument, as he had many times before, that what the United States and Great Britain were after in their war was not Iraq's weapons of mass destruction—for they knew that Iraq had none left—but its vast oil reserves, which he claimed were the largest in the world, something over three hundred billion barrels.

"They have decided to occupy and colonize Iraq," said Aziz.

"They want to reshape the whole region to the benefit of Israel." He said that the U.S. government had been hijacked by a small group of Jews and Christian Zionists, the oil lobby, and the military-industrial complex, which had promoted the war in Iraq for their own selfish aims. Then, for the next forty minutes, he tackled the claims made by the Bush administration about what was happening on the battleground. "First, they said this war would be devastating, incapacitating Iraq's armed forces and the leadership, and that the people would revolt," said Aziz. "And Cheney said that the people would receive the American troops with 'music and flowers.' On this point, I remember telling the U.S. media, 'Don't cheat yourselves and U.S. public opinion: The troops will be received not with flowers, but with bullets.'"

Aziz flashed a laconic I-told-you-so grin. "They said Saddam Hussein was totally isolated, supported only by Tikritis [the people of his hometown] and the Republican Guards. But in Um Qasr, there were no Republican Guards. The regiment fighting the Americans and British there is an ordinary Iraqi regiment. . . . And those fighting in Nasiriyah and Basra, Najaf and Samawa, are not Tikritis. The majority of these people are Shia, not Sunnis or Tikritis. Anyway, in just a few days all those false assessments and assumptions on those two points have collapsed. Shamelessly, and forgive me because I don't want to be harsh, but they are behaving in a very shameful manner. . . ."

Dryly, Aziz added: "When they attacked their target of opportunity on Wednesday, attempting to 'decapitate the Iraqi leaders . . .'" Aziz paused for emphasis, adding: "Please note the term, as if we were a bunch of chickens to be decapitated." Aziz paused again to smile as the audience tittered. "They said, God forbid, that President Saddam Hussein was killed or injured; they wanted to sell this idea to their poor soldiers who they'd pushed into the battlefield. And yet here we are."

Aziz was clearly gloating now. He mentioned hearing that General Tommy Franks had said he "didn't plan" to take Basra for the moment. Aziz smiled jovially. "I laughed when I heard this. It reminded me of the story of the fox and the grapes, when they asked the fox: 'Why don't you take the grapes and eat them?' and he says, 'Because they are sour.'" Aziz's implication was that Franks was afraid of entering Basra because of the fierce resistance offered by the Iraqis there. He warned: "Everywhere the Americans are fighting, they are not yet fighting the Republican Guards. In the south, those fighting are Shia. This is Iraq. We've been telling them: 'Don't fool yourselves. The Iraqi people are united under Saddam Hussein and the Arab Baath Socialist Party.' We said this with good reason; we've been ruling this country for decades."

An air-raid siren began wailing outside, warning of another bombing run over Baghdad, but Aziz ignored it and went on, telling the story of the Iraqi peasant man who, the day before, had supposedly used an ancient rifle to bring down a U.S. Apache helicopter gunship. The peasant had been made an instant hero, interviewed on Iraqi television, and Aziz lauded him again, saying: "With his old Czech Brno gun—made before the time of Havel and the others—this peasant used it to welcome the Americans. Not with music, not with flowers. He had no instruments, just the gun, and he used it in the best Iraqi way, to welcome the invaders."

A journalist asked Aziz what concessions Iraq's government could make in order to spare Baghdad the bloodshed of a siege. "I don't have candies to offer them, only bullets," he said. Another reporter asked him how Iraq's regime intended to defend Baghdad. "Stay in Baghdad, and you'll see," he said coyly, and left the room. The security men closed the salon's doors behind Aziz so that we could not see which way he had gone.

On the sixth day of the attacks, Tuesday, March 25, another turab engulfed Baghdad. Yellow dust was mixed with the smoke from the oil fires, which had been burning for several days. The sky was a blackish purple. It looked as if the city were enduring a nuclear winter. I could hear bombs exploding somewhere, but I could no longer see them.

In the past few days the war had acquired a new pattern. Until Sunday the bombers had come only at night. My brother-in-law in England had begun e-mailing me daily to relay the times that the American B-52s took off each morning from their base there at Fairfield. On the basis of this information, I was able to calculate more or less when in the evening the bombers would arrive over Baghdad. Paul and I always tried to eat and to take turns having a wash in the bathroom before then, because it was difficult to count on having electricity or doing much of anything once the bombing began.

Ever since Sunday, however, when the bombers began striking Baghdad around the clock, our routine had been thrown off. There were now explosions at all hours of the day and night. Usually, sirens sounded, and about twenty minutes later there would be a short series of noises, big, reverberating, crashing roars that rolled into a gritty rumble. Sometimes the bombs fell nearby and sometimes far away. There must have been a pattern to the bombing, but it wasn't apparent to me. Thunderclaps seemed to fall randomly on this or that part of the darkened landscape.

On Tuesday morning, the mood in the streets was muted. People seemed to have resigned themselves to their fates, the way people in the Caribbean do before a tropical storm hits. Civilians had stayed indoors, and the soldiers seemed to disappear into the murk. Strong winds whipped the date palms, tore the branches off trees, and rattled shop signs. Most of the stores were shuttered. On Sadoun Street, only a few places were open: a couple of cheap and cheerful kebab houses, a pharmacy or two, and, oddly, a luggage shop. As I drove down the street, keeping an eye out for familiar shops and restaurants, I became disoriented. Several places I knew well seemed to have vanished. It wasn't that they had been bombed or were simply shuttered up. They were gone. Then I spotted the signboard of a restaurant I knew and saw that where the glass front doors and windows had been there was a brick wall. It covered the entire front of the establishment. As we drove on, I saw many more businesses that had been bricked up. It was as if they were trying to avoid being noticed, like soldiers wearing camouflage.

That morning I went for my first session of physical therapy, which Ala Bashir had arranged for me. The therapy session was only partially a deceit, because in fact my lower back was a chronic low-level problem. (A few months earlier I had suffered an acute muscle spasm after leaving Baghdad and spent ten days flat on my back in Amman receiving medical treatment, but the pain had not gone away entirely.) When I arrived, Bashir called one of his orderlies to take me across the street to the adjacent Al-Wiya Maternity Hospital, where the physiotherapist was expecting me. He told me to stop in after my session.

The therapist, a congenial man named Nabil, gave me heat treatments and applied some pulses of electricity. There didn't seem to be any other patients on his ward, a gray, poorly lit wing of the hospital full of empty beds. Nabil explained that his wing was set up to receive bombing victims, but as yet there had been no patients. He asked me if I was planning to stay in Baghdad, and when I said yes, he laughed and said, *"Al-hamdulillah,"* which translates, more or less, as "Glory to God," meaning that one's fate is out of one's hands. I had heard the phrase frequently in recent days. Nabil said that he was married and had several children. I asked how they were. "You know how it is," he said in a man-to-man way. "Small children don't understand. For men, it's OK. But it's hard for women and children."

When Nabil was finished with me, he walked me out of the hospital and into the street. A few raindrops were plunking down, scattering the dust. Nabil turned to me and said: "Today

the turab is a good thing. I hope it doesn't rain. Rain will clear
the skies and make it easier to bomb. I pray for no rain." He
smiled and shook my hand and told me to return for my second
session the next day.

Several other doctors were sitting in Ala Bashir's office. They
were discussing the competing battlefield claims of the coalition
forces and Iraq's regime regarding the fighting in places like Um
Qasr, Nasiriyah, and Basra. They spoke calmly, exchanging the
information they had heard on radio broadcasts and from friends
or relatives. One of them was a British-trained heart surgeon. He
was a fastidious man who wore a conservative green tweed blazer
and diagonally striped tie and who spoke excellent English. He
mentioned that he'd talked on the telephone that morning with
a colleague at a hospital in Basra. The news was bad. British
troops were exchanging artillery fire with the city's defenders,
and there were many dead and wounded civilians. He turned to
me and said: "They thought this would be a cakewalk—that's
the American term, isn't it?—but it has not been one, and now
it is Iraqi civilians who are paying the price." There was a tone of
rebuke in his voice, but he left it at that.

Ala Bashir's deputy, Dr. Waleed Abdulmajid, a stocky man
with kindly brown eyes whom I had met several times, asked if I
knew what was going to happen. I said that I probably knew no
more than he did, but I feared that a bloody siege of Baghdad
was imminent. Iraq's leader, I said, appeared to have adopted a
survival strategy that involved causing maximum bloodshed. By
situating his military forces in towns and cities, he was trying to
draw the coalition forces into situations where, in order to advance, the Americans and the British would be forced to kill so
many Iraqi civilians that the war would become untenable and
an international outcry would force them to call a halt. The doctors listened and nodded. Bashir's attendant, Sunduz, the woman
with the burned face, brought us tea.

In the afternoon John Burns, Paul, and I revisited the Al-

Rasheed. We had heard that a few Greeks and Spaniards, perhaps unaware of the threats that the Pentagon had made against the hotel, had moved back in there, and we wanted to warn them. We did not find them, but we did locate an Italian, an older man, who seemed to be the only guest in the hotel at that moment. He was absolutely clueless. After we spoke with him, he said he would move out immediately. Still concerned for the other reporters, we asked a young clerk at the main desk to pass on the warnings and to try to be outside the hotel himself after nightfall. He nodded dumbly.

Next we went to the Ministry of Information, because we'd heard that a few television crews were still going over there to do their live feeds. We found it deserted except for three Turkish journalists standing on the roof, illuminated by some klieg lights, doing a standup. It was a bizarre spectacle. The turab was whipping through, blowing sand and dust and trash everywhere, and the sky was darkening fast. The Turks heard us out and said they would leave after they had finished transmitting. Finally, we stopped at a little general food store called Pyramids to stock up on more provisions; it was the only food shop we knew of that was still open in central Baghdad.

Back at the Palestine, we heard the unsettling news that during the previous night several reporters had been rousted from their beds and taken away by security men. They included our friends Matthew McAllester and Moises Saman, the American photographer Molly Bingham, and also an American peace activist and a Danish photographer. Supposedly, they had been put on a bus headed for the Syrian border. Since all of them had come into Iraq on questionable peacenik visas, we assumed that this was the reason they had been singled out for expulsion. But this was supposition; no one knew what had really happened. Their rooms were empty, stripped of any sign they had ever been there, and no one on the hotel staff had seen them check out. The Ministry of Information officials in the hotel claimed to know nothing about them or their whereabouts. But some reporters who had been up in the early hours of the morning whispered they had seen security agents in the hallways and, in one case, pounding on the door of Molly Bingham's room.

Sunset fell suddenly, like a black curtain dropping, well before 5:00 PM. Half an hour later the curtain ascended briefly, and a few fat raindrops fell, turning the dust-caked surfaces of cars muddy. Sirens blared briefly around eleven o'clock, just as a moist fog rolled in. The air smelled curiously like dirt, and it was so dark that even where there were streetlights you couldn't see much beyond a couple of blocks.

Bombs were being dropped somewhere outside the city. We had been told that advance units of the American invasion force had come to within fifty miles of Baghdad, and that B-52s were bombing the Republican Guard forces at the city's southern perimeter. That night there was almost no sound except for the bombs and the hum of a generator in a building close by. No people's voices, no dogs barking. Once or twice I heard a car's tires sweep slowly along the wet road outside my window.

The next morning Baghdad was thickly coated in a layer of yellow dust; the day had a phosphorescent white glow, almost as if snow had fallen. The storm had died down a bit, but there was a cold wind and an intermittent drizzle, so the dust became mud, then dust again, in a miserable cycle. People were wearing kaffiyeh headscarves as masks to cover their mouths and noses. The Iraqi Radio and Television Corporation, about half a mile away, had been bombed during the night. I had learned about it at 3:00 AM, when John Burns called my room to ask if my television set was working. I had checked it and found only static on the screen. He said he had just learned of the attack from Dan Rather, in New York City, who had called him to make comments for his *CBS Evening News* broadcast and was waiting for confirmation from him on his satellite phone line.

By midmorning a huddle of people had gathered around a television set in the hotel lobby, watching the image of a uniformed Iraqi news announcer speaking on a crackling screen. The broadcast, I was told, was coming from an emergency backup transmitter, which had been activated in the past few hours.

I went back to the Al-Wiya Hospital for my second back treatment, but Nabil had not been able to come to work that morning, so I took advantage of the opportunity to drop in again across the street to see Ala Bashir. This morning we were alone, so we chewed more freely over the events of the last few days, especially the news that the American and British invasion forces were becoming bogged down in sideshow battles on their march to Baghdad. He scoffed at this. "Let's be realistic," he said. "What percentage of a chance, really, does Iraq have to win this war? Zero. These battles in Um Qasr and Basra and Nasiriyah, these are small things, which always happen in war. This is what war is, killing and dying. It is only a few days, and already they are, what—fifty miles from Baghdad? I don't think anything the Iraqi Army does can alter the outcome in the end, not with all the armor and firepower the Americans and the British have."

He predicted a bloody battle for Baghdad. Nodding toward the bust of Saddam Hussein on his desk, he said: "It is obvious to me that what he wants is to cause as many civilian casualties as possible. He is going for maximum bloodshed. This is his way." On the eve of a previous war, he told me, Saddam had announced: "'Let the invaders come. But when they arrive in Baghdad, they will find only ashes.' He said this." For Bashir, the only big question remaining was how much resistance the Republican Guard would put up. There was a great deal of fear about this, he told me, not just among ordinary Iraqi civilians, but among the troops too—and with good reason. He said he'd been watching the Iraqi television news the night before, and a member of the Saddam Fedayeen, the fearsome, balaclava-wearing brigade of fighters commanded by Saddam's elder son, Uday, had been interviewed on camera in the northern city of Mosul. The fedayeen had said: "We are here first to kill Americans and second to kill any Iraqi that doesn't fight them." Bashir shot me a look. "This was a message that was being sent to everyone in the army: Fight or die. You see?" Saddam's coercive measures to hold his army together might work, he reasoned, if the coalition forces were slow in getting to Baghdad and continued to have trouble seizing the cities in the south. But if they managed to quell these places and surround Baghdad rapidly, the unity of the army would begin to crumble. The Americans and British would then regain the psychological balance of power, and many soldiers in the army would soon realize there was nothing left to fight for. But there would still be a battle for Baghdad, he believed. "It will be very bloody."

At about 11:30 AM we heard two short, sharp explosions to the north. There was nothing particularly distinctive about them; we merely paused to register the fact and resumed our conversation. A few moments later there was a gust of wind, and a burst of cool air came into the room. "The sandstorm is coming back," Bashir remarked. I asked him how he knew, and he sniffed the air. "You can smell it," he said. "It smells like earth. Whenever I smell this, it reminds me of dead people. Think about it. Think of Iraq's history. What is that history but thousands of years of wars and killing? This is something we have always done rather well, and a lot, right back to Sumerian and Babylonian times. Millions of people have died on this earth and become part of it. Their bodies are part of the land, the earth we are breathing."

A couple of hours later I stopped by the Ministry of Information. I'd heard that something big had happened and that people were gathering there. A crowd of journalists milled around confusedly and began piling on board a couple of buses. I hopped on one of them. Invariably these trips, laid on by the ministry, were inspection tours of freshly bombed sites involving civilian targets; it had become a daily ritual since the war began. We were never shown any damage done to military installations or to the buildings in the presidential complex. I had gone along on some of the trips and stayed behind for others. There was little advance warning of these tours and rarely any information given beforehand about the destinations, merely cryptic hints from minders or ministry officials such as: "We're going to see a school," "a hospital," or "a bomb site."

As we drove off, the word went around that we were being taken to a place where many civilians had died just hours earlier. The buses crawled through the dismal murk. The turab had resumed with full force, and it was raining, but the water had not cleared the skies of dust. The day became dark, illuminated only by an eerie orange light. We drove north through slummy suburbs on the main road leading north out of Baghdad toward Kirkuk. Along the way we passed several oil fires burning from pits dug in the wide median strip of the road. After about twenty minutes the buses pulled to a halt alongside some grubby apartment buildings with ground-floor workshops in the working-class district of Al-Shaab. Large throngs of men and boys milled about on both sides of the road. At first glance, in the strange light and muddy rain, I could see nothing wrong, and then my eyes adjusted, and I noticed that sections of the buildings on either side of the road were scorched, the windows of other buildings were broken, and their facades were pitted and blasted. There was debris everywhere, which looked shorn, as if a giant rake had come along and torn off the top layer of earth. Twisted strips of aluminum panels lay all over the ground. The siren of an approaching police car wailed.

I joined the melee; knots of people were moving in a kind of frenzy of shocked curiosity from one place to another, picking their way with caution over the mangled debris. There was a crater at the roadside where one of the bombs had hit; the tarmac of the road was ripped outward from it in a striated pattern. A family carried furniture and other belongings out of their apartment in one of the buildings and loaded them onto a small truck. I saw what I thought was a bouquet of white carnations lying on the sidewalk, but it was a pair of dead chickens. Men stared wordlessly into the ripped-out interiors of workshops, their contents hurled and tossed and twisted around inside as if by a tornado. A car had been smashed and turned upside down; some people were looking at that. A group of men stood around one of several completely blackened, carbonized vehicles and began singing and dancing, some of them holding up Kalashnikovs, chanting a ditty that had become de rigueur at all of Baghdad's bombing sites whenever TV crews arrived, "Long live Saddam, we will sacrifice ourselves for you," along with epithets in Arabic against Bush and Blair. No one seemed angered by the arrival of Westerners; they looked at us in curiosity, and some approached to explain what had happened, in an effort to be helpful.

I crossed the boulevard through six lanes of slow-moving traffic to join the crowd on the other side. Another bomb had hit at the roadside there, leaving a shallow pit. The destruction to the apartments and workshops there appeared to be identical to that across the road. There was a lot of rubble to climb over, broken plaster and mortar and more twisted aluminum siding, and as I did, I noticed a couple of young men nearby. They must have been in their late teens. One was standing motionless, staring blankly, and as I watched, he began dry-heaving. His friend took him by the arm and led him away. Nearby, a couple of dozen men were gathered in a circle looking at something. I pushed my way through the circle until I could see what it was: a man's hand severed below the knuckles, sitting like a kind of macabre prop on a green metal window shutter that was lying atop some steps. The hand was thick and gray, and the red and white guts of it, at the messily severed stump, spilled out like electrical circuitry from a crudely cut cable. Scarlet blood had drenched the steps below. One young man crouched very close to stare at the hand, his face just a couple of feet away from it. He stayed there for a long time. Someone told me that the man's brain was visible, sitting on the floor just inside the nearest workshop, but I didn't go to look at it.

I walked away and fell into conversation with a pleasant-faced young man who was standing by himself on a pile of rubble. He spoke a little English and explained that he was a student of the College of Arts at Baghdad University. "In the English department," he added with a proud smile. He asked me where I was from. When I told him the United States, he said, still smiling politely: "Welcome." We shook hands. He explained that he had not been there when the bombs struck; he had just come over to see what had happened from his home, several blocks away. Quite a few people, maybe as many as thirty, had died, he said, many of them in their cars. He and I looked around. There were a dozen or so destroyed vehicles on both sides of the street. The dead had included an entire family of five people, he added, pointing to the scorched-looking apartment directly above us. All the bodies had already been taken to the morgue, and the many wounded people had been taken away to hospitals. I asked him how he felt about what had happened. He said, in clear, careful English: "I just feel very sorry for the people who died."

Another man, a little older, approached me. He had an open, friendly face, and he too spoke some English. He told me his name was Muyad and that he was a "librarian." I think he meant that he was a stationer, because he explained that he sold school copybooks and also ran a photocopy machine. He pointed diagonally across the street to the next block, where he said he lived. I asked him if he knew any of the victims. He did, he nodded. He pointed to one of the blackened cars across the street. It had been bombed when the man, a mechanic, was underneath it, working on it, he explained. "His name was Abu Sayaff; he was my friend."

We remained silent for a long moment, as I nodded my sympathy and absorbed this information. Muyad spoke up: "Bush and Blair . . . they said this would be a clean war." He smiled tentatively. I waited for him to continue. He said: "This is not clean. This is dirty—a dirty war."

He was still smiling. Then he asked me where I was from. "America," I told him. He turned away for an instant and then looked back at me. He said: "Welcome." I told him I was sorry about what had happened. He said: "No, don't be sorry. It's not the American people, we know. Most are against this war, we know this." He added, by way of clarification: "I saw the director Michael Moore on TV last night." I was nonplussed. I had no idea what Muyad was referring to. He must have noticed my confusion because he told me about the Oscars ceremony in which Moore had spoken out against the war. Muyad explained that he watched a lot of American movies, which was how he had learned his English. He liked American movies very much. I asked Muyad what he thought was going to happen next; did he think the war could be stopped? "No," he replied. "Nothing can stop this. Only God." Then he added, with a hopeful expression: "God will stop Bush's army."

I said good-bye to Muyad and moved away. I passed a couple of young men. One of them, wearing a kaffiyeh over his face like a mask and carrying a Kalashnikov, looked at me and said, in English: "Welcome." I waved to acknowledge his greeting and walked on. His friend caught up with me and stopped me. He pointed to my rear pocket, where I had stuck my open notebook. He pointed up at the sky, indicating the muddy rain. I understood: He was trying to tell me that my notes were getting smeared in the rain. I thanked him, and he said, *"Afwan,"* which means, more or less, "You are welcome."

*

In the evening, Muhammad Said al-Sahaf, the information minister, made an appearance, the first of what would become his
daily press briefings. Sahaf was a short, corpulent man in his sixties who took great care about his appearance. He wore large
spectacles, his hair was dyed jet black, and his large-featured face
was scrupulously depilated. He also had very bushy eyebrows
and large, rather womanly lips. With his uniform, beret, and
holstered pistol, Sahaf looked rather like an aging actor playing
a role that did not suit him. He spoke English with a quaint,
slightly rusty British accent, but he had a colorful vocabulary
and an entertaining penchant for dramatic humor. He delighted
in referring to the Americans and the British as "villains, mercenaries, and war criminals." With his deputy, Uday al-Taiee,
glowering beside him, Sahaf held up what looked like a car hub-
cap and announced that it was a piece of an American missile.
"We shot it down," he boasted proudly. He explained that it was
one of several missiles fired overnight at the Iraqi Radio and
Television Corporation, the now-shattered-looking building
next to the Information Ministry where the poet Farouk Salloum
used to work.

Sahaf denounced the bombing that had occurred in Al-Shaab
that afternoon. The carnage there, he claimed, had been caused
by cluster bombs, the use of which proved that the British and
Americans had become "hysterical" over their setbacks in the
war. They had not even been able to take Um Qasr, the first
point of entry to Iraq on the Arabian Gulf, he crowed. "We are
now on the seventh day of the invasion"—Sahaf giggled—"and
they are now, until now, only in Dock Number Ten, not even in
the town. They are in a very bad situation. They are now in a
trap. We will drench them, and why not? This is classical and
should be taught in military schools—" Sahaf was interrupted by
the noise of bombs exploding in the city. The lights in the conference room flickered briefly. After a moment he carried on:
"Yesterday we heard this villain called Rumsfeld. He is, of

course, a war criminal and one of the worst American rulers. He said the American and British mercenaries are defending themselves inside Iraq. Well congratulations, Mr. Villain, for defending yourself in our country! We shall show you what defense means."

The turab died down during the night, and the next day, Thursday, March 27, was crisp and bright. Baghdad was still covered with pale yellow dust, but already, here and there, people had emerged to clean up, throwing pails of water over their cars, their shopfronts, and the sidewalks outside their houses. The statues of Saddam, which stood all over town, remained covered by dust, however; the workers who used to be visible most days cleaning the most prominent of them—a new bronze of Saddam on a plinth in the traffic island of Fardous Square, next to the Palestine Hotel—had disappeared. Some of the businesses downtown reopened, and traffic and people were once again on the streets. The money-changers, who had closed their businesses for most of the past week, also reemerged; the dinar had fallen sharply against the dollar, to three thousand, from around twenty-five hundred. Prices had also risen in the little corner shops. But with the majority of the shopkeepers and their families having evacuated to outlying villages and towns, most of Baghdad's commerce consisted of farmers selling their own produce on the sidewalks. Men stood behind piles of freshly harvested onions, lettuce, beetroot, potatoes, eggplants, and tomatoes, grown in the welter of patchy truck gardens that are visible in vacant lots and the odd tilled field all over the city.

In Iraq, there are no clear-cut boundaries between the city and the countryside, and in the heart of Baghdad, which is big and sprawling and not really "urban" at all in the conventional sense, except for the downtown area, rural ways of life maintain a tenacious hold. Vegetables are grown on a vacant lot a block away

from the Ministry of Information, and there are date palm orchards, some of them quite large, just a couple of miles away.
Iraqis are very proud of their dates, which they say are the best
and sweetest in the world and which are exported as delicacies to
other countries throughout the Middle East. Somewhere very
near the Palestine, a donkey brayed loudly several times a day. In
the early hours of the morning I heard roosters crowing.

Baghdad has none of the shiny glass and steel skyscrapers that
have sprouted up in most other capital cities in the past few
decades. In the Saddam era, everything "modern" was rendered
out of reinforced concrete, and except for a few ten- to twenty-
story ministry buildings and hotels like the Palestine and the
Sheraton, most of the city consists of low, single-family town
houses and stumpy three- to five-story apartment blocks. The
majority of Baghdad's big buildings, such as Saddam's two great
unfinished mosques, and his other grandiose palaces and monuments to war and to himself, lay to the west of the Tigris, and
over the past week quite a few of those had been transformed into
ruined hulks. Many of the bombed buildings had caved in on
themselves, with wreckage spilling out onto the streets or with
their insides eviscerated but the basic structure intact. The Al-
Rasheed had so far been untouched, but right next to it a small
building that I was told had been a police computer center had
been entirely flattened, its concrete slabs crunched down onto
one another like a sandwich. Across the street, another large
building, which supposedly housed a department of the
Mukhabarat, had also been hit. A telecommunications center
next to the Saddam Tower had been hit the night before and cut
off all the telephones on the western side of the city. It had been
disemboweled by warheads that entered it through the roof. Several apartment blocks just next to it were practically untouched;
their sides were lightly sprayed by the dust of the explosion, and
they were missing a few windowpanes. I noticed that people
were still walking by these places as if nothing had happened.

They walked around the new piles of rubble as they would around a tree knocked down by a storm.

The people of Baghdad seemed to have taken in stride the new reality of war, which, so far, consisted only of the steady bombing of buildings associated with Saddam Hussein and his power, although the civilian casualties caused by the Al-Shaab bombing were a foretaste, most people believed, of what was to come. This, together with the reports that the invasion was slowing down, the reappearance of Saddam and Tariq Aziz, and their defiant promises to bloody the American and British invaders when they arrived in Baghdad, indicated that there would be a prolonged siege.

On Thursday afternoon, for the second time in two days, I returned to Pyramids, the little general store, to buy more food. This time I bought long-term essentials like pasta and sugar and tinned tomatoes and even more bottled water. I had begun to face up to the prospect that if there was a prolonged siege of Baghdad, I might be stuck there for many more weeks or even months. I also went to see Nabil, the physiotherapist, again, for my second session of heat treatment. Afterward I dropped in on Ala Bashir, but he was busy. He had been placed on twenty-four-hour call and suggested that I return later, in the evening, if I could, so that we could talk.

Shortly after I arrived back at the Palestine, I witnessed two large explosions in the distance, near Saddam's fanciful Al-Salaam Palace—the one with the four huge bronze busts of Saddam wearing a helmet meant to symbolize Jerusalem's Dome of the Rock mosque—which had already been partly destroyed. A few minutes earlier I had sent Sabah off in that direction to find some lunch for us from a restaurant that was still open in the same neighborhood. When he returned, about an hour later, he said he had been driving near the palace when the bombs hit, and the concussion had made his car leap several centimeters off the road. Not long afterward Paul McGeough, who was in another room facing south at that moment, saw what looked like a heat-seeking antiaircraft missile shoot out from some buildings a couple of blocks away and twirl off into the sky. Presumably there was a bomber flying around somewhere up there, but we couldn't see it.

There would be no visiting Bashir that evening. Many more bombs were dropped, including one that exploded spectacularly as it hit one of the buildings in the presidential complex. There was no discernible pattern to it. Sometimes there would only be a bomb or two, followed by a gap of time. At other times they came in waves. But I noticed that whenever the bombing started, I could hear a dirge of men's voices intoning deeply and soulfully, *"Allahu Akbar,"* over and over again, in a steadily rising crescendo, from a nearby mosque.

Few people in Baghdad slept well that night. The bombs continued to fall all over the city until just after dawn, when there was a phenomenal explosion that rocked the buildings downtown, including the Palestine. A number of massive forty-seven-hundred-pound "bunker busters" and cruise missiles had hit several of Baghdad's telecommunications facilities. We went to inspect the Al-Wiya telephone exchange, about three blocks from the hotel. Viewed from the front, the building appeared to be untouched. But at the back there was a great hole where it had been ripped open. Several of its floors were exposed, and their contents had been heaved onto the street. The bomb had penetrated deep into its bowels, carving a pit some thirty feet down and creating a slag heap of broken masonry and twisted metal. A persistent ringing noise that seemed familiar came from somewhere deep inside. It took a moment or two before I recognized it as the sound of a disconnected telephone, but much, much louder, as if a hundred phones had been left off their hooks.

Iraq's minister of transport and communications, Ahmed Murtaza Ahmed, showed up to inspect the damage. He was very angry and declared: "We will fight to the end. We will fight them forever. We will fight the Americans soldiers, we will fight the British. We will not let them penetrate Iraq. We will fight to the last drop of our blood."

Methodically, with each passing day, Baghdad was being rendered a less livable city than it had been the day before. For three nights the Americans bombed Baghdad's telecommunications facilities, comprehensively, and sometimes came back for second and third strikes against places they had already hit. In the space of three days, virtually all the telephones in Baghdad ceased to function. Happily, there was still electricity and running water. At night, from the parklands inside Saddam's ravaged presidential compound, hundreds of street lamps continued to glow with yellow lights. With almost all the government offices closed, the functional aspects of Iraqi statehood had been stripped down to the barest essentials—defense and security, mostly. Baghdad's parks, vacant lots, and the median strips had become armed bivouacs, the sites of foxholes and gun emplacements for thousands of soldiers, policemen, and militiamen. Tanks and armored personnel carriers squatted in traffic islands camouflaged under torn-off tree branches.

The Palestine had now become the public face of the regime, or what remained of it. Virtually all the Westerners remaining in Baghdad were congregated there or at one of the two smaller hotels that were right next door, the Al-Fanar—Patrick Dillon's old haunt—and the adjacent Al-Andalus. The majority were journalists, but there were also some human shields and peaceniks, including one lost-looking figure with long dreadlocks and pierced ears who wore an embroidered jacket and black Kurdish pantaloons with a saggy rear end. I heard that the two Turks who had chained themselves to the trees on Abu Nawas before the war began were still around, but I no longer saw them at their usual post, and I guessed they had given up their arboreal protest. In Fardous Square, on the stone columns that encircled the traffic island with the statue of Saddam, members of a Korean feminist group had hung a banner protesting sexual abuse. There was also a sizable contingent of Japanese shields. They seemed to spend inordinate amounts of their time in the lobby of the Palestine, taking digital pictures of one another, or else marching across the parking lot carrying antiwar banners.

A dozen or so Muslim jihadis—holy warriors—from other Arab countries had moved in with us too. I had first noticed them a few days earlier, while riding the elevator in the Palestine. They had different facial features from Iraqis and wore the beards and fervent expressions of true believers. They were dressed in robes and headscarfs or else paramilitary-style clothing, and they stuck to themselves. They were not outwardly hostile, but their unexplained presence in our midst made me very uneasy. I began asking around and found out that most of my colleagues had seen them too and felt similarly anxious. When I asked one of the Information Ministry minders about the jihadis, he dismissed them as harmless. "They came here to die killing American soldiers, not journalists," he assured me, twizzling his finger against his forehead, indicating that he thought they were crazy. "Believe me, the government won't let them touch a hair on any journalist's head, and right now the government is strong. Anyway, don't worry, I have a big gun in my room." He laughed.

I did not feel reassured, especially since the mysterious disappearances of our friends Matthew, Moises, and Molly on Monday night. They had not been put on a bus to Syria after all, or reappeared anywhere for that matter. The Iraqis still denied knowing anything about them. We had begun to feel serious fear for their safety. Led by Larry Kaplow of the Cox News Service, a number of us met to swap what information we had and to relay it to people outside Iraq who we thought could help. We learned that the International Red Cross had been contacted, and on the outside, pleas for help were being made to people known to have good access with Saddam in the past, who might act as intermediaries. They included Ramsey Clark; the former British Labour member of Parliament Tony Benn, who had met with Saddam just before the war began; and the controversial Scottish Labour MP George Galloway, who had a long and close relationship with Iraq's regime. We were also in regular discreet telephone and e-mail contact with Joel Simon, at the Committee to Protect Journalists in New York, who was trying to help coordinate things.

The Voices in the Wilderness peace group led by Kathy Kelly was staying at the Al-Fanar. They had draped a large white banner from an upper floor of the building which read LIFE IS SACRED. From some of the balconies they had also hung poster-size photographs of Iraqi children. Kelly and her fellow activists were conducting what they called peace patrols, visiting hospitals and bombing sites and paying goodwill visits to civilians living in affected neighborhoods. I learned from some of her followers that they too had come under the control of Qusay Hussein's security apparatus and were having problems. Their presence in Baghdad was being questioned, and their movements around town had been curtailed. Kelly had been told that she had "too many people" in Baghdad, that her group needed thinning out. It seemed that now even she was regarded with suspicion.

The ninth day of the war brought some bombing, but it was desultory, mostly on the fringes of the city, and a flurry of normality returned to the streets. A few people came out to shop, and a smattering of businesses reopened their doors, but most of the business was still being conducted by sidewalk vendors. On Sadoun Street, the most popular items for sale seemed to be kerosene lamps and plastic jerricans for water and fuel.

In the late afternoon I went for a drive with Paul and John Burns. A few men were still out, buying bread and eggs and vegetables for their families from the stallholders around Al-Tahrir Square. In a dusty strip of park, a group of teenage boys played soccer, and a man was shining shoes. A couple of shops selling used military uniforms were just packing up for the day. At dusk we stopped in one of the ancient coffeehouses on Al-Rasheed Street, in the old Jewish quarter. It was filled with old men playing dominoes and smoking narghiles (waterpipes). Some watched the television set, which was showing scenes of Iraqi civilians and soldiers around the country dancing and waving weapons, singing poems to Saddam Hussein, and chanting slogans against George W. Bush. The atmosphere in the café was calm and meditative. Except for the television images, it felt almost as if there were no war.

At about nine o'clock, after dinner at one of Baghdad's two restaurants still open for business, word reached us that there had been a bombing in which many civilians were said to have been killed. We raced out to the place, which was on the northern outskirts of Baghdad. About twenty minutes later we arrived at the Al-Nur General Hospital in the suburb of Al-Shulla, where the director, Dr. Haq Ismael Razuki, who received us in his office, told us that a warplane had struck a marketplace just a few hundred yards away. Razuki was polite but angry; he told us he believed the attack had been deliberate. The bombing had occurred a couple of hours earlier, at the same time people had been out doing their evening shopping. Thirty-five dead and forty-seven injured people had been brought into his hospital, he said, but more had been taken elsewhere. (The final death tally came to sixty-two.) Razuki's assistant led us into the hospital, through hallways filled with people—soldiers, relatives—and out into a rear garden. There we passed a man who had his face turned to the wall. He was sobbing in a loud, grief-stricken way into his folded arms. We walked on. A few moments later, still sobbing, he came up behind us fast, and then, breaking into a run, he overtook us.

We arrived at an aluminum hut. The sobbing man was there, with some other men. They were standing next to a young attendant wearing a filthy hospital smock. The attendant opened the door, and a blast of cold air came out. It was the hospital morgue. The weeping man dived wildly inside, crying disconsolately, but another man, a friend of his, pulled him back out and away from the doorway. Inside, I could see four dead men. Their bodies were torn up and bleeding, and they lay in contorted poses. Their clothes were ragged and dirty. There was a lot of blood on the floor. Some nurses appeared: older women wearing white headscarfs, and they began keening quietly.

One of the dead men was placed on a metal stretcher and brought outside. Other men arrived carrying a plain wood coffin and placed the dead man inside it. Several of the men broke down in tears and held their heads with their hands as this took place, calling out the dead man's name—Haydar—over and over again. They placed the lid on the coffin and hoisted it up on their shoulders. As they set off, they all began singing "La-Illaha-Ila-Allah"—"There is only one God." The morgue attendant came and stood next to me, and I gagged at the stench that came off him, which was of dead bodies.

Down the road, in the mosque, where the relatives were taking their dead ones to be washed and prayed over, people stood around quietly. Men smoked or just stared. No one said very much. A black banner on the wall inside was vividly illustrated with an image of the decapitated head, gushing blood, of Imam Husein, the paramount martyr of Shiite devotion. I followed one of the coffins as it was taken outside, the bearers singing their praise to God, as before, in the hospital. On a vacant lot just outside the mosque, they set down the coffin and prayed together. Red tracer fire from an antiaircraft gun floated into the sky above us.

I left them and walked down the street to the scrubby little marketplace where the bomb had hit. I found the crater, which was small, just a meter in diameter, at the edge of a little plaza surrounded on two sides with humble market stalls. The stalls were ravaged-looking, their tin roofs torn up, and a burst water pipe still gushed water, feeding a growing pool. I could hear a woman crying inside a house across the narrow lane from the marketplace. Soon other people began weeping too, and as they did, the woman's cries became screams.

EIGHT

One morning in late March, I thought I saw Saddam Hussein. The Ministry of Information had bused us over to Adhamiyah, an old Sunni district built on a loop of the Tigris in northwestern Baghdad. Overnight, several missiles had devastated the local telephone exchange and also flattened a house just down the street. An apartment building and several smaller dwellings next to the telephone facility were severely damaged by the blasts. An elderly man sat in a chair, wailing about his calamity, in the crumpled mess that had been his home. He made some insulting remarks about George W. Bush. The press corps stood dutifully around him, recording his comments and taking his photograph.

I strolled away from the ruined building to the edge of the boulevard that ran past it. There was a pretty line of shade trees growing down the median strip, and quite a few people were out and about, walking and driving. I could see a few shops open. It was a lovely, sunny morning, with just a nip of freshness in the air, and except for the smashed buildings behind me it felt almost like a normal day. I attempted to cross the street, but there were cars passing, and I hovered, waiting for an opening. An olive-colored Nissan Patrol SUV, its rear windows covered with gray curtains, came slowly past. There were two men in the front. The passenger's window, which was nearest to me, was

mostly rolled down. The passenger was a man with short hair
and a mustache. He had the look of a security agent. He was
looking away from me, in an attentive way, at the driver sitting
next to him. It was the driver's face that caught my attention. He
was a large, tall man, wearing a red-and-white-checked kaffiyeh
draped loosely over his head, as Bedouins do, and he was peering
out at the destruction behind me. He was laughing, which
seemed odd. And he looked exactly like Saddam Hussein. He
looked about the same age as Saddam, had the same full-toothed
laugh, the same mustache and jowls. Just as I registered these
details, he was gone, while the SUV rolled slowly past my line of
sight. I was flabbergasted and walked across the street feeling a
little dazed, wondering if in fact I had just seen Saddam Hussein,
while simultaneously dismissing the thought as ridiculous. But
the notion lingered, because from all I had ever heard about him,
riding around Baghdad in a car during wartime was exactly the
kind of thing Saddam did. He was known to enjoy driving himself, using a variety of ordinary-seeming cars, and to wear a variety of common-man disguises. He famously liked to surprise
Iraqis in the streets by popping up suddenly in their midst. Later
on, when I told my story to Ala Bashir and several other Iraqis I
knew, they all said it was very likely that the man I had observed
was Saddam Hussein.

Sometime during the night of Friday, March 28, the Americans finally got around to destroying the Information Ministry. The warheads that crashed through into its upper floors
made a mess of the satellite dishes and antennas on the roof, blew
out most of the windows, and shredded much of the building's
interior. Many of the windows in surrounding buildings were
blown out as well. It was destruction that had been foretold, of
course, and the ministry's officials had prepared themselves for
the moment. The next day, when someone asked Muhammad

al-Sahaf how his ministry would continue to function, I heard him reply: "*You* are the Ministry of Information."

Sahaf was in fine fettle that day. He described the Americans and British as "the new condottieri" of the world, saying: "They come and kill your family, and the next day they come to the funeral and give their condolences and say, 'We will help you.'" Meanwhile, he said, the "patriotic Iraqi resistance" had killed so many enemy soldiers that Iraq's government had issued a directive to its forces to bury "all killed American and British in the field, according to the laws of their religions. We cannot have their bodies lying around in the open or in refrigerators." Sahaf wore an expression of morbid delight.

Afterward Uday al-Taiee announced that because of the bombing of the ministry, the Palestine would henceforth officially become the press center. The Sheraton was also going to be opened up to journalists who wished to live there, he said. Then he laid down some new rules. The two hotels were the only places authorized for journalists to stay. There was to be no photography or filming from the rooms. A flat-roofed area on a lower floor of the Palestine would be made available for that purpose. Beginning the very next day, everyone was going to be required to apply for new press IDs, and all of the drivers and minders had to be newly accredited and authorized by the ministry. Our accumulated bills for the "ministry's services" had to be paid in full before we could be accredited. Al-Taiee spoke about the understandable need—because of the war situation—for some kind of "control" over the use of satphones, but he left this topic unresolved, with what seemed like intentional ambiguity. He also referred to "expulsion" several times. I had the impression that he was allowing himself some wiggle room to kick out people whose presence made the state security people uncomfortable. We had heard that seven of Kathy Kelly's peace activists had been expelled earlier in the day; we didn't know why.

Al-Taiee told us that he was working closely with Iraq's military authorities so that we could be taken on visits to the front lines. There would be group visits, on buses, he said, perhaps within two days. No one could leave Baghdad on his own, and even moving around the city without a minder was forbidden— "Even to have lunch," he added pointedly. This was for our own good, he explained. Because the city was now on a war footing, a journalist out on his own in certain parts of the city might be mistaken for an American pilot, for instance, and find his "physical integrity in danger." Anyone who broke these rules, al-Taiee said, was out.

Vice-President Ramadan also came by for a chat. He was very boosterish and said that Iraq was winning the war. He confirmed the news that a suicide bomber had killed four American soldiers in Najaf the day before and hinted strongly that it might be only the first of many such actions. "Any means that will stop the enemy will be used. If they want to avoid that, let them go! Why are they on our land? We are happy to have relations of convenience, but must we remain as slaves?"

Ramadan defended the use of suicide bombers, but said he didn't like the term *suicide*. He said it sounded "desperate." He preferred *martyrdom,* he said, explaining that it meant giving your life in defense of your people and your homeland. "Martyrdom is something Arab history is full of; it's a state of mind, and spiritualism. . . . All the people can do now is turn themselves into bombs. If the B-52s can carry bombs capable of killing five hundred people, I am confident that our freedom fighters have the capacity to kill five thousand people." Ramadan also confirmed the arrival in Iraq of many "volunteer martyrs" from other Arab countries, among them the characters I had seen hanging around the Palestine, I guessed.

That evening Sabah seemed unusually buoyant and chirpy. He had watched Sahaf's and Ramadan's performances on television and appeared to believe everything they had said. He began to regale me with his own versions of stories circulating about supposed Iraqi battlefield victories: an American tank blasted here, an F-16 downed there. Grinning hopefully, he said: "Maybe Bush won't come to Baghdad after all." I asked him why he thought so. "Because Iraqis are strong," he said, lowering his voice to a baritone and pounding his chest manfully. Sabah laughed as he did this, but there was pride in his voice. It was a comprehensible reaction. To be an Iraqi living in Baghdad at that moment must have been a very humiliating experience. Faced, as Sabah believed he still was, with a choice between the safe and routine life he knew under Saddam—notwithstanding his deep hatred of him—and the unknown new life that was coming with the Americans and their terrifying bombs, Sabah instinctively preferred the devil he knew.

At the announcement that the Sheraton was no longer out-of-bounds, Paul McGeough and I leaped at the opportunity to acquire a room there. On Sunday, March 30, we rented a spacious two-room suite on the twelfth floor and moved across the street. (Just in case, however, we hung on to the keys to our room in the Palestine.) The Sheraton stands directly across the street from the Palestine, and our room commanded sweeping views of the Tigris River and across over the entire presidential complex, with its parklands and bombed-out palaces.

The hotel was an unappealing eighteen-story brown concrete affair, built in a style characteristic of the early eighties, with a central indoor atrium, brown-tinted Plexiglas, and bulbous glass elevators. Its room decor was faux Mesopotamia: Fragments of old kilims hung in frames on the walls, and there were patterned carpets and bedspreads reminiscent of ancient Sumerian designs. The rooms had balconies with latticed wooden shutters that were intended to mimic the hanging balconies of old Baghdad. But the hotel had a cavernous, empty-soul ambience, having lost most of its customers, as well as its trademark franchise, many years earlier.

That evening U.S. warplanes carried out some unexpectedly fierce new bombing raids against the palace complex, hitting it at least three times. After a couple of minutes they struck another two targets in the city center just six or seven blocks away. The exploding bombs caused large fireballs, followed by black smoke, which poured up into the sky. The Sheraton rocked back and forth, as in an earth tremor, and the glass in its windows buckled but did not break.

The next morning I awoke to enjoy my new balcony views, which were splendid. It was another fine spring day, and the water in the Tigris sparkled in the sun as it looped gradually downriver in an arc to the southwest. I noticed new damage to the domed roof of the Republican Palace, just across the river. It looked as though debris were strewn across the flat roof around the dome. I counted thirteen oil fires, which appeared to have been newly lit, pouring huge clouds of black smoke into the sky from different points south and west; there must have been at least as many behind me, on the other side of the building. As I looked out, there was a roar, a terrific bang, and an explosion in the palace complex perhaps a half mile in front of me. A brief burst of flame and a huge column of gray smoke. A minute or two later it happened again, a second blow, as a coup de grâce. I heard a rattling, clomping sound and looked down. A man on a donkey cart carrying jerricans clattered along Abu Nawas Street just below me.

Later that day, which was Monday, the last day of March, I went to see Dr. Osama Saleh, an orthopedic surgeon who was the head of medical services at Baghdad's Al-Kindi Hospital. I had met him a couple of days earlier while visiting wounded people at his hospital after the Al-Shaab bombing. Saleh spoke only faltering English, but I'd discovered that we could converse with each other in Spanish. In the 1980s, it turned out, Saleh had studied in Cuba, where he was a pupil of Cuba's foremost orthopedic surgeon, Dr. Rodrigo Álvarez Cambras. By coincidence, I had met Saleh's mentor in Havana a couple of years earlier. Álvarez Cambras, a Cuban revolutionary veteran who was close to Fidel Castro, had told me that he had treated Saddam Hussein for various undisclosed ailments over the years. He had also taken charge of the rehabilitation of Saddam's son Uday after the assassination attempt on him in 1995 and claimed credit for getting the virtually paralyzed Hussein son walking again.

Saleh was a tall, robust man of forty-eight with a receding hairline and a professional manner. He wore a white doctor's coat over his clothing. I told him I was interested in how he was dealing with war casualties. As he walked me down the long halls of the hospital toward his office, he lit up a cigarette, which he puffed along the way. Women in traditional black abaya robes squatted on the floor outside some of the rooms, and the halls were full of patients and nurses and visitors. We bumped into three European doctors from Médicins du Monde, who were also smoking.

Several Iraqi women in abayas were waiting for Saleh when we arrived at his office. He said hello to them and invited me to sit down in a chair. He pulled out an X-ray of one of the women, who was his patient, before having her sit on a bed in the same room as me. A nurse pulled a paravan, a folding curtain on wheels, in front of the bed for privacy, while Saleh briskly examined her. When he was done with her, he turned back to me. Without comment, he invited me to look at some photographic images his assistant, a young woman, was pulling up on her computer screen.

The first image she popped up showed a boy lying naked on a bed in the emergency operating theater. The child's legs were untouched, but there was a catheter and tube attached to his penis. His torso was entirely blackened, and both of his arms had been burned off. At about the biceps, the flesh of both extremities became charred, black grotesqueries, one of the hands twisted and burned into a hideous melted claw, the other much shorter and apparently burned off below the elbow, with two long bones sticking out of it. It looked like something that might be found in a barbecue pit. The child's face was covered with a mask. Saleh spoke: "This is Ali, twelve. He was wounded in a rocket attack. He lost his mother, his father, and one of his brothers. It happened night before last in the southeastern part of Baghdad, about fifteen minutes from here. Four homes were destroyed; in one of them, the whole family, of eight people, were killed. In all, four families were destroyed."

It was hard to conceive that the human being in the photograph might somehow have survived. I asked Saleh if the boy was still alive. Without a beat, his tone flat, he said: "Oh, yes, he's alive. He's conscious, but I don't think he will survive. These burned people have complications after three or four days; in the first week they usually get septicemia." His assistant was pulling up new images, which showed Ali again, on the same bed and in the same position as before, but this time without his charred stumps. Both his arms had been amputated, and his stumps had been covered in white bandages. His blackened torso was covered in some kind of transparent grease. I could see his sleeping face (the mask had been removed). It was beautiful. In another picture Ali was awake, staring at the camera. He had gorgeous hazel eyes, but they were completely expressionless.

With an intake of breath, one hand covering her mouth, Saleh's assistant ran through a series of other images, which showed Ali's family after they had been collected from their home and deposited in the hospital refrigerator-morgue. It was difficult to make out that they had once been human beings. But there was a lot of colorful clothing and patterned cloth—lots of bold reds and greens—amid the carnage there, and there were bits of straw sticking to them as well, so I was able to conclude that they had been farming people, who wore traditional clothing. Saleh confirmed this for me and pointed out Ali's mother. Her face had been cut in half, as if by a giant cleaver. Her mouth was open. In other images, which Saleh said showed pieces of Ali's father and younger brother, all I could see was a macabre jumble of pieces of human beings burned into charred masses that were black and red. The body of his brother was all there, but from the nose up the head was gone, simply sheared off like the head of a rubber doll. The teeth in the mouth were white, and the mouth was opened, like a person screaming.

"Have you seen enough?" the assistant asked me. I didn't say anything, so she showed me more.

After a few minutes of this, Saleh said: "OK. This is just part of the tragedy." He asked me if I wanted to see Ali.

I followed Saleh down to the burns unit. Some men helped us put on green smocks and face masks, gauzy hairnets, and shoe stockings. Saleh told me to follow him down a hall. It was bare and totally quiet. It reminded me of a prison corridor. Nothing adorned it except for a framed portrait of Saddam Hussein on the wall. Saleh opened a door, and we walked into a cell of a room where there was an older woman, Ali's aunt, sitting in a chair. She wore a black abaya. There was a tiny window in the far wall that let in some sunlight. The aunt was sitting next to a bed on wheels that had a hooplike structure over it. It was covered with a coarse gray blanket. Saleh carefully pulled back the blanket, and there was Ali, awake. I could see his naked chest, his bandaged stumps, and his face. Close up, I saw that his large eyes were hazel, flecked with green, and he had long eyelashes and wavy brown hair. He was an absolutely stunning child. I didn't know what to do or say. Saleh asked Ali how he felt. "OK," he said. Wasn't he in a lot of pain? I asked Saleh, in a whisper. I spoke in English. "No," he told me. "Deeply burned patients don't feel as much pain because of the damage to their nerves." I stared back at Ali, who looked wordlessly back at me and at Saleh. His aunt got up and came over, to stand behind his head. She said nothing either.

I asked Saleh to ask Ali what he was thinking about. Ali spoke for a moment, in a soft boy's voice. "He doesn't think of anything, and he doesn't remember anything," Saleh translated. Saleh explained that Ali did not know, nor had he been told, that his family was dead. I asked Ali about school. He was in the sixth grade, he said, and his favorite subject was geography. As he spoke, his aunt began stroking his head. Did he like sports? I asked. Yes, he replied, especially volleyball, and also soccer. Was there anything he needed? No, nothing. He looked at me then and said something. Saleh didn't translate. I asked him what Ali had said. "He says: 'Bush is a criminal and he is fighting for oil.'" Ali said this as he had said everything else, expressionlessly. Ali's aunt began to cry silently, out of sight behind him. I asked Ali what he wanted to be when he grew up. "An officer." At this, his aunt cried out, "*Inshallah* [If God wills]," and I noticed that Dr. Saleh had begun to weep quietly behind his mask. As he tried to compose himself, we quickly said good-bye to Ali and left the room. Neither of us said anything as we walked down the hall and back into the sterile room, where the orderlies took off our smocks and masks and other apparel. Saleh rubbed his eyes and cleared his throat. We walked silently back to his office, where he washed his face in the sink and took a deep breath.

I said: "So it's untrue what they say about doctors being able to suspend their emotions."

He looked at me. His eyes were pink. He said: "We are human beings."

We talked about Ali for a few minutes. Saleh told me that Ali knew that he had lost his arms, but he had not yet acknowledged the fact, nor had anyone talked about it with him. "But he knows. He is conscious. He can see the stumps." In all likelihood, he said, Ali would die within three weeks. "I give him a thirty percent chance of survival."

I asked Saleh about his other cases of war casualties. He told me that Al-Kindi Hospital, which served the eastern flank of

Baghdad, had received about three hundred patients wounded in the bombings since the war began. So far he and his colleagues had managed to save all their patients. About twenty other people had arrived at the hospital already dead. I asked Saleh what his feelings were. He sighed. "Well, as a medical man I feel very bad. Really I don't think that this is a human job to attack civilians. I don't like war. War always brings tragedy, fear, pain, and psychological trauma, for all people. Personally, I feel that we can solve problems by discussion and negotiation and collaboration, and when you use military power, this means your brain has stopped. And when your brain has stopped, you convert into a wild person, without laws and regulations or controls. So the brain and thought should always be above power, to control it. Otherwise we'll end up in a world full of tragedy and pain. As an Iraqi I feel that this is my country and that I should work to maintain it and protect it from invasion, whatever invasion it is. And I think any person would take this position when his country is attacked and invaded."

Saleh was married and had three sons and a daughter. His children were young; the oldest was twelve, the same age as Ali. Saleh confessed to fretting constantly about his family's welfare when he was away from home, at the hospital, where he put in extremely long hours. Since the city's telephone exchanges had been bombed, he could no longer call home during the day to see how they were doing. His eyes met mine quickly. He looked very worried.

For the past few days, a procession of tribal sheikhs and clan elders had been arriving in Baghdad from all over Iraq to show their loyalty to Saddam Hussein. During the day dozens of them, dressed in traditional robes and wearing flowing headscarves with agaals, the thick black rings of cord that hold them in place, could be seen coming and going in minibuses and gathered in groups outside the Baghdad Hotel, an old 1950s Deco pile about eight or ten blocks from the Palestine and the Sheraton. I had heard that the sheikhs were also receiving money and weapons from the regime, in return for which they were expected to rally their kinsmen and fight the Americans and the British in their home areas. At a time when Baghdad's streets had mostly emptied of civilians, and there were virtually no new visitors to town, the sheikhs were an intriguing group. I had tried to visit their hotel a couple of times but been turned away by security men and soldiers. The third time I went, on Tuesday, April 1, I finally managed to speak to some of the sheikhs.

I had brought along a new minder, a dapper man named Sami, whom I shared with Paul McGeough. Sami approached a pair of sheikhs, Salman Amoud Jumeil, of the Jumeil tribe, and Khalil Salah al-Mushaqi, of the Mushaqi tribe. Both men were in their forties. They had come from Diyala, a rural area near the border with Iran, east of Baghdad. They were visibly suspicious of me, but Sami stepped in to explain that I was a journalist and was authorized to talk with them. (Obeying Uday al-Taiee's new strictures, we had obtained written permission to leave the Palestine for the purpose of speaking to the sheikhs.) Hearing this, Sheikh Jumeil, a tall man with a thick mustache, spoke up. He represented about a thousand people, mostly farmers, he said, and had come to Baghdad because he felt it was his obligation. "It is a duty," he explained. "The duty of all of the sheikhs is to defend their lands." When I prompted him to tell me more, Jumeil added: "We are here supporting our leadership, and when we return home, we will tell our families, our people, to be ready to fight. We say no to the aggression being carried out against our country."

I asked Jumeil whom he hoped to see in Baghdad. Would he meet with Saddam Hussein? He exchanged a glance with his friend, Sheikh Mushaqi, and replied: "Maybe we will meet with someone important in the government to explain that we are ready to fight."

Other sheikhs had wandered up to listen and had formed a circle around us. One of them, a rather regal-looking dark-skinned man wearing a fine green robe and a white headscarf, interrupted to say: "We are here to renew our promise to fight for the government." As an afterthought, he added: "If the Americans come as guests, we welcome them. But if they come to occupy our country, no, we will kill them. You have seen what is happening, because you are here living with us." He motioned with his head around us, as if to take in the bombed buildings, just out of sight, all over Baghdad. "No one has done anything to them, but the Americans have come here. Why?" He looked questioningly at me, as if he were not merely asking a rhetorical question but were genuinely mystified.

Before I could reply, Sheikh Jumeil spoke again: "You have seen the airplane attacks on our country. This attack has made people much more anti-American."

An old sheikh, who wore a brown manteau with gold embroidery over his dishdasha, asked if I was an American. When I told him that I was, he asked: "Why has America attacked Iraq? Because it is afraid of Iraq or because of its oil?" He appeared to be genuinely mystified. All the men craned to watch my face. The old man didn't let me answer but asked again: "Is America coming to free the Iraqi people, like they say, or to control it?" He waited intently for my reply. I began to try to explain that in my opinion the September 11 attacks had transformed the security considerations of the United States, and it appeared that President Bush, and other Western leaders, had decided that Saddam Hussein's regime in Iraq was hostile and potentially dangerous and that for this reason he had to go.

All the sheikhs nodded when I said, "September eleventh"; it seemed no translation was needed. Before I could continue, the old sheikh demurred. He said: "I think America comes just for the oil and to protect Israel." All the sheikhs nodded in agreement.

Sheikh Mushaqi appeared to be shy. He had to be prodded by Jumeil to speak up. He began by telling me that he was a Shiite, a follower of Imam Ali, and that the name of his village was Kala, near the Iranian border. He echoed Jumeil's explanation about his reasons for coming to Baghdad—to meet with the Iraqi leadership—but added that he, as a Mushaqi tribal leader, would also be meeting with all the other Mushaqi sheikhs who had come from around the country. The Mushaqis were spread all over Iraq, he explained. I asked whether he and the other sheikhs expected to be given weapons to fight with before they returned to their homes. "We have weapons," he replied. "So we don't expect to be given guns, but yes, directives on what to do." I asked him what he thought was going to happen. Mushaqi gave an ambiguous reply: "We don't expect America to end this problem easily, but we must be united anyway." I pointed out that in most wars, there was a winner and a loser. Which side would win in this war? Mushaqi said: "We are sure America will lose, because we have right on our side. We are in our houses, on our land." Another man interrupted to say: "Now, even the children hate the Americans. This is because civilians are the victims. This is not right. So even God does not agree with them. So why do this?"

A sheikh who said his name was Hassan al-Daraji, from Ramadi, a city fifty miles west of Baghdad, spoke up. "I am the leader of seven hundred people," he announced. Motioning to the dozens of robed men who were milling around nearby, he explained that all his fellow sheikhs represented similar numbers of people. "We elected our president, which means we want him, so why is America coming here to change him? If we want to change him, we can do it ourselves."

How did he think the war would end? I asked Daraji.

"Only God knows," he said, pointing skyward. "God decides whether we die or live. He gives the soul, and he takes it away."

A young man sidled up next to me. He was strong-faced,

muscular, and bareheaded. He said his name was Mujabel Sahel Awad al-Halaj, and he was the son of one of the sheikhs. He was from the village of Al-Hawijah, near Kirkuk. In a loud voice, he declaimed: "All of the people in Al-Hawijah support Saddam Hussein, and we are ready to defend great Iraq. Bush and Blair and Sharon are looking first after the safety of Israel, because our great leader, Saddam Hussein, always threatens Israel, and secondly they are looking for oil. We elected President Saddam Hussein and we love him and we are ready to do anything for him."

When he finished his speech, I asked Halaj how things were in Al-Hawijah: Was it quiet, was there fighting? He made a dismissive hand motion. "Only the Kurds are threatening, but we don't worry about them."

"So, you are an Arab then?"

"Yes, Arab!" Halaj replied proudly.

Halaj, who said he was twenty-five, expressed his eagerness to kill American and British soldiers. "If we catch any American soldiers in Hawijah, we will cut them"—he made a slicing motion—"and kill them like sheep."

"You won't take prisoners?"

"No," shouted Halaj. His eyes were flashing. "We'll just cut them"—he made the slicing motion again, more forcefully than before—"and then throw them away to the dogs." He made a contemptuous throwing motion with one of his hands, as if he had just tossed a severed head to a waiting pack of hungry dogs.

At that point two rough-looking men in civilian clothes came up and asked what we were doing. They were unfriendly and suspicious. The sheikhs began moving away. Sami told me we should leave. At the hotel entrance, a large number of sheikhs were climbing into a pair of waiting minibuses, on their way, I assumed, to an audience with someone in a position of authority.

That evening Vice-President Ramadan made his third appearance since the beginning of the war. This time he criticized President Bush and Prime Minister Blair for the arguments they had used to justify their invasion of Iraq. Ramadan repeated, as so many Iraqi officials had in recent months, that his country no longer possessed any illegal weapons. "Iraq is completely free of weapons of mass destruction," he said in his soft way, "and it is shameful for people, particularly the aggressors, for perpetuating this lie." He was worried, he said, that the invaders would "plant" such weapons in Iraq so as to justify their claims.

Ramadan rallied bravely on the issue of the war itself, warning the American and British troops that they had thus far only fought against Iraqi tribesmen and Baathist militiamen; they had yet to meet Iraq's army in battle, he reminded them, and pointed out that it was well armed with "up-to-date equipment." He then issued a call to Arabs in other Middle Eastern countries. "Your brothers in Iraq do not need food or medicine. Do not allow your government to turn you into charity collectors. Rather, turn up the pressure on those governments who are collaborating with the aggression, and send your volunteers for martyrdom to Iraq." Already, he said, there were more than six thousand volunteers in "this battle of honor, more than half of them for martyrdom, and you will see news of their actions in the coming days."

A reporter asked Ramadan what plans Iraq's regime had for the six thousand volunteer martyrs. "Each will do his duty with the objective of killing the maximum number of enemy soldiers possible," he explained. "They are being organized according to a plan, and we are not going to reveal its details. Wait and see what they do if they try and plan an occupation of our country."

Sabah's friend the barber Karim had shuttered his little shop when the bombing began, but on April 1 he had reopened for

business. That afternoon, taking Paul along with us, Sabah and I
went there to get shaves and trims. First, we had to get permission from the ministry's Mukhabarat official, Khadum. After
questioning Sabah carefully about who the barber was, where he
was located, and how long he had known him, he turned to me,
smiled thinly, and said: "You may go." When we arrived, Karim
was just finishing up with a couple of clients, older men who had
had their hair and mustaches freshly dyed black. Iraqi men are
fastidious about their personal appearance and don't like gray
hairs. Mustaches are de rigueur. One of the men was done. He
was standing around letting the thick black coloring ointment
in his mustache and hair dry; the other was still in the barber's
chair. He was an army officer, to judge from his uniform. He said
to us, in English, "Hello, hello," and a moment later, when he
got up, he saluted us again. He had a gold-plated revolver in a
holster. He said: "Iraq just needs peace. Only peace." Then he
said good-bye, and he and his friend left.

Out on the street, everyone began looking up to the sky. You
could hear the high, slow-rushing roar that B-52s make when
they are overhead. A few moments later there were a couple of
loud explosions, and the rattletrap building opposite shook, and
its plastic-covered windows flapped violently. (Later we found
out there had been a spectacular hit on one of the palaces in the
presidential compound, supposedly a mansion belonging to
Uday, Saddam's elder son.) But Karim stolidly ignored all this,
and one by one, along with our shaves and trims, he depilated
our cheekbones and ears and foreheads. I hated this part of
Karim's ministrations, but he always insisted on doing it, because otherwise he felt he had not done a complete job. This day
he also gave me an extremely close haircut—practically a crew
cut—in the same way that many Iraqi men wear their hair in the
hot months. He was very pleased that I had allowed him to do
this.

Driving over to Karim's along Abu Nawas, we had passed my

old hotel, the Al-Safeer, and I noticed that where its large ground-floor windows had been, a freshly built cinder block wall had arisen. Coming back to the Palestine along Sadoun Street, I could see that almost all the businesses had their accordion steel security shutters locked tight, and big taped X's on their windows. A few blocks farther on, I saw that the Air Defense Ministry had been totally flattened; it was now a messy horizontal pile of gray concrete pads and columns. A column or two and an archway still stood, leaning at odd angles, and out in front, the great statue of Saddam stood perfectly untouched.

With our movements around Baghdad strictly curtailed, my sense of the city also became more circumscribed. It was a dismal, disorienting feeling. It was officially taboo for journalists to visit recently bombed sites on their own. This meant that each day, if we were even allowed out, our drivers and minders had to invent new routes in order for us not to see what had happened during the previous night's bombings or else try to dissuade us from traveling at all. Our lunch outings, which formerly had provided some sense of freedom by involving travel through various neighborhoods, were all but over. There were only two sit-down restaurants in Baghdad still open for business, and now even they required the presence of a minder. Most days, to avoid the hassle of requesting permission, I simply dispatched Sabah to buy us takeout meals from one place or the other.

Ever since the Information Ministry was bombed, it had become a no-go area. Two reporters, an Australian and a South African, who had gone over on their own to inspect the destruction the morning after the second air strike, had been summarily expelled from Iraq. Afterward, instead of simply driving across the convenient Sinak Bridge, which crosses the Tigris on the road that runs past the ministry, Sabah began using other, more distant bridges.

Once we had moved into the Sheraton, Sabah exchanged the room he had there for one next door to mine. Every two or three days he went home for a visit but always returned after a few hours. It was impossibly overcrowded, he complained. Besides his own wife and children and those of several of his sons and a couple of brothers, as well as his elderly mother, all of whom lived in two adjoining houses, he now had one of his sisters and her four children staying in his house. They had left their house because they lived near the Al-Doura oil refinery, the site of a lot of bombing. Then, on March 31, some pieces of a missile landed in the street outside the home of his sons Safaar and Diyah, who lived together a block away. The next day they moved in with the rest of the family. By my calculation, there were now thirty people from Sabah's immediate clan living in the adjoining houses, with a total of five bedrooms between them.

As the days of bombing wore on, I noticed that many of the people around me were developing minor health complaints, such as headaches and backaches. Most also suffered a loss of appetite and were eating less food than before. Cigarette smokers were smoking more than usual. An Information Ministry official named Walid appeared at work one day wearing a neck brace and wincing a lot. Everyone complained of exhaustion; no one, including me, was getting much more than three or four hours of sleep a night.

Sami, our new minder, was a diabetic. I discovered this one evening when we were out chasing down a reported bombing that involved dead civilians, and he went into a badly timed state of insulin shock, rendering him incapable of speaking or comprehending what anyone was saying to him. This happened just as we arrived in the affected neighborhood. We had found some local Baath Party militiamen gathered on the street and stopped to ask them what had happened. Sami had been unable to explain what they were saying and did not answer me when I spoke to him. It was a bewildering moment and became a little alarming, because the militiamen did not know who we were and seemed wary of us. They began speaking sharply in Arabic to

Sami, who was unable to respond to them. It was well after dark, and we had driven there without first obtaining official permission.

Fortunately, we had been tailed. A large GMC Suburban pulled up next to us after a few minutes, and two men got out. One of them strode over and spoke peremptorily to the militiamen, who fell back a bit. Then he turned to me and said that we should follow him in our car. I asked who he was. He said he was from the Ministry of Information and had followed us because it was not wise or safe for us to be where we were. Some antiaircraft fire popped off, arcing red tracers into the sky, not far away from us. We got in our car and followed him back to the Palestine. Apparently, he did not report our transgression, for I heard nothing more about it.

The next morning I took Sami to see Ala Bashir. I'd last seen him several days earlier, the morning the Ministry of Information was bombed, when I had my third and final session of physiotherapy with Nabil. Afterward Nabil said I didn't need any more treatment for a while. My back did feel better, but I had the impression that he was trying to dissuade me from coming for some other reason, something to do with the war. I had stopped in to see Bashir, but he was with other people, and I noticed that the atmosphere in his hospital had changed. There was a tension in the air, but I didn't know why. We could not speak freely, and it seemed awkward to try to arrange an appointment. Now Sami's condition gave me a valid excuse to return and see him.

With Sami present, I explained what had happened. Bashir said that the symptoms I described were very serious and warned Sami that he could fall into a coma if it were to happen again. He advised Sami to see his own specialist and find out whether he was taking the right insulin dosage; he suspected that was the source of the problem. I thanked Bashir, formally, and said I hoped I could return in the coming days and see him. He nodded and said very cordially that he hoped I could as well. It was all very stiff. I had the distinct feeling that my visits had become uncomfortable for him and that I should probably not return anymore.

Later I asked Sami what he wanted to do. He explained that this was a bit of a problem. His specialist had closed his clinic and left Baghdad for the duration of the war. But he said he knew of another doctor and promised to go and see him. He did so and told me the next day that his doctor had suggested he alter his dosage and try to get more sleep. A day or two later I asked Sami if he was feeling any better. He nodded. The change in his dosage had helped, he said. But he was feeling very tired. He was unable to get more than three hours' sleep a night because of the bombardments. Because of his diabetes, he normally needed ten hours' sleep. He shrugged. There was nothing he could do about it, and that was that.

That night we heard some wonderful news. Matt McAllester, Moises Saman, Molly Bingham, and the two others who had been taken with them from the Palestine had arrived safely on the Jordanian border. The reports were that they had been held incommunicado in Abu Ghraib, the prison outside Baghdad, for eight days before finally being released. They had been accused, evidently, of working for the CIA. A couple of days earlier I had found Uday al-Taiee on his own, standing outside the Palestine, smoking a cigarette, and seized the opportunity to bring up the case of the missing journalists. Nearly a week had gone by, and there was still no news of them, but all the indications were they had been arrested and were being held secretly somewhere. That was the assumption we were working on. I told al-Taiee that I needed to talk to him about something important. He said curtly, "You may talk," and stood sideways to me, looking away, but occasionally darting a glance at me. I told him that those of us who were still in Baghdad were very worried about our friends, whom I named, and said that if anything happened to them, it would be very bad publicity for Iraq. Al-Taiee interrupted me. He complained about recent news reports in which it was being said that Iraq was holding journalists in prison. He was very upset about this, he said, because as far as he knew it was untrue. He knew nothing about the case. I said, as pointedly as I could, that the people we were talking about were journalists, nothing more, and that if there were "other people" who thought they might be "something else," then they were making a big mistake. Anything he could do to help return our colleagues to safety would be in the best interests of everyone. Very soon, I said, every journalist in Baghdad would be obliged to go public with what he knew, because, as he had pointed out, their disappearance had become an international news story. When I was done, al-Taiee nodded sharply, said, "I will look into it," and wheeled away.

Despite the heartening news about our missing friends, we were still under duress. A few nights earlier John Burns's officially appointed "translator," Saad, whom he had not seen for several days, burst into his and Tyler's room at the Palestine. He was accompanied by several security agents. After slapping around both John and Tyler, Saad revealed that he was, after all, an intelligence official, and he accused John of being a spy. After Saad made some more threatening statements, John's computer and satphone, as well as a good deal of his cash, were taken from him. Thereafter John led a kind of clandestine existence, moving from room to room within the hotel, staying out of sight, and borrowing friends' satphones and computers in order to be able to file his stories. (At one point John arranged for an encounter with Uday al-Taiee, and spoke to him about the incident. Al-Taiee, as usual, pretended to know nothing. John warned him of the possible consequences if anything were to happen to him. A few days later, as sphinxlike as ever, Uday al-Taiee gave John the all-clear, and his equipment, but not his cash, was returned to him.)

*

On Wednesday, April 2, the fourteenth day of the war, I joined a bus tour laid on for journalists by the government. It took us south about sixty miles, to the town of Hillah, near the ruins of ancient Babylon. It was the first such trip arranged outside the capital, and with reports reaching us that American and British troops had crossed the Euphrates River southeast of Karbala and were quickly advancing toward Baghdad in a thirty-mile-long armored column, none of us knew quite what to expect. But apart from roadside knots of soldiers and their sandbagged bivouacs and occasional groups of camouflaged tanks and gun emplacements hidden along the road in the sparse copses of eucalyptus trees, it was as if the war had not yet arrived.

It was a pretty day, sunny, and the sky was blue. I had not seen a truly blue sky in many days because of the smoke from the oil fires around Baghdad. Near Hillah, I spotted Saddam's great limestone palace, which overlooks Babylon, several miles away. Hillah was a fairly typical Iraqi town, a grid of brown, flat-roofed houses and some older villas surrounded by farmlands. Its streets were like a vision of things past. Men, women, and children were out, all the shops were open, and I saw very few soldiers.

We were taken to a hospital and shown scores of civilian victims of an apparent bombing raid in a nearby village, which had occurred two days previously, and also the survivors of a bus that had been torn to shreds by shrapnel. Many people were said to have died in both incidents. In one room, a man who had lost his leg lay next to another whose arm had been amputated. The man whose arm was gone was being looked after by his wife, who had brought their tiny baby, perhaps a month old, with her. It lay on the bed, tied up with ribbon and cloth like a little papoose, asleep. The mother pointed to her baby, to a covered part of its head, and told me that it too had been hit by shrapnel. Her husband explained that they had been in their car when an American convoy appeared. "We were not afraid because we knew that the Americans do not attack civilians," he said. But then a tank had fired at his car. The man with the missing leg protested rather mildly about the American attack: "If Americans want to come here as tourists, like they used to, we welcome them. But they shouldn't do this." As for his missing limb, he dismissed it with bravado: "I am an Iraqi. We are used to such things."

Driving back to Baghdad, I noticed a scorched, blasted section of trees where some Iraqi Army trucks had been concealed. Up in the sky, a vapor trail came from an American warplane. We all watched the trail, on our guard, until it became obvious that the aircraft was heading away, not toward us. I nodded off and didn't awake again until we were back in Baghdad. As we approached the city center, a couple of powerful explosions came from just across the river; we could see the plumes of gray smoke rise into the air. We craned to see where the bombs had hit, but our driver drove us away from the area, zigzagging through unfamiliar streets until we were back at the hotel. When we got there, we learned that in our absence, warplanes had bombed the Baghdad International Trade Fair and badly damaged the Red Crescent maternity hospital across the road from it, killing seven people. An Iraqi man I knew named Muhammad was very worked up about it. He had been driving along the street near there with his wife at the time of the bombing, he said, and had watched as the windows of other cars blew out, and a bus in front of him was crushed, he said, "like a pack of cigarettes." Wide-eyed, he described how he had left his car engine running and fled with his wife for cover into a nearby building.

Sabah drove us in his car to see what had happened. A large section of the Trade Fair, a fairground with permanent pavilions from such countries as Turkey and Syria, had been obliterated. Perhaps a dozen structures had been flattened. Smoke poured out from the heaps of collapsed concrete and metal girders. All the buildings around, including the Red Crescent hospital, had been badly damaged. All the windows had been blown out in a two-block radius, and broken glass was everywhere. We circled, thinking we might stop and talk with people, but noticed a group of wild-looking Iraqi fighters sitting on a couple of battle wagons—heavy machine guns mounted on swivels on the beds of pickup trucks—and decided it was probably not wise to hang around.

As we drove back toward the Palestine, I felt a new electric tension in the air. Soldiers at sentry positions and on the roadsides held their guns in their hands and appeared anxious; they scrutinized us keenly as we drove by. Others stood looking up into the sky. Sabah drove very fast—too fast—to get us back to the hotel. I noticed that all the shopfronts for three blocks along the road that cuts past the perimeter walls of the Republican Palace were torn up. Glasses and pieces of metal lay tangled on the sidewalks. Some of the shops looked as if they had been looted. I saw that the interior of a little Kurdish restaurant I knew, which had served a delicious roast lemon chicken before the war, had all its windows blown out. Its metal accordion security shutters lay collapsed in a heap in front of it, and it had been gutted of its contents.

Later on I heard the BBC news on a shortwave radio, which reported that Karbala had fallen to the coalition forces and that they had also attacked the town of Kut. The BBC was saying that the battle for Baghdad was imminent. In the evening Salaar, my old minder, came up and asked me if I knew what was going on. I told him what I had heard on the BBC. His eyes widened, and he exclaimed: "Karbala! You mean the town? They have taken it?" I nodded, repeating that this was not confirmed news, but it was what the BBC was reporting. He appeared shocked. He came to stand closer to me, and in a low voice, he asked: "So, tell me, what do you think they are going to do? Will they lay siege to the city or will they enter it and take it by sections. I ask because if it is the first, then this will be very bloody. I am not worried about dying myself, but I am concerned for my family."

I told Salaar that I honestly didn't have any idea, but that I hoped, for everyone's sake, that the Americans and British had a plan of action that would avoid a siege of Baghdad. I felt angry about the prospect of carnage in the city, however, and could not contain myself. A bit unfairly, I used the opportunity to take it out on Salaar. I reminded him that it was his government that had chosen to hunker down for a last-stand fight in Baghdad. This was a very cold-blooded thing to do, I said, because it meant that large numbers of civilians would die. Salaar nodded and said: "Yes, I know." His eyes looked pained. He said, speaking in a very low voice: "Some of the army will fight. Some will run. I hope this will be over quickly."

That evening Sahaf said that the kinds of civilian atrocities we had seen in Hillah were happening all over Iraq. He also accused the coalition of air-dropping booby traps in the shape of pens and pencils on Iraqi towns and villages. Iraqi officials were issuing warnings to people in the affected areas not to pick them up. With a look of outrage, he said: "Pencil booby traps, to kill children and anybody else! What kind of criminals are we facing?" He also accused the Americans of flying their jets low over the holy tombs of Imam Ali and Imam Husein in Najaf and Karbala respectively, so as to damage them. "They are trying to crack these holy tombs," he said, "and this will be scorned by Shia Muslims all over the world." Meanwhile the "heroic Iraqi resistance" was inflicting defeat on the "invading mercenaries" all over Iraq. He gave a province by province tally of their losses in a telegraphic style that sounded uncannily like the BBC's late-night shipping forecast.

The next day was warm and pleasant, except for the smoke. The sun shone, and birds sang and twittered all over town. Even the jihadis, more of whom had begun appearing lately around the hotels, seemed fairly relaxed. One of them was standing on the steps of the Sheraton as I came into the hotel. He had a broad face, slanted eyes, and a wispy beard, and his green turban was tied so that the cloth hung down like chain mail around his shoulders. He was dressed in a calf-length robe, a military-style webbed belt at the waist. The silver hilt of a long, curved dagger protruded from the belt. It was as if one of Genghis Khan's soldiers had been transported through time and deposited there before me. He looked like a Central Asian, an Uzbek perhaps, but I found out later that he had come from Yemen.

Sahaf appeared for his usual press briefing at the Palestine. He laughed at the notion that American forces had taken Karbala or were anywhere near Baghdad. "They are not even a hundred miles away," he snorted. "They are on the move; they are trapped everywhere; they are nowhere. . . . They are a snake in the desert. It's just an illusion. They are not even in Um Qasr! Their allegations are a cover-up for their failure. They are not in hold of any Iraqi towns. We are in a war of attrition with this snake, and I think we will make it very tired."

By late afternoon the skyline was almost totally obscured by smoke. Minarets, domes, and Saddam's samovar-shaped trophy buildings were barely visible through the haze, which turned from brown and black to blue and gray as daylight faded. The bridges that spanned the Tigris downtown began to vanish in the fog, and the river turned a brilliant gold. The Thames must have looked like this in Victorian times, shrouded in mist and the smoke from a million coal fires. From somewhere not far away came a steady thump-thumping sound, the noise made by artillery. The barrages got louder, and suddenly all the lights in the hotel went out. The city on our side of the river was completely dark. It was as if someone had thrown a switch. Then the whole city became black, except for the flying-saucer-shaped Tomb of the Unknown Soldier, illuminated with its fluorescent light strips in the colors of the Iraqi flag. It glowed for some minutes, and then its lights also went out. All of Baghdad was dark, except for the odd headlight and the flames from oil fires.

What we were hearing, as we found out later, was the battle for the Baghdad airport. The next morning, April 4, I drove over to Yarmuk Hospital, just south of the city center, where many of the wounded had been taken. Very few civilians were out on the streets; it was mostly men with guns. The hospital wards were full of young men with short-cropped hair in bloody hospital smocks. One of them said that he was a member of the Special Forces of the Republican Guard and had been shot in the lung at the airport. His name was Omar Bahaldin, and he was twenty-three. Fluid was being drained from his lung into a plastic jug on the floor. His knees were raised, and he jiggled them back and forth. I thought this was because he was in pain but was trying not to show it. "We are not afraid," he said. "I am injured at this moment, but when I get better, I will fight and fight, again and again, until I am a martyr."

A man on an adjacent cot was writhing and groaning in pain. He appeared to be semidelirious. Blood was dripping into a pot from a tube attached to his body. The wounded man groaned and said, over and over again: "I can't take it anymore." His brother was squatting on the floor next to him, holding his shoulders, tears rolling down his cheeks. "You must withstand more. You're a good man. Hold on." An older man, his uncle, held on to his feet with both hands. "You are a lion," he said to the wounded man. "We are proud of you."

Outside, in the hall, a group of distraught women in black sat huddled together. As I walked past, they keened, and one wailed, to no one in particular: "We are so sad, so sad." A man with a blood-drenched leg stood by himself, weeping. Nurses with bloody smocks wheeled wounded men past me on gurneys, trailing a stench of acrid sweat behind them. I paused at the doorway of a ward in which a man was shrieking. A doctor was digging into the man's wounds with a pair of forceps. The man was beside himself with pain. A relative had placed his head on the wounded man's chest to comfort him.

Sahaf showed up for his briefing later than usual that day. He excused himself and explained that he had been delayed because he was trying to get the most up-to-date information possible for us. He confirmed that American and British "criminals" had been air-dropped into Saddam International Airport, south of the city, and several places west and south of Baghdad. "All of these groups have a target, Saddam International Airport, which is now their graveyard. We have decided to allow the invading forces to remain in these places, to nail them down," he said. The battle had now been joined by the Republican Guard, he said, and the invaders were cut off from one another and "bogged down" in little islands, where they were growing "weaker by the hour." Sahaf then made a somewhat confusing reference to the movie *Wag the Dog.* He seemed to think that the movie helped explain why the Americans had attacked the airport. "To air-drop these men is a showy operation, an exhibitionist attempt to show the world that their shock and horror is succeeding," he said. "But they have thrown their desert animals to be killed." He predicted a slaughter there. "Maybe tonight we will show them another Dien Bien Phu. Initial estimates are that it will be difficult for any to come out alive." He promised "unconventional attacks, not necessarily by our armed forces." He confirmed that he was talking about suicide attacks—"martyrs' operations." Asked about reports that a car bomb had killed three Americans that day north of Baghdad, Sahaf retorted: "I am very sad, because it wasn't thirty of them."

Leaving the briefing, I picked up a copy of the *Iraq Daily,* which had shrunk from eight to four pages since the war began, but which was still being printed and distributed. The paper always published an aphorism attributed to Saddam Hussein on its front page, and I noticed that Saddam's piece of wisdom selected for the day also had a snake theme. It was one of the paper's favorite quotes, apparently, because I had seen it published there many times before. "Don't provoke a snake before you make up your mind and muster up the ability to cut off its head. It will be of no use to you to say that you have not started the attack if it attacks you by surprise. Make the necessary preparations required in each individual case and trust in God."

The electricity had been off all over Baghdad for twenty-four hours, but oddly some lights came back on that night in the Republican Palace complex and in several other neighborhoods on the west side of the river. Our side of the Tigris was still blacked out. We could hear the rumble of artillery from the outskirts of the city again. What sounded like a firefight, with machine guns and mortars, broke out inside the palace grounds. A bomb was dropped on the compound, and the weapons fire continued for a bit, then died out. It seemed as if almost anything could happen in Baghdad that night.

Once a war begins, it acquires a kind of organic life of its own. It has unpredictable ebbs and flows and a way of expanding and contracting too. Some days the balance that weighs the war's progress one way or another begins to shift, and it becomes clear that a new pattern has begun. This was what happened when the Americans took Baghdad's airport after heavy fighting on Friday, April 4. I awoke at dawn early the next morning, Saturday, the fifth. A cool breeze was blowing. A rooster crowed. I could hear what sounded like artillery in the distance.

At around that time, a column of American tanks and armored cars was entering the city from the southeast along the road from Hillah and driving through Baghdad's southern outskirts in a great loop (the one I had traveled on just two days earlier) before joining the Americans already entrenched at the airport in the southwestern suburbs. They engaged Iraqi military

forces along the way, leaving a ragged line of blasted and smoking wreckage in their wake.

I knew about this only through rumor, and through news reports from abroad, because all day Sahaf and the ministry's senior apparatchiks kept up a wall of denials and obfuscations about
what was really happening. But among the entourage of Iraqi
minders, drivers, and translators that was part of our marooned
existence at the Palestine and Sheraton, word had spread, and
with it, a general air of panic. The fighting around the airport
had caused many civilian casualties in adjacent neighborhoods, it
was said, and as rumor of this got around, people with families in
the south of the city were fleeing. That morning Sabah found a
room for one of his daughters and her children at the Sheraton, as
did many other Iraqis working with journalists. Safaar and
Diyah evacuated the rest of the family, including Sabah's wife
and aged mother, to a friend's apartment building in northeastern Baghdad, which was said to be safer. Those Iraqis who could
do so were belatedly fleeing the city altogether. Many were going to the town of Baquba, an hour's drive northeast of Baghdad,
which seemed to be the only point of the compass where American troops had not yet penetrated.

In the afternoon the ministry laid on a Potemkinish bus tour
of the suburb of Mansour, a couple of miles to the south, across
the river. We were driven around the bomb-damaged Trade Fair,
then straight back again. The whole trip lasted about twenty-
five minutes. It seemed that there was less and less of the city
that it could safely show us and maintain its claim of being in
control. By now most of us understood what was really happening, and we openly goaded our escorts to take us to the airport,
which they were now claiming was back in their hands. They
promised to try to arrange something.

On Sunday, April 6, the fate of Baghdad hung in an inconclusive limbo. Iraq's regime no longer seemed entirely in control of
things, but the Americans had not yet shown up either. Uday al-

Taiee authorized us to travel in our own cars, but with minders, to a spot in the southern suburbs where, he said, we would see "something special." When we arrived, we found a group of Iraqi soldiers staked out around a destroyed American tank that sat in a blackened, cratered patch of highway that led, a few miles down the road, to the airport.

Together with Salaar, my old minder, who had volunteered to come with me, I dutifully walked over and stared at the hole in the road and the hulk of the tank and listened to the claims of one of al-Taiee's men that the wreckage proved what they had been saying all along: that the Americans had been sent packing under withering fire from the Iraqis and were holed up at the airport, surrounded and under sustained attack. Some children and men who lived in neighboring houses gamely told us how they had seen the tank destroyed by Iraqi soldiers firing antitank rockets—and how the other American soldiers in the convoy had then turned tail in headlong flight. But the large crater in the road by the tank seemed to suggest that it had been hit by a missile fired from the air. (As indeed it had been. From news reports, we had heard that the Pentagon was saying that the tank had been disabled, and to prevent it from falling into Iraq hands, it had sent its own jets to destroy it.)

As soldiers posed on the wrecked tank and journalists clambered around and filmed and took notes and pictures, a pair of U.S. military jet fighters suddenly hove into sight and dived to roar past over our heads, a few hundred feet above our section of the road. The sky was clear and blue. As they did, the Iraqi soldiers became terrified and ran away to conceal themselves on the edges of the highway. After a few minutes most of them wandered back. About five minutes later the jets reappeared and screamed past us, flying in the other direction—and again the soldiers fled. The behavior of the soldiers convinced me that the war was all but over, the endgame rapidly approaching.

As we walked back to the car, Salaar whispered that he could sympathize with the terror of the soldiers, who after all were mostly young conscripts. Then he asked me, nervously, how quickly I believed the Americans would seize the rest of the city. He appeared to be genuinely mystified as to why they had merely "probed" the southern suburbs and then vanished again. "Why don't they just come?" he asked. "I am sure if they did in a massive way, this would be over very quickly." The Iraqi Army, he added, was virtually nonexistent; many of the soldiers, including his own younger brother, had already deserted and were in hiding. "The regime is in decline; it is finished," Salaar explained. "Why should they risk their lives for it now?" There were still Republican Guards who would fight, he conceded, but even among them there were deserters, and he did not feel they could stand up for long to the overwhelming American firepower. "They should do it and get it over quickly," he said. "There are too many civilians dying." Salaar was also very concerned about the safety of his own family. The Iraqi Army had placed antiaircraft guns in a spot very near to their home, and he was worried that the neighborhood, like other parts of the city, would be bombed by the Americans.

Salaar then asked me anxiously what he thought the Americans planned to do with people like him. "I suppose I might be detained," he speculated. "They might believe that I am in the intelligence service or something like that. I don't know what to expect. I don't know, what do you think?" He scanned my face for an answer. As best as I could, I tried to reassure Salaar that if he was merely a civil servant, he would probably be all right. He listened and nodded, but the anxious look on his face did not go away.

That night we could hear the noise of battle coming from southern Baghdad. Later, in the early hours of Monday morning, a firefight erupted inside the presidential palace complex, just across the river. Just before dawn, I fell asleep.

NINE

I was awakened by the sound of heavy combat nearby. It was 8:00 AM. I looked out from the balcony to see explosions inside the palace grounds on the opposite bank of the Tigris. There were bursts of flames and sudden bursts of black smoke rising quickly from the gardens and from some of the palaces. My ears rang with the sound of many weapons being fired, machine guns and tanks and rockets, and of bombs being dropped.

On a wide sandspit that stretches along the riverbank below the palace complex, I saw several dozen Iraqi soldiers in uniform, some walking, some trotting. As I watched, all of them broke into a run, making for the road that extends along the top of the concrete embankment at the river's edge. As they ran, they formed a long ragged line of perhaps fifty men moving at different speeds. A couple of them were wearing only underwear. Some swam into the river and clambered through the bulrushes to get around a metal security fence that ran down the embankment from the palace grounds into the water. I did not understand what the soldiers were running from. Then I noticed that four big khaki-colored tanks, American ones, had driven up and parked along the top of the embankment, just a few hundred feet away from the running soldiers. A withering fire of bullets began to kick up dust from the embankment and the sandy beach below it. There were more explosions, and black smoke began billowing out from what looked like two oil fires set on the beach. After a few more minutes I could just make out the figures of some men, American soldiers, who were crouching and shooting guns, it seemed, from behind their tanks; it was difficult to see, exactly. There was too much happening all at once to absorb. I peered through binoculars and thought I could see what looked like Iraqi soldiers still down on the beach, their heads just visible above the ground in foxholes. One or two appeared to be shooting back. I noticed for the first time that the whole beach, especially along the river's edge, was honeycombed with trenches and fortifications.

I looked down below me to Abu Nawas. It was empty except for a pair of large dogs running side by side down the middle of the road. A few minutes later I saw an Iraqi man, a large fellow in civilian clothes, walking cautiously along my side of the road, carrying a weapon in one hand. He passed an older man who was carrying some bags in his hands, as if he had been out doing the morning's shopping. Then a cameraman and a reporter I recognized as Germans walked out from the Palestine and crossed the street toward the river. They ventured a short distance into the fringe of parkland there and began filming the battle. I saw some Iraqi men approach them, followed by a soldier with a gun. As they converged on the journalists, a furious altercation began. The soldier grabbed the cameraman and hauled him away. He appeared to be trying to force him into a pickup truck driven by another soldier. The other German, the reporter, was trying to stop the soldier. There were angry shouts, and I could see the soldier point his weapon. I thought the soldier was going to shoot the cameraman. The other Iraqi men joined in the commotion. It looked as though they were trying to rescue the journalists. Everyone was shouting and pushing and shoving. Finally, the soldier reluctantly loosened his grip and lowered his weapon, and the Iraqis who had helped the Germans escorted them back to safety in the Palestine Hotel.

The noise of battle became a wall of sound. There was a symphonic quality to it. Much of it was boom and bang—heavy concussive sounds from tanks and planes, the ripping bursts of rockets—but there was also a rhythmic noise, like a great steel drum being pounded mechanically, and, several times, a massive grinding sound. Underneath it all, now and then, came the light clatter of automatic-weapons fire. Several times I heard a huge crackling roar, like metallic popcorn popping, which went on and on and became very loud; I realized later it was probably an ammunition dump exploding. This was a new sound for me, like the grinding noise, which turned out to be coming from the guns of low-flying A-10 Warthogs, which fire four thousand bullets per minute. There were also roars from low-flying F-18 fighter jets, or what sounded like them. These jets, which were very fast and loud, had begun flying over Baghdad in the past two days, replacing the high-flying B-52s of the past fortnight. Once or twice they dropped bombs or rocketed the palace grounds and screamed off again.

The smoke from the fires on the beach was picked up by a sudden gust of wind from the south. It came billowing out across the river toward the hotel, and within a few minutes we were enveloped in a yellow pall of haze and dust and smoke. It was the onset of a new turab, which had, bizarrely, coincided with the palace battle. The dust storm obscured almost everything from sight, but the battle carried on for most of the day.

At around midmorning I decided to leave my balcony perch and go down to the Palestine to find out what was going on. The Sheraton's elevators were no longer working, so I ran down the twelve floors to the street. There were reporters milling around the entrance of the Palestine. I learned that Muhammad al-Sahaf had appeared and given a brief press conference—his briefest ever—in which he had flatly denied that there were any American troops whatsoever in Baghdad. "They are really sick in their minds," he'd said. "They have said they entered with sixty-five tanks into the heart of the capital. I inform you that this is too far from reality. This story is just part of the sickness in their minds. There is no entry of American and British troops into Baghdad at all." They were being "slaughtered" and driven back, he'd claimed, and added colorfully that they were "committing suicide on the gates of Baghdad. We will encourage them to do their suicide. As President Saddam Hussein has said, 'God will grant them their burial at the hands of Iraqis.'" Less than five hundred meters from where Sahaf spoke were several U.S. Abrams tanks, but this fact seemed not to matter to him. He then gave a little sermon to the media about the need for accuracy and truth in their reporting of the news, and he singled out journalists, and especially Al Jazeera, for telling lies about what they were seeing. It seemed that Al Jazeera had been broadcasting live news of the fighting from its own villa on the opposite shore of the Tigris, a few hundred meters upriver from the palace complex. Before leaving, Sahaf had told everyone present: "Be assured that Baghdad is very secure, very safe; Baghdad is great."

In the last few days I had wondered with increasing curiosity about what motivated Sahaf, the last senior Iraqi official anyone had seen since the airport seizure, to make his astonishing claims. I could only conclude that he believed we were not so different, after all, from Iraq's citizens, who had long since lost the ability to call a lie a lie or to contradict anything they were officially told. Perhaps Sahaf thought that if he spoke with enough bonhomie and apparent conviction, we would believe him.

A bus tour for the press corps was organized. Intrigued, I joined it, wondering where we might be taken that could bear out Sahaf's incredible claims. The bus drove down Sadoun Street, one block farther away from the river than Abu Nawas. (From Sadoun Street, you could not see the river or the American tanks on the other side.) I was shocked to see that there were still cars out on the street, and that a couple of sidewalk cigarette and candy kiosks had stayed open for business. When it came to crossing the Tigris, our driver avoided the closest bridge, the Jumhuriyah, which crossed the Tigris at a point just outside the palace walls, and drove on until we came to the second bridge upriver, the Sinak, on the road that runs past the Information Ministry. The city was mostly deserted except for a few fighters here and there in groups of two and three, mostly dressed in civilian clothes with red-and-white-checked kaffiyeh head-scarves wrapped like turbans around their heads. Some, carrying rocket-propelled grenade launchers and loaded up with extra rockets, were crossing the road, walking in the direction of the presidential palace. They flashed us the V sign. The bus took us three blocks past the Information Ministry, took a rightward turn for a couple of hundred meters, to the central bus station, which was empty, and then came back again. The road was blocked off by soldiers where one would normally drive on to the Al-Rasheed Hotel. The rumor was that the Al-Rasheed had been seized during the night by the Americans. Our tour was over ten minutes after it started.

Back at the Palestine, I asked one of the few ministry officials still on hand (many had disappeared since the airport was seized) what the point of the tour had been. He told me that it had been to disprove American claims that they had seized the Informa-tion Ministry. When I asked about the Al-Rasheed, he merely shook his head and pretended not to hear me. Then he said, with enthusiasm, that the ministry hoped to take us to see a place in the southeastern suburbs where the Iraqis had killed "hundreds of Americans."

"Their bodies are everywhere," he told me gleefully. "We would have taken you there already, except that the Americans have left many cluster bombs. So it is too dangerous for you. We have to clear them up. As soon as we do, you have my word, you will see what I am talking about."

I couldn't tell whether this official actually believed what he was telling me himself, as Sahaf seemed to, or was just performing.

In his case, I decided, it was probably a performance. He had an insincere look, and his eyes could not hold mine for very long.

In the late afternoon the dust cleared, and I could see across the river. Two tanks were still there, and I thought I could see the figure of a man sitting with his legs dangling from the embankment wall just in front of the tanks. I looked through a pair of binoculars. It was an American soldier. He appeared to be resting, gazing out at the river, apparently unconcerned about snipers. A moment later he was joined by another soldier. For a time the two of them sat there together, dangling their legs over the embankment. It was one of the most surreal moments I had ever experienced. I could see my countrymen, but a river separated us from one another. For the moment we inhabited two entirely opposite realities on either side of a war. I was still inside Saddam's Iraq. If there had been a footbridge over the river, I calculated, I could have walked over to them in the space of about ten minutes. My reverie was broken by the sounds of more explosions coming from behind the Americans in the palace grounds. Through the binoculars, I could make out the two soldiers getting up and walking along the top of the embankment toward a building half concealed by trees, where they joined other soldiers. Then I lost them from sight.

Someone, an American, I assumed, shot at something on the beach where the Iraqi soldiers had been entrenched earlier in the day. An intense fire broke out at that spot, and then came the sounds of many small explosions—another ammo dump, most likely. Once again I heard the popcorn-crackling roar, and as it picked up tempo, white sparks and projectiles that formed rapid tracers of light flew off in all directions; some arced high up and out in loops like fireworks and landed in the river.

In the middle of the afternoon Sabah offered to fetch us some lunch from Al-Saah, a popular restaurant in Mansour, across the river, where we had eaten many times. It was one of Sabah's favorite places, with its interior done up in shiny black marble and chrome and its dishes showcased on neon signs. Its offerings ranged from Iraqi cuisine to imitation American fast food: fried chicken, referred to as "Kentucky," and hamburgers and french fries. It was, along with Lathikia, where we had bumped into Uday al-Taiee at the beginning of the war, one of the only restaurants remaining open for business in Baghdad. Sabah took a very long time to return, and when he did, he was upset and breathing heavily, as he always did when overcome with emotion.

Once he had recovered his breath and calmed down, Sabah explained that Al-Saah had been bombed just five minutes after he'd left it. He had placed our food order—chicken tikka for two—and had something to eat himself while he waited. He had spent about twenty minutes there, until our takeout was ready, and then began driving back to the hotel. He had gone about a half mile, he said, when there was a tremendous explosion behind him. Like everyone else on the road, he instantly pulled his car over to the side. Everyone was looking back and saying that Al-Saah had been bombed. He hadn't gone back but had driven straight to the Sheraton. We drove over there as soon as we could, after getting permission to go in our own car from Uday al-Taiee.

The windows of Al-Saah and all the buildings around it were blown out. There were clods of earth and debris and shards of glass everywhere; the mess stretched for blocks. Curtains billowed out of broken windows; shop signs were broken and askew, and the interiors of the shops were covered in powder and knocked around as if they'd been hit by a tornado. I saw a young boy pick up a trophy, an ornamental streetlamp, lying on the sidewalk outside Al-Saah. People walked around in a daze. Many of them were going down a side street, and we followed them. On the corner there was a wedding dress shop, its windows shattered. Several mannequins in white satin frocks lay side by side on the floor, like people sleeping together. The side street led into a residential neighborhood of private houses. The street was covered in chunks of masonry and more clods of earth and glass. About a hundred yards in, next to the front garden of a devastated house, its garden heaped with debris and dirt and great chunks of brick and concrete, a large crowd of people had gathered in an open space. They were standing looking at something. I climbed over the mess of debris to join them. What they were looking at was a huge pit. On the other side, some rescue workers were pulling at a section of rubble that was smoking, as a bulldozer growled around, trying to clear it away. The pit was about thirty-five feet deep and about sixty feet across. I noticed the metal headboard of a bed in the pit and an advertisement for a billiard table. What looked like the roof of a car was just visible, covered in mud and rubble, above the surface of a pool of muddy water at the bottom. The houses around the pit all seemed to have their upper stories blown off, and their facades were pocked by the explosion and spattered with earth.

Disoriented by what I was seeing, I asked an Iraqi man who stood next to me what had been where the pit was, before the bombing. "Four houses," he said quietly. It was an extraordinary idea to contemplate. There was nothing discernible anymore that resembled even one house. Just the great hole and the piled-up mess around it, on which people—frantic rescue workers in their blue overalls, photographers, and curious onlookers—were clambering.

A wide-eyed middle-aged woman who spoke English approached. She said her name was Maria Marcos, that she was a secretary at the German Embassy in Baghdad, and that she lived just down the block. She said she had just been switching off her generator when the explosion occurred. The four houses that had been there had vanished, and along with them the families who had lived there. She said there were about nine people altogether who had died. Only one body had been retrieved so far. "We are not afraid of them," she repeated several times. She seemed to be in a state of shock. Nearby a man wept disconsolately into the arms of another man. He held on to the other man with both arms and his whole body, like someone trying to save himself from drowning. Three other men sat on the curb of the street, tears streaming down their faces. Then came the overhead roar of what sounded like an F-15 fighter jet, and many of the people standing around the pit took off running. The fighter passed overhead and did not return.

In the trashed garden of the house next door to the pit, a young man who said his name was Ayad, a college student of twenty, explained that he had been down the street when he heard a roar and saw a great yellow missile, about the size of a date palm, crash into the street and explode in a white light. It had hit the house next door to his grandfather's. He pointed to an old man who was wandering around on the veranda of the house with a bloodstained shirt, his head partly covered with a bloody bandage. The house where the missile had struck had belonged to Um Salman, a widow, he said, and she had lived there with her two sons and two daughters. They had run a printshop nearby. I noticed that Ayad, who had a checked shirt on, was wearing army-style fatigues and boots, and I asked him if he was involved in the defense of Baghdad. "No." He chuckled, adjusting his glasses. "It's just fashion." As we spoke, a neighbor came up and said: "Only an animal does this; a human doesn't do this," and wandered away again.

Ayad's mother, Neda, a pleasant-faced woman in traditional dress, invited us into her father's ravaged home. She said that her father, a retired engineer, was seventy-five years old. He had built the house himself and lived there for the past forty-three years. She said she was trying to convince him to leave it, but he was still saying he wanted to stay. I could see him wandering outside. Neda showed us around. The interior had been mostly destroyed. There was rubble, broken plaster, and dirt everywhere, and the stairs were inches deep in broken plaster and cement. The plaster had come off most of the walls, leaving the brick exposed. Smiling, and in broken English, Neda said: "I think this is from God. I think maybe God wants us to suffer this. I am satisfied with this." I took her to mean that she was thankful no one in her immediate family had died and that she bore no hatred for anyone for what had happened.

It was only later, back at the Sheraton, that I heard the news from abroad that the Pentagon had confirmed that it had dropped four "bunker buster" bombs on a house in Mansour after receiving intelligence that Saddam and his sons, Qusay and Uday, were meeting there. It sounded plausible. Mansour was the neighborhood where Saddam Hussein had done his impromptu videotaped walkabout a few days earlier, which had later been shown on Iraqi television. The video had shown him getting out of a car and walking around in the street, high-fiving excited residents. Viewers had identified the area as a part of Mansour. Some news agencies were also reporting that Saddam and his sons had been having lunch at Al-Saah.

I asked Sabah what he thought of these reports. He shook his head in disbelief. He didn't think the reports were true. He had heard, in the way that Iraqis do—by word of mouth, through friends and neighbors—that Qusay, Saddam's younger son, had eaten lunch at Al-Saah, but not with Uday, or their father, Saddam. And it had been the day before. (The clients of Al-Saah were mostly young and upper middle class, but families also went there, as well as military officers. Saddam Hussein's sons were said to be regulars, but I had never seen them there.)

Amazingly, no one in Al-Saah had been killed, although many people there had been cut by shards of glass. On the next block, an eight-year-old girl had her neck severed by flying shrapnel.

I awoke the next day to the sounds of heavy combat coming from the direction of the presidential complex. I heard bombs dropping and saw explosions across the skyline. A red and black fireball shot up from the open roof cavity of the Baath Party headquarters, a massive stone building under reconstruction since its destruction by American bombs in 1998. There were more blasts near the Al-Rasheed Hotel, and all up and down the riverbank opposite the Sheraton and between the two nearest bridges, the Jumhuriyah, next to the palace, and the Sinak, which crosses the Tigris near the Information Ministry. Everything in that area seemed to be getting bombed, rocketed, strafed, or machine-gunned.

On the Jumhuriyah Bridge, two tanks emerged into the open. They advanced tentatively and then stopped, crouching there like great predatory beasts, swiveling their guns to and fro. All around them, behind them, and in the skies above us, the battle continued. I could see white tracers arcing out into the air toward them, apparently coming from Iraqi forces. I saw an airplane, clearly visible in the sky above me, a stubby-looking AC-10 Warthog, flying a slow upward loop over the river, and I heard the great grinding sound of its guns. The plane made five more passes, and each time it made that grinding roar. With each pass, it seemed to hit a different quadrant of the city. On its third or fourth pass, I saw the facade of the Planning Ministry, a big oxblood-colored ten-story building at the edge of the Jumhuriyah Bridge, explode into a thousand bursts of white light and what looking like flying glass. Then a fighter jet appeared, roaring low, to bomb a building on the opposite bank, causing a great explosion and a rush of black smoke, which continued to billow out for the rest of the day. I thought I could hear the sound of helicopter rotor blades, but I could see nothing.

There was a knock at my door. It was James, the Sudanese room cleaner. I was amazed to see him. Most of the hotel services, including the laundry, water, and electricity, had faltered or stopped altogether. The elevators had not worked for several days. But James had come to clean my room. In a circumspect way, he asked me if I had seen the two helicopters. He motioned to me and, wielding his master keys, opened the door of another hotel room on the eastern side. He pointed through the window to a spot about five miles away. I could clearly see two helicopter gunships, Apaches the color of gunmetal, circling like dragonflies over a part of the city. As we watched, the ground below them exploded in a dozen or more bursts of flame and smoke. James explained that they were attacking the Al-Rasheed military garrison, which had its own airport.

I went back to my own room, and from the balcony I watched as the tanks on the bridge and others hidden from view behind them began a fearsome barrage of the Board of Youth and Sport, one of Uday Hussein's fiefdoms, a large building on our side of the river. They seemed to have been taking sniper fire from the building, and for several minutes they fired shells into the building, hitting most of its floors. The building began to blaze in several places. They swiveled their cannons and began firing into the city on our side of the Jumhuriyah Bridge. Dust and smoke rose from the area around my old hotel the Al-Safeer and the neighborhood near where Karim had his little barbershop. The city resounded with the noise of explosions.

Someone in the hall shouted that the Palestine had taken a hit. I rushed to look out and saw a great knot of people, mostly journalists, pouring out of the entrance. It looked as though they were carrying people on stretchers. I raced down the stairwell to the street and ran across to the Palestine. The same Iraqi official who had gloated about the dead American soldiers the day before stopped me to exclaim jubilantly: "Now even the journalists aren't safe from the Americans!"

A crowd stood around in the driveway, looking shocked and upset. I learned that the Reuters room, on the fifteenth story of the hotel, and another room on the fourteenth floor, just below it, had been hit by something, no one knew what, and that there were three badly wounded reporters. Those were the figures I had seen being carried out. They had been rushed off to the hospital by the time I arrived. Most of the reporters I spoke to believed it had been an Iraqi attack and worried what it might mean for our safety. Everyone was wearing his flak jacket, and those who had helmets were wearing them. As we milled around, word came that the offices of Al Jazeera and Abu Dhabi television, both located in villas on the opposite bank of the river, where the fighting had been taking place all morning, had also been bombed, and that at least one Al Jazeera reporter was dead. A car pulled up, and a friend, the French photographer Jerome Delay, spilled out of it in a rush. His features were distorted. He immediately collapsed into the arms of several friends, shouting, "I lost him, I lost him," and weeping grievously. He had gone to the hospital with his close friend Taras Protsyuk, the Ukrainian cameraman for Reuters, the most badly injured of the reporters. Protsyuk had just died. No one yet knew the fates of the other wounded journalists, José Couso, a Spanish cameraman with Telecinco of Madrid, and Paul Pasquale, a British satellite technician with Reuters.

A scuffle started between a distraught Spanish reporter and Uday al-Taiee. The reporter was accusing the Iraqis of firing a rocket into the Palestine. This was vigorously and heatedly denied by al-Taiee, who insulted the Spaniard and then stormed away in a huff surrounded by several of his flunkies. What was interesting about the exchange was that it was the first time that any of us had seen an Iraqi official challenged in an open and angry way in public, and although al-Taiee maintained a kind of ugly composure, he appeared rattled. I noticed that he was the only ranking Iraqi official still around. All the others, such as Khadum, the ministry's Mukhabarat overseer, and Mohsen, the titular head of the Foreign Press Office, had vanished.

I walked around the Palestine to inspect the damage. To my

eye, it looked as though the hotel had been hit from behind, from central Baghdad, which could only have meant Iraqi fire. At any rate, I could not conceive that the Americans had fired on a hotel where they knew the international press corps was congregated.

(I was wrong. Later we heard that the hotel had, in fact, been hit by a shell fired by one of the tanks on the Jumhuriyah Bridge. The Americans thought they were receiving sniper fire from the Palestine and said they had no idea there were journalists in the hotel. No one in the Palestine believed this to be true.)

With several other reporters, I drove over to the Al-Kindi Hospital, where, it was said, there were a great many civilians who had been wounded in the fighting that day. It was also where José Couso had been taken for emergency treatment. When we arrived there, we found a Spanish photographer standing outside in a shocked state. He said that Couso was still on the operating table. He had lost a large chunk of one of his legs, but the femur was still intact and the doctors were saying it could be saved. Couso and he had spent the previous evening together, drinking and talking, the man told us. He said this several times, in a dazed way. We went inside.

We bumped into Dr. Osama Saleh, the doctor who had taken me to see Ali, the mutilated boy, a few days before. He recognized me and shook my hand. Saleh was very distraught. He said it was the worst day he had ever spent as a doctor. At least a hundred wounded people had been brought in since the morning. Three children had died in his hands. One of them, he said, was only three. He asked us, in a tone of cool, calm fury: "Do you think this is justified? Do you?" Saleh went on to say that nothing, no kind of motive, justified warfare that targeted children. "The child that died could have been my own," he said. He told us that he had brought his own family to live with him in the hospital. He became tearful but controlled himself. I asked Saleh about Ali. He said he didn't know how he was, that other doctors were caring for him now. He looked overwhelmed. We said good-bye and wandered out to the morgue.

The morgue was a small house with double steel doors located in the rubbish-strewn rear area of the hospital. The concrete pathway to it was spattered with blood. Here and there I noticed discarded hypodermic needles. Outside the morgue stood an attendant in filthy clothes. There was a big bloodstain on the ground near him, along with a large clump of black human hair and couple of bloody gurneys on wheels. The attendant was talking to two men I recognized as reporters for Al Jazeera. They had come to identify the body of Tareq Ayoub, their friend, who had been killed that morning. Ayoub was a Jordanian reporter who had just arrived in Baghdad a couple of days earlier, and had done me, John Burns, and Paul McGeough the favor of hand-carrying in some badly needed cash for us. His body lay inside the morgue with about twenty other bloody corpses in a confused heap. The bodies were intertwined willy-nilly, like so much discarded offal. One of the reporters began explaining to us that before the war Al Jazeera had provided the U.S. Central Command with the exact location of its offices in Baghdad and had been assured by the Pentagon that it would not be targeted. The network had taken this precaution, he said, because during the war in Afghanistan, the Americans had bombed its office in Kabul. He began to speak about his friend Tareq Ayoub, but he erupted in tears and walked away.

In the emergency ward, about two dozen doctors and nurses were dealing with eight or more simultaneous emergencies in adjoining white tiled cubicles with green curtains. It was pandemonium. From one of the cubicles I heard an anguished woman's wails and the sound of fists thumping on a wall. Nurses walked around crying openly, and the faces of the doctors looked stricken. A man was wheeled out on a gurney and left in the corridor next to me. He was burned from head to toe, his skin a black and red mass of damaged flesh. His face was covered with bandages. I assumed he was dead, but then I noticed that he was still breathing, because his naked chest rose and fell. A man with a hugely swollen and bloodied face was wheeled out in a wheelchair. In one of the cubicles, a woman who was naked from the waist down and covered with blood was being sponged down by a nurse. As much as the nurse scrubbed, she did not seem to be able to get rid of the blood. The woman's body was left a smeared orange color. A great sobbing erupted. I saw two children, a brother and sister, being covered up by attendants on a gurney where they lay together. Before the cloth covered her, I saw that the girl was covered in blood. Her brother looked as though he were sleeping. But they both were dead. Their mother was there, beside herself with grief. She was the woman I had heard wailing and hitting the walls. Then almost all the onlookers around the mother, including the doctors and nurses, broke down and cried. I was overcome and went outside and sat down. I wept. The children's father was sitting a few feet away from me, disconsolately sobbing into his arms.

Two soldiers who looked as if they had come fresh from combat rushed up to the entrance, asking about a friend. The doctors told them they could come in but only if they left their weapons behind. They were festooned with antitank rockets, and both carried automatic rifles. They argued but then agreed to leave them behind. After about ten minutes they emerged again, looking upset and angry, and collected their guns.

On the drive back to the hotel, the streets seemed unusually empty of people, and there were almost no soldiers manning the sandbagged bivouacs along the streets. A family moved slowly on foot along the sidewalk, carrying bags and suitcases, heading away from the city center. At the Palestine, we heard the news that José Couso had died. Paul Pasquale, the other wounded man, was said to be awaiting the amputation of one of his legs in another hospital. People said that the U.S. Marines had secured the Al-Rasheed military garrison and were moving into the city from there. Another contingent was reported to be coming in from the north. The tanks that had sat all morning on the Jumhuriyah Bridge and fired on the Palestine were gone.

There was a cool breeze now, and I sat on the balcony of my hotel room, watching large black long-necked birds wheel around. White terns flurried around the bulrushes on the Tigris. A lone hawk, or maybe an eagle, drifted high above me. As dusk approached, two fighter jets came past and repeatedly soared and dived and struck at the Board of Youth and Sport building, sometimes singly and sometimes together. I watched as one of them came ripping out of the sky in a downward spike. A rocket burst out of its pod and gleamed sharply through the air and plunged directly into the building and exploded. The jet raced on and lunged upward and away again after making its strike. On one of the jets' passes, there was a sudden whoosh from the trees on the riverbank about three hundred yards east of us, just down Abu Nawas. It was a heat-seeking missile, and it swooped up in a white vapor trail, chasing the closest American jet. After a few seconds it vanished into the clouds. It had missed. The fighter came out of the clouds and raced on unscathed. The two jets came and went for about forty minutes and then flew away. Night fell, and on the front lawn of the Palestine Hotel, a candlelight vigil was held for the journalists killed that day.

On Wednesday morning I went outside to find out what was happening. Everything seemed a little too quiet. At daybreak there had been a short barrage of tank fire by the American soldiers who were parked across the Tigris inside the Republican Palace compound. They directed their fire against a leafy section of the riverbank about three hundred yards down Abu Nawas from the Sheraton. It was where I had seen the antiaircraft missile fired off at the fighter jet the previous afternoon.

At the Palestine there were no officials to be seen at all, only a few of the low-level minders, and they looked adrift. Sungsu Cho, a young Korean photographer who had begun working with me, told me he had heard that widespread looting had begun in Saddam City, a large Shiite slum in northeastern Baghdad. Saddam City had a reputation as a hotbed of Shia discontent. An uprising had taken place there in 2000 that was quelled brutally by Saddam's Republican Guard; it had always been a difficult place to visit as a foreign journalist. With Sungsu's devil-may-care driver, who was from Saddam City and who owned a BMW, we raced through the city. There were no soldiers or policemen anywhere. A white pickup passed us. In the back were a dozen or so young men who looked like soldiers, but they were wearing civilian clothing. There was a machine-gun mount in the back, but the gun was gone. They looked as though they were escaping. We passed a truck that was pulling a white Mercedes sedan without tires behind it, making a terrific din as the bare rims scraped along the concrete. Cars were driving erratically in both directions on either side of the divided highway, and everyone seemed to be in a particular hurry.

We passed the Ministry of Oil and then, a little farther on, the Ministry of Transport. Just before the road circle that leads into Saddam City was the Ministry of Trade. The Saddam billboard at its entrance had been shattered, and a stream of youths and men were pouring out of the building and onto the main road, wheeling office furniture loaded up with air-conditioning units and ceiling fans. Several were driving along slowly with purebred horses, tied to the cars by ropes, trotting behind them. A boy cantered bareback along the road on a gorgeous black Thoroughbred.

At the traffic circle, pickups were being loaded up with all manner of goods by frenzied men and a few women. As we turned off into Saddam City, a bomb exploded in a warehouse a couple of hundred meters ahead of us. We passed what looked like a police station, where a fire had been set. There were people looting there too. We pulled up just behind a group of men who were loading things onto a truck. Sungsu got out of the car and approached them on foot. As he did, a number of men came running toward him. One of them, a bearded man wearing a gray dishdasha and an unfriendly expression, approached and called out something in Arabic. Khifa, a translator who had come along with us for the ride, told me the man was saying that if we didn't take Sungsu away at that moment he would kill him. Khifa called out urgently to Sungsu, who reluctantly returned to the car. As he did, an Iraqi youth ran up from across the street to say, politely, that the behavior we were observing was not representative of Iraqis or of the people of Saddam City. We thanked him, did a fast U-turn, and drove out of there quickly.

As we made our way back, I saw that the Ministry of Transport's upper floors were on fire. There was smoke coming out of the Iraqi Olympic Committee headquarters as well, a modern office block some ten or so stories high set back off the main road. Its director had been Uday Hussein, and people were said to have been tortured and killed regularly in the building. Uday had a large stable, and as I saw more horses being led out of the walled grounds on ropes, I realized that they were probably his.

After returning to the hotel, I retrieved my flak jacket and, with John Burns, Tyler Hicks, and Paul McGeough, prepared to make a second run at Saddam City in two cars. (Sabah refused to go, saying it was too dangerous.) Before we left, I noticed a large group of young Iraqi men in civilian clothes sitting in the entrance to the Palestine. They were, I learned later, deserting soldiers, who came there looking for refuge, and asked a few people for money, before leaving again. Out in front of the Sheraton and walking down the street away from it was a large group of jihadis, Arab volunteers from other countries who had come to fight for Saddam Hussein. Now they looked intent on escape. None of them carried weapons or made eye contact with us as we drove by. I counted about sixty of them.

In the forty minutes or so that I had been away, the looting
had metastasized. Large mobs of people were now ransacking
warehouses belonging to the Ministry of Trade. The fire in the
top floor of the Transport Ministry had spread, and the Olympic
Committee building was being quickly gutted by a raging fire.
We could see people on the roofs of other buildings, frenetically
prying loose air-conditioning units. Along the roadside were
more stolen horses and more men and boys pushing swivel chairs
loaded with office equipment. Other people had piled up furniture and were loading it into pickups. Trucks passed us towing
stolen cars behind them. We reached the bridge overpass that
marked the frontier between Baghdad and Saddam City and noticed that a group of U.S. Marines had arrived.

They were still pulling up as we came upon them, a group of
four or five green hulking Light Armored Vehicles that were
covered with rucksacks, boxes of meals ready to eat, and assorted
weaponry. Out of them emerged a couple of dozen athletic-look-
ing young American men wearing helmets and flak jackets and
holding weapons. Their faces were covered in dust. Their commander was reading a map and telling them where they should
deploy. Two groups immediately occupied abandoned Iraqi
sandbagged bivouacs on either side of the intersection, while
others ran back and forth to receive orders.

We said hello to the marines and explained who we were, and
they all said hello back but kept their eyes on the chaotic traffic,
made up almost entirely of looters, which surged up the road
toward Saddam City. The marines began to try to block the traffic. Two marines went out with their weapons into the road. As
the drivers realized who they were, they began honking and giving thumbs-up signs and shouting, "Bush good," and smiling
and waving. Others looked uncertain. When they didn't stop
their cars in time, the marines got into ready-to-fire positions
and pointed their rifles directly at them. One car dragging another behind it by a rope caught one of the marines in the rope

and almost dragged him off his feet before it could stop. The driver was very apologetic and with sign language tried to say he was very, very sorry. The marine brushed himself off and shook his head. A car coming in the other direction stopped, and a man inside it called out repeatedly, "Welcome, my friend!" and dispensed happy kisses to Paul's and John's cheeks. It seemed not to matter to them who we were, or else they were unable to distinguish reporters from soldiers. An Iraqi youth walked up to me, showed me some kind of a military medal, and said, in English, "Saddam animal," then walked away. Groups of young Iraqi men would wander up, smile, give the thumbs-up, say, "Down Bush," or, "America good," before walking on. It was unclear to me whether they meant what they said or thought this was a ritual they should perform.

The marines were having difficulty getting things under control, and they were getting jumpy. "Godammit, get over here right now!" one of them yelled to several others who were standing around on the other side of the road. He wanted them to help stop the traffic. When one car kept crawling forward after it was motioned to stop, one of the marines put his gun in the firing position and screeched: "Stop your fucking car right now." The car stopped.

As the marines redirected traffic away from the entrance to Saddam City, a carnival-like atmosphere took hold. People shouted and waved white flags. One man leaned out of his car window and ostentatiously tore up a 250-dinar note embossed with Saddam's portrait and threw it on the ground at the feet of one of the marines. The marine looked nonplussed. I explained what it was, and the marine said: "Oh, damn. I wish he hadn't torn it up. I was supposed to get one of those as a souvenir for one of my friends." I told him not to worry; there were plenty of dinar notes around. He said, "Good," and went back to directing traffic. One man came along in the traffic pushing a wheeled sofa set and waving happily. A boy driving a forklift that seemed out of control spun in circles near the marines, making them jump back; the boy smiled ecstatically while making facial expressions to show he meant no harm. A truck came by pulling a stolen police car, its rear window smashed. A man pushing an executive's chair piled up with air-cooling units stopped and yelled, "Mister good good!" before heading off down the highway with all the other happy looters. In the background, flames were pouring out of the Transport Ministry; the fire had engulfed the entire top floor.

We left the marines and took a drive through the government district that was being sacked. Outside the Olympic Committee building, which had become an inferno, a man who said his name was Abu Montazar stopped to say, "I am very happy Saddam is finished. We got rid of Saddam with your help, but why should we destroy our country?" He motioned to the burning building, the chaos all around. "The Americans are welcome to stay here for a while to help Iraqis rebuild the peace, but after that they should go. Middle East peace should not be secured on the backs of the Iraqi people. The Americans should see us as human beings, not only as oil."

There was great activity on the streets outside the warehouses of the Ministry of Trade. As we approached, a flurry of gunshots made some looters race off in their loaded-up pickups. Someone had left behind several boxes of Very brand sports shoes from China, and immediately other men came rushing up to try them on. Most of the boxes had only one shoe left in them, however. Some men and boys emerged kicking soccer balls, still wrapped in plastic, to relatives waiting by a vehicle. A procession of American marines, a different group, came by on their great beastlike armored vehicles and tanks. They had spray-painted names on the barrels of their guns, among them Assassin, Carnage, Cold Steel, Crazy Train, Rebel, and one that read: "Got Oil?"

I asked Khifa, the translator, how he felt about everything we were seeing. "I am very, very happy," he replied. "But I don't know why, I also feel like I want to cry. OK, Saddam Hussein is gone, but I am afraid the Americans will need to put another Saddam Hussein in power to keep control here. This is exactly what happened in 1991, and this is why Saddam was needed afterward. You know why? Because he represented the police station. Now, look around, there is no one, no authority, no police. And this is the result." Khifa looked distressed. A moment later he added, more calmly: "I can't be certain that things have changed until I see the head of Saddam Hussein."

We returned to the marines' roadblock outside Saddam City. They appeared to have finally gotten things under control. They now had their armored vehicles parked across both lanes of the highway, so we got out and walked toward them to avoid problems. We reidentified ourselves and told them we wished them to allow our cars to drive past their roadblock. They agreed, and we told our drivers to creep forward slowly. As they did so, the drivers waved and smiled excessively at the marines.

I fell into conversation with a pair of friendly young corporals. They said they were from the First Marines out of Camp Pendleton. Each of them, I noticed, had writing pens and toothbrushes tucked into the front pockets of his uniform. One of them, Jim Higareda, was a Mexican-American from Redlands, California. He was olive-skinned and wore large glasses. He said he was twenty-three. His friend, Pete Regan, was a slim, blue-eyed, and blond youth with freckles. He was twenty-two, he said, and from Brooklyn. He said that his father had been a firefighter from Rescue Three, in the Bronx, and had died on 9/11. He said this in a matter-of-fact way, in the same way he had told me his name and age.

Pete Regan acknowledged not having much of a clue where he was. I tried to give him a brief idea, but he shrugged, uninterested.

He said: "We came in from the east, through some abandoned military crap, and they just dropped us off here." I asked him what he meant by getting "dropped off." He nodded to the Light Armored Vehicles parked nearby, and he explained that each one carried about twenty-one marines, who sat inside and never knew where they were going. Only the commanders and the pilots did; that was how it had been this morning. One minute they had been outside Baghdad, at night, and then the hatches were open, and now here they were, on this intersection outside Saddam City. They had been moving like that all the way from Kuwait for the past three weeks. I asked them what they thought of Iraq so far. Pete Regan smiled and said: "It's a dump; it sucks." Jim Higareda said to Pete: "Well, there was that place we went through yesterday afternoon, what was it called?" Pete shrugged blankly. Jim Higareda said: "That was pretty nice." He turned to me and explained: "It reminded me of some parts of deep down in Mexico."

Both of them were looking forward to getting home. Neither had been able to talk to his family since February, they had been on the move so much. Jim Higareda said he was looking forward to going up to Big Bear Lake in the High Sierras—"and do nothing, for like two days." He smiled at the thought of it. He had very white teeth.

A hundred yards away, at the traffic circle, some of Jim Higareda's and Pete Regan's comrades were trying to hold back a swelling crowd of enthusiastic Iraqi men. A hundred or more Iraqis, mostly adolescents and young men, were swarming and surging forward, and all of them were gesticulating and cheering and gabbing away at the young marines. The marines seemed to be in a tolerant mood but were having trouble controlling the crowd. In the midst of this, one of the marines was holding a little piece of paper with Arabic words on it, and he was trying to study it so as to come up with an intelligible phrase. He was not having an easy time of it, because a group of friendly young

Iraqis kept jostling him and asking him questions in Arabic. He tried to explain what the paper in his hands was. He repeated the word "translation" loudly to them, in English, several times. The Iraqis seemed very curious and delighted by this, and when I left, they were still waiting anxiously to hear what he would tell them.

Down the road, the looting was continuing. Most of the major buildings along it were now on fire. But, at the Oil Ministry, a squadron of marines had taken up combat-ready positions on either side of the entrance, and the looting there seemed to have mostly stopped. Some excitable and edgy Iraqi boys still hung around, trying to engage the marines in conversation. One of the Iraqis placed a rubber tire around the outstretched arm of the statue of Saddam Hussein that stood outside the ministry, as if to burn it. A young horse trailing a rope came darting by, chased by men, and pranced off out into the highway, where it was nearly hit by a passing car. Spooked, it cantered into the next lane, where more cars swerved to avoid it, and more men joined the chase. On the horse went, zigzagging all over the highway, narrowly missing cars and trucks and the men chasing it. The last glimpse I had of it, the horse was still free and was trotting down the shoulder of the road. It seemed to have outrun its pursuers.

An obese man in a flamboyant suit appeared at my side. He spoke a rather stilted English and looked like a well-off Iraqi merchant but said that he was a pharmacist. He said that his name was Muhammad Samarrai. "Please," he exhorted. "All educated persons are not satisfied by the sequence of events in the country." I asked him what he was trying to tell me. "The thieving," he said, gesturing around us. "This is by the uneducated people." He had a chastising look on his face that I did not appreciate. I told him that I was not a soldier but a journalist. He looked unconvinced and kept repeating what he had said. As I left, thanking him for his insights, Samarrai called after me: "We just want people to live under any system. Any system is better than this." It seemed to me that Samarrai was probably a loyalist of the ancien régime and was upset with the Americans. Because of them, I understood him to mean, Saddam was no longer around to keep the people in their place.

We drove back downtown and along Abu Nawas Street. Our original team had gone in different directions, and I was traveling now with John Burns. Sabah had agreed to drive us; he felt guilty about not going with me to Saddam City. The Al-Safeer Hotel's windows had been blown out, but I was gratified to see it had not been hit by the tanks in the battle the day before. Near Karim's barbershop, several men were trying to push a brand-new white government-issue Toyota Land Cruiser into a garage in the street to conceal it. It looked as though the whole neighborhood had gathered to watch them. The looting had spread to the city center. Out on Sadoun Street, there was broken glass everywhere. Some boys were carting off rolled-up Persian carpets in a wheelbarrow. We approached the Jumhuriyah Bridge, wondering if we might cross it, but it was blocked by a barricade of debris and looked unsafe to try. At the next traffic circle, near the entrance to the Sinak Bridge, some jumpy-looking youths and young men with weapons crouched behind sandbags on either side of the road. Clearly, the Americans had not arrived there yet. We traveled on, through a poor district where the shops were being looted and large numbers of rough-looking young men stood around, looking predatory. Sabah began protesting about the danger of our outing; a couple of hours earlier, he said, in the same place, a mob had stopped the car of some other reporters, beaten them, and robbed them of their equipment, their car, and all their money.

We turned left onto the street leading to the next bridge, about a kilometer farther on. It was one of the colonnaded streets of the old downtown. The street was deserted. We drove to within a halfblock of the bridge, where the street was blocked by rubble and debris. A man with a severe limp came up to us and told us that it was dangerous there. The Americans had shot and killed someone who had tried to cross the bridge. He led us to the corpse. The bloodied body of a young man under a burlap sack, buzzing with flies, lay in the sun on the street corner. Shots began to ring out here and there from the adjacent streets. We walked back to our cars and drove on one more kilometer, to the fourth bridge leading over the Tigris, looking for a safe way to cross over to the western side. On the way, we swerved around an old crone in a black abaya who was pushing a chrome-plated hat-rack, obviously looted, down the middle of the street.

At the traffic circle that led onto the next bridge, there were a half dozen men wearing civilian clothes. Some wore kaffiyeh headscarves. They carried automatic weapons, and some had an-titank rockets. They didn't stop us. We saw cars going over the bridge, and we followed them. On the other side, we found our-selves on the avenue that led down to the Ministry of Justice. About 250 yards down the avenue, we could see the large lum-bering shapes of several Abrams tanks. They seemed to have stopped, but their cannons were pointed toward us. A man ran out into the street and waved us back. We turned the cars around quickly, lest the tanks shoot at us, and drove back down the main street leading from the bridge, out of sight of the tanks. We were surrounded almost immediately by a dozen or so men, one of whom said to us that Saddam or no Saddam, they would fight the Americans. The other men yelled their agreement with this, and some briefly chanted "Down Bush."

Two men wearing kaffiyehs like balaclavas over their faces and carrying rocket launchers darted furtively across the street at our side. They were looking in our direction and yelled something to the men around us before they vanished down a side street in the direction of the American tanks. Clearly, they were going to try to ambush them. Sabah and Khifa told us urgently to get in the cars. The men who were around us also made shooing movements with their hands. We wheeled around again and raced back across the bridge. Khifa said that the men were fedayeen and had yelled, "Clear the area," and that one had whispered to him warningly, "Get them out of here now."

As we traveled back toward the hotel, we passed the first group of gunmen we had seen earlier near the Sinak Bridge. One of them saw us and yelled angrily, in English, "Go! Go! Go!" Sabah said that these gunmen were not Iraqi, but Arab jihadis from other countries. A pair of white Toyota Land Cruisers were being slowly pushed down Sadoun Street by looters who didn't have the ignition keys to start them. Two blocks away from the Palestine and Sheraton hotels we saw that both sides of the boulevard ahead of us were blocked by tanks and armored vehicles. The U.S. Marines had arrived downtown.

Telling Sabah to drive forward very slowly behind us, John and I got out of the car and walked toward the marines. An Iraqi man who was standing with a huddle of other men and women and children gathered at the side of the road called out to ask us if we were Americans. When we said yes, that John was English and I was American, the whole group began cheering and applauding us, clapping their hands as if they were at a performance in a theater. "America good," the man called out several times.

The name stenciled on the barrel of the first tank we reached was Kitten Rescue. The marines had surrounded Fardous Square and the Palestine and Sheraton hotels with their war machines, and the atmosphere around them was festive and expectant. A crowd of excited young Iraqi men and boys had gathered. Everyone looked up at the great bronze statue of Saddam Hussein on its plinth. A couple of Iraqi boys clambered up and tried pushing at the statue to knock it down. After a few minutes of this futile effort, some marines drove an armored vehicle with a winch up the steps of the plaza. The steps broke under its metal treads. As the winch was raised, a marine emerged from the hatch of the vehicle, shinnied up the winch, and produced an American flag, clearly planning to hang it on the statue. He retrieved the flag after a minute, however, as if someone had told him this was not a politic thing to do. An Iraqi flag was soon produced and hung on the end of the winch. One of the Iraqi youths on the plinth helped place the winch cable around Saddam's body and climbed down. After a great chugging of its engine and backward and forward movements, the vehicle pulled it until it toppled forward, facedown. The statue hung suspended in the air for a few minutes until the marines gave it another good yank, and it came completely off, minus Saddam's bronze feet, which remained on the plinth. The crowd of Iraqi men and boys rushed forward, excitedly yelling, jumped on Saddam's statue, and began hitting it with their shoes.

An hour or so later I was in the lobby of the Sheraton, waiting for the elevator, which had mysteriously begun working again. Two middle-aged Arab men, perhaps Iraqis, waited for it with me. They eyed me carefully. One of them, who had the look of a middle-class businessman, was busily cramming rice in his mouth from a paper plate with a plastic fork. When he was done, he threw the plate and the fork on the floor. This seemed like unusual behavior, but somehow in keeping with the altered reality of the day. After he had finished chewing and swallowing, the man looked at me and said, in perfect English: "Well, the Iraqis really put up a stiff resistance, didn't they?" His tone was barbed, and so I merely nodded noncommittally. The elevator opened, and the three of us entered it. We were silent all the way up to the tenth floor, where they got out.

After they stepped out, they turned around to face me. The second man, who had the appearance of a government functionary, held the elevator door open with his hands. He was frowning. He asked: "So, the war is over, *khalass*—finished?"

I shrugged and said, "Maybe, so it seems."

"Really?" he replied. "What about Saddam Hussein?"

"I don't know," I said neutrally. "Maybe he is dead."

"Dead? You think so? Really?" His eyes were cold, and his smile was tight and sarcastic. He let the elevator door go.

TEN

By Thursday morning most of downtown Baghdad was being plundered. On the east side of the Tigris River, where the marines had arrived the day before, the looting had become a free-for-all. Only the west side of the city was still free of looters, because the bridges over the river were blocked by Abrams tanks of the U.S. Army's Third Infantry Division, which had taken the east side of the city. Two blocks from the Palestine, I came across throngs of people raiding shops and carting away merchandise. New buildings were being set on fire. It was chaos.

Hoping to find Ala Bashir, whom I had not seen for a week, I set off for his hospital, the Al-Wasati. The road leading to the hospital was lined with several other medical facilities, which were being brazenly ransacked. Trucks were loading up equipment of every description, and people were frenetically pushing or pulling items away. There was trash everywhere. I heard occasional gunshots, and I could see some smoke rising from a couple of the buildings. I saw no American marines anywhere.

In the lobby of Bashir's hospital there were many wounded people lying in cots against the far wall, their relatives looking after them. Two dead men covered with blankets lay on cots on the floor near the main entrance, and three badly injured men lay next to them. One of the wounded was the driver of a Red Crescent ambulance; he had been shot by marines at a roadblock. The damaged ambulance was parked in front of the main door of the hospital. I was met by Sunduz, Bashir's attendant; she looked weary and anxious but smiled in relief upon seeing me. I asked about Ala Bashir. She shook her head, frowning, and led me hurriedly into the anteroom of the emergency operating theater. After a minute Bashir's deputy, Dr. Waleed, emerged. He looked exhausted. His hands were sheathed in green surgical gloves that glistened with fresh blood. He held them up in the air. He had been working nonstop for over thirty-six hours without sleep, he told me. A steady stream of wounded people was being brought in for treatment, and he was all on his own. Most of his medical staff had not shown up for work for two days. He didn't know how much longer he could keep going. He didn't know what to do. The Al-Wasati was the last hospital functioning in central Baghdad, he said worriedly. All the others had been plundered, and now it too was in danger of being overrun. Several raids had been made by marauders during the night, and another attempt had been made just a few minutes before I arrived. The hospital had no sentries anymore; the usual guards had all vanished two days earlier. The Al-Wasati's only protection was a young medical student who had volunteered his services. During the night the student had stood guard and thrown rocks at the attackers to keep them at bay, but it was only a matter of time before they came back with more men and mobbed the place. Waleed asked me for help. I promised to return to the Palestine to see if I could get the American marines to do something.

Waleed thanked me, then pulled me close to him and whispered urgently in my ear. He said that six days earlier, on Friday, April 4, the day the Baghdad airport had fallen to the Americans, Saddam Hussein had sent for Ala Bashir. Waleed had sent Bashir off to his rendezvous in a car with his own driver. Neither Bashir nor the driver had reappeared. Waleed feared the worst. I asked whether he thought Bashir might have been with Saddam at the time of the bombing that had taken place in Mansour three days earlier. Waleed didn't know, but he said, "I don't think Saddam Hussein is dead. I don't know about Ala. But I am very worried about him." He proposed that we go together and look for him. He said he knew where a sister of Bashir's lived, on the west side of the city. If Bashir was still alive, he speculated, he might be there. We agreed to make the trip the next morning, if the bridges across the Tigris were open.

Before I left, Waleed told me that he had a British patient. He told Sunduz to take me to see him; he had to return to the operating theater. She led me to a dingy ward. The patient turned out to be Paul Pasquale, the Reuters technician who had been wounded in the tank attack on the Palestine on April 8. He looked terrible. His face was peppered with shrapnel wounds; bigger wounds on his torso had been stitched up, and his legs were heavily bandaged. But he had not lost a leg, as was initially reported. Pasquale was conscious but seemed disoriented. A couple of his Iraqi Reuters colleagues were at his bedside. They told me they were trying to have him evacuated from Iraq, but with all the chaos going on, it looked as though it would take a couple of days. I asked if they had talked to the U.S. Marines. They shook their heads; they had not yet been able to find anyone in authority to approach. One of them took me aside to tell me that Pasquale didn't know that his friend Taras was dead; he begged me to keep it a secret. I chatted with Pasquale for several minutes. He told me that the previous night several wounded Palestinian jihadis had shared his room. He had spent a sleepless night, fearing that their presence could provoke an American attack on the hospital. In the morning some men had come and taken them away, which was a relief. But he was aware that the hospital was unguarded and that there were looters trying to break in. Then Pasquale asked me point-blank about his friend Taras. How was he? I lied. I told him that Taras had been injured and taken to another hospital. I had not seen him myself, I said, but I'd heard he was going to be fine. Pasquale nodded, visibly relieved by this news. I left, telling him I would be back soon.

I hurried back to the Palestine. A Humvee stood out front with what looked like a couple of senior-looking American officers standing next to it. Marine sentries stopped me from approaching. I explained who I was and that it was an emergency. One of the officers, a big strapping man with a cigar in his mouth, beckoned me forward. He said his name was Lieutenant Colonel Bryan McCoy. I didn't know it at the time, but he had led the Marines' charge into the city and was at that moment the senior commanding officer in Baghdad. As I explained the situation at the Al-Wasati to him, McCoy listened attentively to me. He seemed completely unaware that the hospitals in Baghdad were being looted; he had obviously never heard of the Al-Wasati. Thinking it might help convince him to send troops to protect the hospital, I told him that there was a British citizen there. I told him that Pasquale was one of the journalists who had been wounded when the American tank fired on the Palestine. He made no comment about this, but he nodded. He and a junior officer pulled out a military map of Baghdad and laid it out on the hood of the Humvee. He asked me to show him where the hospital was. I tried, but it proved difficult to explain. He told me to wait for fifteen minutes, until he could put together a platoon of men. Could I lead them there? I said I could. While I waited, I spotted a Frenchman I'd met before who worked for Première Urgence, an organization that supplies emergency aid to hospitals. The Frenchman had volunteered his services during the war at Bashir's hospital. I explained what was going on. He agreed to come with me. With Sabah driving, the Frenchman and I drove at the head of a convoy of three or four Humvees and a couple of armored vehicles, with fifteen or twenty marines, to the hospital.

The looting had intensified in our absence. A truck and a refrigerator nearly blocked one side of the road, and Sabah's car just made it through the gap. The vehicle behind us pushed the refrigerator out of the way, then half crushed it as it drove on. The marines pointed their guns at the looters. When we arrived at the Al-Wasati, the marines leaped out and got into crouching combat-ready stances facing the hospital. Sunduz and some nurses and civilians stood in the doorway looking absolutely petrified. I quickly called out to the marines that it was the hospital that needed protection. They instantly turned around and took up positions at the entrance gate, this time facing the street. I led the platoon commander, a young lieutenant named Danner, into the hospital to see Dr. Waleed, whom we found in the operating theater. He was immensely relieved to see us and thanked Lieutenant Danner profusely for coming. He said there had been a drive-by shooting of the hospital entrance during my brief absence. Fortunately, no one had been killed or injured. I took Danner to see Pasquale. The lieutenant spoke to him comfortingly and reassured him about his safety. The marines secured the perimeters of the building and promised to stay there for the night. I told Waleed I would return the next day to go with him to look for Ala Bashir.

The west side of Baghdad was still a no-go area for us. A few people appeared to have been able to get across, but others had been repelled by American gunfire. Sungsu Cho, the Korean photographer, had tried to make his way across one of the bridges over the Tigris but been shot at by American soldiers on the other side. Some Iraqi civilians who had tried to cross in their cars had been killed. From my hotel room, I could see their shot-up vehicles sitting in front of the tanks. There was still some heavy fighting taking place in pockets around the city. It was not yet entirely clear which parts of Baghdad were in American hands and which were not.

I joined several photographers on a drive to Jadiriyah, a residential neighborhood in southern Baghdad that had the virtue of being on the same side of the river as the Palestine. It was an area where many senior Baathist officials, including Tariq Aziz and most of Saddam's relatives, had villas. We were looking for a palace complex that Uday Hussein was said to have lived in. It took us a long time to get there, because several main avenues were blocked by vigilantes with guns who were aggressively stopping cars from entering, to stop looters. We took side roads and shortcuts to avoid them.

Several dozen marines had set up ambushes at a traffic circle where another large statue of Saddam had been toppled. We drove around the burned-out carcass of an Iraqi ammunition truck. It was surrounded by hundreds of rockets, some of which looked as if they had not yet exploded. I recognized the traffic circle as one near the Al-Hamra Hotel and realized that it was my only point of reference to the neighborhood. It had begun to dawn on me how little I actually knew Baghdad. Our knowledge of Saddam's city had been so strictly circumscribed before the war that few of us even knew the names of many of his palaces or the purposes of many of his government buildings. Over the past forty-eight hours I had been discovering places that I had not even known existed. On one of our drives to Al-Wasati Hospital, for instance, Sabah and I had gone past a medium-size hotel, the Al-Sadeer, which stood a mere five blocks or so away from the Palestine. The hotel was ablaze, and a guard was running around, shooting his gun to chase some looters away. Casually, Sabah remarked that the hotel was where most of the Arab ji-hadis recruited by Saddam had been living during the past few weeks. I asked Sabah why he had never told me before. He shrugged and smiled. He pointed to a large apartment block, just off Sadoun Street. That building, he said, had housed some of the guerrillas of the Iranian Mujahedin-i-Khalq organization, which Saddam had subsidized. He chuckled.

When we were within a few blocks of the palace, we left our car on the main road and set out on foot through a residential neighborhood. All the streets were barricaded and guarded by suspicious-looking residents with guns. They looked at us warily but said hello when we did. A woman in her forties wearing Western clothing came up to me; she looked very angry. She said: "Please, I want to say something to you, please!" I stopped. She yelled: "What is America doing to Baghdad? Why has it come?" There seemed little to say to her, so I said nothing. She stomped off, yelling: "America is stupid."

We arrived at the gates of a large palace complex. A group of young marines who were lounging around the entrance waved us through. Inside, we found five neoclassical domed palaces built of limestone. Each had an ostentatious pillared entrance. There appeared to be a palace for each member of Saddam Hussein's family. Two of them had been heavily bombed, and parts of their roofs had caved in under slag heaps of debris. We found American marines everywhere, poking curiously around the interiors or else outside lying around in the flower beds, listening to radios and hanging out. They told us they had arrived the night before. Pieces of ornate fretwork and carved wooden door panels with ornamental brass and enamel inlay lay scattered around. A great crystal chandelier had crashed onto the rubble in the foyer of one palace. It was covered in gray dust.

On the entrance wall of one of the palaces, a marine had scrawled "Texas" and "Suicide 1/7" (First Battalion, Seventh Regiment). In the rear garden, I saw a swimming pool and a reproduction stone statue of the Venus de Milo. Two snarling porcelain leopards guarded the entrance to the palace next door. This palace had marble inlaid floors and a solid white marble staircase that divided triumphantly halfway up and was overlooked by a huge family portrait of Saddam, his wife, and his two daughters and sons in earlier, happier years. From the ages depicted in the tableau, I guessed it dated from the early 1980s. The portrait had been rendered in different colored laminates of fine marble; pink marble had been used for the Hussein family's faces and hands.

The palace had a private dental clinic and a beauty salon

decorated in tones of mauve and pink. Pictures of Britney Spears lay randomly on the floor. Upstairs were several huge bathrooms with gilded taps and step-down baths. The furniture was mainly chinoiserie and reproduction antique French pieces, heavy on the gilt. In one bedroom a carved teak love seat covered with a little girl's doll collection sat near a large window with a view out to the Tigris. Another bedroom was entirely pink and reeked of perfume. I noticed that all the bedrooms' river views were obscured by high spiked metal fences. Children's scooters lay around the floors in some of the reception rooms. In one bedroom, a brand-new McCullough chain saw sat on a sofa next to the bed, its yellow box on the floor. There were four more chain saws, still in their boxes, in the walk-in closet. A refrigerator in another bedroom was stocked with rows of Clarins Extra-Firming Concentrate, Gentle Night Cream, and Eye Contour Gel; there was also a crate of Iranian kiwifruit and tins of Korean red ginseng drink. In that same bedroom, there was a large-screen Sony television, a PowerJOG exercise unit, several Christian Dior eyeglass cases, and, on the floor next to the bed, a picture book titled *A Day in the Life of Spain*.

I did some looting of my own. Spotting a back-support seat cushion in a bedroom, which appeared to have belonged to one of Saddam's daughters, I picked it up and took it with me. I had been without the able ministrations of the physiotherapist Nabil for ten days or so, and my backache had returned.

We moved on to another palace, where a marine told the photographers with me not to take any pictures of the troops, because they were "intel." We walked past a marine officer defecating into a milk crate while reading a copy of *Playboy*. He waved at us as we passed. Some young marines were hanging out around a Humvee festooned with photos from what looked like a perfume ad showing two women in an intimate pose, and one of them called out to ask whether I had any news of the war. "We don't have a clue what's going on," he said. I told him what I knew. He appeared keenly interested, but his friends looked bored. One asked me whether it was true that Madonna and J.Lo had died together in a car accident. Not that I knew of, I said. The marine said: "That's good. Boy, I sure wish Madonna was here right now." He laughed in a lewd, boyish way, and so did his friends.

As we left the compound, we passed some marines sitting on the curb of the palace driveway, eating MREs. Most of them were also smoking cigars. They waved in a friendly way. "Are those Cuban cigars?" I asked. "From the Man's private stash?" A few of the marines smiled slyly and gave me the thumbs-up sign. "Only the best for us," one of them said with a laugh. Outside the palace, on the avenue running along the line of riverside villas, there were thuggish men in cars cruising by. Some of the cars were loaded up with loot. The men stared at us. We darted across the traffic and made our way back through the side streets. The men at the barricades were unsmiling, but they let us pass. We heard gunshots here and there.

On the drive back to the hotel, I noticed that the sky was blue again. Saddam's oil fires had stopped burning. But on the skyline I could see new plumes of black smoke, billowing up from government buildings that had been set on fire. No one appeared to be putting them out. Motorists were racing up the wrong side of the roads, straight into oncoming traffic, and overtaking on any side they liked, as if there were no rules anymore.

At Fardous Square, the marines had established stringent new security measures. Razor wire had been looped across the road approaches to the Palestine and Sheraton. Marines manned roadblocks on Sadoun Street, stopping and searching all cars trying to enter the zone. Sabah tried to get around this by driving past the line of waiting cars toward some marines in the road. Smiling ingratiatingly, he waved and called out, "Hey, Gus!" (Gus and Jim were names Sabah had suddenly started using the day before interchangeably, calling them out loudly whenever he

came across a marine) and gave them the thumbs-up signal. The
marines looked blankly at him; then one curtly ordered him to
back up and pull over like everybody else. Sabah did so, but then
he threw a fit. He braked his car angrily and yanked his door
open. He spluttered with fury. That was it, he said, he would
take no more, he was going home, he had had it. I told him to
calm down, explaining that the marines were only doing this for
security reasons, that they had just come out of battle, that they
were young, were afraid of suicide bombers, and so forth. "But
they know me!" he yelled. "I've just been through here an hour
ago." He pointed to one young marine standing nearby: "I talked
with him."

Sabah's pride was deeply wounded. For years his life had re-
volved around the same safe and familiar rituals. Every day for
many years he had earned his living by driving from his home to
the Al-Rasheed to the Ministry of Information and back again.
He had derived great satisfaction from the small ways he had
found to bend the rules to his own whims, such as his illegal U-
turns on the highway in front of the Al-Rasheed, and parking his
car in the hotel's reserved VIP spaces in exchange for small
amounts of baksheesh to Iraqi policemen. All of that had precip-
itately ended, and now he was having to submit to orders given
by gun-toting nineteen-year-old boys from Kentucky and Ten-
nessee who didn't speak his language.

Back at the Sheraton, the hotel manager stood in the doorway,
looking distressed. I asked him what was wrong. He said: "I have
seen my beautiful city destroyed, first by Saddam Hussein and
now by these people." He pointed outside to the marines on the
street. "Why must this happen? Who will rebuild it? Why does
this happen always to Iraq? Is it because of our oil?"

On Friday morning, April 11, the U.S. Army withdrew its
tanks from the bridges over the Tigris. Almost immediately

a flood of vehicles poured across the river, and the plundering of western Baghdad began.

I had been up until dawn that morning. After a few hours' sleep I woke up at midday but still felt exhausted. I sent word to Dr. Waleed that we should wait for one more day to begin our hunt for Ala Bashir. In the afternoon I decided to go see how Ali, the burned and armless boy, was doing at the Al-Kindi Hospital. When Sabah and I got there, we found its gates chained shut and a group of Iraqi men with turbans and robes standing around them. A male nurse among them informed me that the hospital had been threatened by a mob of looters, and its staff had fled. Al-Kindi's patients had since been evacuated to other hospitals. He told me that the boy, Ali, was still alive and was now in a hospital in Saddam City. I asked Sabah to drive me to Saddam City. We argued about this. Sabah said that it was too dangerous to go there. I became angry with him and said that if he wasn't willing to take me, I would find another driver who would. At last, Sabah shut up and began driving, but he was furious with me.

We passed through a checkpoint manned by marines on the outskirts of Saddam City and drove in. Almost immediately, the paved road fell apart into a badly patched track with large potholes and huge puddles of standing water. We passed hundreds of people heading on foot to the slum, burdened with stolen goods from their looting expeditions in the city. I began to feel uncomfortable when I saw roadblocks on the road ahead—crude, zigzag gauntlets made out of oil drums and furniture and cement blocks. Rough-looking youths stood alongside them holding iron bars. In the alleyways between the hovels lining the road, I saw men with guns. In one alley, I spotted a stolen fire engine; in another, a big red double-decker Faw bus, one of the new city passenger buses Saddam had recently imported from China.

At the first roadblock the men standing there yelled at Sabah and tried to open my door and pull me out. He spoke to them urgently. They let my door go, and we drove slowly on. Sabah looked fixedly ahead and did not speak. He was breathing in a tight way through pursed lips. We made it through a couple of more such roadblocks and arrived at the first of Saddam City's two hospitals. A large group of armed youths were standing around behind the closed gates, and some of them surged toward us as we approached. They looked unfriendly, but after Sabah spoke to them, explaining why we had come, they opened the gates, eyeing me intently all the while. They locked the gates behind us. I got out of the car and was immediately surrounded. I noticed that men were searching Sabah's car. They began asking me questions in Arabic. They were very suspicious of me. Who was I? Was I American? Why had I come? Sabah spoke to them, but he was behaving in a strangely passive way, and he stood away from me.

I became very afraid but tried to conceal it. A young man with the look of a religious student marched up to me and shouted at me, in English, that Saddam City and its hospitals were now under the control of Islamic religious scholars. Was I aware of this? he demanded.

I began to relive a particularly terrifying experience I'd had many years before, in Gaza, when a mob of Palestinian men had grabbed me in a moment of confusion, during a standoff with the Israeli Army in which a young Palestinian man had been shot and bled to death. His friends had hustled me down an alleyway to a construction site behind a half-built mosque and thrown me against a wall. They accused me of being an Israeli, a Jew. They did not believe me when I told them that I wasn't. They kept shouting: "*Yahud, yahud*—Jew, Jew," and all of them began picking up pieces of concrete and stones. I felt sure they were going to stone me to death when someone at the edge of the mob spoke up. He said he recognized me. That person, I am convinced, saved my life.

The religious student in Saddam City looked at me expectantly, waiting for my reply. No, I told him, I had been unaware of the Islamic takeover of the hospital. I repeated that I had come to see Ali, the burned boy. He told me that the boy was not there, but at a different hospital. Would I like to meet the sheikh who was now in charge of the hospital? Yes, I replied, trying to look interested. After a minute or two a couple of imams with turbans and robes and scraggly beards came through the crowd. One of them appeared to be the figure of authority. I nodded as he spoke, but I did not really listen to what he was saying, except to register the fact that he and the men around us were the followers of the militant Shiite cleric Moqtada al-Sadr. The sheikh said that it was their belief that the United States had maliciously orchestrated the sacking of Baghdad, which was still going on, and that because of this, they were assuming the control of public security and essential services in Saddam City. (Within a couple of days, Sadr's men had secured the slum, with its population of some 2.5 million people, and renamed it Sadr City, after his late father, the revered imam who had been murdered on Saddam's orders.)

After saying his piece, the sheikh went back inside the hospital, and I was left with the mob. Just then a man walked through the crowd toward me. He had a familiar face and did not appear to be Iraqi. I recognized him as an Arab presenter for Al Jazeera television. He walked up to me and in good English, in a low voice, he said: "What are you doing here?" I explained why I had come but told him that now all I wanted to do was leave. He muttered: "I do too." Then he asked me, very quietly: "Are you an American?" I said I was. He shook his head from side to side, looking cross. He explained that he had come out to the slum because he'd heard about the Sadr takeover of the hospitals but didn't like the atmosphere. He was trying to negotiate with the vigilantes for an armed escort to get out. He had an anxious look on his face. He told me to stay where I was. I had managed to maneuver myself through the crowd until I was standing next to Sabah's car, but there were still militiamen all around me, staring at me and talking among themselves. The Arab returned a moment later and said tersely: "Get in your car and follow us."

The Sadr men had apparently refused to send an escort vehicle but agreed to send one of their men in the Arab's car. Sabah and I drove out of the hospital behind his car and tried to stick as close to him as we could. We watched as they had a shouting match at the first roadblock, where the vigilantes seemed reluctant to let them through, but after a few minutes they waved them on, and allowed us to follow. After the last roadblock the Sadr man hopped out of the Arab's car. Once we were out of Saddam City, the Arab's car roared off at high speed. Sabah and I drove on in silence for several minutes. Then he shot me an I-told-you-so look and said: "Mr. Jon Lee—" and broke off to shake his head significantly. He twizzled one finger against his temple and said: "Sabah, he crazy? Or Mr. Jon Lee crazy? Who crazy? No more Saddam City. OK?"

(I never saw the burned and mutilated boy, Ali (whose full name was Ismael Ali Abbas), again, but I eventually learned that he survived his wounds. After extensive treatment in a Kuwait hospital, Ali was taken to London, where he was fitted with prosthetic arms. In April 2005, he traveled to the United States for further medical care. I never saw the Arab Al Jazeera man again either, but several months later, I was watching the evening news at home in England and recognized his face on my television screen. He was identified as Tayssir Allouni, a Syrian-born Spanish émigré. He had been arrested at his home in Granada, Spain, on charges of being a high-level "messenger" for Al Qaeda.)

The next morning, Saturday, I returned to the Al-Wasati hospital to collect Dr. Waleed. The American marines were still there, guarding the place. Waleed looked much more relaxed than he had two days before. He told me that the marines had promised him they would stay at the hospital indefinitely, until the situation had calmed down. I asked about Paul Pasquale. Waleed said he had been evacuated back to Great Britain the day before.

As we left the hospital, I noticed that some of the marines were standing guard over four Iraqi men kneeling on the ground and facing the wall, their hands clasped behind their heads. Dr. Waleed explained that the men had been driving a stolen Red Crescent ambulance, and the marines had captured them. We came across several other marines talking with an excitable group of young Iraqi men. One of Waleed's doctors was translating what they were saying. The Iraqis were asking the marines to help them look for their relatives. They were pointing to an especially ugly and sinister-looking building next door to the Al-Wasati, which I had never really noticed before. It stood about four stories high but was entirely windowless above the ground level. It was a Mukhabarat building, they were saying, and there was a prison on the top floors. It had been evacuated, and the cells had already been searched, but they believed there was a secret underground prison beneath the building. Neighbors in the area claimed they had heard men's cries coming from the building as recently as a couple of days before. The Iraqis wanted the marines' help to find the secret dungeon.

Led by a young lieutenant, six or seven marines carrying their guns and flashlights set off toward the building with the Iraqi men. Dr. Waleed and I followed them. The place was dark, without electricity, and the ground floor was awash in several inches of stinking raw sewage. We climbed the stairs and looked through some of the cells, the doors of which were open. They were horrid dank cubicles. A powerful stench emanated from them. It was a familiar stink, and then I realized why: I had smelled it in certain zoos in very poor countries, the reek of accumulated filth and sweat and excrement.

We found the dispensary, and the marines began examining some of the medicines and the ledger. Dr. Waleed translated the labels for them. The young Americans speculated aloud about the possibility that the prisoners had been used as guinea pigs for secret medical experiments by Saddam's regime. Dr. Waleed dismissed the notion, but he observed that many of the prisoners had been prescribed medicines for the treatment of parasites and infections and gastroenteritis, which he explained were characteristic complaints for prisoners held in Iraq's jails.

The marines began clambering down the dark stairwells, intent on looking for a trapdoor or some secret chamber that might lead them to the dungeons. The Iraqi men who were hunting for disappeared brothers and fathers and cousins followed them in a state of thrall, with unwavering eyes; they dogged the Americans' steps like people who believed they had found their saviors. In one of the stairwells we came across a big box filled with long strips of cheap cloth: prisoners' blindfolds.

Waleed and I had seen enough. As we said our good-byes, Dr. Waleed told the young American lieutenant leading the group that he appreciated what he and his comrades were trying to do, but that it was pointless, because he really didn't think there were any underground cells. As we walked away, Waleed told me: "Everyone in this country wants to believe there are these underground prisons, because they hope to find their missing relatives alive. I don't think there are any. The people they are looking for are probably dead."

As we walked back toward the hospital, Waleed told me the story of a hospital colleague who had vanished after being inexplicably picked up by the Mukhabarat a few years before. After about two years he had reappeared, gaunt and unwell. He had lost half his normal body weight. The doctor had informed Waleed that he had been held in that very same prison, right next door to the hospital. Once or twice, for one reason or another, he had been taken to a lower-floor room with tightly grilled windows, and his blindfold had been removed. He had spotted Dr. Waleed and some of his other colleagues obliviously coming and going from the Al-Wasati. During all that time, said Waleed, neither he nor any of his fellow doctors had any idea that their colleague was there.

Sabah drove us across the river to the west side of Baghdad without incident. On the other side of the river, virtually every government building we passed was being looted, and a number of them were ablaze. As we passed the Al-Rasheed Hotel, we saw that, despite all the warnings, it had survived the war intact, but now it too was being looted. A number of cars and trucks had pulled up to the front steps, and we could see men carrying furniture out the front door. Sabah was shocked by this sight. The Al-Rasheed was the last bastion of his former life that had remained untouched. We all had expected the Americans to take it over and to use it as one of their bases. But we saw no Americans anywhere near the place. "Why, Mr. Jon Lee?" Sabah exclaimed in plaintive bewilderment. I had no answers for him. I was dismayed and angry that my countrymen were simply standing by and watching as Baghdad was sacked and burned. It made no sense at all.

Just past the Al-Rasheed, we drove by a group of men who were wheeling stolen hospital gurneys, complete with attached IV bottles and drip tubes, along the side of the highway. We passed another group behaving merrily and dressed as if they were heading off to a costume ball, with ornate peaked hats and dress jackets with epaulets and brass buttons, like those worn by a military marching band.

We proceeded cautiously through the city, with no clear sense of which areas were safe and which weren't. Here and there gun battles were still taking place. Dr. Waleed asked if we could stop in at his family's home, which was nearby. He explained that it had stood empty since the week before, when he had evacuated his wife and children to Samarra, a town to the north of Baghdad, near Saddam's hometown of Tikrit, where he had relatives. He was beginning to get worried, however, because of news reports that the Americans were about to launch an offensive against Tikrit. He had not heard from his family since they'd left and had no means to contact them by telephone.

Waleed's house was still intact, thanks to some watchful neighbors. As we spoke with them, we watched looters cruise by in both directions. Shots rang out. Waleed explained that the residents were shooting off their guns to warn the looters away. Along the side of the road, scores of young men were trudging past on foot. Most of them looked as though they had already been walking for hours. They looked thirsty and hot. All were headed south. "They are soldiers," Waleed said. He pointed to some discarded pieces of military uniform lying along the road. His neighbors nodded and said that since the previous day, many hundreds of soldiers had been walking by, on their way home from Baghdad and cities farther north. They had handed out bread and water to as many of the men as they could. All of them were from frontline army units that had chosen to lay down their arms and abandon their positions rather than fight. Most had already changed into civilian clothes. Waleed stopped a couple of the walking men. They confirmed they were askari—soldiers. One said he had come from Kirkuk and was on his way home to Basra, in the far south of Iraq.

As we took our leave, Waleed noticed people moving around in the garden of a house two doors down from his. He called out to them in a friendly fashion. They waved back. Smiling broadly, Waleed remarked: "This is remarkable. This was the house of an old friend, Ali Bilal, whose son was picked up by Saddam's secret police in 1980, accused of what we don't know. He never returned. He was obviously killed. Afterward the regime made the family leave the house and prohibited them from ever living in it again. It has been twenty-three years since it was inhabited. These people must be family members, but it has been so long I don't recognize them." He pointed out some fresh graffiti that had been spray-painted on the garden wall. He translated: "This is the house of Ali Bilal. His family returns with their heads held high." As we walked away, Waleed smiled happily. Over and over, he repeated: "This is good. This is very good."

When we were back in the car, Waleed gave Sabah directions to the home of Ala Bashir's sister. We crossed a traffic circle that was heavily shot up from a firefight the previous day between Arab fedayeen and the Americans. We drove down some residential side streets into a middle-class neighborhood and negotiated a couple of ad hoc roadblocks manned by local men, some with guns. We drove into the street where Bashir's sister lived, and Dr. Waleed pointed excitedly ahead of us to an unremarkable two-story house behind a garden wall and said: "That's it." He craned forward to look as we drove up alongside. "I am afraid he is not there." Waleed's words carried an ominous portent. We had discussed what we believed might have happened to Ala Bashir. Both of us feared that he had been spirited away by Saddam and was either already dead or else with him, living as a hunted fugitive on the run. There were no cars out front, and no one was visible in the front garden. Just across the street was parked a large truck that looked as though it had been stolen.

Dr. Waleed told me to wait in the car. He got out and went to the front gate of the house. A young woman, who I later learned was one of Bashir's nieces, appeared and opened the gate. Waleed went in. A few moments later he was back at the gate, smiling broadly and waving to me to come in.

As I walked in, Ala Bashir came striding up the driveway, dressed in jeans and a checked shirt. He was wearing a big smile, and his face wore a look of immense relief. Normally an undemonstrative man who shied from public displays of emotion, Bashir embraced me and Waleed and kissed us both on the cheeks. I noticed that his clothes were disheveled and he was unshaved; it looked as though he had about a week's growth of beard. I had always seen Bashir looking scrupulously clean, smooth-shaven, in freshly laundered and ironed shirts. He said he was very glad to see me and waved me inside. I asked him about his stubble. He grabbed his chin and laughed, looking embarrassed. "I meant to shave today. I will shave tonight." It occurred to me that perhaps he had no razors, and I said I could bring him some. He said: "No, no, I have razors, it's just . . ." He didn't finish; he waved his arms as if everything that had happened to him was too much to explain.

Ala Bashir's sister, Soheila, greeted me shyly and a bit watchfully. She was a short, pleasant-faced older woman with intelligent eyes and close-cropped white hair under a black headscarf. Her husband, Abu Ahmed, a thin man with glasses, a retired English teacher, shook my hand. Abu Ahmed ushered us into the living room. His wife and daughters stayed in the kitchen, preparing tea.

For several minutes Bashir could not stop smiling. He explained that on Friday, April 4, he had gone, as usual, to the presidential hospital on the western side of the city, inside the palace complex. He explained to me, for the first time, that he was one of the members of Saddam's private medical team and that once every week he reported in for a twenty-four-hour stint of duty, which ran from 8:00 AM one day until 8:00 AM the next. His duty-call had coincided with the battle for the Baghdad airport, which he knew about from listening to BBC radio reports. He had obtained permission to leave early on Friday—at 6:00 PM—because his elderly mother, who lived with another of his sisters, was unwell, and he wanted to go see her. Bashir was told to stay in the western part of the city, however, so he agreed to go afterward to his home, in the Al-Jihad neighborhood, not far from the airport. He was to remain there on call until further notice.

Bashir understood this order to mean that he was on some kind of presidential alert because, as he said, "I know that the president never left the west of Baghdad, which means he wanted me to be close by." While he was at home on Saturday, he could hear the sound of fighting coming from the airport, and he also heard news reports that the airport had been taken by the Americans. At about 6:00 PM one of the president's top security men came to his home. When he saw who the officer was, Bashir understood that Saddam had sent him personally. The officer instructed Bashir to come with him "immediately, immediately," to Kadhimiyah, an outlying neighborhood on the western side of the Tigris, where there was a secret presidential medical facility used only in times of national emergency. The man told him to pack a bag with some clothes and bring it with him. The officer's order and his tense demeanor alarmed Bashir, and he resolved to try to escape. He explained: "I knew that if I went, this meant I'd never come back." He didn't believe he would really be taken to the clinic, he said, but to some secret hiding place of Saddam's. He knew that Saddam had many safe houses in Baghdad, because he had been in some of them with him during the Gulf War.

Bashir told the officer to go on ahead; he would collect a few of his things and follow him in his own car within a few minutes. "Please go as quickly as you can," the man said anxiously before he sped off. Instead Bashir told his driver (Waleed's missing chauffeur) to take him to his sister Soheila's nondescript house, more or less confident that Saddam's people did not know its location. He had been there ever since, in hiding.

(After dropping off Ala Bashir, the driver had gone to his own home in eastern Baghdad. The next morning the Americans had entered the city, and he had been trapped there. That was why he had been unable to return to the Al-Wasati Hospital.)

I had brought my portable Thuraya satphone along with me. I asked Bashir if he wanted to call his wife and daughter in Amman. "Oh, yes, thank you," he exclaimed gratefully. "They have no idea about me." He had not spoken to them in ten days. We went outside into the garden, where we could get a clear satellite signal. I dialed the number he gave me, then handed him the phone and walked away to give him privacy. His relatives had gathered outside the front door of the house to watch. Ala Bashir spoke in a soft, reassuring voice and laughed a lot. After a few moments he ended the call. "They were so relieved," he said, laughing. "Everything is good now; they know I am fine." In an affectionately scolding tone, he added: "What is it about people, why they have to cry when they are happy? I have never understood this." He shook his head, still smiling.

As we sat talking, another visitor arrived. It was Samir Khairi, Ala Bashir's friend from the Foreign Ministry. I had not seen him since the eve of the war. Samir was dressed in a suit and looking very dapper. He greeted us warmly. He too had come in the hopes of finding Bashir. After they had caught up, the conversation turned to the latest news, which was that the Americans had bombed the family home of Barzan al-Tikriti, Saddam's half brother, in the town of Ramadi, west of Baghdad. Barzan was the former chief of Iraqi intelligence, and I knew him to be an old friend and acquaintance of Ala Bashir's. The Americans were speculating that Barzan had been killed in the bombing. Samir turned to me and said: "I know this is not true. Barzan is still alive." He did not say how he knew this. Later, after Samir departed, Bashir told me that Samir was in fact a long-term Mukhabarat official and had worked off and on with Barzan for many years. His recent Foreign Ministry posting was just a cover. Both Samir and Bashir said they believed that Saddam Hussein was still alive too.

Bashir explained that the Adhamiyah mosque, where Saddam had been sighted on Wednesday, April 9, at around the same time as the U.S. marines pulled down his statue in Fardous Square, was in a neighborhood right across the Tigris from Kadhimiyah. That was where Bashir had been ordered to go on April 5. He said he believed Saddam's choice of these adjacent neighborhoods to be very significant. He pointed out that Adhamiyah was an old Baathist stronghold, easily accessible to Kadhimiyah via a bridge. Both neighborhoods were along the river, and both were situated at the outer edges of the city, offering an easy means of escape. He pointed out that north of Baghdad, the Tigris River valley led all the way to Saddam's hometown of Tikrit and that a large area of countryside along the way was the fiefdom of a tribal leader who was a very close ally of Saddam's.

After spending several hours with Bashir, I left, promising to return the next day. Sabah and I returned to the Sheraton, where John Burns and Paul McGeough proposed we take a trip to visit the Salaam Palace, which, like most of the other palaces, was in the process of being ransacked. The palace was one of the most emblematic of Saddam's trophy buildings, the one with four bizarrely helmeted bronze heads of Saddam staring out from its star-shaped parapets, and this was our first opportunity to see inside it. It had been hit by cruise missiles a few days into the American bombing campaign, and we had seen its dome wrecked, but only from a distance.

The palace gates were open, and we drove in past looters wheeling booty out. We entered by the front steps, where a gang had hauled out an entire baroque imitation Louis XIV living room set, done up in gilt with gold-colored cushions. It was ready to be loaded on a truck and taken away. Inside, various groups of men worked methodically in rooms they had apparently seized as their respective turfs, stacking up and hauling away gigantic couches, mirrors, banquet tables, and wall decorations. Others were busy removing bathroom fittings and light fixtures from halls and rooms that had already been stripped bare. Here and there, in dark recesses of the palace, fires had been lit so that the men could see in the darkness. We climbed up to the top floor, where the missiles had punched through the dome. The view of the city was glorious. Saddam's massive bronze busts still stared out in all directions.

We decided to drive over to the Triumph Leader Museum, which was nearby, where Saddam's priceless gifts were exhibited, including the gun I had seen that had killed Colonel Gerard Leachman. As we approached, coming up a divided boulevard, we passed a van that looked as though it had crashed into the small trees in the median strip. Its tires were blown out, and it had settled messily onto the verge there. As we drove around it, I noticed a man and two boys, clearly his young sons, wielding a shovel and some other tools. I saw that there was a dead body, or perhaps two, lying sprawled half out of the van. At first I thought the father and his sons were there to retrieve a relative who had been killed or were planning to bury the dead people. Then I realized that they were trying to dig out the van, to put it up on blocks. They had a small flatbed truck nearby. I assumed they were going to try somehow to get the van onto the back of the truck. They were looters. About two hundred yards away, a U.S. Army Bradley Fighting Vehicle was parked on a side street in the shade. I could see the shape of a helmeted American soldier on top, manning the turret machine gun, apparently resting.

We drove up the lane to the entrance of the Triumph Leader Museum. A large truck and several cars had pulled up, and a couple of dozen men were coming and going, industriously carrying items out of the museum and loading them into the vehicles. Some of them appeared to be workers, hired by other men, who were standing outside. They looked at us furtively. We walked in. A man walked along the empty glass display cabinets in the foyer, smashing the glass with a metal rod. Smoke was coming out from the lower recesses of the museum, where the pendulum clock swung. The gilded Kalashnikovs that had adorned it were gone. Fires had been lit down there, and some men were working on something with torches. We did not linger. Almost everything was gone from the exhibition rooms: all the jeweled watches and throne chairs and priceless guns. Only some paintings of Saddam remained, in a variety of poses. We went back outside.

One of the workers was carrying a gold-plated sniper rifle I thought I recognized as the one that had been given to Saddam by the former head of the Soviet KGB. I walked over to examine the gun. The men stopped what they were doing and looked warily at me. I made placatory gestures to indicate that I merely wanted to see it. They let me look at the weapon for a second and took it away again. One of the men in the truck brandished another trophy weapon. It was a much older, long-barreled rifle and looked a lot like the Leachman gun, but it may not have been. I saw that one of the men standing near me had a revolver tucked into his trousers under his shirt. He was eyeing me in a way I didn't like. I thanked them, walked back to where John and Paul and Sabah waited, and told them I thought we should leave. The smoke was pouring out of the museum now. Several cars with men inside them patroled up and down the lane watchfully.

We drove past the van with the dead bodies, where the man and his sons were still hard at work in their preparations to steal it. The Bradley was still parked just down the street.

I visited Ala Bashir every day for the next two weeks. He was still uncertain what to do with himself, and for the time being had resolved to lie low. He seemed grateful for my company, which gave him a kind of lifeline to the outside world. He also agreed to talk to me about his long relationship with Saddam Hussein. We usually sat in the family room, left alone by his relatives, who periodically interrupted us to bring us small cups of Turkish coffee and, in the early afternoon, to call us to lunch. Bashir's brother-in-law, Abu Ahmed, pottered in the garden, which had a fig tree, a date palm, a love seat, and a bed of fresh red carnations. Bashir's sister, Soheila, was very protective of him; she worried about his safety and did not want him to stray from the house. One day, when Bashir suggested that we go talk in his own home, for a change of scene, she adamantly opposed the idea. He shrugged and said that it was up to me; he didn't mind one way or the other. He dismissed any notion that he might be in danger, although I had my doubts about this.

Abu Ahmed had already confided to Sabah that Ala Bashir was so identified in people's minds as "the doctor of Saddam Hussein" that he and his wife feared he could be an assassination target. He mentioned the incident several years before when Bashir had been attacked and stabbed twice by a man who was later caught and sentenced to several years' imprisonment in Abu Ghraib. The stabbing had been politically motivated, he told Sabah. Worryingly, the assailant had been released into the streets during Saddam Hussein's postreferendum victory amnesty in October 2002, and Bashir's relatives thought it was possible that the man might seek revenge. This was not the first I had heard of the attack; a couple of months earlier Bashir had told me about it but claimed it had been carried out by one of his patients who was mentally imbalanced. Knowing Bashir's tendency to downplay everything, I imagined that his brother-in-law's version of events might be the truer one, and so I told him that I thought it best that we stay put for our conversations.

In one of our first meetings I challenged Bashir on his friendship with Iraq's dictator. "How could you, a man of culture and education," I asked, "have such a close relationsip with Saddam Hussein, knowing about all the things that he had done?"

Bashir closed his eyes briefly and after a pause, said: "Maybe, very briefly, I can tell you. . . . It was my talents as an artist that brought me to this situation. In the late seventies I got to know the military adviser to Saddam Hussein when he was still the vice president. His name was Ghassam Ibrahim. He was a very brave and honest man; he was killed later by Saddam Hussein, of course. . . . I had done an art exhibition, and Saddam Hussein had written about it in the newspaper. He had written that my art was 'unique.' Ghassam told me that Saddam Hussein was talking about me, and he offered to take me to see him, but I refused. I don't like this thing of meeting people because they are powerful. Barzan al-Tikriti also used to come to my exhibitions, and he told me the same things about how much Saddam Hussein admired my work."

Bashir's first meeting with Saddam did not come until 1983. "In the early eighties, during the Iran-Iraq War, I did a lot of work on the war wounded, and I invented some new techniques in plastic surgery. I did the first reimplantations of hands and fingers in Iraq. In 1982 the health minister invited twenty-five of Iraq's most outstanding doctors to meet the president, and I was included in this group. 'The president wants to praise your work,' he told me. So I went. The president gave a speech and shook hands with everybody. That was it. Afterward one of his guards came to me and told me to go and speak with the president. I did. He said: 'I was really surprised to know you were the same Ala Bashir as the artist.' He praised my work and said: 'We are very proud of you.' Soon afterward I was chosen as one of the doctors in his medical team.

"It was strange, you know, because he looked down on doctors. But he always saw me as something else. And he always told me, and several times, in public in front of other people: 'I see you not as a doctor but as an artist, as a man of culture.' Sometimes, on a few occasions, he'd call me to him just to talk. One day he came to the hospital—I was there with other doctors, doing something—with his son Qusay. We were standing up because this is the custom in the regime; you couldn't be seen sitting down if the president was there. Then he came up and said of me, in front of everyone: 'He is a brilliant surgeon, a great artist, and, above all, a great man.' Then he left. Afterward Qusay returned and said: 'What have you done for my father? This is the first time I've heard my father speak this way about anyone!' He was very surprised.

"Once, in the late eighties, a lady interviewed me on TV, and the next day the chief of the presidential guard sent for me. He told me the president had watched the program and had been very impressed. And he said the same thing as Qusay. So then I began to wonder what it was about this interview that interested him. In the television studio they had hung a painting I had done of man's destiny; it showed a man holding up a grim-looking bird, like a raven, and the bird was trying to bite the man's face. It's a very strong image. I had explained to the interviewer that the painting represented man's struggle with destiny, and that in this battle man always lost. I also said that when men came to have a lot of power and began to think of themselves as immortal, then it's all over, they lose the battle. To find an example of what I meant, I quoted a famous Iraqi poet, Mutanabbi, who is perhaps one of our greatest poets ever: 'The most bitter experience for a free man is to make a friendship with someone he doesn't like.'

"Saddam Hussein had liked the interview, but his guard chief told me that he was very upset with the lady announcer because she had asked me about my baldness. He thought she had upset or embarrassed me. He sent orders for her not to be allowed on TV for six months. But I am not upset by such things. I told the president's man this, but he said: 'The president has ordered this.'" Ala Bashir shrugged.

"On February 1, 1991, during the Gulf War, which I remember began on January 17, Saddam Hussein had some kind of accident, and I used to see him every other day. He never said precisely what had happened, but it looked to me like a car accident. He had a sharp, deep cut on the left side of his chin, right down to the bone, and the small finger of his right hand was almost hanging off. His son-in-law Saddam Kamal, the brother of Hussein Kamal—both of whom, as you know, he later had killed—was also wounded, in the lower lip, and a lady, whom I knew to be his second wife, Samira Shahbander, was also wounded. She had a facial fracture and a deep cut in her right eyebrow. So I treated him and them too, and I saw him every other day for a time, and we had long chats. One day he said: 'I came to know you very well from the TV interview you gave in 1986. You said only a few things, but they were all things which are essential to life.' "

I noticed that Bashir had not answered my question. He was telling me why he thought Saddam Hassein had been attracted to him, but not his own motivations. I changed tack and asked him about Saddam Hussein's personality. Bashir said: "He is really very sensitive and emotional, although he looks very tough. And he has a very suspicious personality. You have to select your words very carefully when you are with him."

"Did you feel afraid of him?"

"No, never in my life did I feel frightened of him. I know many others did, but I don't know why, I just didn't."

"But you knew about the things he did."

"I knew, yes," replied Bashir.

"So, how did you feel toward him?"

After a very long pause Bashir replied: "I think he has done a lot of evil things to Iraq. . . . But in our conversations he respected me a lot, and I spoke to him freely in a way I don't think anyone else did. Barzan al-Tikriti told me that not even he dared to speak to him in such a way. 'He deeply respects you,' he told me once. 'Did you perform magic on him?' "

"Did you ever use this respect he had for you to try and influence him?"

"No," replied Bashir. "Because he was very suspicious of everything, and he measured everything you said to him." He looked thoughtful, as if aware that his explanation was unsatisfactory. After a moment he said: "He was very depressed about the uprising of the people against him in 1991. He really believed the people of Iraq loved him. I went to see him in Radwaniyah, the palace near the airport. He spoke of the uprising, and he said: 'I don't think they are really Iraqis.' I said nothing. I was very surprised. He had never spoken in this way to me before. He asked: 'Why do you think these people have done this?'

I replied: 'I don't know. I am a doctor, and my relationships with other kinds of people are very limited.' He said: 'OK, but I want your opinion about what has happened.' I said to him, 'Do you remember five years ago, when you chose a painting from my exhibition and afterward you asked me to come and see you? Well, I did, but you were in a meeting with your generals and were very busy, so I never got to tell you what I wanted to say. I would like to have told you this: 'If you enter a room and see two dead men, both of them shot, and are told that one is a martyr and one is a traitor, how can you tell the difference between them?'

"Saddam looked at me and asked: 'Do I know them?' I said: 'No.' He said: 'So how would I know the difference?' I said: 'The truth doesn't show itself on the surface, superficially. What appears is not always the truth. If we trust people through what they say to us, then we will make mistakes.' Then I told him: 'If you ask me right now what I think of you, I would say: "You are our president, our leader, and we will sacrifice ourselves for you." How do you know I am really telling you the truth?' He didn't say anything; he just stared at me for a long time. Then he said: 'Let us go walk in the garden.' It was beautiful, springtime—this time of year—and it had just stopped raining. That palace has very large gardens. We walked, and he kept silent for a long time. Then he said he wanted to ask my opinion about something he'd been thinking about for three days. He talked for more than twenty minutes. He talked about the uprising and he said: 'These people who are in the south are not originally Iraqis.' I didn't follow exactly what he was getting at. Then he said: 'They have no morals, their women are loose, and if they have no morals, it means they can do anything.' I think he was referring to his feelings about the Shia, although he didn't say so openly. The intifada had just started, and at this time he'd not reacted yet. Then he referred to Islam, and he said that the people in the south were not true believers in Islam. He asked me what I thought. I said, 'Right,' that's all."

"Why did you say, 'Right'?" I asked Bashir.

"Because he expected me to say something, and I couldn't say, 'You are wrong!' I remember as he was speaking I was looking at his ear. The sun was coming right through it, and it looked like wax. Because of this, I wasn't really listening to him, concentrating on what he was saying. But he was talking about being an Arab, about Islam, and he seemed to be trying to come up with a reason for their uprising against him. . . ."

"Why not say to him, 'You are wrong'?"

"I didn't think he was in the mood for someone to oppose him. I noticed that . . . You know, this is our history, long before him, for hundreds of years, people in Iraq have not been able to give their opinions frankly."

"What do you think he took away with him from the story you told him?"

"I think he gathered from what I had said that people are hypocrites. Then I told him: 'I think the Iraqi civilization is rooted deeply in the past; this country's civilization goes back five and six thousand years. Even though their religion is Islam, I think that when the Arabs of Iraq adopted Islam fourteen hundred years ago, they took some of it, but they retained much of their own culture.' He didn't say anything. Then he asked me why it was I had named my eldest son Sumer. I told him that it was because I thought Iraqis should be proud of our civilization.

"The next morning, and for two consecutive days, articles appeared in the Baathist newspaper, *Al-Thawra*. They were unsigned, but they were written by him, and everything in the articles was exactly what he had told me in the garden. I think he was making his argument to justify his repression in the south."

Ala Bashir's account of his walk in the palace garden with Saddam Hussein and his fixation on Saddam's ear rather than on what he was saying rang true to me. It seemed consistent with the man I had come to know. He was sensitive and distracted much of the time, a man who lived in his own head, more an artist than a man of science. But I wondered if his distraction at that moment, when Saddam seemed to be rationalizing what would soon be the brutal suppression of the Shia intifada, wasn't also an act of will. No doubt it must have been an unexpected and terrifying glimpse into the mind of the tyrant he was obliged to serve, and by focusing on the Great Leader's ear, he was able to escape briefly back into the illusion of his neutral role as the doctor who checked up on Saddam's corns and who was occasionally obliged to humor his questions about art. But Bashir hadn't forgotten that moment, and the fact that he recalled it to me a decade later seemed to indicate that perhaps the issue of moral compromise was not so abstract to him after all.

Most days Samir Khairi dropped by for a visit. Other people began showing up too. The word was out that Ala Bashir had survived Saddam's fall, and a stream of friends and colleagues and advice seekers came to see him. One was a male nurse I recognized from the Al-Wasati Hospital. He was wreathed in smiles and kissed Bashir, who accepted his greeting embarrassedly. We sat down together at Soheila's kitchen table. A few minutes later the nurse informed "Dr. Ala," as most Iraqis respectfully addressed him, that he was in mourning. His wife, he explained, had died of illness the previous day, and he was also about to bury his son, who had been killed in the city of Kut. Bashir murmured some words of sympathy, and I also expressed my condolences. The nurse closed his eyes and nodded his head in gratitude. I asked if his son had been killed by accident by U.S. troops while he had been out driving around. There had been such incidents ever since the Americans had entered Iraq's cities. The nurse shook his head. No, his son had died fighting the Americans. He had been a member of a Baath Party militia unit in Kut. He explained this matter-of-factly and without reproach. His son was dead, carrying out his duty, and it was over.

Another day Bashir's visitor was a senior officer in the Iraqi Army, a stern man in his early sixties. He was wearing civilian clothes. After introductions, Bashir explained that his friend was a major general and the former head of cardiac surgery at the Al-Rasheed Military Hospital, which was part of the complex I had seen rocketed by helicopter gunships on April 8. The military doctor told me that he was sitting in his home waiting, like a lot of his colleagues, for a summons by the Americans to return to work. But he did not know where that would be. His hospital had survived the rocketing but then been completely sacked by looters. We discussed the ongoing sacking of the city. He and Bashir traded conspiracy theories; both seemed to give credence to reports that the American military had in some cases allowed the looters, even assisted them, but laid the ultimate blame, as a lot of Iraqis were doing, on "Kuwaitis" who were said to be accompanying the Americans and who, widespread gossip around Baghdad had it, had orchestrated the looting in a spirit of revenge for the sacking of Kuwait City in 1990 by Iraq's army. I was circumspect about these allegations, which I didn't believe, but expressed my sorrow about the looting, particularly of Iraq's National Museum, the pillaging of which had become news in the last few days. I said that I hoped the Americans could soon get things under control, before more of Iraq's patrimony was stolen or destroyed. Looking unconvinced, the military doctor flashed me a sour smile. "What do these things matter? They've already stolen the whole country."

In these conversations, Ala Bashir always adopted a sanguine perspective. He gave credence to some of the rumors carried by his friends, such as the one about the Kuwaitis, but he laid the final blame on his fellow Iraqis. He did not mince his words. "I think this looting is part of the indigenous nature of Iraqis," he intoned. "Before Iraq was a state, this land was a desert inhabited by Bedouins, and they survived by raiding one another's camps, carrying off their belongings and their livestock. Nothing has changed. Every time there is a war in Iraq, and among all the Arabs, in fact, they rob and loot. This is unfortunately part of our nature."

One morning, a doctor from Bashir's hospital showed up with news of many gunshot patients in the Al-Wasati's wards. Bashir listened to him with visible impatience and after a few minutes saw him off. He turned to me and said disgustedly: "These people are all looters. Our patients are now all thieves. Why should we treat them? I told the doctor he should refuse to treat them." He shook his head. He was angry, but his face was impassive.

A few days after our reunion Ala Bashir left his sister's house for the first time to have lunch at Samir Khairi's home in Mansour. We went in my car, with Sabah driving, the protective wartime "TV" letters in yellow masking tape still attached to the windows. Ala Bashir made it clear that he preferred to be less obtrusive by sitting in the backseat.

At Bashir's request, we made a stop at the house of the secretary who worked at his private clinic. A short woman with dyed blond hair, she was overjoyed to see that he was safe. She asked timidly if she could use my Thuraya satellite phone to call her relatives in Detroit. When her call went through, she and her sister and mother took turns talking and weeping tears of happiness. Everyone laughed when the secretary's mother, a large, rough-voiced older woman, got on the phone, because she positively bellowed into it, and whatever she said had everyone blanching and tittering. Ala Bashir laughed too and told me she was telling her concerned relatives: "Don't worry, we are safe, and anyway, we have machines guns to defend ourselves!"

Over the next few days Bashir began making his first short trips out alone, checking on the state of his house in Al-Jihad and visiting the Al-Wasati Hospital to say hello to his colleagues. One of his former drivers, the former POW called Jihad, had reappeared, and he now drove a small white nondescript Japanese pickup truck, rather than the brand-new white government-issue Toyota Land Cruiser that he had chauffeured "Dr. Ala" around in before the war. The Land Cruiser would immediately have identified Bashir as someone of privilege from the Saddam era. As it was, whenever we were stuck in traffic, quite a few people in other cars recognized Bashir and stared at him.

On April 19, we went off together to visit Bashir's hospital and his house. He sat in the back of my car, as always, and had his driver, Jihad, follow us in the pickup. Before we left his sister and brother-in-law's house, I could see that they were fretting about his leaving, and I reassured them I would bring him back safe and sound. They smiled but looked worried. As we drove away, I asked Bashir whether he felt he had any reason to worry, and as always he dismissed the idea that he faced any real danger from anyone.

We drove past Ala Bashir's monument *The Union,* which sits in a traffic island at the western edge of the city, a kind of gateway to Baghdad for travelers arriving by road from Jordan. The Jordanian Embassy itself was situated just a couple of hundred yards away. I noticed that the monument was gouged with bullet holes, and someone had added some painted graffiti in Arabic around its base. Bashir did not comment on the defacing of his work; he looked entirely unperturbed. I asked him what the graffiti said. They were political slogans, he told me; one said "Long live Talabani" (one of the main Kurdish political leaders) and the other "Long live Sistani" (the grand ayatollah of the Shiites). He remarked, "You know, Jon, the real problems are just beginning here in Iraq. The Americans have now conquered or liberated Iraq, or whatever it is, but now they have a really tough job. I think it is going to be very, very difficult for the Americans to deal with all of the parties and the ethnic groups. They need to move fast to get things working again and to prevent these different groups from moving into the vacuum."

We saw some people walking along the side of the road, carrying green and black flags. They were Shia pilgrims, walking from Baghdad to Karbala, fifty miles to the south, as part of the annual religious festival of Arbayeen, to commemorate the end of forty days of mourning for the death of their revered marytr Imam Husein. The sight of the pilgrims unsettled Ala Bashir. "The biggest problem they must deal with quickly are these religious people. The Americans must put them in their place quickly or they will cause a lot of trouble." By birth, Bashir was a Shiite, but he was virulently anticlerical. In recent days he had told me repeatedly that he thought it was very important that post-Saddam Iraq remain an officially secular state, and he fretted about the Shia resurgence, such as Moqtada al-Sadr's takeover of Saddam City, that had begun to manifest itself since Saddam's downfall. He believed it to be orchestrated by Iran's hard-line clerics to expand their influence in Iraq and said he would not be averse if the United States decided to launch an invasion of Iran next. "It is not just me," he said. "I think many, many people in Iraq would support this, because everyone knows that Iran is the biggest troublemaker in the whole region. This is a fact."

When we reached Bashir's house, I noticed that all the cars were missing from the carport of his front garden, which was walled off from the street. He had moved them to a safe place, he told me, before the looting began. One of his sculptures, an abstract bronze of a man, stood by the front door. The face was shorn off, and he was holding it up, like a mask, in one of his hands. In the living room, I saw that Bashir had taken down most of the pictures from his wall, including those of his family, his son's wedding pictures, and the one of him standing with Saddam. Broken glass was on the floor near his living room windows, which had big gaping holes in them—"From the bombing," he explained. He led me into the kitchen, where the refrigerator doors were wide open. Before the war he had emptied them of their contents and given everything in his freezers to his neighbors. There had been no electricity in Baghdad for the past two weeks, and the house was dark.

We went through the back of the house to his studio, which was in an annex across a little open space. His painting studio was downstairs. There was a large bookcase stuffed with art books—I noticed one on Russian icons and another on Max Ernst—and medical tomes. On the floor were buckets filled with paintbrushes and paints. A large canvas on an easel faced his desk. The painting was one of his, he said, painted in 1980. It featured a reclining nude woman with voluptuous buttocks reaching up to hold a bird. A man stood above her. It was reminiscent of Rousseau's *The Dream*. A framed newsmagazine clipping hung on the wall. It showed him standing smiling next to a patient's bed. He explained that it was from an operation he had done in 1983, in which he had successfully reimplanted the hand of the man in the picture. His patient was a Hungarian technician who had been working in Iraq and who had lost his hand in an industrial accident. "It was the first successful limb reimplantation in the Middle East," he said proudly. This was the operation for which he had been selected as one of the outstanding doctors of the year and been invited to meet Saddam Hussein. He and all the other doctors had been given new cars by Saddam Hussein. He told me that it was the one and only time he had ever accepted a gift from the dictator.

We went upstairs to another room, where Bashir kept a stock of framed paintings and some small terra-cotta sculptures. Most of them featured human heads, many distorted in surreal ways, and ravens. He showed me one piece, of a raven with an open beak and three more beaks coming out of its maw. He explained: "This to me expresses the need to scream, to call out. Sometimes you feel that no matter how much you call out, it is not enough." Another piece showed a pair of heads, a male and female, side by side. The male's eyes were closed, and the female's open. A raven was tucked into the clay beneath them. He said that the piece had been inspired by a couple he knew, old friends who had been very close for many years but who then had become inexplicably divorced. The wife had later confided to him that she had never been able to sleep in their years of marriage but had lain awake, thinking. The work symbolized their dilemma, he said. As for the raven, it was the "keeper of secrets," he explained, a device he used to depict the unspoken gulf between the couple.

As we drove away from his neighborhood, a large suburban enclave of desert brown houses, most of them modest but comfortable single-story houses with walled gardens, Bashir told me that this area had been an allotment bought by the Medical Union of Iraq in the 1960s for its members. In those days, he said, it was just desert and lay well outside Baghdad. Doctors who wished to live there were able to buy lots and build houses subsidized by their union fees. Many had sold their lots in the years since, and other people had moved in, but there were still many doctors there, and it was still solidly middle class. We drove out to the main highway. Across the road I pointed out a line of nouveau-riche trophy mansionettes of the New Babylonian style favored by Saddam's cronies, gaudy places with flamboyant facades, decorated with domes and outsize pillars and gigantic front doors. It was a new neighborhood, and there were many other mansions, some only half-built, in the open land behind the houses flanking the highway. "All of those houses," he said, "belong to Saddam Hussein's guards."

At the Al-Wasati Hospital, the staff greeted Ala Bashir with surprise and characteristic reverence. Sunduz followed him around with adoring eyes and then rushed off to boil us some tea. The lobby was full of hospital beds with wounded men and boys on them, most with quite bloody wounds. I noticed a young boy with a freshly amputated arm. He had been wounded, we learned, in one of the last bombing raids by the Americans the week before, but most of the others, Bashir said, were looters who had been wounded while they were caught stealing or else in gunfights with one another. He was upset by the spectacle and told me with irritation that he didn't want to stay long. "A hospital for reconstructive surgery, full of thieves," he said with a bitter irony. We went into his office, where the Saddam portrait on the wall had been removed. A yellow rectangle marked the place where it had hung on the pale green wall. The bust of Saddam was gone from his desk.

Sunduz brought us our tea. She had been sleeping in the office since the war had begun; her cot, carefully made up, sat in the corner. Bashir told me he was worried about her future because he didn't know whether he was going to be able to keep working at the hospital. There were those on the staff who were jealous of her because of her close relationship to him. He would have to see what he could do for her.

Bashir chatted with Waleed and other members of his staff and he inquired about some of their patients, but he seemed ill at ease and anxious to leave. His brother-in-law Abu Ahmed appeared in the waiting room. Ostensibly he had come out to check on his own business, a custom furniture shop, but I had the impression that he was protectively trailing Ala Bashir around town. I asked him about his shop. He told me that he had been there, and everything was fine. It had not been looted; he had taken the precaution of removing the furniture from the showroom before the war arrived in Baghdad. But he was going to keep it shuttered for now, he said. There was no point in reopening because there were no customers to buy anything. He shrugged. When we left the hospital, Abu Ahmed climbed into his own car to follow us home.

The last time Bashir had seen Saddam Hussein had been ten weeks earlier, around the time that Colin Powell was presenting the American case against Iraq to the UN and King

Abdullah of Jordan was trying to get the United States to offer Saddam safe haven in an Arab country. "Saddam had come to the hospital to visit his aunt," he explained. "She was seriously ill. He asked me how I was, and how the construction of the new Saddam Center [a plastic surgery facility] was going on."

Saddam caught Bashir staring at a nevus, a mole, growing on his left cheek. "We'd been supposed to remove it a few months earlier," Bashir explained, "but he'd postponed the operation. He had said: 'If I do it now, people will say I have cancer or am having plastic surgery, and there will be a lot of rumors.' This time he said: 'I see you are staring at it; we'll remove it when this problem'—he meant the war—'is over.' I thought he looked tired. And he looked older to me, and in fact, from the condition of his skin and the wrinkles on his hands, I think he was actually older than his declared age. Officially he was born in 1937, but I believe he was older. A person's hand can tell you a great deal about his true age."

I pressed Bashir again on his relationship to Saddam Hussein. I asked him if he had ever been concerned about how his proximity to the dictator appeared to other people.

Bashir conceded that Saddam's constant flattery of him had made him uncomfortable and had not done him any favors. "This extra attention was bad for me," he said. "His guards and his son Uday, they didn't like me. They knew I didn't care for them. But they knew he respected me, and this was why they were afraid to touch me." He added that he had considered leaving Iraq "many, many times."

"So why didn't you?" I insisted.

"Well, I thought this was my country, and also, it is the easy thing to leave. . . ."

I became impatient. I told Bashir that for his own good he needed to confront honestly his past relationship with Saddam. He listened to me, nodding. He said: "I will tell you the truth. I don't know about Saddam Hussein, but all the people around him made a mistake. They all helped him to become who he looked like. Those surrounding him, praising him, especially the leaders of the Baath Party—they created this. And yes, of course he didn't stop this, and this . . . was his mistake, I think. . . . One day I asked him about all the pictures of himself erected all over Iraq because in fact, you know, many of these are ugly. . . . He didn't discourage this. He said to me: 'Let them express their feelings.' But the essential thing is, those who encouraged this cult of personality were the leaders of the Baath Party and the security services. . . . In later years I think he reached a point where he didn't think of himself as a president but as a sheikh, the leader of a tribe, and he acted as such, and he pushed the laws of the nation aside. He thought he was the father of the nation and what he said and did was right."

"What did you really think of Saddam?" I asked. "Was he a good man underneath it all? Did you respect him?"

Bashir pondered this for a long time. "To be honest, I think he was a victim of himself and the people surrounding him. He's like any other human being. He has something good and something bad. I think it depends upon the circumstances and the environment that make these characteristics come out more one way or the other. I think his fatal mistake was to allow the supreme power he had to overcome all the other good things inside himself. He came to power when he was young—only in his thirties. This was very young, and to have absolute power in a rich country like Iraq, this is not an easy thing. People had been suppressed. They were illiterate, overcome by superstitious ideas and thoughts. It was as though the nation were living outside the twentieth century, and even now many have ideas as if they were still living in the seventeenth century. So if you were to judge this man as if he were someone from Western Europe or the States, I think this is not fair. He had no scientific knowledge. He had never lived in the West."

Bashir became more relaxed when I asked about Saddam's

personal habits and daily life. When he was at home, he said, Saddam dressed casually. He wore jeans or else an Iraqi dish-dasha. "He almost never slept in the same house on consecutive days, and he tried not to follow routines. He never slept in the palaces, like everybody imagines, at all. He just went to them for visits and short periods. He was always on the move. To pass the time, in the last few years, he received people. He read all the newspapers, and he read books, mostly about politics. In the last few years he followed everything that was written about him, and in the last two years he wrote three books. He wrote them himself and then gave them to someone for polishing. And he was always on the television, talking for long periods about any-thing at all, even very trivial things. I did not think this was very wise. One day I told him: 'I don't know how you are able to talk for so long about such small subjects.' He looked at me. I don't think he was very pleased. He said: 'From my days in prison, when I read a lot, I have a lot of ideas about things.'"

"Do you feel sorry for him now?"

"Well, I was expecting this—that he'd be overthrown—if not this year, then the next. If not by the Americans, then by the Iraqis. Because the system was corrupted from top to bottom. I must say this: He did not agree that his guards and his relatives abused their posts. But in the end they did what they did. No-body dared tell him about Uday's corruption, for example. Uday was not just violent; he was a criminal. One day Uday sent a man to come and take one of our elevators from the hospital, to his hospital, the Olympic Hospital, which he had taken over, stolen from the state, actually, without his father's knowledge. He turned it into a private hospital, to make money. And he brought in French surgeons to do operations for him there. But he had no equipment for them to work with, so he began taking instru-ments from other hospitals. I refused when he tried to take from ours. One day his assistant came and said: 'I'd like to take your elevator, which isn't working, to Uday's hospital.' I refused. I said it was going to be fixed and that we needed it for our hospital. Uday got mad. He sent back his assistant, who threatened me. The president heard about this and formed a committee to investigate how Uday got his hospital. In the offices of the palace administration I saw a letter from Saddam Hussein to his son telling him to refrain from these actions and to leave public property alone. 'By your actions, people are talking not just against you, but against me,' it said. But in the end nothing was done, and the Olympic Hospital was even made official. Letting Uday do what he did was one of Saddam's greatest mistakes because he humiliated many Iraqis, many officials. Uday, I think, was ninety percent of Saddam's problem."

I asked Bashir whether he now regretted having been Saddam's doctor. "As a doctor you must treat a person whether he is good or bad," he replied. "It is just like being an electrician. You are doing your job as a doctor, and that is it."

"But you knew the things he'd done—"

"Yes!" said Bashir. "Sometimes, even, I would think to myself: He's a criminal. And I'd have a dialogue with myself: 'Is this the same man who does these things?' I concluded that he must have a double personality. . . . One day he asked me to treat a burned boy who had been brought to him for help by his mother. It was an old burn, on his face, which was badly disfigured. So he called me and, describing the boy to me, asked me what I could do for him. And he started crying. Really! He took tissues and wiped off his face. He was really crying."

Only once, said Bashir, had he ever witnessed Saddam's "other" personality. "Once I was asked to go see him. It was around ten AM. He was different. Normally he has a very pale skin, you know, a kind of lemon white skin, but this time his face was dark, bluish and congested, and he looked very tired. I said hello. He didn't smile; he didn't say anything. I was there to check up on him for an operation I'd done on his foot a few days before. Normally he would say hello and ask about my family and ask me to sit down, and we'd chat about current things, maybe drink some tea. . . . This time, though, there was nothing. So I had to get down to business directly. The only thing he said was: 'I am very tired; I want to go to sleep.' Later that day I realized what it was. A very important army leader was executed. Saddam himself may have been involved in his questioning. His name was Kamal Sachet. He was accused of treason. This was around 1998. . . . Sometimes, you know, he would have people executed and later it was discovered that it was false—a mistake—and the person was officially resurrected from 'traitor' to 'martyr.' These things are dealt with in low profile, and the family is usually apologized to and given compensation and a full allowance. If the man is a traitor, the family gets nothing, not even a pension."

Ala Bashir evinced a certain pride in his recollection of Saddam's words of praise. I couldn't help thinking that constant flattery from the dictator had had a seductive effect. When I asked Bashir what he thought Saddam saw in his art, he said: "I don't know. He never explained. . . . He always praised it, saying it is 'genuine.' He said: 'I don't understand it, but it is genuine and honest, and I think it is the best art in this country.' Once he even said: 'In the history of Iraq.'" Bashir chuckled ambiguously. He added: "And he never, ever forced me to do things. But he asked me to do things, very politely. For example, in 1991, he told me he had had a dream.' He said: 'I dreamed that I was walking in a forest. It was dark. Suddenly I saw a huge snake rushing toward me. My guards and I killed the snake. I cut off its head, and a few drops of its blood stained my clothes.' He said: 'I would like you to do a painting about this dream.'" Bashir had agreed to paint his dream, but like the *Epic of Saddam,* later on, he took his time about it. "After six months he saw me and asked me about the painting, and I said I had done a few sketches, but the truth was, I don't like to do portraits or to do what someone tells me. Then, in 1996, I was seeing him about some skin lesion he had, and he said: 'Look, Ala, what about that painting? You keep saying, "Two or three months," and we've been waiting a long time; it's been five years.' He seemed a bit cross. I said: 'I am almost finished with the sketch.' So then I went and finished it, and I asked a friend, a good painter, to help me execute it. He painted it, in fact, and I did the final touches. So then I gave it to him, and he was very happy. He hung it in the Triumph Leader Museum, where all his personal gifts were displayed." I told him about my visit to the museum and how all the artwork there had been either stolen or destroyed. He nodded in silence.

Except for that painting of Saddam's dream, Bashir told me, he had never done a portrait of Saddam Hussein. He believed himself to be the only Iraqi artist who could make that claim. He blamed the national frenzy of Saddam portraits and sculptures on the sycophants around Saddam. The art in his palaces and their decoration were not chosen by Saddam either, he said. "It was the people in the palace administration office, those who were in charge of furnishing his palaces, who selected the art for them. They bought from a lot of Iraqi artists. . . . The only thing they ever asked me my opinion about was the Salaam Palace, with the four heads, where he is wearing the Al-Aqsa mosque—the Dome of the Rock—on his head. While it was being completed, the palace administration people told me that the president had come and looked at these and said he didn't like the way they were fitted on the building, and he said: 'Tell Ala to come. I want his opinon.'

"So I did. I thought it was rubbish. They had the bronze heads poking out over the side of the building, and they were placed so that they had to be supported by metal bars. It looked like a commercial billboard for Mitsubishi or something! And they had crossed swords made out of bronze and bronze palm trees set along the roof between the heads. It looked very ugly. And I said these things didn't fit with the palace, and I recommended that they all should be removed, including the heads. So a week later the palace guy said the president had come and heard what I had said and said, 'OK, maybe he's right.' He ordered the removal of the palm trees and the swords, but he kept the heads." Bashir gave one of his ambiguous laughs.

A few days later I found Bashir looking rather preoccupied. This was very unusual, since he normally masked his feelings so well. I asked him if there was something wrong. He nodded. He told me that he had been watching the Al Arabiya channel on his nephew's satellite TV and had seen footage of the looted and vandalized interior of the Saddam Arts Center, Baghdad's national gallery. Nearly two dozen of his best paintings had been in the gallery's permanent collection. He saw that his works had been slashed to ribbons, and this had depressed him. "I have trained myself not to be sad because everything in life is temporary. But the destruction I saw confirmed to me how ignorant human beings are. Basically, we are not very far from the Stone Age." He mentioned that Barzan al-Tikriti had owned twelve of his paintings and guessed that they must be gone too, because Barzan's house in Baghdad had also been looted and burned.

Ala Bashir told me of a dream he had had about eight years earlier. "There was a huge sky and desert. Thousands of people were spread out in this desert. They were naked. They were standing, and each one was washing a naked body lying on a table in front of him. I was behind them. In the foreground, I saw people digging in the ground, looking for bodies. They were digging them out and taking the bodies of their beloved. There were women and children and men, all weeping, and they were all trying to take the bodies to a table and wash them. I was very frightened. Then I was digging too, for my father, and I was very scared, and my heart was beating fast, and my chest was tight. I was wondering what his body looked like. Finally I found him. He was only bones, covered by skin, but I could recognize him, and I took him to a table to wash him. Then my wife was shaking me and telling me to wake up. I saw that my sleeves were rolled up. I was sweating and exhausted. It seems I'd been shouting and had rolled up my sleeves so as not to be splashed when I was washing. That dream has always stayed in my mind. I don't know, but maybe this was a vision of Iraq now. People everywhere are searching for their missing loved ones." He mentioned that his sister-in-law had been all over Baghdad with her daughter, helping her search for her husband. He had been missing for a week. They had finally found him, he said, a couple of days earlier, buried at the side of a road.

I arrived at Soheila's house one afternoon to find the whole family gathered in the driveway, looking distraught. One of the cars in the driveway was covered with bloody handprints. They explained that they had slaughtered a sheep to thank God for a miracle that had occurred. The ritual, and the handprints, were an old Iraqi custom. Soheila pointed to the back window of the car and the rear left side window, where there were several bullet holes. The previous afternoon one of Soheila's daughters, her husband, and their young son had taken the car to go to the nearby market. The son, who was about seven years old and quite short for his age, had sat in back, behind his father. Suddenly shots had rung out. It seemed that they had driven right into a shoot-out between two armed criminal gangs over the spoils of an armed robbery. A bullet had entered the car an inch or two above the child's head and exited out the back window. If he had not been such a small boy, the bullet would have taken off the top of his head. (A few days later one of Soheila's nephews by marriage, a man I had met on one of my visits to the house, was killed in a similar incident.)

Ala Bashir was becoming increasingly concerned about the continuing chaos in Baghdad and the apparent unwillingness, or inability, of the Americans to restore order. He was especially worried about the growing public presence of Muslim fundamentalists, whom Saddam had always managed to keep under wraps. Bashir said he had watched satellite television images of an anti-American demonstration that had taken place the day before (within a few days of the toppling of Saddam's statue, these had become a daily event in Fardous Square) at which the people had shouted: "Islam! Islam! No America! No Saddam!" This kind of slogan, he said, alarmed him greatly. He said: "For the Americans now begins the second stage. The first stage was the change of Saddam's regime, and that seems definite. It's over. Now comes the next part, where they extend their influence over the different parts of Iraqi society. The thing is that Saddam was very tough and also very sharp, and even he had problems with the different ethnicities and sects of Iraq. So how are the Americans going to deal with them? They came with the language of liberty and human rights, so they can't be too tough, or they'll be accused of being the same as Saddam. The thing that worries me is that they don't appear to have a plan. Why have they left everything so loose? They've left everything with no order, no security, for almost a month now. Jon, the mobs are wandering Baghdad, and no one is opposing them. It's very strange."

On the morning of April 20, as Ala Bashir and I talked in the living room of his sister's house, the Americans showed up. One of his nieces came to the door to tell him someone had come to the front gate. Bashir excused himself and walked up the driveway to the gate. I looked out the window and saw three white Western men standing next to an SUV with "TV" taped to it. But these were not journalists. One of them was wearing khaki trousers and had on a kind of black combat harness and a contraption on his head with a microphone attached, arcing around to his mouth, and he was holding an assault rifle. He walked back and forth, hovering at the open gate of the garden and looking out into the street while the other two talked with Ala Bashir. The men all looked like Americans. They were wearing American sports boots and the kind of casual clothes that Americans wear. One of them had a beard. They were out of earshot, so I couldn't hear what they were saying. After about twenty minutes they left, and Bashir came back in.

He seemed rather excited. He said: "That was Charles." Charles was the name of an American man who was a friend of his cousin Faleh, in the United States. The second call Bashir had made on my Thuraya after I had found him had been to Faleh. The last time I had seen Bashir, during the bombing of Baghdad, he told me that his cousin had called and warned him to try to leave the city if he could. But it was too late by then. Until I found him at his sister's house, Bashir had had no further contact with his cousin or anyone else outside Iraq.

After speaking with Faleh, Bashir had thanked me profusely and said that his cousin was very grateful to me and had told him that he wanted me to call him back, so that he could thank me personally. Faleh had also wanted to know if it was all right if some friends of his, "people who he says want to help me," could make contact with Bashir through me. Later on I had called Faleh. He had been gracious and said that he appreciated my help and that what he wanted most of all was to be sure that his cousin was safe. "There are some other people who care about Ala who want to help him," he told me. They would be getting in touch. The next day, when I was with Bashir, I had a call from an American who said his name was Charles and who asked for Ala Bashir. I handed over the phone. Afterward, Bashir explained that Charles was a man he knew from his several trips to the United States, a friend of Faleh's whom he had met socially a couple of times.

Charles told Bashir that he was in Kuwait and would be in Baghdad soon. He said that he and some "other people" who were already in Baghdad wanted to come see him. Bashir said he had also asked if I wouldn't mind sending him the Global Positioning System coordinates of Bashir's sister's house using my Thuraya, so that they could locate him. I did so. About four days later Charles and his two friends showed up.

"So, who is Charles?" I asked Bashir, after he had returned from his meeting out at the front gate.

"He told me that he worked for an oil company," he replied. I shot Bashir a skeptical look. He caught my look and said: "But I guess they are probably CIA."

Animatedly, Bashir remarked that he had been surprised to recognize the second man—not the one with the gun but the other man in civilian clothes. "He came to my art exhibition in New York, in 1998," he said. Bashir had had an art exhibition that year at the UN General Assembly sponsored by the Iraqi delegation, and he had been allowed to travel there to attend its opening. Looking perplexed, he added: "But the thing is, though, he was always with the Iraqis from the UN. I assumed he was working with them. At first I didn't recognize him because he has a mustache now. He speaks perfect Arabic, with a Lebanese accent."

I suggested to Bashir that it was possible that the second man was an intelligence agent who had infiltrated Iraq's UN delegation. He pondered this and said: "Yes, it's possible. I remember that about six months later two of the Iraqis at the embassy asked for asylum."

He then told me, laughing, that he had invited the Americans inside, saying that he had a friend inside, another American, and had mentioned me by name. Charles had declined, saying: "No, thanks, we'll just stay here." They had told him they had just come to make initial contact, on his cousin's behalf, to see that he was safe. They would have come earlier, they said, but they had been very busy. They would return later that same evening, they told him. He added: "They said they wanted my opinions about a number of things." They had also asked him if there was anything they could do for him. "I told them that if they could help me visit my family in England"—where two of his three sons were (his wife and daughter were still in Amman but had UK visitor's visas)—"I would be very grateful. They said we could talk about that and many other things when they returned."

I told Bashir that I suspected that our days together were now numbered. If his visitors were, as I believed, from the CIA, they intended to debrief him and no doubt to ask his assistance in helping them find Saddam Hussein and other Iraqi fugitives. He laughed, dismissing the notion, and assured me that whoever they were, he was his own man, and they could not stop him from talking to me. I was pessimistic and told him so.

It was just as I thought. Once Ala Bashir's meetings with the Americans began—sometimes at Soheila's house, but usually at his own house in Al-Jihad and unspecified locations elsewhere—we began meeting less frequently, and he became increasingly vague about the substance of his discussions with them. He became uncomfortable when I probed, so I stopped probing. I felt certain that they had asked him not to talk to me. After a few days, however, I asked him point-blank what they wanted from him. He told me that they hadn't been very specific, but one of their ideas was that he could be useful, for instance, by helping to resurrect Iraq's damaged Health Ministry. Bashir had an insincere look on his face and did not seem happy. He clearly felt guilty about lying to me, so I no longer obliged him to. We continued to meet, without tension, for midday meals with his relatives and to talk about his past life, his family, Saddam, and his views on life. Every other day or so we went to Samir Khairi's house.

With the fall of Saddam, Samir's house became a kind of Harry's Bar, with a crowd of friends constantly coming and going and hanging around, gossiping about the Americans and the most recent events, and also intriguing and ruminating about their own futures. As usual, the TV blared away, and everyone watched the satellite news channels, alternating among Al Jazeera and Al Arabiya and CNN and the BBC. Whenever Bashir and I stopped by, Samir usually obliged us to stay for overly abundant Iraqi meals of rice and lamb and salads and egg-plant and red beans cooked in various sauces, followed by coffee or tea and more conversation. In the evenings, there was arrack or whiskey.

Most of Samir's friends were people like him, nomenklatura of the ancien régime, most of them long-standing Baath Party members, military officers, or Foreign Ministry officials who were suddenly jobless and wondering what the future held for them. One was Samir's own brother, an air force captain who had fled Tikrit before the U.S. Marines arrived and who was awaiting a summons to report back to work. Another day it was a former Iraqi Air Force fighter pilot. He told me about a friend of his who had been in prison and just returned home. For years he had served as a kind of pimp or procurer of women for Uday Hussein. Some months before, they had had a falling-out, and Uday had punished his friend by having the tip of his tongue amputated. Amazingly, the officer said, his friend was beginning to make sounds and to speak again. It was difficult to understand him, but each day he was sounding more and more comprehensible.

Another of Samir's regular visitors was Muhammad Jaffar, a neighbor of his who spoke very good English. He was an irritat-ingly voluble man, a publisher of trade and industry journals and a former diplomat who delighted in pointing out everything the Americans had done wrong since they had arrived. He predicted nothing but doom and gloom for the Americans in Iraq. "The fu-ture is bleak," Jaffar told me one day, smirking. When I asked him why he thought so, he said it was because the Americans knew nothing about Iraqi society and were making a lot of mistakes. "They are sitting on a time bomb," he said, pointing out the growing restiveness of the Shia clerics and the fact that the Americans weren't moving quickly enough to clip their wings. In the next breath, he told me that at the same time, for people who were savvy like him, the "new Iraq" posed good opportunities for business. He hoped to expand his publishing business and, if everything went well, even launch a magazine on Middle Eastern economies. I told Jaffar that he seemed to be contradicting himself. He smiled and said something about "the duality" of the Iraqi character. "This is another thing the Americans don't understand." He smiled at me, as if he were withholding a secret that he might divulge at some future time.

Great snorts of derision went up from Samir and his friends, including Bashir, on the day that the Iraqi finance minister was captured and taken into custody by the American military. When the CNN newscaster quoted Bush administration officials as saying they hoped the capture would help them trace the billions of dollars Saddam had allegedly stolen from Iraq and stashed away in foreign accounts, Bashir scoffed: "This man is a nobody, a nothing. They will not find anything through him. Do they really think Saddam Hussein and his family used this man to hide their money?" All that sort of business, he said, was handled directly by Hussein family members or their personal representatives.

On the day that Barzan al-Tikriti, who had not, after all, been killed, was captured by the Americans and the news was relayed on television, Samir was ecstatic. "Good! Good!" he shouted out. Later, when I left his house, he walked out with me. As my car drew away, he came forward and motioned for us to stop. He walked up to my side of the car and leaned in and said in a low voice: "If the Americans want to know anything about this man, tell them I am willing to help."

Samir had made many references to Barzan in recent days. He had muttered that Barzan had once been his best friend but had betrayed him, throwing him in prison for no reason, and he could never forgive him for that. No other details were forthcoming. But a few days after he spoke to me outside his house, I managed to get him to sit down in a quiet corner of his living room, as Ala Bashir and other friends sat watching Al Jazeera, and to talk frankly with me about Barzan and about his own career in the Mukhabarat.

Samir was born in Mosul in 1951, the son of a police colonel. He had studied law in Baghdad and obtained a doctorate in constitutional law in 1981. By that time he had also gotten involved in journalism, which he called the other great love of his life, working as the editor of a newspaper in Baghdad. Just before he got his PhD, Barzan al-Tikriti, who was then the chief of Saddam's intelligence apparatus, called him and asked him what he planned to do with himself. Samir told him that he wanted to teach in the law faculty of Baghdad University. "He asked me to be the editor of a new Arabic language magazine in Paris, called *Kul al-Arab* [*All the Arabs*], with an international distribution. The money came from Iraqi intelligence, but they told me it was not to be an Iraqi organization, but a journal for all Arabs." Samir accepted the post, moved to Paris, and served as the editor of the magazine from 1983 to 1991. "It was a great success, with distribution all over the Arabic-speaking world." Samir smiled, obviously proud of his achievement. Then, in 1991, when the Gulf War began, he was arrested by French police, accused of espionage. They held him two days and then deported him back to Iraq.

After his return to Baghdad, Samir was made the director of the Department of Research in the Presidential Institute, a branch of the Mukhabarat, where his official work was drafting summaries of foreign books and publications for Saddam Hussein and also providing analysis for the president about international affairs. He was at this job until 1993, when Barzan, who by this time was Iraq's ambassador in Geneva, was appointed Saddam Hussein's political adviser. Samir went to work as the director of Barzan's office in the Foreign Ministry. His real function, he explained, was to serve as the liaison between Barzan and the president. He stayed there until 1998. "Then Barzan came back to Iraq, and the problems between us began. He wanted me to get involved with him in a bid to become a political force against Saddam's son Uday, whom he hated. Uday had married his daughter, and after only three months he had left her. I didn't want to be part of his problem with Uday. He had hopes of becoming the number two man after Saddam, but this was not realistic. After his sons, Uday and Qusay, who were two and three, there were several other people who were ahead of Barzan, more important than he was. Because of this, in 1999, he made a problem for me and had me put in prison. I was in prison for two months and four days. The president's men were afraid to tell him about me; the president never learned about it. Finally they told Barzan that I had to be released because he had no cause to hold me. I was held in the Mukhabarat prison in Mansour, and to be honest with you, it wasn't so bad. I was given a good room, with satellite TV, and they let me go home discreetly every two or three days. This kind of thing was one of the strange things of our dictatorship, my friend." He chuckled confidingly, in the manner of a schoolboy telling a friend about having played hooky.

Only six months after his release, Barzan invited Samir to attend a bereavement ceremony for his deceased wife. She had died of cancer two years before in Switzerland, and her body was kept there in a refrigerator while he prepared a shrine for her in Owja, the village of the presidential clique near the city of Tikrit. "He insisted that I come," Samir said. "I did not want to go. I went and talked to my father, and for one of the few times in my life I took his good advice. He said I should go, that it was obvious that Barzan wanted to apologize to me. And so I went. And that was exactly what happened. He apologized."

Having made his formal peace with Barzan, Samir returned to his job in the presidential research office. By this time Barzan no longer had any connection with it. Meanwhile, said Samir, Saddam had come to esteem his work. "The president respected me too much. He always read everything I wrote, and three times he sent me a half million dinars as rewards for my work." He had stayed at the post until December 2002, when, as a commendation for his labors, he was told he would be made an ambassador and was seconded to the Foreign Ministry, where he worked as Naji Sabri al-Hadithi's press adviser.

Samir boasted a little about the work he had done for Saddam Hussein. His analyses had focused on Iraq's relations with the United States. "I can't show it to you now because I am still faithful to the state, but I want to tell you that I wrote three assessments for the president in the last year, the last one only three months ago. I told the president that the Americans would attack Iraq and that we had no chance to resist them." But Saddam's right-hand man and chief bodyguard, General Abed Hamoud, had refused to give his reports to Saddam, Samir said. "Like everyone else, he was afraid to tell him the truth."

I asked Samir why he was ready to collaborate with the Americans against Barzan. "It's not because of anything he did to me," Samir said emphatically. "Believe me. It's because when he was head of the Mukhabarat, he killed too many innocent people. And you must tell this to those responsible in the United States. . . . He should be taken to Guantánamo; he's a criminal. He killed many, many people; how many exactly I don't know, but hundreds."

"Personally?"

"He was present in the ceremonies of killing, yes."

"So, how could you work for him, and for Saddam, knowing what you knew about them and what they did?"

"Really, I had no choice." Samir stared intently into my eyes, and his voice had a beseeching tone. "Because once they knew me, I was afraid for my family, my mother, father, brothers, sisters, even my cousins. If I were to leave the country, they'd hurt them. And if I stayed here and didn't work for them, they could kill me at any time. You know, they killed too many people, Jon Lee."

While Ala Bashir had never joined the Baath Party, Samir was a Baathist and very proud of the fact. "I joined the Baath Party in 1973, and until now I believe in the principles of the party," he told me. "The principles of Arab unity, socialist economy, and liberty. But these have never been fulfilled because of Saddam Hussein's takeover of power in 1979, when he became president. Until then he had pretended to respect those principles. But when he took over the party in 1979, he executed more than twenty-two people who were the real leaders. For years Saddam Hussein has said that the Baath Party was the ultimate authority in Iraq. This was not true. It was one family—his—that had the power, and it used the party to give itself political legitimacy. The party became like an intelligence apparatus; this was the role it exercised in Iraqi society. Saddam Hussein built up the command class of the party as the only one with authority in the society, but actually he never gave an opportunity for the intelligentsia that had been part of the party in 1968," the date of the Baathist revolution. "Those who were given command posts were nothings. In truth, Jon Lee, the principles of the Baath Party are very good for our society, upholding the principles of freedom and liberty and respect for all religions. . . . That's why so many of the educated people, like me, became Baathists in university." It was his fervent hope, Samir told me, that the Americans would see that the Baathists had a role to play in Iraq and would keep the party alive.

One morning Ala Bashir and Samir and I were sitting and talking at Soheila's house when Sabah suddenly came barging into the living room. This was unusual behavior. Sabah normally waited for me outside with his car or else in the garden. He was clutching a manila folder filled with papers, and he was very agitated. He walked right up to Bashir and thrust the file into his lap. He was talking excitedly. His face was flushed with emotion, and his voice was raised. I could hear the words "Taher" and "Mukhabarat." Bashir was immutable as he began looking through the papers in the folder, as Sabah was clearly asking him to do. Samir seemed to have frozen in his chair.

Sabah walked over and sat heavily down on the sofa next to me. He was breathing in a choked way. He grabbed my arm, and in his broken English he told me that he had bought his missing brother Taher's dossier from a Mukhabarat official who lived around the corner from his house. The agent was selling the files of prisoners and disappeared men to their families. Taher's had cost him one hundred dollars. "Jon Lee," he said, his voice breaking, "they killed Taher like this, with rope." He circled his neck with both of his hands. Sabah sobbed a little but managed to control himself and looked expectantly over at Ala Bashir. He wanted to know what had been done with his brother's body, but he was too overwhelmed to read the documents properly. Bashir soon found the relevant page. He read it aloud. It was the death certificate. Taher had been executed, Bashir said, for being a member of the Iraqi Communist Party. He had been executed about a year after he had vanished, but the document did not say where his body was buried.

Sabah hung his head for a moment. Then he got to his feet, thanked Bashir, retrieved the file from him, and walked out. Bashir and Samir sat in silence.

One day Ala Bashir took a book, *Lenin's Embalmers,* from his library and asked me to read it. It was an account of the mummification of Lenin, written by a man, a Russian Jew, who had helped his father carry out the embalming and run the laboratory in the mausoleum dedicated to maintaining Lenin's body in perpetuity. Bashir had been struck by the similarity between Stalin's Russia and the Iraq he was living in. "It is exactly the same, exactly!" he exclaimed. "I was amazed." There was a photograph of the embalmed body of Lenin on the cover, and photographs inside the book showed the construction of Lenin's mausoleum in Red Square. In the 1920s, an architectural competition had been held for a new mausoleum, and a few of the entries were reproduced in the book. It seemed to me that there were uncanny parallels between the fanciful drawings for the Soviet übermorgue and the necromantic bestiality of the *Epic of Saddam* monument that Bashir had designed. I asked him if he thought of himself as, in a sense, Saddam's embalmer. Bashir looked at me quickly and then looked away. He laughed but didn't say anything.

Bashir explained that he had read the book when he went to Moscow to visit the embalming institute. He had gone there at the request of his friend Barzan al-Tikriti. Bashir expanded on the story Samir had told me about Barzan's keeping his wife's corpse in a refrigerator in Geneva for years while he built a kind of mausoleum for her in Tikrit. "Two years ago it was still incomplete, and he told me he had already spent more than five million pounds on it. It is an incredible thing. So he asked me to explore the idea of having her embalmed by the institute in Moscow. The idea was he would put her on display in the mausoleum, but just for family and friends."

It had not been easy to obtain permission for the visit to the institute, Bashir said, which was one of the most highly secure buildings he had ever entered. On every door there were locks that needed to be opened with special keys. The only other people there were a few attendants. He described being led down an empty hall to a chamber that was lined with decapitated human heads. In the inner sanctum, they showed him a body that was being embalmed. The heirs of Lenin's embalmers explained that they were surviving by performing similar services for Russian mafiosi. The pièce de résistance of his visit was when the embalmers pressed a button, a section of the floor opened up, and a platform rose from the depths. Lenin was perched on it in his glass coffin. He was periodically removed from the mausoleum in Red Square and refreshed by the group of scientists who were preserving him for posterity.

I asked what had happened when he reported back to Barzan al-Tikriti. "It seemed too expensive to him," Bashir said. As he recalled, the embalming would have cost about five million dollars.

At the end of *Lenin's Embalmers,* the author speculates that he and his father escaped death during one of the most dangerous periods in modern history because, ironically, they were so close to the source of the awful power that destroyed so many people. They were useful. I asked Bashir whether he regarded his relationship to Saddam as a self-protective collaboration similar to that of Lenin's Jewish embalmers. He brightened and warmed to the theme. "You are very clever to have noticed this," he said, smiling broadly. As he continued talking, I realized that his elation was due to a misapprehension that I had finally swung around to his views about the Jews' stealthy opportunism and age-old plan to rule the world. Bashir said: "The book shows that the Jews everywhere, even in Europe, where they are rich, have to be useful, whether deliberately or unconsciously, to protect themselves."

I tried to steer Bashir back to a discussion of the parallels between his condition in Saddam's Iraq and that of the Jewish embalmers in Soviet Russia, but he was having none of it. "There is really no comparison," he said. "First of all, I come from a very strong tribe here, so it would have been hard for Saddam's people to hurt or harass me. But the truth is that what gave me protection from his guards was the fact that Saddam respected me so much; he really did."

Bashir remarked that he regarded it as a strange quirk of destiny that he had been chosen to have an unusual relationship with Saddam Hussein for two decades. He had saved documents and letters and written things down, he said, and he hoped to be able to tell the story of what had happened in his country so that it could not happen again anywhere else. "It is strange how a system can become so bad that no one, not a single person, can change it."

For several weeks after Baghdad fell to the Americans, the city remained suspended in a bizarre limbo between its past and its future. There was no single defining moment of national catharsis that signified a break with the past. The toppling of Saddam's statue in Fardous Square had symbolized a great deal to people abroad, and perhaps especially to Americans, who witnessed the moment on their television screens and who believed it to have marked the end of the war in Iraq. But to most Iraqis, who knew that Saddam himself had eluded capture and was still capable of inflicting great harm, the event had been a largely irrelevant sideshow. Meanwhile, they were being forced to watch, as passive spectators, the wholesale looting and vandalism of their capital city. Their liberators, the Americans, watched passively along with them.

On the same day that General Tommy Franks arrived in Baghdad and gave President Bush a congratulatory telephone call from the ransacked grounds of Saddam's bombed-out presidential palace complex, knots of looters, not far away, were still working over some government warehouses next to the Baghdad

Trade Fair. They were carrying out fifty-kilo sacks of sugar and tea on their backs, loading them into cars, and selling them at knockdown prices to passing motorists. I noticed a young donkey lying dead on the sidewalk leading over the Jumhuriyah Bridge across the Tigris. I wondered if it was the same donkey I had listened to braying throughout the bombing campaign. I hadn't heard it since the war had ended.

That night, the Planning Ministry, which had already been strafed from the air and then thoroughly looted and partially burned, somehow caught fire again. At twilight a big column of black smoke poured from its upper windows. The next morning, crossing the Jumhuriyah Bridge over to the western side of Baghdad, I noticed a young russet-colored camel on the loose. It was walking around the street next to a small park with a bronze fountain sculpture depicting Iraqi girls carrying jugs of water. The camel was standing placidly in the street as a small group of people held out freshly cut grass for it to eat. I found out later in the day that it had escaped from the zoo in Zawra Park, about a mile away. A unit of marines stationed there were feeding the lions and the tiger and a bear. A couple of days earlier looters had pried open the cages of most of the other animals and stolen them, except for the monkeys, which had escaped into the park, where they had taken up residence in the trees.

One evening Madame Sabah sent over a specially cooked Iraqi meal for Paul and me. Sabah collected it from his house and brought it to the hotel. He came in the door and set down the pots of food. Then, suddenly, he began bawling like a child. The tears flowed down his cheeks, and he wept with a full voice. His body shook, and he wailed, racked by sobs and gasping for air. Over and over again, he called out the name of his brother Taher. I embraced him and comforted him until he stopped.

The Al-Rasheed had been saved after all. After a day of looting, the Americans moved in, cordoned it off, and guarded it with their tanks. Sabah was very pleased to see this, even if he could no longer work there. In his excitement, he let slip that the Al-Rasheed Car Service, the company he had worked for, had been run by the Mukhabarat. For years he had been forced to turn over a percentage of his salary to it. "No more Mukhabarat, no more commission." He chuckled. He was looking forward to being his own man for the first time, he said, and with any luck, he would now be able to save up enough money to buy the car of his dreams, a GMC Suburban like those used by TV news crews and the drivers who took passengers across the desert from Baghdad to Jordan.

After the fall of Saddam's hometown of Tikrit, my friend Thomas Dworzak, the photographer, arrived in Baghdad in a jeep driven by a couple of Iraqi Kurds, with whom he had come down from the north a few days earlier as the government-held cities there began to fall. Thomas thanked his escorts and paid them off and told them they were free to return to the north. They smiled and looked at a loss as to what to do. It was late in the day, they said, so they thought they should find a hotel for the night. I told them about my little old hotel, the Al-Safeer, just down Abu Nawas Street, which had just reopened. They looked confused. Saba wrote them some directions on a notepad that they produced with official lettering on it. When I asked where the notepaper was from, they laughed delightedly and said they had looted it from the police station in Kirkuk. They looked blankly at the directions Sabah had given them, so I told them that if they got lost en route to ask anybody they saw where the Al-Safeer was, and they would point them the right way. They threw up their hands apologetically and said, "We don't speak Arabic, just Kurdish and English. And we've never been to Baghdad before."

While this was going on, a young American woman, Marla Ruzicka, whom I had last seen in Kabul after the fall of the Taliban, wandered by. In Afghanistan Marla had spearheaded efforts to seek compensation for the relatives of civilians killed in

American bombing raids. She had once organized an angry demonstration outside the recently reopened U.S. Embassy there, a feat that had earned her a place on the embassy blacklist. She had become well known among Western journalists and re- lief workers there for such efforts and for her social skills in ar- ranging several memorable dancing parties. She had come to Baghdad to do the same thing she had done in Kabul, Marla said, but, she added, with a daunted look, Iraq's problems were looking "a lot more complex" than Afghanistan's had been. She handed me her card. It read: "Iraq Victims Compassion Cam- paign." Marla joked that that she was also having talks with the management of the Palestine Hotel about opening up a night- club there and waved a cheery good-bye.

Nearby, some marines stood guard behind the long looping coil of razor wire they had unfurled across the streets leading into the Palestine and Sheraton hotels. In addition to housing the Western press corps, which had swollen by hundreds of people since the fall of the city and brought media luminaries like Dan Rather and Christiane Amanpour to town, the neighboring ho- tels had become the temporary headquarters for the U.S. Marines in Baghdad. They were everywhere. Their brown plastic MRE wrappers littered the ground, and their tanks and armored per- sonnel carriers and Humvees were parked all over the place. Most of them were young and polite and said "sir" and "ma'am" and apologized when they told journalists entering and exiting the cordoned-off hotel complex that they had to be frisked. Most of them also said that they were tired and ready to go home.

None of the senior officials of the former Information Min- istry had been seen since the night before the marines arrived. There were many stories going around about their final hours at the Palestine. I heard that before he fled, Uday al-Taiee had gone around to the major television networks with some of his thugs and demanded huge sums of cash from them. By some counts he had made off with two hundred thousand dollars. His deputy,

Mohsen, had reportedly tried to steal the sequestered French TV crew's expensive Kuwait-registered SUV from the hotel parking lot but had been thwarted in the act and then chased on foot down the street until he ran out of breath and was run to ground. There, in an act of final cowardice, Mohsen had begged his confronters to let him leave, ostentatiously torn up his Baath Party membership card, and walked off, alone and defeated.

I did spot a number of our former official minders, however. Some of them had stayed on and hired themselves out to journalists as freelance guides and translators. They appeared to have weathered the transition from the era of Saddam Hussein to life under American occupation without too much trouble. One morning I bumped into Salaar, my original minder. He looked like an entirely different person. He had always been a rather nervous man and dressed very conservatively, but now he was looking casual and sporty in jeans and some very hip dark sunglasses. He was working for a major American newspaper, he told me. He wore a big smile.

One day Karim, the barber, showed up at the Sheraton. He had brought a little satchel with all of his tools, and he wanted to cut my hair and shave me. His barbershop had not been damaged or looted, and his family was well, Karim reported, but there was no longer any electricity for him to operate his hair clippers. He needed to work, so he had taken it upon himself to come to me. When he was finished with me, Karim cut Sabah's hair and then Paul's. Afterward we introduced him to other friends of ours, several of whom agreed to let him give them trims and shaves and even his excruciating facial massages. Everyone liked him and tipped him well, and Karim was very happy.

Some of the Iraqis I knew didn't survive the final days of the war. One of them was Salaah, a polite, humorous, and handsome man in his fifties. He had once been the chief steward for Iraqi Airways, but since the Gulf War, and the UN sanctions that had

grounded the fleet afterward, he had become a driver for Western journalists. I had seen him the day before the fall of Baghdad
in the foyer of the Palestine. He had his young teenage son with
him and had introduced us. Four or five days later I heard that
Salaah's family was looking for him; he had not come home since
the day the marines had arrived. A few days later his wife and
daughters came across his car at the side of the road. Salaah was
inside it, dead, apparently shot in a crossfire between the Americans and fedayeen. He had apparently gone to fetch the laundry
of the British journalist he was working for at the time, and was
on his way back to the hotel to tell him that it was too dangerous to keep driving for him, and that he was going home for the
duration of the war.

A week after the fall of Baghdad, Sabah went home to see his
family. He returned the next morning looking as if he had been
crying. His mother, his wife and children, and his brothers and
sisters all were back at home, he reported, and they were fine.
But one of his nephews, a truck driver, had been killed, apparently hit by a rocket or strafed from the air by the Americans on
the day the city fell, or perhaps the day before. He had been
missing for several days. His body had been found after a neighbor who happened to be driving by recognized his truck at the
roadside, all shot up, and found him lying in the street. He had
apparently bled to death of his wounds over a two-day period. In
all the chaos, no one had stopped to help him.

EPILOGUE

Baghdad was filthy, unkempt, and baking hot when I returned there in the third week of June 2003. There were fewer overturned tanks and burned-out vehicles on the city's streets than there had been two months earlier, but great heaps of rubble still spilled out from bombed buildings, and tin cans and plastic bags were strewn about everywhere. Traffic was dense, and most of the major intersections were gridlocked, but there were no traffic cops in sight. Driving into the city, we passed an armored convoy of American soldiers in full combat gear, their guns at the ready. As Issam, the driver who had brought me in from Jordan, negotiated a back street to reach my hotel, the Al-Safeer, on the east bank of the Tigris, we encountered a large man carrying a revolver, walking belligerently down the middle of the street. Issam edged carefully around him.

Within a few hours of my arrival, Sabah heard that I was in town and came to see me. He gave me news of what had happened while I was away. None of it was very good. His wife had been in the hospital with a blood pressure crisis, and the wife of the barber Karim had suffered a partial stroke. A few weeks earlier Sabah himself had been arrested and then detained for two days at Baghdad airport, where high-ranking military and intelligence officials of Saddam's regime were being held. He'd been picked up when American soldiers who were sweeping his neighborhood had searched his house and found a large bronze plaque decorated with a bas-relief of Saddam's head. It was a souvenir I had picked up during the fall of Baghdad and left with Sabah for safekeeping. He said that he hadn't been treated badly, but he'd had to sit with hundreds of other men in what he described as a large hangar, and there had been only crackers to eat and water to drink. Once he was questioned and had been able to explain why the Saddam plaque was in his possession, he was released and allowed to take it home with him. But while he was away, his wife had had her blood pressure crisis, and she had not been able to do much since but rest.

There hadn't been any electricity in the city for four days when I arrived. The official explanation for this was that a substation had been bombed and no one had been able to fix it. The lack of electricity had caused a shortage of running water and, of course, had shut down refrigerators and air conditioners. There was also a fuel supply shortage, and huge lines of cars and fractious drivers waited in front of gas stations for hours at a time. Since these calamities had coincided with the onset of the abysmally hot Iraqi summer, with temperatures well over 120 degrees Fahrenheit, tempers were seriously on edge. Security had deteriorated as well. It was no longer safe to walk around Baghdad's downtown streets, to sit and drink tea in its coffee shops, or to prowl through bazaars and chat with shopkeepers. These were activities I had grown used to during Saddam's rule, when, paradoxically, Baghdad was an extremely safe place to visit. Now American soldiers were being killed at the rate of about one a day, and not long after I got to town, a young British journalist, Richard Wild, was shot at point-blank range in the back of the head by an assassin near the Museum of Natural History. The next morning an American soldier standing outside Baghdad University was killed in exactly the same fashion. Immediately afterward, at the scene, his furious comrades aggressively pointed their guns and shouted curses at onlookers and reporters who tried to approach the scene. On their Humvee one of them had scrawled in chalk: "The Guilty must be Punished."

A couple of mornings later I rushed over to Baghdad's Mustansiriyah University, where a U.S. Army Humvee had just been attacked by someone firing an antitank grenade. Several soldiers had been wounded. Fidgety young American soldiers with guns had arrived and cordoned off the area around the blasted, burned-out vehicle and were busy conducting searches of cars and people in the area. Most of the Iraqi onlookers, I noticed, wore dispassionate looks, and a few appeared to be amused. Later that day, when I described the scene to some Iraqi friends, one of them retorted pitilessly: "What do the Americans expect! This will continue as long as they do not resolve the situation. Where is the electricity, the water, and where are the jobs?"

By ten o'clock at night, an hour before the start of the regular curfew, which lasted until four in the morning, Baghdad had become an eerie place, almost pitch black, and silent except for the occasional barking dog and exchanges of automatic-weapons fire or the clatter of helicopters along the river. One night, just before curfew, as Sabah drove me back to my hotel, we came upon a pickup truck parked sideways across the street, blocking our way. Several men in civilian clothes were standing in the bed of the pickup, and others had fanned out on the street around it. They were holding automatic weapons. Sabah stopped our car about twenty feet from them, and for a moment they stared at us and we at them. Then, with an almost imperceptible hand motion, one of the men waved us on. Wordlessly, and very slowly, we drove past them, and as we did, I saw that the truck was crudely decorated with what appeared to be a police car emblem. It looked suspicious to me. "Who are they?" I asked Sabah.

"Maybe police," he said tentatively. "Or maybe Ali Baba," the generic term in Iraq for thieves. Sabah made it clear that it made no difference to him.

*

When I'd left Baghdad at the end of April to go home to my family in England, things were still tense, but the widespread looting had begun to wind down, and it had looked as though the Americans were gradually asserting control over the situation. Then, over several days at the end of April, just after I left, American soldiers had fired their weapons into crowds of demonstrators, killing at least seventeen of them. The killings, which occurred in Fallujah, an unremarkable city of two hundred thousand people, fifty miles west of Baghdad, turned out to be a historic watershed. Iraqi attackers retaliated, killing two Americans and wounding others in successive attacks. Simultaneously, the violence spread to other towns north and west of Baghdad, throughout the predominantly Sunni Muslim area known as the Sunni Triangle, and into Baghdad itself. By the end of spring it was becoming clear that the Americans were faced with an intensifying guerrilla insurgency in Iraq, queering their ambitious plans to reshape the country into a friendly democratic state.

In early June, while I was home in England, I received a telephone call from Ala Bashir. His wife and daughter were still in Amman, he told me, awaiting visas to travel to the United Kingdom. Bashir told me that the situation in Iraq was "very bad." He said he was thinking of leaving soon to join his family, as they were pleading with him to do, but that for the time being, he was staying on in Baghdad at the request of the Americans. He said something vague about their wanting his help in getting Iraq's Health Ministry, which had been badly looted, up and running again. I still suspected that there was more to the Americans' interest in Bashir than he was letting on, but he was clearly uncomfortable speaking on the phone, so we left it at that. "We'll talk when you get back to Baghdad," he said.

A few days after Ala Bashir's call, I decided to return to Iraq. I flew from London to Amman, the starting point for the six-hundred-mile road journey through the desert to Baghdad.

While I was there, I went to see Bashir's wife, Amal, and daughter, Amina, who were staying in a small residential hotel. Amal confided that her husband had come to see her the previous week. It had been a very brief trip, she said, and he had been accompanied by two American men, Charles and David, who rarely let him out of their sight. I asked her what the Americans seemed to want from him. Was it to do with the Iraqi Health Ministry? Amal smiled and shook her head. As far as she knew, she said, their main interest seemed to be what he knew about Saddam Hussein. She arched her eyebrows in a skeptical way. She told me she didn't trust her husband's new friends and resented them for making him stay on in Baghdad. By coincidence, Amal added, the American named David had telephoned her to say he had just arrived in Amman from Baghdad and planned to come and see her. She was expecting him at any moment, she said, and urged me to stay.

Out of curiosity, I lingered. After about half an hour a thin American man wearing casual clothes walked up the street to the outdoor café where we were seated. David appeared to be in his mid-forties, and he carried an object wrapped in a plastic shopping bag in one hand. He greeted Amal Bashir and Amina politely, shook my hand with a wan smile, and sat down at our table. Thereafter he avoided direct eye contact with me. Exaggerating its weight, he placed the package he was carrying heavily on the table and said to Amal: "This is from your husband." He raised his eyebrows in an expression of mock suspicion and quipped: "I don't know what it is; maybe it's the weapon of mass destruction we've been looking for." Both Amal and her daughter tittered awkwardly at the heavy-handed joke. Amal thanked David and explained that the package contained some of her jewelry, which her husband believed was no longer safe to leave in their home in Baghdad. David nodded and then, still ignoring me, began speaking to Amal in heavily accented Arabic. After a few minutes of this, I tried to initiate a conversation by introducing myself and asking him his name. He replied simply, "David," without supplying a surname, and turned his attention back to Amal.

I had the distinct impression that David worked for the Central Intelligence Agency. I spoke up again, and asked David if he'd just come from Baghdad. He rolled his eyes theatrically, nodding, and said: "Oh, yes, indeed I have." How were things looking? I asked him. "Very bad," he said, giving me a direct look. "Very, very bad." Seeming to relax a bit, he ran through a checklist of the problems: rampant crime, severe electrical, fuel, and water shortages, and an upsurge in attacks on U.S. military forces. "It's a mess," he concluded. He added that morale was low among the American experts who had been brought in to govern Iraq in the Coalition Provisional Authority. "Whether because of the situation, the heat, or both, a lot of people are leaving before their time is up." Would it all come right in the end? I asked. David threw his hands up and shot me a bleak look. I asked him if he was returning to Baghdad. He nodded. I asked whether he was someone I could talk to when I arrived or whether he would be off-limits to me. "Oh, I think I am very much off-limits to you," he said, flashing me a thin smile.

I told David that I intended to drive to Baghdad, leaving Amman early the next morning. He wished me luck and advised me to watch out for bandits on the stretch of highway west of Baghdad between the cities of Ramadi and Fallujah, at the western edge of the Sunni Triangle. The road had become dangerous immediately after the fall of Baghdad, and apparently nothing had changed. A couple of journalists I knew had been attacked and robbed by armed gunmen in the same area just the week before. Inexplicably, the American military didn't patrol the road, so the bandits operated with impunity. I asked David if he could give me any special tips to ensure my safety. He shrugged and shook his head. "It's pretty much down to luck."

On the journey the next day, everything went well until we

reached a spot in the desert about 120 miles west of Baghdad, where the right rear tire of the GMC Suburban I was riding in suddenly exploded. We were traveling at about 90 miles an hour, and the car immediately began careening, but my Jordanian driver, Issam, with whom I always made the trip, managed to bring it to a grinding, metallic halt. He jumped out and began putting on a new tire while I kept an eye on the road in both directions. I saw, with relief, that there was what appeared to be an American military outpost about half a mile away. Several Humvees and Bradleys were visible around the walled compound. Then I noticed two cars on the highway traveling in our direction suddenly pulled over and stopped. I imagined that the men inside the cars were bandits calculating their odds: Would the soldiers prevent them from robbing us, or could they get away with it before the soldiers reacted?

Before anyone made a move, Issam finished changing the tire, and we were off again. A half hour later, as we approached the dangerous stretch of road between Ramadi and Fallujah, Issam began sweating profusely. He nervously jerked his foot on and off the brake and accelerator and asked me where I had hidden my cash. I pointed to the box of facial tissues he kept next to his seat, and he said, "Good. But keep something small in your pocket to give them, just in case." We drove on in a tense silence for about thirty minutes, until we had passed Fallujah and the desert began to give way to the scrubby outskirts of Baghdad. Finally Issam sighed audibly, mopped his brow, and said I could retrieve my money from his Kleenex box.

A day or two after my return I called on Bashir at Soheila's house. He was as warm and friendly as always, but he seemed preoccupied, fidgety. I asked him how he was occupying his time. He told me he had been extremely busy overseeing the installation of new security grilles for the doors and windows in his house, which had recently been broken into and burglarized. He'd been performing a few plastic surgery operations as well, mostly as favors to old friends. He was also considering whether or not to accept an invitation from a relative of the emir of Qatar, whom he knew personally, to become the director of plastic surgery at one of the top hospitals in Doha. The offer came with a good salary and free housing. Bashir confessed that he was feeling tired and needed a break, and he saw nothing further he could do in Iraq. Everything was a mess, and he held out little faith in the Americans' ability to restore Iraq to stability soon. Maybe the Qatar job, he said, which came with no strings attached, was something he could do for a couple of months, until he decided what to do next. Meanwhile he would resume painting and perhaps begin writing his memoirs. Maybe he'd join his family in England, or maybe not. It was his wife's greatest wish that they settle there, he said, but he still wasn't convinced.

Bashir was more circumspect about his dealings with the mysterious Americans Charles and David, but he acknowledged that he had, at their request, stayed on in Iraq and assisted them by participating in meetings with Iraqis he knew. From the way he spoke, I had the sense that Bashir had been operating as a broker between the Americans and Iraqis who might form alliances with them and could help them hunt down Saddam Hussein. He told me about one of the meetings, which had taken place a few days earlier. Bashir said that he had accompanied David and Charles to a meeting with Sheikh Ibrahim al-Jubour, an eminence of the Jubour tribe, one of Iraq's biggest traditional clans. (Estimates vary, but overall, the Jubouris, with their numerous clans and subgroups, which include both Shia and Sunni Muslims, are believed to number as many as five million people, or nearly 20 percent of the Iraqi population.) Bashir said that he had participated in the visit grudgingly because he disdains Iraq's tribalism and had long since eschewed his own tribal links, but that because he was, by blood, a ranking member—technically a sheikh—of the Jubouris, his presence was seen as useful by the Americans.

It had been a goodwill visit, Bashir explained, in which David and Charles had introduced themselves to Sheikh Ibrahim and an assemblage of lesser sheikhs. The sheikh, according to Bashir, had welcomed them with a barbed admonishment, by reminding them of the size and influence of the Jubouri people in Iraq and saying how surprised he and his fellow sheikhs were that it had taken the Americans two full months since their arrival in Iraq to pay them a visit. He had gone on to say that the Jubouris had nothing in principle against the Americans, having suffered greatly under Saddam's repression, and were grateful to the Americans for ousting him from power. They were willing to help the Americans restore Iraq to stability, if that was what they had come to do. "But there is still confusion over your intentions," the sheikh had said. "Is the U.S. intending to restore Iraq to peace and prosperity, or is it planning to occupy Iraq? Because if the U.S. is planning to occupy Iraq, then the Jubouris will work against you."

Having been thrown this gauntlet, Bashir told me, the Americans had not given a direct reply but dissembled, making a hash out of the varying definitions of what exactly constituted an occupation. Bashir shook his head in dismay. Sheikh Ibrahim and his fellow elders had not appeared pleased by the Americans' obfuscations. "Their lack of sincerity, or their lack of authority to speak clearly, was very obvious to everyone," said Bashir. The meeting, he said, had ended on this inconclusive note. Such unsatisfactory encounters and the lack of any other visible progress on any front that he could see, Bashir said, had made him lose confidence in the Americans' ability to put things right in Iraq. David and Charles seemed well intentioned, but they appeared to have little power to do anything. Both of them, he added, were very depressed and had told him they were thinking of resigning their jobs, but first, they'd asked him to come with them to Washington, D.C., to talk to some "important people" there. They'd told him that they believed his insights could help their cause. When I asked him what their "cause" was and which agency of the U.S. government they worked for, Bashir claimed not to know.

Bashir sat there in silence, looking abstracted. I asked him if he felt himself to be in danger in Baghdad. I told him that his wife believed that he was. He gave a small, unconvincing laugh and said: "No, I don't feel unsafe." He didn't elaborate on this, but he acknowledged that the rumor mill about him was going strong. In recent days some Iraqi newspapers had run articles about him, repeating the old saw that he had performed plastic surgery on Saddam during the war and helped him escape; also that he had been the creator of Saddam's "doubles." Laughing bitterly, Bashir said that another of the stories going around was that he had escaped with Saddam, performed plastic surgery on him, and then been killed by Saddam in order to keep his new identity a secret. Before I left the house, Bashir told me he was probably going to accept the Qatar job but had not yet made a final decision. He promised to let me know in a few days.

As we drove away, Sabah told me that while I'd been with Bashir, he'd been speaking with his driver, Jihad, who had confided that a week earlier a gunman had walked into the lobby of Bashir's hospital, the Al-Wasati, looking for him. The gunman had said he was looking for Ala Bashir—the *charmuta* ("whore")—in order to kill him. Ever since, Bashir had stopped his visits to the hospital and kept an even lower profile than usual.

Three or four days later Bashir called me on the Thuraya satellite phone that the Americans had given him. There was a lot of background noise. He was in a car, he explained, en route to Baghdad airport, and was being flown out of the country. He apologized for calling me at the last minute, but his departure had come up unexpectedly; he had not even been able to let his sister, Soheila, know he was leaving. When I asked Bashir where he was headed, he said he was going first to Amman; after that he wasn't sure. I asked how long he would be gone. "At least a couple of months," he said. "But I'll be in touch, from wherever I am."

Afterward I went to see Dr. Waleed, Ala Bashir's deputy, at the Al-Wasati Hospital. He didn't know that Bashir had left the country, and when I broke the news, he seemed surprised and a little wounded that Bashir had not called him to say good-bye. I asked him about the assassination threat against Bashir. Waleed confirmed it. A gunman had come into the hospital the previous week looking for Dr. Bashir, he told me, and had said "many bad things" about him.

I asked Waleed whether he had any idea what Bashir had been doing with the Americans over the past couple of months. Had it anything to do with Iraq's Health Ministry? Waleed laughed. "Was that what Ala told you?" he asked, smiling. I said that it was, although I had not really believed him. Waleed nodded. Then he told me that to his certain knowledge, Bashir had been personally involved in arranging for the surrender to the Americans of at least two of the "most wanted" Iraqis on the Pentagon's famous deck of playing cards. Waleed added that he knew this because both men were blood relatives of his, a cousin and an uncle. One had been a senior military officer, and the other had been a high-ranking Baath Party official. "Ala drove them to the airport himself," Waleed added. (The Americans had established a prison at the Baghdad airport, where most of their high-level prisoners, men like Tariq Aziz, were being held.) Waleed stated this matter-of-factly, without offering his judgment on whether the arrest of his relatives had been a good or bad thing.

After a pause Dr. Waleed said reflectively: "I am sorry to see Ala go, because he was my close friend for many, many years, but it's probably best for him to leave. He was in danger here. He has a big problem, you know. His big problem was that he was the close friend of Saddam Hussein. Everybody in Baghdad knows this. And it was true, he was."

Dr. Waleed confessed that he too was thinking of leaving Iraq because of his growing doubts about the Americans' capacity to restore law and order. Over the past two months, he said, he had been summoned repeatedly by Americans seeking his advice. They had ranged from civilian experts who worked with Paul Bremer to senior military officers and several men he suspected were CIA agents. At their request, he had spoken about a wide range of topics and offered tips on how to deal with Iraqis, including the people of Fallujah, whom he described as famously xenophobic and rebellious toward any outside authority, even during Saddam's time. The problems the Americans had encountered there, Waleed insisted, had arisen mostly out of cultural misunderstandings. For instance, when the American soldiers had occupied the school that was their first base in Fallujah, he said, they had posted sentries on its rooftop. This had infuriated the local men, because it meant that the soldiers could look down into the private courtyards of their houses and spy upon their wives and daughters. "You know that for a traditional Iraqi man, their women are the most sacred thing," Waleed explained. "For another man to see his woman in this way is a terrible dishonor."

Once the killings began in Fallujah, the cycle of violence had become difficult to halt. For the families of the dead men, it had become a matter of tribal honor to exact blood vengeance, and Waleed predicted that the Fallujans would not stop killing Americans until they had evened the score. In order to halt the cycle of violence, he'd advised the Americans to seek out and make friends with two of the city's most influential imams. If they had done that, he said, Fallujah could possibly have been pacified. He shook his head in frustration. "The Americans are very good listeners, but they don't seem to do anything." He confessed that he felt totally bewildered by their behavior. He added: "Until now the Americans in Iraq are wearing blinders; they don't see. They know this, and they know there is a big gap between themselves and the Iraqis, and that they must bridge this gap, but until now, they have not. Why, I don't know. Do you?"

Dr. Waleed's views were typical of many of the Iraqi professionals I had known from the Saddam era. Most were now jobless, frightened by the enduring chaos and violence, alienated by the changes taking place, and angered by the Americans' incompetence, or unwillingness, to set things right. There were those who, like Ala Bashir, were fatally tarred by their past associations with Saddam or the Baath Party, and for whom there was no place in the new Iraq. Whether they liked to admit it or not—and most wouldn't—Saddam's ouster had cut many Iraqis loose from their moorings. The steady certainty of their previous lives, however tedious and oppressive they had been, had been lost, and with it their sense of purpose and belonging in their own country. In some cases, their dilemmas were poignant; in others, simply pathetic. I found Samir Khairi sitting at home in a bathrobe, drinking arrack and idly channel-flipping on his television set. His previous aspirations of going to work for the Americans, which he'd told me about just after the fall of Baghdad, had gone nowhere. On top of that, he'd been struck off the Foreign Ministry's rolls by its new coalition administrators because of his Baath Party membership. The party had been banned, and this meant Samir would receive no back salary and no future pension. He was thinking of trying to get a teaching post abroad, he said, trying vainly to appear enthusiastic. He mentioned Abu Dhabi and Algeria as two possibilities.

One day Farouk Salloum, the poet from Saddam's hometown of Tikrit, came to see me at the Al-Safeer. For years Farouk had held various senior posts at Iraq's Ministry of Culture, but his real status derived from the fact that Saddam Hussein liked him. In recent years, Farouk had in fact become Saddam's pet poet. I had last seen him in mid-March, on the eve of the war, at the dinner party he had thrown at his house, when he had become maudlin and played his lute and sung sad songs and told his guests that the very next day, he was sending his young wife, a beautiful former ballerina, and their daughter, a toddler, out of the country. They would be going to Damascus, he said, while he himself was leaving on an official visit to Spain. At the time, it seemed fairly obvious that he would not be coming back.

We drank Turkish coffee in the lobby of the Al-Safeer, and Farouk, who smiled and chatted warmly, but nonetheless seemed ill at ease, confirmed that he had spent the war in Damascus with his wife and child. He explained that he had decided to evacuate them after he'd learned that people like Barzan al-Tikriti, Saddam's half brother, and Tariq Aziz were getting their families' passports revalidated in order to send them to Syria. He had returned to Baghdad alone, he told me, on April 31 and had immediately presented himself to the American authorities. "They knew of me, of course; they had a security profile of me," he said, smiling somewhat embarrassedly. "And they knew I was not a Baathist." Seeing my questioning look, Farouk added: "I had been one, until 1991, but then I gave up my party membership."

The Americans had authorized Farouk to resume his old job for the time being, he said, and they had given him a credential, which he pulled out of his top pocket to show me. It gave him access to the Coalition Provisional Authority headquarters, which was located in Saddam's Republican Palace complex. He was still officially the director of music and dance of the Ministry of Culture and was receiving his old salary, so things weren't all that bad. But Farouk didn't know how long it would last. "I understand that the ministry will be dissolved," he said, "and that there will be an arts council or something in its stead."

I was interested in hearing what Farouk really thought of

Saddam Hussein, now that we were speaking freely for the first time. He nodded uncomfortably. "You know, for the past ten years it has been a kind of nightmare," he began, "because Saddam changed after 1991"—after the Gulf War—"and he lost his feeling for humanity." He trailed off, and I didn't press him to go on. Farouk said that he had offered to help the Americans in their dealings with the Tikritis, his people, and also to help hunt down Saddam, but no one had ever taken him up on it. He didn't know why.

I asked Farouk how he was adjusting to the new Iraq. He said he felt dismayed by some of the changes, especially by the many "new Iraqis" on the streets of Baghdad, the returned refugees and exiles, and the poor people who had poured in from the outlying slums and countryside to live as squatters in the abandoned houses and apartments of regime apparatchiks. "When I see their faces, what I see are the peasants of Sumeria, and they should return to the land," he said. "They are looters, thieves!" He thought that the Americans were insufficiently in touch with Iraq's educated class, and he blamed most of the current violence on the Shias, as many Sunnis in Baghdad did. "The resistance is a combination of Al Qaeda and Shia religious fundamentalists backed by Iran," he declared. Farouk said that he still hoped things would work out with the Americans—anything was better than the religious fundamentalists—but he wasn't very optimistic.

Farouk also had safety concerns. While he was abroad during the war, he explained, he had given an interview to the BBC in which he'd said something about Saddam's being the past and the Americans' being the future. Afterward, Tikriti friends told him Saddam had heard the broadcast and felt betrayed by him. Farouk had also heard that he was a target of the Shia radicals in the northeastern Baghdad slum of Thawra, formerly Saddam City. (I'd noticed that, in general, Shiites tended to use the slum's new name—Sadr City—while Sunnis like Farouk insisted on calling it by its original name, Thawra.) "I have heard that in the Imam Ali mosque in Thawra my name is on the wall as someone to be assassinated," he said. I asked Farouk whether he was worried and what he was doing to protect himself. He was taking care, he said. "I am staying at home a lot." I noticed that he was accompanied by a bodyguard, a heavyset man who sat nearby as we spoke.

A week later, at Farouk's invitation, I attended a musical performance that he had organized. It was held in the convention center inside the coalition compound, the Green Zone, and I sat in the audience with Amal Jubouri, an Iraqi poet who was an old friend of Farouk's. Amal had left Iraq in the mid-1990s to live in self-imposed exile in Germany and had returned after the war. Amal told me she had known Farouk in the old days. After the Gulf War, he had confided that he wanted to flee Iraq, but somehow he had never made the leap. Amal thought he had paid a high price for his indecision. She believed Farouk was deeply depressed about this and that he was now having a hard time finding himself again. But she knew that there were many Iraqis who were not as sympathetic as she was to Farouk's dilemma. They could not forgive him for his close relationship to Saddam; he was a pariah to them.

We looked around the theater to see if we could spot Farouk, but he was nowhere to be seen. Then, about halfway through the performance, we saw him. Farouk had entered the room quietly toward the back of the seating gallery, through a side door, and was sitting alone. He was dressed entirely in black. Amal became distressed at seeing Farouk on his own. She proposed that during the next lull we go and sit with him as a display of our friendship. I agreed. But by the time the piece that was playing, a violin quartet, was finished, Farouk had vanished.

One morning I paid a call on Uday al-Taiee, who had been Saddam's capo for the foreign media. Curious to see how he had fared after the fall of the regime he had served so well, I tracked al-Taiee down at his apartment. It was on the top floor of one of the ugly concrete apartment blocks that sat near the former Information Ministry. The electricity was not working, so I had to walk up ten flights of stairs, past pools of urine and uncollected bags of garbage. Al-Taiee's apartment was large and comfortable and impeccably clean, however, and al-Taiee, who was dressed in a casual dishdasha, welcomed me in with an amnesiac's display of warmth and good grace. He introduced me to his wife and teenage son and bade me sit on a couch across from him. His wife brought us refreshments. We chit-chatted politely about things for a while, and then al-Taiee's underling, Mohsen, showed up. Mohsen looked surprised to see me, but he too behaved as if everything were normal and shook my hand as if we were friends.

Mohsen was carrying a file of papers, I noticed, and after he and al-Taiee had conferred in Arabic for a few minutes, al-Taiee turned to me and explained that they were making representations with the coalition on behalf of the five thousand employees of the Information Ministry. They had all been left in limbo, without salaries, waiting to know whether their ministry was going to be abolished or not. As he spoke, al-Taiee became indignant. It was their right, he said, as long-serving government employees, to be paid what was owed them. He began intoning darkly about the foolish arrogance of the new coalition administrators. His wife and Mohsen both chimed in with their own complaints about crime and the lack of electricity and the aggressive behavior of American soldiers. Al-Taiee began speaking over them to talk about the penuries of his new life without a salary. His family was living off the small amount of money he had managed to save, he said, but soon it would run out, and he would have to start selling the furniture in their home. I recalled the reports I had heard about al-Taiee's robbing Western television networks of large amounts of cash the night before Baghdad fell. As if he had read my mind, al-Taiee began saying that he knew that "falsehoods" were circulating about him. He fulminated angrily about this for several minutes, peppering his harangue with protestations about how he and Mohsen had been the friends and allies of the Western media and had gone out of their way to protect journalists from harm. Al-Taiee even claimed, with Mohsen nodding his earnest agreement to everything he said, that he had opposed some of Saddam's policies. He concluded by saying: "My conscience is clean."

I sat there, politely attentive, for quite a while, but listening to al-Taiee carry on was galling, and finally I could stand it no longer. Addressing the issue of their unpaid salaries, I suggested that perhaps, as former employees of Saddam Hussein's government, he and Mohsen and their colleagues were not on the coalition's list of urgent humanitarian priorities. I added that if, as they were now claiming, they'd really been against Saddam Hussein's regime, then why had they served it until the day of its collapse?

"But we did, privately," al-Taiee protested, while Mohsen nodded.

"Where is the evidence?" I asked.

They looked at me blankly. "There are people who know," al-Taiee said vaguely. "As God is my witness, I know what I did," he added staunchly, and fell silent again.

I replied: "Maybe so, but that's not really good enough, is it?" I pointed out that while they had worked for Saddam, his henchmen had murdered tens of thousands of people. Their loyalty to his regime understandably made both of them seem complicit with its repressive policies in many people's eyes. Couldn't they see that? (Both were frowning and shaking their heads in disagreement as I spoke.) Perhaps, I added, they should have left the country and gone into exile, as so many other Iraqis had done over the years.

They argued back. "But we could do nothing; we had families to protect," said al-Taiee.

I could hardly believe my ears when Mohsen added: "We were

only following orders." (A couple days later I heard the news that the coalition had decided not to revive the Information Ministry. Al-Taiee and Mohsen were out of jobs.)

Another official from the old days, Khadum, who had been the senior Mukhabarat official assigned to the foreign press at the Information Ministry, came to visit me one afternoon at the Al-Safeer Hotel. He brought his thirteen-year-old son along with him. Khadum greeted me warmly, as if we were old chums, and then he introduced his son. With paternal pride, he patted the boy on the head and informed me that his son had been born in Virginia. Khadum explained that he'd been stationed at the Iraqi Embassy in Washington, D.C., until its closure following Iraq's invasion of Kuwait. He said he was hoping to get his son's U.S. passport for him as soon as possible and meanwhile was encouraging him to learn English. The boy smiled at me politely as his father spoke but said nothing. Finally, Khadum brought up the real reason for his visit. He was jobless, he explained, and wished to offer his services to me as a translator or, he added, "for whatever you might need." He knew people, he said, who, in exchange for some money, would be willing to give me incriminating government documents, papers that revealed illegal past business dealings between Western governments and Saddam's regime, for instance. He also knew many former intelligence and military officials, he added hopefully. They too would be prepared to talk for money. I thanked Khadum for his offer but reminded him that I was a journalist, not a CIA agent. He nodded, but I could see that he didn't really understand the difference. (Sometime later I heard Khadum had been hired by Fox News.)

As the months dragged by, and more and more of Saddam's fugitive cronies surrendered themselves to the Americans or else were captured or killed (as his sons, Uday and Qusay, were in July), Naji Sabri's whereabouts remained a mystery. Sabri was not wanted for war crimes, nor was he one of the "most wanted" Saddam officials on the Americans' deck of playing cards. Sabri had not been seen in public since the eve of the American air strikes against Baghdad, when he gave his last press conference. Since then, many rumors had circulated about his fate: that he had been killed, that he had been wounded, and so forth. All of them turned out to be false. A few weeks after the fall of Baghdad, however, I had heard credible-sounding reports that Sabri was alive, somewhere outside Iraq. He had evidently called some personal friends on a cell phone that had been traced back to Vienna. The speculation was that he was living in Austria under the protection of Jörg Haider, the far-right Austrian politician, with whom he had become friends during his tenure as ambassador. It wasn't until April 2004 that I found out, from a friend of his, that in fact Sabri was living in Qatar and that for the time being he had decided to keep a low profile.

On July 6, I drove to Fallujah to find out what was going on there. It had been unusually quiet for several weeks. At the military base outside town, I met with Lieutenant Colonel Eric Wesley, the executive officer of the U.S. Army's Second Brigade, Third Infantry Division. At the outset of our conversation, Wesley, a slim, intense, bespectacled man in his thirties, surprised me by declaring boosterishly: "I would argue that Fallujah is a success story." He informed me that since his troops had taken over the city from the Third Armored Cavalry Regiment of the 101st Airborne Division in early June, relations between the Americans and the Fallujans had gradually improved. As proof of this, he said, he had not lost a single man to hostile fire. (This was strictly true, although a few days earlier an Australian journalist had died of wounds he had suffered when one of Wesley's patrols, which he had been accompanying, came under fire.)

Wesley attributed the turnaround in Fallujah to his use of the "carrot and stick." Enthusiastically, he explained how it worked. "It's a very focused stick and a very broad carrot. First, we go

after the bad guys and get rid of 'em. And second, 'It's the economy, stupid!' The stick only gives me linear results. What this
means is that if I bust one guy with an RPG, what I get is one
RPG off the street. The inverse of the stick is the carrot. Part of
the carrot is to work closely with the police chief and the authorities of the town. We hear the people out and try and get 'em
what they need. For example, we've gotten the police some new
patrol cars. And we're working closely with the mayor on
Democracy 101. But he's no American stooge; he was selected by
the sheikhs of the community. Now that's not ideal, I know, but
it's one of the ways we are trying to use the culture of the region
to promote success. We also meet weekly with the local imams.
If we are successful, these leaders can go to those who are disaf-
fected and say: 'Hey, the Americans are hooking you up.'" Wesley shot me a satisfied smile.

At around midday I went out on a patrol with some of Wesley's soldiers. Beforehand, they explained that we would be patrolling an area of Fallujah they called Little Detroit. I asked why
they had given it that name. "Because the people there don't
smile," one of the soldiers said, laughing. On their map, they
showed me the various sectors of Fallujah, for which they had
code names like Charlie and Foxtrot and their own psychological
profiles of the inhabitants. Little Detroit, in the southern part of
town, was not Fallujah's most hostile neighborhood, for instance.
They pointed to a district farther north. "They are really unfriendly up there." When I asked why certain parts of Fallujah
were hostile and others weren't, the soldiers looked mystified.
"Who knows?" said one of the men with a shrug.

The unit's commander, Lieutenant Dan Ganci, of Staten Island,
New York, was a short, wiry young man with a deep voice and a
ready smile. He was a West Point graduate from the class of 2000.
Ganci told me to ride in the lead vehicle in the convoy, which consisted of three armored personnel carriers and three Humvees. I
climbed aboard and met my new companions, Specialist Travis

Wilhelm, a husky young fellow of twenty-six from Pennsylvania, and his skinny comrade, Private First Class Zack Freidl, who was chewing a cud of Red Man tobacco. An older soldier sat above us inside the gunner's mount, manning the .50- caliber machinegun. Everybody carried an M-16 assault rifle and a liter bottle of cold water. It was a very hot day, around 130 degrees Fahrenheit.

We journeyed the three or so miles down the highway toward Fallujah. The armored personnel carrier clanked on its metal treads, and its engine gave off a loud roar, which made it difficult to talk. The heat was intense. The city's outskirts were a dismal, refuse-strewn welter of auto repair shops, metal scrapyards, and factories. This panorama gradually gave way to the city itself, a low-slung jumble of mud-colored squares and rectangles overhung with a skyline of television aerials and the minarets and domes of a dozen or so mosques. In the center of town, we turned off the main road into Little Detroit. On a street corner where there was a gaggle of shops, Ganci halted the convoy and dispatched some soldiers to distribute handbills printed in Arabic for the storekeepers to post on their shopfronts. Lieutenant Ganci explained that the handbills outlined the Coalition Provisional Authority's intentions to phase out the Iraqi dinars in circulation—known as the Saddam notes because they featured the former dictator's visage—and replace them with an up-dated version of Iraq's pre–Gulf War currency. These were vintage Saddam-less notes that were legal tender in the autonomous northern Kurdish territories. The idea was that by the end of the year all Iraq would have a single currency, and nary a Saddam would be seen.

As the soldiers fanned out on the streets, a loud commotion erupted. Iraqi men and boys had crowded around in front of a small kebab house. I walked over and saw that a heated exchange was taking place between the owner of the kebab house, a young

Iraqi man with a clipped beard and a white dishdasha robe, and the unit's psy ops (psychological warfare operations) officer, a beefy man in his thirties who wore a floppy olive green hat. His Iraqi translator, whom Ganci had pointed out to me as his unit's "interpreter asset," stood ineffectually by his side. He was a slight man in civilian clothing who had a pistol in his belt. Surrounded by a group of youths, the shopkeeper was standing about two feet away from the psy ops man and appeared to be openly defying him. He wore an expression of contempt, and he was speaking in rough English and pointing challengingly to the handbills in the officer's hands.

"What is this?" the shopkeeper shouted. "I don't want this. Go away! Why are you here?" He turned and said something in Arabic to his friends, who laughed and leered at the psy ops man.

Looking confused, psy ops asked his interpreter: "What's he saying?"

Before he could answer, the shopkeeper, coming closer, said in English: "You should leave. Go away. I hate you."

Turning his back, psy ops said, "I hate you too," and walked off.

The crowd was giddy now, a little wild, and there was a lot of shouting and loud commentary going on. I wandered over to where some teenage boys were besieging a couple of soldiers who were bearing stacks of the handbills. They were grabbing the leaflets and darting off again, laughing. The soldiers looked befuddled, and it was obvious that they hadn't a clue what was being said to them. I heard more shouting behind me and saw that the psy ops man was back at the kebab house, where he and the shopkeeper had renewed their standoff.

The Iraqi was jabbing crudely at the American's face with a finger. I noticed for the first time that the psy ops man's tongue was pierced.

The Iraqi shouted, in English: "What is this? Are you a woman? Why do this?" He made a crude gesture with his tongue. "Aren't you a man?"

The psy ops man, smiling, replied: "Sure, I'm a man."

"No!" retorted the Iraqi, who turned and said something in Arabic to his friends, who laughed and yelled things at the American.

Psy ops began to turn away.

"No, don't turn away!" the Iraqi shouted at him. "Aren't you a man?"

Psy ops turned back to him. He wore an uncertain look.

"Only women do this," the man yelled, sneering and poking him again in the mouth with his finger.

Psy ops stared at the man for a moment, and then he told his translator, "Tell him it's for eating pussy." He grinned and waggled his tongue lewdly at the shopkeeper.

The interpreter was shocked, and he shook his head; he didn't want to translate this.

"Tell him!" psy ops insisted.

Looking embarrassed, the translator said something in a low voice to the shopkeeper in Arabic. As he did, psy ops turned his back and began walking away, and called out loudly: "Have a nice day."

"Have a bad day!" the shopkeeper shouted at his retreating back.

I followed psy ops over to the opposite side of the road, where the convoy's vehicles were parked, and several soldiers stood guard with their weapons. He stood there silently, hands on his hips, looking back at the kebab house, where the shopkeeper who had insulted him still stood talking loudly with the crowd of youths. I asked him how he felt about what had just happened. Without looking at me, he said defensively: "Well, so the guy fucking hates me, so what? And I'm allowed to hate him back." He said no more. Nearby, Lieutenant Ganci stood quietly watching as his soldiers handed out the last of their handbills.

Two older, sun-darkened men wearing kaffiyeh headscarves approached, pushing a bicycle. They came up to Ganci and said they wanted to speak to him. They were smiling. He greeted them politely, but they couldn't understand one another, and so he called the interpreter over. One of the men explained that they had a question. "Sure, whatever you'd like to ask," replied Ganci. The Iraqi asked how old his soldiers were. Nodding obligingly, Ganci said: "They're between twenty and twenty-five years old."

The men exchanged a look, and one of them spoke again. His face wore a look of exaggerated sympathy. He clucked his tongue and wagged his head. "Ah, so young! And in this hot sun . . . They should be far away from here, enjoying a different climate." He and his friend stared at Ganci, as if expecting a reply. He stared back at them, realizing that they were taunting him. He asked the interpreter if there was anything else they wanted to discuss. They began complaining about the scarcity of propane, of gasoline, and of water. Ganci nodded and smiled. He had heard it all before. He thanked them for their time and moved away. They walked on, pushing their bike and grinning to each other.

Next, a husky young man, a teenager, pushed up to Ganci. He gestured to a rubbish pile that filled a vacant lot next to the shops and houses. In an overly loud voice, he asked Ganci: "Why don't you Americans clean up the garbage?"

Sighing, Ganci replied: "Why don't you clean it up yourselves?"

The boy said, theatrically: "Oh, because we are not like you Americans. We are savage and primitive people." His eyes were laughing. He went on in this fashion for a minute, until Ganci grew tired of it. He interrupted the youth and called his men back to their vehicles. He told them to start moving out.

We moved slowly out of Little Detroit through a grimy neighborhood of scrap metal yards. As we passed people on the street, we received mixed reactions. Among the adults, they ranged from blankly neutral stares to glances of mild curiosity and a few expressions of frank hostility. Small children jumped up and down, yelling excitedly. Some gave the thumbs-up sign, others the thumbs-down. Specialist Wilhelm, who stood next to me in the armored personnel carrier, smiled pleasantly at everyone we passed, giving a languid thumbs-up signal.

As we clanked along, Wilhelm confessed that he and the other men of his unit were weary and ready to go home. They had been in the field the longest of any of the army's soldiers, since the previous September, when they had been deployed to Kuwait. Their morale was pretty high even now, he said, because they'd been told they could go home soon. "We have only eleven days to go, and we're counting them down, I can tell you." He smiled and added: "Actually we don't have it too bad right now. Here in Fallujah is the first time we've been able to sleep indoors. Until we got here, it was all in tents."

Wilhelm pointed to a winchlike metal affair in the bed of the vehicle and told me that it was the mount for a mortar launcher. They had taken it out because they didn't really need a mortar in Fallujah, where they mostly just patrolled. But they had used it a lot during the war, he said, and added proudly: "We scored two hundred kills with that."

I asked if he was referring to vehicles or personnel. "Personnel," Wilhelm clarified emphatically, smiling at my ignorance.

Once, he explained, their advance scouts had detected a group of a hundred Iraqis hiding behind a berm, and so the unit's gunners had done their measurements and launched their mortars at the spot. "We killed them all, man; that was something."

Next he pointed to the machine-gun turret and said that once, during the war, outside the city of Najaf, he had been manning the .50-caliber when an SUV had suddenly come hurtling down the road toward them. "We didn't know whether it was fadaheen [as he called the Saddam Fedayeen] or what. They were coming straight at us, so we just lit 'em up!" Wilhelm shook his head, re-membering the moment. He paused and then laughed. "I've got some pretty good stories, so I guess I'll be drinking for free for a while back in my hometown bar."

Wilhelm said his experiences in Iraq had made him more curious about world affairs. When his enlistment was up, he hoped to go to the University of North Carolina at Chapel Hill and study international relations. The GI Bill would pay for it. I asked him what he hoped to do when he got his degree. "I was thinking I might try the CIA," he said musingly. "Or maybe I might like to try and be an ambassador one day. But I guess I'm jumping ahead of myself there. Who knows?"

I returned to Baghdad that afternoon, but a few days later I drove back out to the Fallujah base. I'd heard Lieutenant Colonel Wesley was going to attend a graduation ceremony for the city's first contingent of U.S.-trained Iraqi policemen, and I hoped to accompany him. When I got there, however, I was told the ceremony had been canceled. I was given no explanation, but the reason seemed to be that Wesley's carrot-and-stick approach had begun to run into trouble. The day before, a remote-controlled bomb had exploded in front of the police station in Ramadi, twenty-five miles down the road, killing seven policemen at their graduation ceremony. Meanwhile, Fallujah's police chief had asked the Americans to withdraw their soldiers from his police station, arguing that their presence was bringing it under nightly attack, and they had quietly agreed to do so.

At the base, morale was not good. Specialist First Class Wilhelm and his fellow soldiers had been informed that they were not going home as planned after all. By orders of the Pentagon, their stay in Fallujah had been extended "indefinitely."

Ala Bashir's kinsman Sheikh Ibrahim al-Jubour turned out to be an imposing figure of a man. He wore a white headdress and flowing black robes with gold-embroidered hems, and he carried himself in a ponderously regal way. He also sported a magnificent handlebar mustache, dyed jet black. Intrigued to hear his version of the encounter with the Americans David and Charles, I had tracked him down at the Baghdad headquarters of his newly formed United Iraqi Party. Entering his office, I noticed a large framed portrait on the floor leaning against the wall. At first glance, it resembled a picture of Saddam, like those that had hung in every office in Iraq before the war. Looking closer, I realized that it was of the sheikh himself, posed in a style not dissimilar to that of the former dictator.

After we had exchanged some ritual courtesies, Sheikh Ibrahim politely but firmly asked me: "You are welcome here, but let's be on the level. Are you an official of the U.S. government, or a journalist, or what exactly?" I explained that I was a journalist and a friend of his relative Ala Bashir. The sheikh nodded and relaxed. I told him I was curious about his meetings with the Americans. He replied: "I am becoming a pessimist, because the Americans come, they listen to our proposals and points of view, but they do nothing. Nothing has come out of our meetings with them. It seems they just come to do reconnaissance." The sheikh raised his eyebrows in a skeptical way and added: "When I asked them what their intention was in occupying Iraq, they remained silent."

The sheikh's chief gripe, as far I could tell, was his sense of political displacement in the new Iraq. Saddam had astutely curried favor with the country's tribal leaders, bestowing patronage on those who supported him and punishing those who opposed him. Sheikh Ibrahim had done time in prison for opposing Saddam, he said, and felt he deserved better treatment from the Americans. On behalf of the Jubour tribe, the sheikh said he had used his meetings with Charles and David to lobby for representation on the Iraqi Governing Council. His initiative had not gotten anywhere, however, so he and his fellow Jubouris had set up their party, with him as its leader. "For now, we have our own political activities within our own party, and we don't seek a role in the council," he explained. "But I predict that in the future the Americans will beg to be close to us."

As I rose to take my leave, Sheikh Ibrahim shook my hand and handed me a photograph of himself, magnificently attired in his tribal costume. Smiling magnanimously, he announced that he regarded me as an "honorary Jubour." When I thanked him for his gesture, he declaimed: "America has great technological power, but it doesn't seem very expert in politics or with people. The Americans came to liberate Iraq, to bring democracy, and to take away the weapons of mass destruction. But when they got here, they forgot about these things and about the people who are influential here. Tell the Americans not to be blind, not to ignore a tribe with so many people, so that its eyes will not be harmed. This is just advice."

There was more to the Jubour tribe than met the eye, of course. One of the sheikh's nephews, a man in his early forties, collared me as I left the building and asked to come and see me in my hotel. Later, he showed up. He said that his name was Khalaf al-Jubour, and that he was a former official of the Mukhabarat, Saddam's intelligence service. "I am one of the old regime intelligence people, and so were a lot of my family members," explained Khalaf without embarrassment. "Two of my brothers were in counterintelligence. My uncle was an administrator of the Mukhabarat. Altogether thirteen of my cousins worked in the same field." He personally had been in charge of the Mukhabarat's French department, he said, adding that he had never been involved in operations against the United States. So, when the war ended, he had presented himself to the Americans, who had investigated him and, he claimed, found him clean of any war crimes. He had begun to cooperate with them, giving them information, and had even helped to arrange the surrender of one of his cousins, an ex-officer in the Saddam Fedayeen, the brutal militia that had been led by Uday Hussein. The cousin had come to him for help after the Americans had raided his house and, not finding him, had taken his father and brother hostage, as well as a large sum of money in cash. The Americans promised to return his money and free his relatives if he turned himself in. Khalaf had personally driven his cousin to the Americans at Baghdad airport, where there was a prison for former regime officials, and handed him over.

"But the Americans have not kept their word," exclaimed Khalaf in a tone of great indignation. "They have kept my cousin's family, and they don't acknowledge taking his money." I found Khalaf's affectation of moral outrage rather amusing, considering who he was. I remarked that I found it interesting that the Americans had adopted Saddam's own time-honored tactic of taking hostages to lure in troublemakers. Khalaf caught the irony in my voice and smiled. He acknowledged that what I said was true. He immediately switched tack and got down to what his real concerns were, and they didn't have much to do with his cousin. The Americans so far had been happy to receive information from him, he said, but they had not hired him. Khalaf wanted a job. "There are thousands of ex-Mukhabarat who are now jobless," he said. "This is a big problem. I've advised the Americans to find a solution to this. And there are thousands more who worked in the secret police. They may all join together in the resistance. My wife, who is an engineer, had a good job in the presidential office, and she is now jobless too. We have children to support. The Americans have told me to go to my house and remain there. What am I supposed to do, open an office and sell information about my country?"

Disenfranchised tribal leaders and unemployed Mukhabarat agents were just part of the complex, emerging mosaic of post-Saddam Iraq, where every imaginable political party, religious faith, and ethnic group was now jockeying for its place in the sun. The transformation was occurring at a vertiginous speed, and with it, Baghdad had become a Tower of Babel. One afternoon, driving past the old Air Defense Ministry, which had been bombed into a pulp by the U.S. Air Force in the war, I noticed a crudely painted new sign by the front gate, which said: IRAQUIAN FORMER POLITICAL PRISONERS ASSOCIATION. The Central Committee of the Iraqi Communist Party had installed itself in a building directly across the Tigris from the Republican Palace, now the headquarters of the Coalition Provisional Authority. Meanwhile the formerly Iranian-based Shiite religious party, the Supreme Council for Islamic Revolution in Iraq—led by Ayatollah Muhammad Bakr al-Hakim, whom I had met with in Tehran before the war—had taken over Tariq Aziz's villa farther downriver, while the Pentagon-sponsored former exile Ahmed Chalabi had commandeered a faux-Chinese-rococo mansion that had been the home of the chief of Saddam's Mukhabarat. Moqtada al-Sadr's Baghdad office was a more humble affair, appropriately enough, and was located incongruously next to Mansour's most popular ice-cream shop. I constantly had to remind myself that just a few months earlier, the members of any of these groups would first have been tortured, then shot or hanged, if they had so much as shown their faces in Iraq.

Since the war, foreigners, ranging from earnest do-gooders to outright carpetbaggers, had also flooded into Baghdad. A group of paramilitary-looking Americans brandishing revolvers and Kalashnikovs, along with their Iraqi bodyguards, moved into the Al-Safeer while I was there. When they were asked what they did for a living, they said mysteriously that their business was "information systems." Some upper-class British college kids in their early twenties turned up and founded an English-language biweekly newspaper, the *Baghdad Bulletin.* It did not last long. Steffa, a middle-aged American woman from California, had used her own savings to travel to Baghdad in order to organize a peace conference. Steffa had never been to the Middle East before and spoke not a word of Arabic, but as she explained it, she felt compelled to "do something for peace." As the weeks of summer dragged by, I noticed that Steffa was spending long hours writing poetry and surfing the Web in the new Internet café at the Al-Safeer. She confessed that she was finding her peace project hard to get going.

One of the most intriguing new faces in Baghdad was Ayad Jamaluddin, an Iraqi Shiite cleric of forty-two. He was a slender, good-looking man in a black turban and a white robe covered with a black manteau. He had a short, clipped beard, and he carried himself with the erect posture and air of serene composure that I had come to associate with Shiite clergymen. But there was nothing ascetic about Jamaluddin. For instance, there was his habit of smoking Cuban cigars, Cohibas, which he drew from a black leather case hidden somewhere in his robes. In his front driveway he had a collection of automobiles that included a convertible Cadillac, several Mercedes-Benzes, and a dark blue Rolls-Royce with cream-colored leather seats and a gold-plated front grille. Nor did Jamaluddin have electricity worries. His imposing riverside mansion had its own state-of-the-art generators, which kept its lighting and air-conditioning systems going around the clock. It had been the home of Izzat Ibrahim al-Douri, Saddam's deputy in the ruling Baath Party, who had vanished during the war and was still a fugitive. The house had been ransacked and totally looted, but Jamaluddin, who had somehow requisitioned it, had obviously taken a great deal of care and expense to restore and refurnish it.

The interior of the mansion, which was done out in glazed green brick and stained glass and decorative Islamic fretwork, had superb marble floors covered with authentic Persian carpets. Two canaries in cages near the front door filled the house with song. In the dining room, a splendid hand-woven Persian tapestry of pure silk hung on a wall. The rear garden, which overlooked the Tigris, was planted with fresh new turf and date palms, and on the lawn stood an arched reed house, a mudhif—the traditional meetinghouse of the Marsh Arabs of southern Iraq—which Jamaluddin had had custom built by craftsmen from Basra. A couple of bodyguards armed with Kalashnikovs stood watchfully by the rail fence at the end of the garden. Some steps led down to a jetty where a long wooden boat with a swooping bowsprit was moored. Jamaluddin told me he had erected the mudhif in order to host meetings where ideas could be freely exchanged between people. He saw it as a symbol of Iraq's new position as a bridge between the Middle East and the West, and he added, smiling: "I love the fact that it is built out of the reeds that come from the marshes that were drained by Saddam."

Jamaluddin had recently returned to his homeland after twenty-five years in exile. In 1979, as the politically active youngest son of a religious scholar of Najaf, the Shia holy city, he fled Saddam's Iraq for Iran, attracted by Khomeini's revolution, which had just triumphed there. After a couple of years, Jamaluddin told me, he had become disenchanted with the Iranian revolution but had stayed on to study Islamic religion and philosophy. Eight years ago he had gone to live in Dubai, where he had served as the representative for the Islamic charity there of the world's highest-ranking Shia cleric, the reclusive Grand Ayatollah Ali al-Sistani, of Najaf. Sistani, who had been kept under virtual house arrest by Saddam since the early 1990s, represented the quietist school of Shiism, which opposed political Islam of the sort espoused by the late Khomeini and his disciples. Now that he was back in Iraq, however, Jamaluddin clearly intended to become a player. He was reputed to enjoy an extremely close relationship with the American officials of the Coalition Provisional Authority, including its newly appointed chief administrator, Paul Bremer, and had already established his own foundation, aimed, as he put it, at promoting "greater understanding between Iraq and the West." He hinted that the foundation would eventually become a political party.

A close friend of Jamaluddin's fleshed out his story for me, explaining that the cleric had been a staunch supporter of the Bush

administration's plan for war against Saddam. In the autumn of
2002 the Americans had approached him and asked for his assistance in building up a Shiite base of support for the United
States once the war took place. He had agreed and, during the
first week of fighting, had been flown into Najaf by the U.S.
military. His job, evidently, was to curry favor with Grand Ayatollah Sistani by offering to provide him with security. (It was an
overture that was politely rebuffed by the old cleric.) Jamaluddin
was joined in Najaf by Abdel Majid al-Khoei, another pro-Western Shia cleric who had been living in exile in London since the
death of his father, Grand Ayatollah Sistani's predecessor, in
1992. Khoei ran the London-based Al-Khoei Foundation, a
well-funded Shiite philanthropy. He was also working closely
with the CIA, and had arrived in Iraq with a large amount of
cash in order to buy favor for himself and support for Americans
in Najaf's clerical circles. Within a few days, however, Khoei had
been murdered savagely in Najaf, by followers of the young, vi-
tuperously anti-American Shiite cleric Moqtada al-Sadr. Khoei's
murder had effectively dashed the American plans of building up
a viable loyalist faction within Iraq's Shiite community.

Moqtada al-Sadr was the son of yet another late Shiite cleric
who had been wildly popular in Iraq and who had been murdered, apparently on Saddam's orders, a few years earlier. Young
Sadr was closely tied to one of Iran's most hard-line clerics and
had emerged as an opponent of the coalition immediately after
the war. Within days of Saddam's ouster, Sadr had set up a power
base in Najaf and in the vast Baghdad Shiite slum of Saddam
City, which he had renamed Sadr City. His followers were mostly
young, unemployed, and uneducated Shiite men, whom he
turned into a vigilante force. Lately Sadr had begun issuing blus-
tering calls for the Americans to leave Iraq and had summoned
his followers to join in an "Islamic army" to oust them. Given
the threat to their plans posed by religious militants like Sadr,
Jamaluddin obviously represented a potentially useful ally of the

Americans in Iraq. Jamaluddin was handicapped, however. Without Khoei to serve as a leader whom he could rally people around, Jamaluddin was isolated. He had neither the late Khoei's venerable family name nor a base of support of his own among Najaf's clerics. All he could really do for the time being was to try to survive and, somehow, build a constituency for himself. Jamaluddin did not hide his affinities. "Without the Americans," he said, "we would have remained as the slaves of one man, Saddam Hussein. Iraq is not exceptional; this is how it is in most of the Middle East. For fourteen centuries Arabs have been slaves to their rulers. They do not know what freedom is. The society has a backward culture, and this society should be changed. The Arab and the Islamic culture should be changed. Saddam Hussein is just the rotten fruit of a corrupted tree. If we do not want another Saddam Hussein to appear, then we must uproot the oppressive and corrupted culture that we live in."

I could see why the Americans liked Ayad Jamaluddin. He was a Dream Muslim, with a transformative, pro-Western vision for the future of Iraq and the Middle East. But to me, Jamaluddin was an anomaly who didn't seem to have a place in the uncompromising new Iraqi reality that was rapidly developing outside the secure walls of his mansion. I could not see him surviving long into the future, not without a lot of luck. Along with the violence, sectarianism and xenophobia were on the rise in Iraq.

One day I traveled to Najaf to revisit the beautiful shrine of Imam Ali, the son-in-law of the Prophet, who had died there in AD 661. Gone were the plainclothes henchmen who had vigilantly prowled the grounds during Saddam's day. The courtyard of the shrine was thronged with fervent and emotional pilgrims from all over the Shiite universe: Lebanon, Pakistan, Iran, and even Afghanistan. Groups of mourners bearing coffins came and went from the shrine, seeking blessings for their dead relatives. As I stood observing the scene, an Iraqi man approached me and asked me challengingly if I was a Muslim. When I told him no, that I was a Christian, he asked truculently what I was doing there. My Iraqi translator, Salih, a devout Sunni Muslim from Baghdad, was shocked at the man's rudeness, and he spoke roughly to him. The man moved away but glared back at me as he went.

Afterward Salih apologized profusely to me. He then began to rail about Shiites, who, he explained, were "not good Muslims," but primitive, uneducated fanatics. I argued heatedly with Salih about his attitude, pointing out that tens of thousands of Shia had been ruthlessly slaughtered over the years by Saddam. Salih shook his head vigorously from side to side. But the evidence was there in plain sight, I insisted. What about all of the mass graves that had been uncovered since the war? It was true, Salih acknowledged finally. Many of the mass graves were filled with the bodies of Shiites, but, he declared, most of them had deserved their fates, because they were "looters and thieves."

On July 18 Salih and I attended a special prayer ceremony for Sunni Muslims. It was held at the Mother of All Battles mosque, which is located on Baghdad's western fringes, on the road leading out of town to the prison of Abu Ghraib and, a little farther on, to Fallujah. The mosque was built by Saddam to commemorate the fact that during the Gulf War, "the Mother of All Battles," he had hidden in a house that once stood on the site. It was set in a moat and had four inner minarets modeled on Scud missiles and four outer minarets modeled on Kalashnikovs. Before the war, in a small museum annex of the main mosque, a special Koran had been on display. Everyone referred to it as the Blood Koran, because it was supposedly written in Saddam's own blood.

It was a brutally hot day, and there were hundreds of men wearing white skullcaps milling around outside, waiting for the ceremony to begin. A small crowd had gathered around a bearded cleric who was giving an interview to Al Arabiya television. Salih approached him and asked if he would speak to me. After we had introduced ourselves, the imam said he recognized my name. He knew that I had spoken to his uncle Sheikh Muther Khameez al-Dhari just before the war began. He was Dr. Muthana Harith Dhari, he explained, an Islamic scholar and a lecturer in sharia law at Baghdad University. His uncle was one of the elders of the tribal clan that lived in Khandhari, across the road from the Abu Ghraib prison, with whom I'd met back in March. They were the descendants of the late Sheikh Dhari, who had murdered the British colonial officer Colonel Gerard Leachman back in 1920. I mentioned this history to the imam, and he nodded, looking proud.

I asked Imam Dhari what the day's prayer ceremony at the mosque was all about. "We will try to call the people to be united and to desist from sectarianism," he explained. "At this time we should not think of ourselves as Sunni or Shia; we should be one. The Governing Council has been founded only to divide us." It was necessary for Iraqis to be united, he added, in order to resist the American occupation. That week the new Iraqi Governing Council of twenty-five Iraqi leaders from a cross section of the country's political parties had been sworn in. Many Sunnis were known to be upset because two-thirds of the council members were Shias. Dhari explained that in making this call, he was fulfilling his religious obligations. "As scholars it is our duty to remind people that they must resist the occupation with all the means they have at their disposal. We don't tell them to use this option or that. Our people are intelligent, and they know what to do."

Imam Dhari said that the prayer ceremony had been organized by a new group that he belonged to, the Association of Islamic Scholars. It was based in the Baghdad district of Adhamiyah, which was predominantly Sunni and which I knew to be regarded by the Americans as a stronghold of Saddam loyalists. The imam excused himself. The prayer ceremony was about to begin, and his father, Sheikh Harith Dhari, like himself a religious scholar, was officiating. I stayed outside the mosque in the sun to listen. Soon an old man's shrieking voice could be heard over the loudspeakers. Salih translated for me. Imam Harith Dhari began with a story about a recent outrage, one of many that he said were being committed by the U.S. military forces. It had to do with a village where the Americans had conducted house-to-house searches. "They even searched the women!" screamed the imam. Then he bellowed out: "Iraqis! Do you agree with this?"

"No," came the resounding cry from the assemblage.

The imam went on: "Iraqis are losing their patience! We warn the occupiers: Our patience will soon be over. And if they continue to insult the dignity of Iraqis, they will see something new from the resistance!" The imam said that the Iraqis knew how to restore their national glory, and as an example of what they were capable of, he cited the 1920 rebellion against the British, during which his ancestor, of course, had become a heroic figure.

The imam warned against sectarianism, reminding his audience that in 1920 the Iraqis had not cared whether they were Sunni or Shia. "They only thought of getting rid of the occupiers. Let them go, and we can choose suitable leaders to lead us. Just leave!" He called for a repudiation of the new Governing Council, spoke against revenge killings of suspected Baathists—"Let bygones be bygones"—and bemoaned Iraq's wounded dignity. "Iraqis!" he screamed. "Wake up, stop sleeping! Be united as you fight against the criminals and looters and those who want this mess to continue."

After the prayers, Dhari and another imam gave a pep talk to the crowd, which poured out of the mosque onto the grounds. There were perhaps five or six thousand men, who chanted, "Down with colonialism," "God is great," and "Down with the occupiers." Despite the appeals against sectarianism, leaflets were handed out that challenged the veracity of the census statistics allegedly used to give the Shias more council seats than the Sunnis on the basis of their percentage of the population. The crowd seemed to be very worked up about this issue, and even Salih told me he agreed with them on this point. He insisted, as the speakers were doing, that Sunnis were not a one-third minority in Iraq, but a two-thirds majority—if the Sunni Kurds were included. The Shias, he said, could not be allowed to take power through an election. If they did, then they would establish a religious regime like the one in Iran. One of the imams yelled out: "We will confront the occupier from the north of Iraq to the south, from Basra and Baghdad, Ramadi and Fallujah!" At the mention of Fallujah, which had become emblematic of the anti-American resistance, there was a huge chorus from the crowd of "Long live the Fallujans."

I left Iraq again in August, just as the gruesome wave of suicide bombings began in Baghdad, causing scores of deaths at the Jordanian Embassy, the UN headquarters, and a host of other targets. One of them was Ayatollah Muhammad Bakr al-Hakim, who was blown to pieces on August 29, along with at least one hundred other people, when two cars packed with explosives were set off by remote control outside the Imam Ali shrine in Najaf. Following his return home in May, Hakim had fulfilled his vow of resuming his clerical life in Najaf and, publicly at least, had abstained from politics. He had just finished officiating over Friday prayers when he was killed. Hakim was succeeded as leader of the Supreme Council for Islamic Revolution in Iraq by his younger brother, Abdulaziz, who already represented the party on the new Iraqi Governing Council.

A couple of weeks earlier I had met Abdulaziz at his new office in Baghdad, in a well-guarded house that had once housed Tariq Aziz's bodyguards. Abdulaziz seemed to have shifted remarkably well into his new role as a de facto political ally of the

coalition, but he made no secret of his displeasure over the foreign military occupation of his country and expressed his hope
that it would not last long. He told me he was very concerned
about the unraveling security conditions in Iraq and blamed
them on the Americans' own mistakes.

A few days before I left Baghdad, I heard a rumor that Samir
Khairi had been arrested by the Americans and hauled away to
prison. I rushed over to his house with Sabah. The metal gates
had been smashed in and were now sealed off from the street by
loops of razor wire. The doors and windows of the house, I could
see, had been broken or removed entirely. We asked some neighbors what had happened. The American military had arrived and
raided the house, breaking into it by force, and had taken Samir
away, they said. Afterward "looters"—they didn't say who—had
set upon the house and plundered it. I attempted to find out
from the Americans in the Coalition Provisional Authority what
had happened to Samir, but got nowhere.

Ala Bashir telephoned me from Qatar. He had accepted the
job offer there, he informed me, and was just beginning to settle
in. His wife and daughter had obtained their UK visas and were
on their way to stay with his two sons in England. We spoke
about Samir Khairi. Bashir already knew about his arrest and
told me he had been trying to get him released through *his* contacts, but he had been unsuccessful. Nobody seemed to knonw
why Samir had been arrested, he said. It was a mystery.

By November, when I next returned to Baghdad, I found that
the feelings of many Iraqis had hardened further toward the
Americans. One day, over lunch at his home, Ali, a Sunni businessman, expressed his views candidly: "The suicide bombers
mostly come from outside Iraq, but I'll tell you, as Iraqis, when we
hear that one of these people has killed Americans, we are happy.
We are all happy. Anyone who says differently is lying to you."

Not only American soldiers but anyone suspected of working for the coalition, Iraqis as well as Westerners, was now considered fair game by the insurgents. Policemen and politicians were the primary victims, but translators and even laundrywomen who washed the clothes of American soldiers were being assassinated. There was no longer anywhere in Iraq that was truly safe. The same morning I arrived, the Palestine Hotel was hit by several rockets, launched ingeniously from a camouflaged donkey cart. No one died, but one of the rockets punctured through the masonry and landed a mere fifteen feet from the bedroom of my friend John Burns, who was staying there. The other hotels, like my favorite place, the Al-Safeer, were either deserted or else guarded by armed sentries and ringed by high reinforced concrete walls to prevent car bombs. I stayed in a friend's house in Baghdad that had its own armed guards and a video surveillance camera permanently trained on the street outside.

By the end of the year nearly 250 Americans and many more Iraqis had been killed since President Bush had prematurely declared "an end to hostilities" at the beginning of May. Britons, Spaniards, Italians, Koreans, Thais, Japanese, Bulgarians, Poles, and a half dozen other nationalities all had contributed their own quota of victims to the growing body count, as well. Saddam's humiliating capture in his "spider hole" in Tikrit in mid-December raised hopes that the anti-American insurgency would finally abate, but within days there were more bombings and attacks all over the country. After months of searching by CIA experts, no concealed weapons of mass destruction had been discovered, but this now seemed less important than the fact that Iraq had become, as President Bush had declared, the new front line in the War on Terror. But perhaps it was only a case of self-fulfilling prophecy. In early December, in Baghdad, I met with some Iraqi men who were involved with the insurgency. One of them, who called himself Abu Abdullah, speaking in perfectly comprehensible English, told me: "The Americans should leave;

that's all we need. There won't be any terrorist operations when they go. We don't need America to fix this country or to build this country. Just to leave, my friend."

I didn't work with Sabah on that trip. I had finally lost my confidence in him during an incident that had occurred in July while he was at the wheel of his new white GMC Suburban. We had been arguing over his choice of vehicle for several days beforehand. I had misgivings about moving around in the SUV; to my eye it looked too much like the coalition's vehicles, which were increasingly being attacked by gunmen. Sabah had dismissed my concerns and stubbornly insisted that his Suburban was safe. I had reluctantly given in to him. Then, one morning, driving through the suburb of Adhamiyah, we'd been caught in traffic as two gunmen appeared on foot behind us and begun shooting their revolvers toward us. It was a not unreasonable assumption to think that we were in danger; Adhamiyah was a hotbed of resistance to the Americans, and there were frequent clashes in the neighborhood. Sabah's reflexes in the huge vehicle were maddeningly slow. At my angrily shouted insistence that he get us out of the line of fire, he'd made the mistake of following the car in front of us off the main road into a dead-end street. The car turned out to be driven by the man the gunmen were shooting at. We realized this when we watched him jerk his car to a sudden halt and run away, while we were forced to make a laborious reverse—again, much too slowly for my taste—backing up in front of the approaching gunmen and racing away again before they opened fire. After that, I didn't feel safe driving with Sabah. With Baghdad becoming increasingly dangerous, I wanted to be driven in a nondescript small, fast car with a driver who had sharp nerves and a steady hand and, above all, who did what I said. The times had changed. It was an issue not of friendship, but of security.

On my way out of Iraq, I stopped in Amman to see Nasser al-Sadoun. It had been a little over a year since we'd first met and he'd made his prescient warnings about the American plans to occupy Iraq after the war. When I reminded him of his prophecy, he smiled wanly. He clearly took no pride in seeing his prediction borne out and proceeded to tell me, with an engineer's eye to practical detail, what he thought the Americans might do to remedy the situation. "I think the Americans should get out of Iraq's cities, into camps, and stay away from road junctions, where they are constantly ambushed. But they must first bring back several divisions of the Iraqi Army"—which the Coalition Provisional Authority administrator Paul Bremer had formally disbanded in May—"and the Iraqi police, and let them do the patrolling. The more they involve the Iraqis, the better. The Americans should not show their faces, and they should leave the Iraqi officers alone to handle things, so that if the fundamentalists start to attack, then they will hit only Iraqis, and this will make the people angry with them. The Americans should come out only when they are needed. The thing about Iraqis is, they are very proud of their responsibilities, but if there is someone else in charge, they don't care about things. So put the Iraqis in charge. The British learned this lesson a long time ago. They gradually pulled their people out, even from the ministries, and by 1930 they were all out." Nasser paused to light his pipe. He puffed on it a little and sat back, apparently lost in thought. It crossed my mind that he was the first man I had met in many years who still smoked a pipe.

Nasser told me he had been giving some thought to politics as well. If the Americans pulled back their troops as he was proposing, he believed that most Iraqis would accept their continued presence in the country to guarantee their transition to democracy. But Iraqis also needed a figurehead of their own, he said, someone to guide them and who had their respect. It was his opinion, said Nasser, that such a role might be filled by a

Hashemite king. His old friend Crown Prince Hassan of Jordan, he suggested, could fulfill such a role, but he knew that Hassan would never agree to being placed on the throne by the Americans. "He will do it," said Nasser, "only if the Iraqi people ask for him." Nasser said he thought that Iraq's Sunnis and a great many of its Shiites would set aside their differences and rally around such a figure, who would be above the political fray. Meanwhile, until elections were possible, he continued, it might be a good idea to install a former military man, someone not accused of war crimes, as Iraq's de facto president. He mentioned Saddam's last defense minister, General Sultan Hashim Ahmed, who had recently turned himself in to the Americans, as a worthwhile candidate. "The army will respect and follow him. Maybe he could be the man who leads the transitional government." Nasser said that he realized that what he was proposing was not an ideal political model, but that Iraq's problems were such that they needed urgent practical solutions, and the first priority was a strong Iraqi leadership. "If there is a weak government, there is a real risk of a civil war in Iraq," said Nasser. "The government must be hard and strict. Killers should be hanged in the streets, so that people can see what happens if they commit violent crimes. It cannot be like the Americans say: 'No more death penalty in Iraq.' This doesn't work there. If you have a strong government with a military impact, the people will follow." I asked Nasser if he had any intention of returning to his homeland. He shook his head. "It has been so many years, and everything has changed so much," he said. "My friends are gone. My life is here now." Maybe, when things settled down, he would return for a visit—"like a tourist," he added, chuckling. His wife, Tamara, he confessed, did not agree with him. He shrugged neutrally. I knew that Tamara had returned to Iraq after the war and was spending most of her time there. We had met some days earlier in Baghdad, where she told me enthusiastically about the work she was doing. She had begun a charity for Iraqi orphans and had many other projects in mind. She said she thought it was her duty to do what she could to help fix Iraq's damaged society. For Tamara, clearly, Amman already lay in the past. With the fall of Baghdad, she had regained a home and a sense of future purpose.

On the evening of March 17, 2004, I was back in Baghdad and in a room of the Palestine Hotel, sipping a coffee, when a powerful explosion shook the building, threw my coffee out of its cup, and knocked me back out of my chair. The sound of gunfire was routine in Baghdad, and explosions were heard almost every day. There had been several recent blasts, but nothing remotely like this one. It was the strongest explosion I had heard since the bombardment of Baghdad during the war, which had begun almost exactly a year earlier.

I rushed out to the balcony, which had a view of a stretch of the Tigris River and, on the other side, of Saddam's Hussein's former presidential complex, which had become the headquarters of the Coalition Provisional Authority, the so-called Green Zone. At first, I could see nothing. I craned my neck out to look toward the city center, to the northeast, and then I saw a great plume of gray smoke billowing upward into the night sky. I went up to the rooftop for a better look. Flames were blazing from a gaping hole in a neighborhood of small hotels and apartment buildings about six blocks away. It looked as if a molar had been violently yanked out of a row of teeth.

I joined a couple of friends, Italian reporters, to take a closer look. As we made our way on foot to the blast site, cutting down a darkened side street, we came across two young men kicking a soccer ball back and forth in the street. One of them stopped what he was doing, picked up the ball, and, in a friendly way, voluntarily pointed the way for us. Then he resumed his game. A little farther on, a taxicab pulled over for us, and we got in. We had gone about two hundred yards along an avenue when we came to an intersection where a scrum of ambulances and fire engines and police cars had converged, blocking the way. Hysterical men in policemen's uniforms and others in civilian clothes ran around, shouting and waving weapons, turning back all traffic. Some men were arguing. One ran around with a pistol in his hand. American soldiers in Humvees and noisy armored vehicles clattered past us, into the melee. It seemed that they were just arriving on the scene. We told the taxi driver that he had better let us out where we were, and he did so, without asking for any money, saying politely, in English, that he "understood" and wishing us good night.

The blast had devastated a couple of family houses and a small hotel, the Mount Lebanon, as well as an apartment building, and it had partially destroyed another small hotel just down the street. The larger buildings were scarred and had their stone fascias peeled away; their guts had been torn apart and twisted. The houses had been almost completely reduced to rubble. One had collapsed entirely. The other looked as though it had been hacked violently in half from above, vertically, like the effect someone trying to cut a cake with a machete might produce. The back half of the house still stood, severely cracked and its remaining walls leaning, seemingly about to collapse, but with its innards visible. A second-story bedroom was exposed to public view in a fashion similar to a dollhouse in a museum; the bed hung over the gaping edge and a carpet drooped down from the former floor. A framed print of an Iraqi pastoral scene was still hanging on the wall. I heard someone say that somewhere under the mess of bricks and mortar there were trapped people who might still be alive. This seemed difficult to imagine.

Where the bomb had gone off, it had left a large crater in the concrete road. It was about six feet deep and about eighteen feet across. There was black dirt everywhere, mounds of rubble, a toppled, shorn tree. Acrid smoke rose from the embers. The air had a dank, scorched smell. Firemen with yellow jackets and hoses were shooting water into the smoking ruins. I counted five carbonized cars sitting on the street. Paramilitary-looking Americans with flak jackets—perhaps FBI agents—came and inspected the crater carefully. The scene was a pandemonium of flickering flashlights and headlamps and shouting, pushing men and confused-looking American soldiers who were trying to clear the area of people. I saw a couple of injured men who were trying to hobble and simultaneously being half carried away by others. Another man, dressed in a bloodied gray dishdasha robe, lay dead or unconscious on a stretcher that was rushed into a waiting ambulance. American soldiers and Iraqi policemen strained to hold back a mob of onlookers, relatives, and reporters. Fire engines and ambulances came and went. Everyone stumbled on the suddenly uneven ground.

An Iraqi friend of mine, Salam, loomed out of the murk. He carefully stepped over to me. He told me it had been a rocket attack. I told him I doubted this, that it looked like a car bomb to me. Salam said he had heard this from a man who had seen the rocket. He said he had heard fifty civilians had been killed. I had learned during the bombing of Baghdad not to believe much of what I heard from people on the street and told him so. It was too confusing and there were many stories that went around on the scene for anyone to know what had really happened.

Eventually I was pushed away from the area along with almost everyone else by American soldiers. Some were polite, some rude. I found myself with a crowd of people being herded forcibly away down a residential block. Among us was a distraught Iraqi man who was pleading with the soldiers to be allowed through. Another Iraqi man who spoke English and who was next to me remarked: "He is trying to tell them he lives just there"—he pointed a few meters away—"but they won't let him go home." He shook his head in dismay. He said to me: "They are your people. Can't you tell them to at least be nice?"

I walked back to the Palestine on my own. It was only about 10:30 PM, but there were no longer many cars out on the roads, and the streets were dark and gloomy. Every shop was closed except for a single roadside cigarette kiosk. The few Iraqis I passed gave me sidelong, neutral glances. I felt acutely vulnerable, and it wasn't until I was back inside the blast walls that had been set up around the perimeter of the Palestine and had been frisked by the sentries who guarded the access point that I truly felt safe again.

Iraq was a much more dangerous place than it had been a year earlier. The Iraqis had been liberated from dictatorship by Operation Iraqi Freedom, but their newfound liberty was not something they could easily cherish. Iraqis now had the freedom to express their opinions, to surf the Web and watch satellite TV, to read any newspaper they wanted, and to join the political party of their choice (except for the Baath Party); but now too terrorists and criminals were free to strike at will, seemingly, against whomever they wanted, whenever and wherever they wanted.

Freedom has only notional value unless a state is capable of harnessing its benefits for its citizens. For that to be possible, there must be security. It seems like a simple formula, but it was the essential ingredient still missing in Iraq a year after George W. Bush declared it to have been delivered from evil. No Iraqi I knew felt comforted or protected by the continued presence of 130,000 American soldiers in the country. Quite the contrary. Because of the risks to their own safety, the American troops lived inside secure compounds like the Green Zone or Saddam's former palaces and military camps, protected by sentries and blast walls. When they emerged, they engaged with Iraqi society from behind their protective coating of flak jackets and Kevlar helmets and weaponry, and they moved around in armored vehicles, guns at the ready. Most days, several of them were killed by ambushes or roadside bombs detonated by remote control. After such incidents the soldiers often opened fire, sometimes wildly, spraying everything around them. All too often they killed Iraqi civilians who just happened to be there, within range of their bullets.

It was no longer safe for Westerners to travel around the country. In the month of March alone a series of targeted ambushes on Iraq's roads resulted in the deaths of about twenty Western civilians, including businessmen, civilian contractors, clergymen, and relief experts. After the bombing of the Mount Lebanon Hotel, which had apparently been targeted because it hosted some foreign guests (a British businessman was among the blast's victims), and subsequent attacks on other small, unguarded hotels, most Western reporters and other civilians remaining in Baghdad moved behind the walls that surrounded the Palestine and Sheraton or else to the Al-Hamra, which now was also surrounded by blast walls and armed guards. Just about the only people in Baghdad living without such protection were the ordinary Iraqis, and for them, life had become just as hazardous. Criminal gangs had proliferated and operated with impunity. The number of murders and rapes had skyrocketed since the fall of Baghdad, as had carjackings and kidnappings for ransom. Frequently, the victims were children.

Sabah's youngest son, Ala, who was twelve, had been kidnapped earlier in the year. I learned about it within days of my return to Baghdad at the beginning of March. Sabah tracked me down, as he always managed to do, and told me all about it. He wept as he recalled the episode. He explained that Ala had been walking from his house to school with several friends one morning, and some men in a car had come along and snatched him. A few hours later Sabah had received an anonymous call from a man demanding he pay fifty thousand dollars if he wanted Ala back alive. It was far more money than Sabah could ever afford. For the next three days Sabah negotiated with the kidnappers and eventually bargained them down to six thousand dollars. He had to sell his white Mercedes to come up with the money. On the third day, two of his brothers drove to a lonely spot proposed by the kidnappers and handed over the cash to a carful of masked men. A few hours later the kidnappers dropped Ala off at the roadside a few blocks from his house, and he walked home. He told Sabah that he had been kept blindfolded in a garage and been fed very little food.

Sabah had not let Ala return to school since his abduction; he was keeping him at home. "He is missing school, but what else can I do, Mr. Jon Lee?" He became emotional again and cried some more. I asked Sabah what had happened to his GMC Suburban. Knowing how much Sabah liked to show off, I half suspected that it was the big flashy car that, along with his Mercedes, had attracted the kidnappers' attention to him in the first place. With a rueful look, Sabah told me that he still had the Suburban but had kept it parked in his garage ever since Ala's abduction. He wasn't driving it around anymore.

On April 4, a huge upsurge in the bloodletting began. Over the next two weeks, at least seventy Americans and as many as seven hundred Iraqis were killed. It was the worst violence Iraq had seen since the American-British invasion a year earlier and showed no signs of abating anytime soon. The unexpected escalation of hostilities and huge number of casualties caused widespread international alarm and raised new questions about the Bush administration's handling of the occupation of Iraq. If there had ever been any doubt, it was now abundantly clear to everyone that the United States was still fighting a war in Iraq.

The new violence was sparked by several events. On March 31, four American contractors were ambushed and killed while driving through Fallujah, and in a sickening spectacle that was filmed and broadcast on Al Jazeera, their charred bodies were hacked to pieces by a throng of men and boys, who then dragged them through the streets and hanged some of their body parts from lampposts and the ramparts of a bridge over the Euphrates. Afterward the First Marine Division (which had recently taken over jurisdiction of the Fallujah area from an army division) surrounded the city with the aim of capturing or killing the men responsible for the contractors' deaths. When they moved in on April 5, however, the marines encountered fierce resistance and took heavy casualties. Their police action soon became a siege, as they resorted to pounding, bombing, and strafing the town with helicopter gunships, F-18s, and tanks. Tens of thousands of civilians fled the city.

Simultaneously, a new front opened up, and for the first time the coalition was confronted with fighting not only Sunni insurgents but Shias as well. On April 4 the armed followers of Moqtada al-Sadr launched an attack on the Spanish and Salvadoran coalition troops stationed in Najaf, killing one Salvadoran soldier. The uprising followed the arrest by American troops of one of Sadr's aides, who was accused of being involved in the murder of Abdel Majid al-Khoei a year earlier. After the fighting in Najaf, Sadr's fighters, who wore black turbans and black clothes and called themselves the Mahdi Army, rose up across southern and central Iraq, attacking and killing coalition troops and seizing police stations in a half dozen cities and several districts of Baghdad, including Sadr City. As the Americans retaliated with tanks and gunships, Sadr called on his fellow Shiites from his mosque in Kufa, a town next door to Najaf, to revolt against the foreign invaders. A few days later he moved to his home, in a back alleyway of Najaf itself, very close to the Imam Ali shrine. Several hundred Iraqis and several dozen coalition troops were killed before Sadr's fighters were dislodged from their newly conquered positions and fell back to Kufa and Najaf.

The Americans announced that Sadr himself was wanted for Khoei's murder and that they would kill or capture him if he didn't turn himself in. The U.S. Army sent a couple of thousand soldiers to surround Najaf. Sadr remained defiant and dared the Americans to come into the holy city after him. If they did, Sadr warned, it would spark off a jihad all across Iraq, which was clearly what he wished for. By the end of the second week of April the heavy fighting had died down to hostile standoffs at Fallujah and at Najaf, as an array of tribal sheikhs, religious leaders, and other figures came forth to mediate. Shiite politicians, including Abdulaziz al-Hakim, attempted to calm things down between the Americans and Sadr in the south, while Imam Dhari and other Sunni clerics emerged as of mediators and political front men for the Sunni mujahideen operating in and around Fallujah. The shadowy resistance groups operating there, meanwhile, heightened tensions by going on a hostage-taking spree, kidnapping around fifty foreigners, including aid workers, human rights activists, contractors, soldiers, and journalists. Some of the hostages were released after a few hours, but the abductors were holding on to others, especially, it seemed, anyone from one of the nations involved in the coalition.

The imposing, gold-domed Kadhimiyah mosque, one of the principal Shiite shrines in Iraq, dominates the eponymous district of Kadhimiyah. It is one of Baghdad's oldest and most pleasant neighborhoods, with wide streets lined with old villas and planted with date palms. There are always many pilgrims, including many from Iran, around the mosque, and shoppers crowd the streets of the old bazaar around it, known for its goldsmiths. A wide pedestrian street forms a promenade to the mosque, and it is normally full of activity, a favorite stroll for families with children and chaste couples, groups of pilgrims and hawkers of ice cream and soft drinks. Small shops along the walkway sell sweetmeats and pickled cauliflower, olives, cashews, pistachios, and carpets and wall hangings with gold

Koranic inscriptions and the images of Imam Ali and Imam Husein woven into them, heroic portraits in which the revered martyrs appear as handsome, robust men with eyes that melt with compassion.

On Monday, April 5, the second day of Sadr's revolt, the area around the mosque seemed unusually quiet compared with the other Shiite neighborhoods of the city. I had already been to Sadr City, where a large mob of people at a funeral had become angry at the sight of Westerners. I was there with Samantha Appleton, a young American photographer who was working with me, and Franco Pagetti, an Italian photographer. When the crowd began to get out of control, we decided to leave. We had gone next to Al-Shulla, another Shiite district of Baghdad, where a hundred or so fighters milled around the front of Sadr's party office. They were heavily armed and looked very edgy. Across the street, a throng of men and boys were jumping up and down and brandishing daggers and yelling atop the smoking hulk of an American military vehicle. A house had been shot up by a helicopter, and smoke still curled up from its roof, where it had been hit. We left when that mob also became crazy and a group of young men began pounding on our cars.

On the approach to Kadhimiyah, a black banner hung on the street with English lettering, which said: PEACE BE UPON YOU, HUSEIN, THE HERO WHO REVOLTED AGAINST TYRANNY. As we pulled up in our car alongside the pilgrims' buses near the mosque, I dispatched our driver, Salam, to go ahead and see if we were going to be welcome. Salam was a savvy and good-humored Shiite man who normally worked with Samantha. On my previous trip to Iraq in November and December, Samantha and I had begun working together, and Salam had stayed with her, operating as our driver and occasional translator. He came back a moment later and waved us forward. He was standing with some men wearing the black shirts and trousers of the Mahdi Army. They were armed. We were received in a perfunctory way and

walked across the promenade to a husseiniyah, a Shiite community center, which had become Sadr's local branch office. Several
hundred meters up the promenade loomed the big burnished
gold domes of the mosque. There were not many people around.
More fighters searched us at the door. The courtyard inside was a
tumult of men and boys with weapons, all of them dressed in
black. Most of them also wore green headscarves, showing their
readiness for battle.

We were shown into a room lined with chairs and posters of
Moqtada al-Sadr. One poster, showing him glowering sternly
and shaking a finger, bore a strong resemblance, but for Sadr's
vaster bulk, to photographs of Che Guevara in his more implacable "Yankees-are-the-enemies-of-humanity" moments. A bearded
black-robed and black-turbaned man who appeared to be in
his mid-thirties introduced himself to us as Sheikh Raed. He
explained that his name, in English, meant "thunder." He seemed
to like this fact very much, and so I duly complimented him.
Raed said that he worked with Sheikh Hazem al-Arraji, Sadr's
top deputy in Kadhimiyah. I asked him to tell me what was
happening. "We follow the word of our leader, Moqtada al-Sadr,
so what you see here today is like a demonstration to show
our support for him," said Raed. "The schools are closed out
of solidarity with us; the university students are coming to ask if
they can join us."

I asked him what he thought about Paul Bremer's vow to capture or kill Moqtada al-Sadr and his description of him as an
"outlaw." He retorted: "Moqtada al-Sadr is not an outlaw. Bremer is an outlaw. Sadr is an Iraqi. Bremer is not. Maybe we will
catch Bremer instead. If they try to do this, they will go to hell."

A young, intense-looking man sitting next to Raed leaned
forward to say to me: "We are *all* Moqtada al-Sadr."

After a few minutes of this, Raed's boss, Hazem al-Arraji, came
in and sat down in the corner. Hazem was a handsome man in his
thirties dressed, like Raed, in black robe, black turban, and beard.

He had a Grecian nose and intelligent eyes. I noticed that he smiled a lot. He shyly spoke a little English, in a reedy, soft voice. He explained that he had lived in Canada for a short time. He had gone into exile after Saddam's killing of Moqtada al-Sadr's father and two older brothers in 1998. Since the late Imam Sadr had been his spiritual mentor, the Mukhabarat also wanted to kill him, he said, and so he had fled to Iran and Syria and ended up in Vancouver, where he had spent two years. He had returned to Iraq after the war last year. Hazem pulled up his black pantaloons to show me a bandage on his left leg. He explained that he had fallen and hurt himself during a shoot-out that had erupted between Sadr's men and Iraqi and American security guards the day before on Sadoun Street, near the Palestine Hotel.

As we spoke, the Mahdi fighters in the courtyard outside began chanting slogans in support of Moqtada. I asked Hazem if a full-fledged uprising had begun. He replied delphically: "Wherever the Americans try to close the Sadr offices, the people will try to defend them." I asked him again. He shook his head, and said: "The people are only acting in self-defense, but if the U.S. forces continue, it will become an intifada. This morning Bremer called Moqtada an outlaw. When he said this, I believe this created an even bigger space between us." I asked Hazem what would happen if the Americans tried to capture Sadr. He smiled and said: "They can't."

"Why?"

"Because there are about ten thousand people around him with guns."

Our conversation was interrupted several times by men coming in to hand Hazem notes or to whisper in his ear. His cell phone rang constantly. A commotion began outside. Hazem explained that he had to go. Apparently an American armored column was approaching Kadhimiyah, and there was speculation that it might be planning to attack. "They will *try*," said Hazem, smiling and arching his eyebrows, as he departed.

I walked up the promenade to the mosque with one of Hazem's men, Haydar Husseini, who spoke English. He was in his late twenties. Several of the Mahdi fighters accompanied us. One of them carried a sword; the rest carried guns. The mosque had been sealed off by American troops the night before. Haydar explained that the Americans had entered Kadhimiyah in tanks and laid down coils of razor wire. "It's the first time it's been closed since Saddam shut it down in 1991," he said reprovingly. A small huddle of Iranian pilgrims stood outside the wire facing the mosque, praying. A woman and an invalid boy who seemed to have come in search of a miracle cure were lying down in a little strip of lawn outside the razor wire. Haydar said: "When you pour gas on the street and put fire on it, what happens? You make an explosion. Last night the Americans tried to do that. They entered Kadhimiyah in tanks and tried to make us fire on them, but we didn't," he claimed. "We want peace. They want to provoke us and make us into terrorists. They closed the mosque. But we didn't shoot." Reflectively, Haydar added: "I don't know what is going to happen, but I don't want war. If it starts, it will never stop. But if they insist, we will say 'Welcome!'"

Haydar told me that like Hazem, he had spent several years in itinerant exile—in Syria and Turkey, Jordan and Iran. He had been a student at Baghdad University's language school—he'd been studying Dutch, he said—when he had to interrupt his studies to flee. His crime had been to strike an officer of the Saddam Fedayeen. He didn't say why he had done so. Haydar chuckled. "Afterward I ran away." He had returned to Iraq just before the war and remained underground. I asked him when he had joined Moqtada al-Sadr. Haydar looked at me intently. "On April 9, 2003," the day Baghdad fell to the Americans and Saddam's statue was toppled in Fardous Square. I asked him *why* he had thrown his lot in with Sadr. "Sadr really, really wants a free Iraq," said Haydar. "He wants us to live freely. The other political parties are all looking after their personal interests. They don't care if people die, are injured, or are captured by the U.S. forces." He blamed the Americans for creating a sectarian divide in Iraq with the proportional representation that had been imposed on the Governing Council. He added: "They tried to create a war between the Sunni and the Shia. But they haven't been able to. We are all of us brothers. All of us"——he stared at me pointedly——"are Iraqis."

The next day, April 6, Samantha, Franco, and I traveled by car to Kufa, where Sadr was said to be holed up in the mosque where he normally officiates over prayers. We traveled in two cars. The roads were full of Shiite pilgrims beginning their walks—in some cases, all the way from Baghdad—toward Karbala, where in four days' time the religious festival of Arbayeen would take place. Arbayeen is the festival marking the end of the forty-day mourning period for Imam Husein, which begins each year on the anniversary of his death. The pilgrims were mostly wearing black and carrying flags of different colors. I saw one group of people wearing brilliant allegorical costumes and leading a camel covered with multicolored cloth. In the towns and villages along the roadside, residents had set up little tents and stands and open-air kitchens with large pots of rice and soup, in keeping with the Shiite custom of offering free food, beverages, and rest to religious pilgrims. Unusually, there were no American military convoys on the road.

There were no signs of trouble, or of Sadr's militiamen, until we reached a leafy curve in the road on the outskirts of Kufa, where we ran into a checkpoint manned by a score or more of armed, turbaned men, most of them masked with kaffiyehs and wearing the trademark black turbans of the Mahdi Army. They had the nervous energy and furtive movements of feral creatures and behaved a bit wildly. They brandished RPGs and Kalashnikovs at approaching cars. We drove up behind a convoy of seven Red Crescent ambulances, which had just arrived. As we waited, a rousing pro-Sadr chant began from the fighters. They were joined by the drivers of the ambulances. It seemed they had decided to join the uprising and had driven their ambulances to Kufa to offer their services. The ambulance drivers were waved on, and then the fighters swarmed around us. We were told to get out of the car. Salam explained that we were journalists. After some debate we were allowed to pass.

We drove over the Euphrates on a bridge and passed a couple of Sadr fighters who were doing sentry duty on its ramparts. One of them was wearing a U.S.-issued flak jacket with the word *police* in yellow letters in English and some Arabic script above. Salam explained that the Arabic inscription was new and read "Mahdi Army" instead of "Iraqi Police Forces." The atmosphere in Kufa was tense, with fighters stationed all over the square around Sadr's mosque, and we did not hang around. Sadr had apparently moved to Najaf, and we drove there after negotiating roadblocks around the shrine of Imam Ali, where Sadr's chief deputy was giving a press conference in a small courtroom in an alleyway. The aide made a number of claims, including, rather unbelievably, that Grand Ayatollah Sistani had given Sadr's uprising his blessing. When the conference was over, Mahdi fighters danced in a circle, shouting, "Down with America, down with Israel," for the benefit of photographers and cameramen.

We decided it would be best if we returned to Baghdad while there was still daylight. One of Sadr's officials gave us a note saying that we had permission to photograph the fighters at the checkpoint outside Kufa on the way back, but when we got there, not everyone was satisfied with the note, and there was a lot of yelling and gun waving. Samantha and Franco took some pictures anyway, and we were about to leave when an older man, apparently a local sheikh, showed up. A new round of yelling and gun waving ensued, the cameras were confiscated, and we were all packed into our cars and driven back to Kufa, where

Salam and the sheikh disappeared into the mosque while the fighters outside watched over us with various degrees of hostility. This was two days before the first foreign hostages, Japanese, were taken outside Fallujah and the rash of political kidnappings began, but it was unsettling nevertheless.

Finally, after perhaps an hour, Salam emerged from the mosque, looking anxious, and we were allowed to leave. Night had fallen, and none of us felt good about being out on the road after dark. When we were about halfway back to Baghdad, Salam revealed that when he was inside the mosque, a belligerent young fighter who appeared to be in charge of things had ordered his men to take us prisoner, but Salam had talked him out of it. Salam also mentioned that he had seen John Burns inside the mosque. I was stunned by this news and asked Salam why he had not told me before. He apologized profusely, saying that it had simply slipped his mind, he was so intent on getting us out of there, and that anyway John didn't seem to be in trouble. This turned out to be an overly optimistic assessment, however, for when we got to Baghdad, we learned that he and several other *Times* staff members had in fact been detained. Earlier in the evening John's translator had managed to get a call out over a satellite phone before it was confiscated.

Feeling remiss about overlooking John's predicament, Salam offered to go to Kadhimiyah and speak with Hazem al-Arraji, the friendly Sadr cleric whom we had met the day before, to see what he could do. He tracked Hazem down at around midnight, and Hazem got on the phone and arranged for the hostages to be freed. Hazem told Salam that the *Times'* people were believed to be spies and that the men holding them had planned to execute them.

A couple of days later I was in my room at the Palestine when Franco Pagetti telephoned me from the lobby to tell me that Hazem al-Arraji was downstairs and was being arrested by

American soldiers. He had come to give an interview to an Italian journalist, and as he left the hotel, someone had fingered him as a senior aide of the fugitive Moqtada al-Sadr. I rushed downstairs and saw that Hazem was in the middle of a crowd of pushing and shouting people, including a cordon of helmeted American soldiers, who were trying to drag him away. He was making calls on his cell phone as the scrum around him grew more and more chaotic. A group of sheikhs in headscarves who had been attending a meeting of tribal clans in a conference room of the Sheraton next door leaped into the fray. They pushed through the mob and shouted that they would not allow Hazem to be arrested. The American soldiers said that they didn't intend to arrest him; they just wanted to "talk" to him. After about fifteen minutes the entire mob, with Hazem at the center, moved into the conference room where the tribal sheiks were holding their meeting. Hazem sat down and kept making calls on his cell phone as the crowd whirled around him, but the soldiers finally managed to get him to his feet and maneuver him out of the room. They spirited him away in an armored personnel carrier.

"Do you realize what is going to happen now?" Iraqi friends said to me incredulously. They predicted violent demonstrations by Shias in Sadr City within hours and, very possibly, reprisal attacks against the hotel complex. Hazem's arrest certainly seemed a political blunder, given that it had been the arrest of another Sadr deputy that had led to the Shiite uprising in the first place. I called John Burns to tell him what had happened and reminded him that it was Hazem who had made the call that freed him. Burns said he would get in touch immediately with some senior officials at the Coalition Provisional Authority. A few hours later Hazem was released, but not before being driven out to the American military prison at Baghdad airport, given a medical checkup, read his rights and obligations as a detainee, and placed in a cell for five hours. Eventually, as Hazem explained later, a senior American military official arrived, told him he was free to go, and apologized for his arrest, which he said had been a "mistake." Hazem was driven back to the Palestine, where he gave some interviews and said that, all things considered, he had been well treated.

At the Sadr office in Kadhimiyah a couple of days later there were no armed men, black uniforms, or weapons in evidence. The courtyard was filled with Mahdi fighters, but they had "stood down." Hazem and I joked with each other about our evolving relationship as hostage mediators, and I asked him what the consequences might have been if his detention had been prolonged. Would there have been, as we all feared, a renewal of the violence? He nodded. "When I was arrested," he said, "many thousands of people came here and began going toward the Palestine. Others were gathering in Sadr City. I am sure they would have fought with the Americans, but I didn't want that." He said he thought the "problem" between Sadr and the United States had been resolved. "This morning I heard Colin Powell saying on television that he just wants the Mahdi militia to be disbanded. The Americans are changing their language."

I accompanied Hazem and a large crowd of his followers to the Friday noon prayers at the Kadhimiyah mosque, which had just been reopened. Pallbearers carried a coffin draped with green cloth past us. They were coming from the mosque, where the coffin had been blessed. Hazem stopped, murmured some words of prayer in deference to the mourners, and moved on. The mosque custodians made way for us, and at the entrance we were all sprayed with rosewater by a man wielding a bottle with a pressure pump. Several thousand men sat waiting in the large interior courtyard of the mosque, and as Hazem made his way around the edge of the crowd, his men, and then all the men in the crowd, began chanting, "Hail Moqtada, down with America, down with the Governing Council," and pumping their fists in the air. The prayers turned out to be a political rally, as first Sheikh Raed and then Hazem spoke at length. Several men held up pictures of Sadr. In the distance, across the courtyard, I could see groups of Iranian pilgrims coming and going. Some of them ignored the rally altogether; others stopped to watch and listen. After about three hours, it was over, and I was swept out of the mosque with Hazem's entourage. A man in the crowd touched my arm as I approached the archway to the mosque courtyard. He said that he was a doctor and asked, in broken English, if I was American. When I nodded, he smiled. "Why is America still here?" he asked, with apparently genuine curiosity. "What is left for America to do in Iraq?" I shrugged. "Thank you for getting rid of Saddam, and OK," he said. "But everybody wants America . . . just to go." Then he shook my hand. "Good-bye," he called out, as I was pushed off by the crowd. "Thank you."

That evening I returned to Hazem's office in Kadhimiyah to continue our conversation. A few hours before, Sadr's militia had again clashed with coalition troops in Kufa, and a number of his men had been killed and wounded. I thought the atmosphere at Kadhimiyah might be chilly, but it wasn't. Hazem was, as usual, receiving constant calls on his cell phone, and at one point he announced that a Canadian hostage being held in the south had just been released. He looked pleased, and I asked him who had been holding the Canadian hostage. "Criminals," he replied. "Our people got him released." He blamed the kidnappings around Fallujah on bandits, and when I pointed out that some of the hostages were clearly being held with political goals in mind, he said that if the "resistance" was carrying out such actions, then it was making a mistake. Hazem looked at me and tried to lighten the tone of the conversation. "Don't worry," he said. "If you get kidnapped, I'll help free you." He laughed.

On April 8, three days into the siege of Fallujah, Samantha Appleton and Salam and I traveled to the western suburbs of Baghdad. We had heard that a huge civilian convoy consisting of ambulances and trucks loaded with donated food and medicines for the inhabitants of Fallujah had rendezvoused at the Mother of All Battles mosque and begun heading to the besieged town. As Salam drove us toward the mosque, we passed through the Sunni neighborhood of Ghazaliyah, where I recognized a block of houses as the street where I had interviewed three Iraqi insurgents in a safe house the previous December. We drove cautiously onto the open highway that leads to Fallujah, and saw that we had missed the aid convoy.

The cars ahead were all stopped. Many drivers were standing outside their cars and pointing at a column of smoke in the distance, which meant that something had been bombed. Some of the drivers were turning around, driving over the median strip, and heading back. That is what Salam did. Our only other alternative to reach Fallujah was to take the old road, which cuts through Abu Ghraib, the community around the infamous prison. I did not have a good feeling about taking the road, however. Two *New York Times* reporters had taken the same route the day before and been held hostage for several hours. I asked Salam to drive instead to the Mother of All Battles mosque. Since the fall of Saddam the mosque had been renamed something anodyne—"Mother of All the Villages"—but it had remained a bastion of that part of Baghdad's Sunni Muslim community that was anti-American and afraid that a Shiite-dominated government would assume power in Iraq.

Outside the gates of the mosque, where a couple of armed guards stood vigil, there were a dozen or so pickups and cars loaded with boxes of food and medicine. There were also a couple of Red Crescent ambulances. Men were milling about. As we

pulled up, another car did too, and a young man with a stricken
expression and clothes covered with blood was bundled out and
half carried into the gatehouse of the mosque. He had been riding in one of the food trucks in the convoy, we were told, and it
had been fired on by the Americans.

We wandered into the grounds of the mosque, where men
were loading up a couple of large dump trucks with donated supplies—flour sacks and cooking oil and rice bags—from a series of
small pickups, which continued to arrive from around Baghdad.
One pickup arrived with two black flags—Shia flags—flying
like battle standards from its stanchions. An Iraqi man who was
standing near me saw my surprise and commented, in good English: "You see that? It's from a Shia mosque." He told me that
mosques all over Baghdad were collecting donated goods from
the citizens, Sunni as well as Shia, and dispatching them to the
mosque to be sent on to Fallujah. He added: "Before, there was
no common ground between Sunni and Shia, but now there is.
The reason is that the Iraqi people are all tired of the occupation
and the humiliation of soldiers pushing their doors and stealing
from them and bothering their women and sticking guns in
their faces." The man smiled. He seemed friendly. We shook
hands. He introduced himself as Mouayed al-Muslih, forty-five
years old, the chief engineer for the grounded Iraqi national airline. He was also the head of the Iraqi airline pilots' and engineers' union, he said. Muslih asked me if I was an American.
When I said I was, he smiled and told me that he had studied in
the seventies at Oklahoma State University, which was where
he'd learned his English. He had had a "great time" there.

Muslih told me that he and most other Iraqis had been pleased
by the American overthrow of Saddam and had had high expec-
tations of what would come next. But they had been sorely dis-
appointed. "Tomorrow, the ninth of April, is the anniversary of
the fall of Baghdad, but now, you know, everyone sees this as the
date marking the beginning of the liberation of Iraq." I under-

stood that what Muslih was talking about was liberation from *American* occupation, in an inversion of the language used by President Bush to refer to the U.S. role in Iraq. Muslih went on: "Iraqis don't have anything against American people or their culture, you know, but they don't want to be humiliated by American soldiers."

We were interupted by the sound of heavy machine-gun fire coming from a spot on the highway to Fallujah a few hundred meters away from us. "That's the Americans," Muslih said, identifying the caliber of the weaponry. He continued with his train of thought: "You know, Iraqis don't like to be occupied, and this will continue, because Iraqis are proud. They don't like to be defeated." Muslih went on saying things I had heard before from many Iraqis, about how he believed that what the United States was doing in Iraq was not its own policy, but something orchestrated by Israelis, who had a nefarious influence on the Bush administration, and how Israel's ultimate intention was to destroy Iraq so that it could never threaten the Jewish state again in the future. Muslih shook his head. "We all wanted change, and we wanted good things from America. But the Americans have shown us their ugly face. Here we are, you and I. I am an Iraqi, and you are an American, and we can talk to one another. There is no difference between us. But don't put a gun in my face. You see the people in the streets. They are quiet when they see the American soldiers, they don't say anything, but in their heads and minds they think something else. There is a lot of hatred. The reason is because you cannot just take away a people's security and give them nothing in return."

Muslih said one of the biggest problems was the lack of legitimacy of the members of Iraq's Governing Council, who were selected by the coalition. Many Iraqis did not believe they had a truly representative voice in the government. "Everyone hates these Iraqi guys on the Governing Council," he said. "Most of them were living outside Iraq for twenty or thirty years. Many were thieves who ran away after committing their crimes, and they came back with the CIA. The Americans didn't need these people. There are twenty-five million people here, and many of them are good, qualified people. Why didn't you choose from among them?" The transfer of power planned for June 30, said Muslih, was not a solution to the problem. "As long as the American Army stays here, all of this is just bullshit! Iraqis don't even think about this date. They know that there will just be a change of faces and that it's just bullshit."

After a pause Muslih took me aback by adding: "You know, there are those of us who don't want the Americans to leave so quickly, but they should behave. Believe me when I say that most Iraqis want freedom and democracy. They want good education and health care. And they want relations with Americans, but as long as the Americans don't behave the right way, there will be problems between us."

After leaving the mosque, Salam drove me to another, smaller mosque not far from his own home in the mixed Sunni-Shia neighborhood of Al-Salaam. Salam himself was a Shiite but had many Sunni friends, and told me he had a good rapport with the imam of the local Sunni mosque of Al-Suheil.

Al-Suheil was a modest mosque. It was bounded by a wall on which I noticed a poster of Sheikh Ahmed Yassin, the spiritual leader of Hamas, who had been assassinated in March by the Israelis, and whose murder had been "avenged," according to a communiqué, by the killers of the four American contractors in Fallujah. On a nearby wall, I saw, was a poster of Moqtada al-Sadr. A couple of pickup trucks were being loaded with food for Fallujah, and the imam, a bespectacled, bearded man named Sheikh Fadel al-Gaidy, whom Salam introduced me to, was overseeing things. Several older men wearing headscarves were sitting in chairs in the entranceway of the mosque, watching.

Above them hung a banner that said, in Arabic: ALL THE CITI-ZENS OF AL-SALAAM SEND FOOD, MONEY AND MEDICINES TO THE MUJAHIDEEN OF FALLUJAH AND RAMADI. As I spoke with Sheikh Fadel, other men and boys gathered around to listen. One interrupted excitedly to declaim: "Sunni and Shia are together. All of Iraq is Fallujah." I asked Sheikh Fadel if this was true. He nodded and said: "The relationship between Sunni and Shia has deepened since the downfall of the regime, because they have a common enemy."

"Is this a jihad?" I asked.

"Yes," he replied, nodding. "It is a jihad."

"How will it end?"

"It will end when the Americans leave Iraq."

I asked Sheikh Fadel what would occur if the Americans acceded to Sadr's demands and if they also pulled out of Fallujah. What would happen then? "The jihad will continue," he replied solemnly. "Because the Americans have lied to the people of Iraq about the reasons for the occupation of Iraq, because they clearly want to stay here a long time, and because the Americans have tried to divide the Sunni and the Shia."

We were interrupted again, by a man who came up and said, "The USA should leave our country," then walked away.

The sheikh nodded. He turned back to me and said: "This is just like 1920." He was referring, of course, to the fateful year of the Arab revolt when the Sunni and Shia tribes of Iraq rose up together against the colonial British occupation forces. Sheikh Fadel added: "In the last year the Americans have killed a lot of Iraqi civilians, including children, and have sent a lot of people to prison. They want to kill Iraqi civilization, and they want to steal the oil of Iraq. But we say that the Americans will surely leave our country because all of the religions of Iraq are now united in one power and because in Islam, for this time, the important thing is jihad. And because none of us are afraid to die. Iraqi people know how to distinguish between truth and lies.

The Americans came to Iraq saying that we had weapons of mass destruction. They did not find them. So now the Americans say the really important thing was that they liberated Iraq." Sheikh Fadel shook his head in disgust. He said: "Iraq's Muslims have a strong faith. We want democratic freedoms, but through Islam."

On April 14 the kidnappers of Fallujah gave to Al Jazeera a videotape that showed the execution of one of four Italian security guards they had taken hostage. In its communiqué, the so-called Green Brigades explained that it had killed the man in retaliation for Silvio Berlusconi's refusal to consider a withdrawal of Italy's troops from the coalition. The Italian's murder cast a pall over every Westerner staying in Baghdad. Afterward our movements became even more restricted. Quite a few journalists' translators quit their jobs, and many drivers, including Salam, began refusing to drive to certain parts of Baghdad, much less outside the city, out of concern for our safety, as well as their own. Just as it had been during the worst days of the American bombing campaign a year before, the Palestine Hotel became our only sanctuary from danger. This time, however, the dangers were much greater.

The day after the Italian was executed, I ventured out to visit Ayad Jamaluddin at his home on the Tigris, in southeastern Baghdad. It was still regarded as a relatively safe part of town and had the additional benefit of being heavily guarded by gunmen working for several members of the Governing Council, such as Jalal Talabani and Abdulaziz al-Hakim, both of whom had homes and offices nearby. I had not seen Jamaluddin since the previous summer, when he had been full of optimism about creating a political base for himself and was speaking out to promote the establishment of a pro-American secular democracy in Iraq. I was curious to know how his fortunes had fared in the intervening months and how he saw things now.

Jamaluddin had more bodyguards outside his house than I re-called seeing before, and there was now a gauntlet of cement-filled oil barrels to negotiate, forcing approaching cars to slow down. Inside the gates were several more new cars, among them an RPG-proof black Mercedes-Benz, which, one of Jamaluddin's aides told me boastfully, had formerly belonged to Jordan's Crown Prince Hassan. Jamaluddin still had the Rolls-Royce, I noticed, but it was covered by a dropcloth. Gardeners were at-tentively watering the clipped green lawn. Jamaluddin's security men ushered me around to the back of the house, on the riverside lawn, where he was sitting on a plastic chair at one corner of the stone courtyard. The tiled fountain was spurting jets of water next to Jamaluddin's woven reed mudhif, and roses and garde-nias blossomed in the beds along the walkways. I noticed that the metal fence along the riverbank had been built up and cov-ered with some roofing material, concealing the river from view. Two guard towers with armed men sitting in them now stood at both corners of the garden overlooking the river. There were some guinea fowl running around freely, and some baby ducks.

Jamaluddin waved me over and patted an empty chair next to his. Several other men, who were not introduced, but who ap-peared to be friends or followers, sat around as well. Jamaluddin had gained some weight. His cheeks were fuller, and he had a slight paunch. He had been positively svelte the previous sum-mer. He also had new gray hairs in his beard. In every other dis-cernible way, however, Jumaluddin seemed unchanged. He was smoking a Cohiba, and he had pulled his bare feet out of his san-dals to sit cross-legged in his chair, as was his custom. He was wearing a white turban and white robes.

After we exchanged pleasantries, I asked Jamaluddin how he saw the situation, and in particular, what he thought about Mo-qtada al-Sadr's uprising. He smiled and said imperturbably: "Creating a new, free, and democratic Iraq is like giving birth." I quipped that to my eye, it seemed a bit more like a cesarean without anesthesia. Jamaluddin chuckled and replied: "It's only like a cesarean for Moqtada." He waved his hand dismissively. "There are always complications to building democracies, especially after long dictatorships. All these fundamentalist issues"—he referred here to Sadr's xenophobic brand of political Islam—"will be aborted."

I asked Jamaluddin what he believed the best approach was in dealing with Moqtada al-Sadr. "Moqtada should be tackled politically," he declared. "I believe in stages. First, the arrest warrant on him should not be served until there is an Iraqi government in place to deal with him. Then his militia and all the other militias in Iraq should be disbanded." Jamaluddin warned against an American military assault on Najaf and said he believed they should desist from their plan to arrest Sadr for Khoei's murder. "At this moment in time, the stability of Iraq is what is important, not the Khoei murder. If the Americans proceed, there will be more violence, a lot more innocent people's blood will be shed. This will lead to a lot of hatred by Iraqis toward the Americans, and I am afraid of that. There is too much hatred already; God forbid this hatred should spread further. It is very hard to plant democracy in Iraq, and democracy is an American product. If Americans are hated here, all their products will be hated too."

The guinea fowl started squawking, making a terrific din. Jamaluddin stopped talking and glanced over to acknowledge them. He laughed. "The guinea fowl agree with me."

At the end of April, when I left Iraq, I flew out of the Baghdad airport, which was still in the hands of the coalition. Most of the roads leading out of Baghdad had been cut by the U.S. military, and driving to Jordan was out of the question anyway, since the road ran past Fallujah, where the fighting still raged, and where many of the foreigners taken hostage had been snatched.

On the road to the airport, we passed the burned-out carcass of an American military fuel truck. It had been part of a convoy that was attacked a few days earlier. Many of the coalition's convoys were getting ambushed lately. On the nearby road that led to Abu Ghraib, past the prison there, and on to Fallujah, more trucks and tanks and Humvees had been destroyed. American soldiers and contractors had been killed, and several had been abducted.

At the military checkpoint for cars outside the airport runway, an American soldier began raging at some Iraqi men in a car over some infraction. They appeared to be coalition employees, but he cursed them violently and ordered them out of their car. They appeared bewildered and very intimidated. He continued to shout at them at the top of his lungs. Another soldier came over to assist him. I couldn't see what happened next because I had to catch my plane. When the plane took off, it flew sharply upward in a corkscrew pattern, to throw off antiaircraft missiles.

A day or two later, the first photographs showing the sadistic abuse and sexual humiliation of Iraqi prisoners committed by American soldiers at Abu Ghraib became public. On May 11, amid the escalating scandal, a video clip was broadcast on an Internet Web site that showed the decapitation of Nicholas Berg, a twenty-six-year-old American civilian. Berg was shown wearing an orange jumpsuit similar to those worn by the accused terrorists held at Guantánamo by the Americans. He was facing the camera, kneeling in front of a group of armed and hooded men. Before sawing off Berg's head with a large knife, one of his captors explained that Berg's execution was in retaliation for the abuse of Iraqis by Americans at Abu Ghraib. Berg's headless body was found dumped on a highway overpass in western Baghdad. It later emerged that Berg, a communications specialist from Pennsylvania who had come to Iraq to look for work, had attempted to fly out of Baghdad at the height of the uprising, but that on the road to the airport he had been taken hostage.

The date of Berg's kidnapping was believed to be April 9, the first anniversary of the fall of Baghdad. A year had gone by, but it seemed as if Baghdad had not really fallen at all—or perhaps it was still falling.

Afterword

In the middle of June 2004, Ala Bashir telephoned me to say that Samir Khairi had finally been released from Abu Ghraib prison. Samir had been freed at the end of February after seven months in custody, but he was gravely ill and remained in bed for nearly two months. When his health improved, he finally contacted Bashir and told him he still had no idea why he had been detained.

Bashir himself was living in Doha, the capital of the Arab emirate of Qatar, where he had spent most of his time since leaving Baghdad. Since I was about to return to Baghdad to cover the end-of-June "handover" by the coalition to the newly appointed interim Iraqi government, I arranged a stopover in Doha to see him.

In Doha, a hot and airless city on the Persian Gulf, I found Ala Bashir living in a guesthouse that belonged to Sheikh Hassan, a cousin of the ruling emir, who had invited Bashir to Doha to work as a plastic surgeon. Bashir told me he had declined a lucrative contract that he had been offered by the sheikh, opting instead to perform operations case by case so as to maintain greater autonomy. For the time being, he was saddened to be separated from his family in England, but he remained reasonably happy because he had free use of an art studio owned by the sheikh. Bashir proudly showed me a series of huge canvases he had painted: dark, surreal works featuring his trademark ravens and masks. He called the series *Masks of Cain,* and explained that it dealt with the eternal struggle between good and evil in human beings and with their relationship to power.

Bashir told me that Samir Khairi had left Baghdad a few days earlier and was now in Amman. Since I was flying there next, we telephoned Samir. He sounded very happy to hear that I was coming, and we agreed to meet as soon as I reached Amman. When Samir arrived at my hotel, I saw that he was much thinner than when last I had seen him, and that his eyes were sunken. For the next several hours, Samir recounted his ordeal. His arrest in July 2003 had been as violent as it was unexpected. American soldiers had surrounded the house, smashed down the doors, seized him from his bed, and handcuffed him. Then a soldier smashed his rifle butt into Samir's side, breaking several of his ribs. After that, he found it difficult to breathe.

At the airport detention center where he was first taken to be interrogated, Samir suffered a massive heart attack. He was saved by American military doctors who gave him emergency medical treatment. Afterward, he was sent to a military prison camp in Um Qasr, in the far south of Iraq. He spent two months there and suffered two more heart attacks. Then he was sent to Abu Ghraib, where he remained for five months, until one day, without warning, he was released. When he left Abu Ghraib, he was wearing nothing but a hospital smock and a blanket. Samir couldn't go to his own home, which had been thoroughly looted, but went to his parents' home instead. Samir wept when he recalled how, three months into his imprisonment, he had learned that his elderly father had died.

Samir was not really bitter toward the Americans. They had not tortured him at Abu Ghraib, he said, although he had heard rumors about the abuses taking place in a special unit there. He spoke warmly about several American officers who had behaved humanely toward him. But he remained mystified and wounded by the terrible living conditions in the prisons, which had seemed needlessly primitive and humiliating. Every Iraqi detainee he met, he told me—including those who had not been opposed to the Americans before their arrest—had become determined to fight them in one way or another upon their release.

To all intents and purposes, Samir was a broken man, although he tried bravely to conceal it. He was fifty-two years old and had a doctorate in constitutional law, but he was now in exile, homeless, penniless, and ill. He had been robbed of all his savings by the soldiers who had arrested him, and he was desperately hoping that one of the universities in Jordan would hire him as a law professor. "Whatever they offer me," he told me, "I will take it." Returning to Iraq was not an option for Samir. He was a marked man because of his past work for Saddam: his name had appeared on a published list of targets earmarked for assassination by a militant Shiite group. Samir was extremely anxious about Iraq's future. He predicted further mayhem and probable civil war in Iraq if American troops remained in the country. "If that happens," he asked, "how will the Americans deal with the situation? Will they return to the towns and cities and destroy them again? They can't, because now the Iraqi people—who were very happy a year ago when they came and got rid of Saddam—don't want them anymore."

On June 28, two days ahead of schedule, the formal handover of Iraqi sovereignty took place in Baghdad's Green Zone, in a surprise move aimed at thwarting expected terrorist attacks. Within hours of the coalition's official dissolution, its outgoing administrator, Paul Bremer, announced that Iraq was better off than it had been when he arrived, and he left Baghdad on a flight back to Washington.

Acknowledgments

My special thanks to Scott Moyers at the Penguin Press, who first conceived of this book, for his unstinting patience, encouragement, and good faith; and to Sarah Chalfant and Andrew Wylie at the Wylie Agency.

Without the respective talents and beyond-the-call efforts of Janie Fleming, Bruce Giffords, and Pearl Hanig at The Penguin Press, this book might never have made it to the printer, and for that I am truly grateful.

Sharon DeLano, my editor at *The New Yorker,* has been a close partner in all of my Iraq experiences, and I owe her a unique debt of gratitude. All of the material in this book has come out of my reporting trips to Iraq for the magazine, and readers familiar with my published articles may recognize some of the episodes and characters I have presented here. I am deeply thankful to David Remnick, *The New Yorker*'s editor in chief, for his constant support. I'd also like to thank Dorothy Wickenden and Pamela McCarthy for their multifarious efforts on my behalf. Many other staff members have helped to make my work possible, in too many ways to be enumerated here, but all of their help has been invaluable. They include Nana Asfour, Daniel Cappello, Gita Daneshjoo, Amy Davidson, Kevin Denges, Perri Dorset, Ben Greenman, Raffi Khatchadourian, Daniel Kile, Risa Leibowitz, Jacob Lewis, Lauren Porcaro, Nandi Rodrigo, and Francine Schore. Andy Young has once again come to my rescue by fact-checking this manuscript, catching my errors with eagle-eyed grace, and delivering his corrections with a wonderful blend of tact and bonhomie.

In the UK, at Time Warner, my thanks to Cecília Durães, Iain Hunt, Ursula Mackenzie and Tim Whiting.

For their steadfast camaraderie during difficult times, my heartiest thanks to Paul McGeough and John Burns. During my comings and goings to and from Iraq, many other people have demonstrated their friendship and solidarity to me as well. They include Waleed Abdul-majid, Samantha Appleton, Ala Bashir, David Blair, Giovanna Botteri, Sungsu Cho, Tamara Daghestani, Adam Davidson, Jerome Delay, Adri-ana Dergam, Patrick Dillon, Robyn Dixon, Francis Dubois, Thomas Dworzak, Farnaz Fassihi, Jeffrey Fleishman, Suzanne Goldenberg, Patrick Graham, Jan Hartman, Tyler Hicks, Haitham al-Husseini, Salaar Jaff, Saad Naji Jawad, Kimberly Johnson, Amal Jubouri, Ranya Kadri, Larry Kaplow, Samir Khairi, Yuri Kosyrev, Melinda Liu, Dumeetha Luthra, Matthew McAllester, Salih Mehdi, Merhdad Mir-damadi, Salam al-Muhammadawi, Wamidh Nadmi, Craig Nelson, the late Elizabeth Neuffer, Bob Nickelsberg, Rod Nordland, Farah Nosh, Heathcliff O'Malley, Franco Pagetti, Scott Peterson, Pablo Ruperez, Marla Ruzicka, Nasser al-Sadoun, Farouk Salloum, Moises Saman, Fran Sevilla, Adel Sheikhly, Ali Shukri, Michael Slackman, Wendell Steaven-son, Tara Sutton, Scott Wallace, and Iva Zimova.

My gratitude also to Soheila and her husband, Abu Ahmed, for their repeated gestures of hospitality; to Issam, for getting me through every time on the runs between Baghdad and Jordan; and to Abdullah, a perfect gentleman from Sudan, for his honesty and unparalleled work ethic. I do not have words sufficient to thank the unknown room cleaner at the Baghdad Sheraton who, just after the fall of Baghdad, found and left untouched the envelope containing ten thousand dollars in cash, which I had left behind in my unmade bed. This action, which took place as Baghdad was being ransacked with impunity, did a great deal to restore my faith in human nature. Thanks also to Jane Scott-Long and Pam Williams, for their greatly appreciated backup support, and to Joel Simon of the Committee to Protect Journalists, for his ceaseless efforts on behalf of all the journalists in Iraq.

My fondest appreciation to Vanadia Humphries and Tony Heaton for helping out repeatedly during my many prolonged absences from home. And, as always, to Erica, Bella, Rosie, and Máximo, my heartfelt thanks.

Index

ABC, 162
Abdullah, Abu, 413–14
Abdullah, king of Jordan, 346
Abdulmajid, Waleed, 224, 308–9,
    311, 317, 320–5, 327, 345,
    383–5
Abraham, 20
Abu Dhabi, 385
Abu Dhabi television, 289
Abu Ghraib, 264, 332, 435, 443,
    445, 446
    prisoner abuse at, 443
    prisoner release from, 3–6, 79, 130
Abu Nawas, 66, 89, 176, 185, 218,
    278, 302, 369
Adhami, Muhammed Mothaffer al-,
    102–4, 108
Adhamiyah mosque, 328
Afghanistan, 40, 41, 44, 103, 291,
    369–70, 407
    Karzai government in, 124
    lack of U.S. follow-up in, 124
    U.S. bombing of, 123–4
agaal, 255
aggression see Gulf War
Ahmed, Abu, 326, 331–2, 345
Ahmed, Ahmed Murtaza, 237–8
Ahmed, Sultan Hashim, 217, 416
Ahmed (author's interpreter), 29,
    31–2
Ahmed (elderly man), 47–8

AIDS, 44
Air Defense Ministry, 261, 402–3
Air Force, U.S., 403
Al-Andalus Hotel, 86, 238
Al-Aqsa mosque, 351
Al Arabiya channel, 352, 358, 408–9
Al-Azamiyah bridge, 191
Al-Dawa see Islamic Call
Al-Doura oil refinery, 2, 88–9, 262
Alexander the Great, 20
Al-Fanar Hotel, 89, 91, 98, 190,
    238, 240
Algeria, 385
Al-Ghazala, 68
Al-Hamra Hotel, 98, 99, 141, 145,
    149, 166, 312, 421
Al-Hawijah, 258
Ali, Imam, 20, 59, 407, 425, 430
Ali, Jawad el-, 29–30
Ali (Iraqi businessman), 412
Ali (Iraqi child), 251–4, 290–1, 317,
    319
Ali (unemployed Iranian), 43
Al Jazeera, 71, 216, 280, 289, 291,
    319–20, 358, 360, 422, 440
Al-Khoei Foundation, 406
Al-Kindi Hospital, 249–54, 290–2,
    317
Allouni, Tayssir, 320
Al-Mansour Preparatory School for
    Boys, 27

Al-Mustafa Center for Islamic Research, 60
Al-Bur General Hospital, 241
Al Qaeda, 25, 320, 387
Al-Rabe Tourism Apartments, 191
Al-Rasheed Car Service, 65, 369
Al-Rasheed Hotel, 65, 73, 84, 85, 96, 98, 141, 145, 162, 165, 166, 169, 175, 176, 177–8, 186, 189, 191, 194–5, 201, 207, 235, 281, 287, 316
  as bombing target, 95, 152–3, 156, 187, 225
  Internet café of, 96, 182
  looting of, 323, 368
Al-Rasheed military garrison, 288, 292–3
Al-Rasheed Military Hospital, 339
Al-Saah, 282–3, 286
Al-Sadeer Hotel, 312
Al-Safeer Hotel, 98, 141, 145, 148–9, 166, 185, 261, 288, 302, 369, 373, 385, 391, 403, 413
Al-Salaam Palace, 236
Al-Suheil mosque, 438
Al-Tabeekh restaurant, 68
Al-Tahrir Square, 241
Al-Thawra, 337
Álvarez Cambras, Rodrigo, 250
Al-Wasati Hospital, 76, 169, 307–11, 320, 327, 338, 340, 344–5, 382
Al-Wiya Maternity Hospital, 223, 227, 237
Amanpour, Christiane, 370
Amiriya air shelter, 82
Amman, 64, 357, 376, 383, 415, 417, 446
Anfal campaign, 162
Annan, Kofi, 213
Ansar (refugee camp), 49
anti-Semitism, 77–8
antiwar groups, 35
Appleton, Samantha, 425, 429, 430, 435

AP television network, 174
Arab Baath Socialist Party see Baath Party
Arab Potash Company, 2
Arab revolt of 1920, 103, 108, 213
Arbayeen, 342, 429
Arif, Abdul Salam, 199
armoured personnel carriers, 393, 398
Army, U.S., 392, 424
  Third Infantry Division of, 307
Arnett, Peter, 84–5, 180
arrack, 122
Arraf, Jane, 7
Arraji, Sheikh Hazem al-, 426–7, 431–4
art, 17–19, 82–4
Ashrafi Isfahani (refugee camp), 50–1
Association of Islamic Scholars, 409
Assyrian dynasty, 20
Australian Foreign Office, 187
'axis of evil', 39
Ayad (architect), 101
Ayad (student), 285
Ayoub, Tareq, 291
Aziz, Tariq, 91, 236, 311–12, 383, 386, 403, 411
  attempted assassination of, 56
  author's interviews with, 7, 21, 24–5, 200
  press conference of, 219–21
  rumour of death of, 212
Aznar, José María, 162
Azores Islands, summit in, 162

Baath Party, 10, 39, 49, 86–7, 105, 190, 338, 347, 358, 363, 371, 383–5, 420
  headquarters of, 178, 287
Babylon, 20, 266
Badr Brigade, 55
Baghdad, 6, 10–14, 16, 64–5, 137, 204, 221
  Adhamiyah neighborhood of, 81, 105, 244, 409, 414

Al-Jihad neighborhood of, 81,
  326, 340, 357
Al-Karamah district of, 191
Al-Shaab district of, 229–32, 233,
  236
Al-Shulla neighborhood of, 425
Bab Al-Mouatham neighborhood
  of, 113
blackouts in, 273
bombing of, 211–12, 217–18,
  229–32, 236–8, 241, 249,
  355
buildings in, 235
businesses bricked up in, 223
clan elders in, 254
clock tower in, 12
destroyed American tank in, 275
dust in, 226, 234
emptiness of, 176–7, 182–5
exodus from, 164–5
explosions in, 417–21
first Internet café of, 96
flood of foreigners into, 403
Ghazaliyah neighborhood of, 435
human shields in, 86–9
intellectual life of, 120
Jadiriyah neighborhood of, 311–12
journalists in, 73–4
Kadhimiyah neighborhood of, 327,
  328–9, 424–9, 431, 433–4
Khandhari neighborhood of, 409
looting in, 307, 310–11, 312, 323,
  339–40, 352, 367–8, 376, 387
Mansour neighborhood of, 81
marketplace bombing in, 241–3
mood in, 215, 222
1991 bombing of, 123, 152
oil fires in, 249
plans to defend, 141–2
possible siege of, 224, 236, 269
prewar mood in, 161–2, 163
prewar preparation of, 182–5
progovernment rally in, 160–1
protests in, 6–7
public monuments in, 11–14

restaurants in, 261
Saddam's statue pulled down in,
  304–5, 328, 367
'shock and awe' bombardment in,
  200–1
Sudanese in, 177–8
suicide bombings in, 411
telecommunication facilities of,
  237–8
thieves' bazaar of, 9
tribal sheikhs in, 254–8
U.S. entry into, 273–6, 277–306,
  327, 367
U.S. Marines in, 370
war preparation in, 169
Baghdad-Basra railway line, 111
Baghdad Bulletin, 403
Baghdad Hotel, 253
Baghdad International Trade Fair,
  267–8, 274, 367
Baghdad Times, 136
Baghdad University, 102, 206, 231,
  360, 374, 409, 428
Bahaldin, Omar, 271
Bakr, Hassan al-, 10
Baquba, 274
Barroso, José Durão, 162
Bashir, Ala, 75–84, 117, 140–3, 146,
  154–5, 164, 167–8, 169–71,
  176, 195–200, 223, 236, 245,
  263–4, 307, 340–2, 345, 359,
  445–6
  art of, 82–4, 146–8, 343–4,
    350–2, 445–6
  attempted murder of, 332
  departure from Iraq of, 382–3
  dream of, 352–3
  family of, 81–2
  hiding from Saddam, 325–8
  interest in telepathy of, 159
  Iraqi Embassy anecdote of, 198–9
  Lenin's Embalmers and, 365–7
  on looting, 339–40, 344–5
  meetings with Charles and David
    of, 335–7, 379–82, 400

Bashir, Ala – *cont.*
  monuments created by, 145–6
  move to Qatar of, 412
  and murder of Sabah's brother, 364
  openness in author's relationship
      with, 144–5
  relationship to Saddam of, 75, 146,
      160, 308–9, 327, 331–8,
      343, 346–52, 366, 377, 384,
      385
  on Saddam's war plan, 227–8
Bashir, Amal, 81, 377–8
Bashir, Amina, 81, 196, 377–8
Bashir, Sumer, 337
basij, 47
Basra, 28–9, 48, 50, 111, 113, 196,
      213, 220, 221, 224, 227, 324,
      405
  air strikes against, 116
BBC, 71, 180, 268, 326, 358, 387
Bedouins, 339
Behesht-e-Zahra Cemetery, 46–7
Bell, Gertrude, 13, 128–9, 135
belly dancing, 164
Beneath the Veil, 99
Benn, Tony, 240
Benson, Ross, 85, 180
Berg, Nicholas, 443
Berlusconi, Silvio, 440
Big Brother, 87
Bilal, Ali, 324
Bingham, Molly, 264
  disappearance of, 225, 239–40
bin Laden, Osama, 40, 60, 62
biological weapons, 23–4, 33–4
bitter almond tincture, 36
Black, Conrad, 179
Blair, David, 165
Blair, Tony, 162, 175, 259
  administration of, 35, 94
Blix, Hans, 155
Board of Youth and Sport building,
      288, 293
Boer War, 125
bonyads, 43

booby traps, 269
Boston Globe, 211
Botteri, Giovanna, 5–6, 330, 331
Bradley Fighting Vehicles, 330, 331
Bremer, L. Paul, 384, 405, 415,
      426–7, 447
bribery, 70, 73
Brown, Private S., 114
bunker busters, 187, 237, 286
Burns, John Fisher, 85, 173, 174,
      176, 178, 181, 189, 194, 200,
      207, 224, 226, 240, 291, 295,
      302–4, 329, 331, 413, 431
  accusations of spying against, 265
Bush, George H.W., 25
Bush, George W., 88, 90, 101, 124,
      133, 152, 162, 164, 175, 259,
      367, 413, 420, 437
  administration of, 25, 34–5, 58,
      94
  State of the Union address (2002)
      of, 39
  ultimatum given by, 164, 168–9,
      186
Bush Doctrine, 88

Camus, Albert, 188
cancer, incidence rates of, 29–30
car bomb, 272
Castro, Fidel, 13, 118, 198, 250
CBS Evening News, 226
Ceaușescu, Nicolae, 10
Cedar Hotel, 148
Centurion Risk Assessment Services,
      35–7
Ceylon Sanitary Section, 114
Chalabi, Ahmed, 403
Charles (CIA agent), 335–7, 377,
      380–1, 400
'Chemical Ali' *see* Majid, Ali Hassan al-
'Chemical and Biological Warfare
      Awareness Training', 35–7
chemical warfare, 36
chemical weapons, 23–4, 30, 33–4,
      36

Cheney, Dick, 220
China, 198
Chirac, Jacques, 13
Cho, Sungsu, 294, 295, 311
choking agents, 36
Churchill, Winston, 127
CIA, 88, 159, 264, 356–7, 378, 384,
    413, 438
Cimino, Michael, 94
Clark, Ramsey, 85–6, 90, 240
Clash of Loyalties, 135
cluster bombs, 233
CNN, 6–7, 71, 84, 95, 188, 358–9
    ejection of, 192
Coalition Provisional Authority, 378,
    386, 403, 405, 412, 415, 417,
    432
Collier, Robert, 179
Committee of Friendship and
    Solidarity with the Peoples, 86–7
Committee to Protect Journalists,
    179, 240
Conrad, Joseph, 92
Council of Ministers Building, 200
Couso, José, 289, 290, 292
Cox News Service, 179, 239
cruise missiles, 104, 200–1, 237
Ctesiphon, 111, 113
Cuba, 198, 250
    dissidentes legales in, 107
'Culture of Change, The' (Salloum),
    120
'currency violations', 174

Daghestani, Tamara *see* Sadoun,
    Tamara, al-
Daily Express, 85, 180
Daily Telegraph, 99, 165
Damascus, 386
Daniszewsky, John, 179
Danner, Lieutenant, 311
Daraji, Hassan al-, 257
date palm orchards, 235
David (CIA agent), 377–9, 380–1,
    400

Dawlat Abad, 51–4
Day in the Life of Spain, A, 314
Deer Hunter, The (film), 94
Defense Department, U.S., 153, 189,
    399
    warnings to media by, 191–2
defense establishment, 91
Delano, Sharon, 179, 191
Delay, Jerome, 289
deserters, 276, 295
Desert Fox, 153, 178
Dezful, 48–9
Dhari, Imam, 409, 424
Dhari, Muthana Harith, 409
Dhari, Sheikh, 128, 129, 130, 132,
    134–6
Dhari, Sheikh Abdul Wahab
    Khameez al-, 130–1
Dhari, Sheikh Harith, 410
Dhari, Sheikh Muther Khameez al-,
    130–3, 409
Dhari, Sheikh Taher Khameez al-,
    130–1
Diaz, Cameron, 154
di Giovanni, Janine, 99
Dillon, Patrick, 91–4, 98, 162–3,
    167, 171, 172–3, 176, 188,
    190, 192–3
    deportation of, 202–3, 211
Diyala, 255
Doha, 380, 445
Donkey Boy *see* Sloan, Gordon
Dorsetshire Regiment, 114
Douri, Izzat Ibrahim al-, 404
Dubai, 405
Dulaimi tribe, 128
Dworzak, Thomas, 216, 369

Eichmann, Karl Adolf, 77–8
ElBaradei, Mohamed, 155
electricity, 238, 343, 374–5, 378, 389
e-mail, 96
Enver, Pasha, 125
Epic of Saddam (Bashir), 146, 168,
    350, 365

Era of Saddam Hussein, 17
Ernst, Max, 343
Essex Regiment, 114

F-15 fighter jets, 285
F-18 fighter jets, 279
Faily Kurd, 52
Fairfield, England, 222
Faisal I, king of Iraq, 129
Faisal II, king of Iraq, 1
Faleh (Bashir's cousin), 144–5, 164,
    355–6
Fallujah, 128, 376, 378–9, 384,
    392–9, 423, 431, 435–6, 439,
    442
    Little Detroit neighborhood of,
        393–7
Fardous Square, 239, 304, 315, 328,
    354, 367
Fatima, 59
Eaw, 196
FBI, 419
fedayeen, 304, 325, 372
*Fire This Time, The: U.S. War Crimes
    in the Gulf* (Clark), 85
First Marines, 299–301
Fisk, Robert, 180
Ford, Harrison, 155
Foreign Ministry, Iraqi, 140, 190,
    328, 358, 361
Foreign Press Office, Iraqi, 6, 71–2,
    289
    personnel changes at, 73–4
Fox News, 391
France, 94, 137
Franks, Tommy, 220–1, 367
Freidl, Zack, 394
friendly fire, 216

Gaidy, Sheikh Fadel al-, 438–40
Galloway, George, 240
Ganci, Dan, 393, 394, 396–7
Garrels, Anne, 99, 179
Gaza, 99, 318
Geneva, 361

Germany, 94, 388
Ghazali, Hamid al-, 171
Ghazali, Majid al-, 171–2
Ghazali children, 163, 167, 171
GI Bill, 399
Gilgamesh, 20
Global Positioning Systems (GPS),
    175, 356
Godard, Jean-Luc, 92
Goldenberg, Suzanne, 180
Graham, Patrick, 179
Great Britain, 7, 8, 10, 27, 36, 51,
    64, 103, 116, 126, 127–30,
    136, 162, 164, 175, 212–13,
    357, 376, 380
    colonial rule in Iraq of, 112–13
    1920 revolt against, 103, 108
    World War I invasion of Iraq by,
        110–13, 196
Green Brigades, 440
Green Party (Turkey), 86
Green Zone, 388, 417, 420, 447
Guantánamo Bay, prison at, 362
Guardian, 180
Guernica, 82
Guevara, Che, 9, 426
Gulf War, 13–14, 17, 24, 25, 27,
    29–30, 34, 37, 100, 106, 123,
    180, 182, 327, 334, 360, 371,
    388, 408
    reign of terror after, 101, 387

Habré, Hissène, 13
Hadithi, Naji Sabri al-, 76, 155, 362
Haider, Jörg, 392
haircuts, Iraqi, 76
Hakim, Abdulaziz al-, 55, 57, 424,
    440
    assassination attempt against, 59
Hakim, Ayatollah Muhammad Bakr
    al-, 54–9, 403, 411
Hakim, Grand Ayatollah Mohsen al-,
    54
Halabja, 36
Halaj, Mujabel Sahel Awad al-, 258

Hamas, 438
hammam, 113
Hammurabi, 20
Hamoud, Abed, 83, 362
Hands of Victory Pavilion, 12
Hashemite dynasty, 10, 129
Hassan, 125
Hassan, crown prince of Jordan, 2, 416, 441
Hassan, Kassim Mussin, 19
Health Ministry, Iraqi, 357, 376, 383
Heart of Darkness (Conrad), 92–3, 167, 217
Heche, Anne, 155
Heckfield Place, 35–7
heroin, 45
Hicks, Tyler, 174, 178, 181, 189, 200, 265, 295
Hidden Imam *see* Twelfth Imam
Higareda, Jim, 299, 300
High Sierras, 300
Highway of Death, 31
hijab, 44
Hikmet, Abu, 29, 31, 32–3
Hillah, 266, 269
Hillal, 73
Hilsum, Lindsey, 180
Hiroshima, 82
history, teaching of, 27–8
Hitler, Adolf, 34, 77, 78
Holocaust, 77
hospitals, obligatory visits to, 29
human rights organizations, 35
human shields, 86–9, 116–17, 152, 166, 167, 175, 190, 238–9
 deployment sites of, 88–9
Husein, Imam, 115, 242, 342, 425, 429
Hussein, king of Jordan, 2
Hussein, Qusay, 160, 162, 165, 166, 175, 240, 286, 333
 death of, 391
Hussein, Saddam, 41, 51, 77–9, 91, 104–6, 117, 146, 220, 236, 254,
 280, 286, 299, 328, 371, 386, 401, 406
 alleged stealing of, 359
 aphorisms of, 26, 273
 appearance of, 349
 assumption of power by, 10
 author's possible sighting of, 244–5
 Bashir and, 75, 84, 146, 160, 308–9, 327, 331–8, 343, 346–52, 366, 377, 384, 385
 birth of, 112
 brutality of, 21
 Bush's ultimatum to, 168–9
 capacity for mercy of, 22–3
 cult of, 17–20
 doubles used by, 190
 gift collection of, 13, 125
 health of, 250
 hostage taking as tactic of, 100
 hunt for, 357, 380
 injuries of, 334
 interest in supernatural of, 159–60
 Iraqi modernization campaign of, 11–12
 Kamal's defection and, 159–60
 loyalty referendum of, 65, 72–3, 79, 102
 monuments built by, 82
 mosques built by, 16–17, 190
 national anthem meeting of, 117–18
 nuclear weapons procurement program, 159
 obsession with Iran, 38
 palace-building obsession of, 14–16
 palaces of, 201, 312–15
 political theater of, 7
 portraits of, 17–19, 313
 post-air strike public appearances of, 197
 post-Gulf War invisibility of, 17
 prisoner release of, 3–7
 public monuments of, 145–7, 235

Hussein, Saddam – *cont.*
    purges by, 10, 21–3
    Rather interview with, 85–6
    rise to power of, 2
    rumors about, 382
    rural values of, 107
    safe houses of, 327
    senior officials as hostages of, 158
    Shiites slaughtered by, 408
    television reruns of, 71
    tunnel network of, 95
    war strategy of, 227–8
    youthful bravery of, 119
Hussein, Sajida, 151
Hussein, Uday, 71, 76, 84, 86, 98,
        160, 250, 260, 286, 295, 312,
        346, 348–9, 358, 361
    death of, 391
Husseini, Haydar, 428

Ibrahim, Ghassam, 332
Imam Ali mosque, 388, 411, 423
Independent, 174, 180
Information Ministry, Iraqi, 6–7,
        69–71, 78, 96, 102, 136, 140,
        165, 167, 175, 177, 181, 189,
        191, 206, 211, 217, 225, 244,
        261, 281, 316, 370, 389–91
    as bombing target, 189
    bus tours of, 228–9
    destruction of, 245–6
    move into Palestine Hotel of, 203
    payoffs to, 173–4
    takeover by security agents of, 165
Inmarsat satellite, 96
International Atomic Energy
        Commission, 156
International Red Cross, 239
Internet, 96
    cafés, 96, 182
    see also e-mail
intifada, 99
Iran, 23, 35, 387, 405, 407, 411
    changing nature of, 41
    distrust of U.S. in, 39–41

drug use in, 44–5
Iraq and, 38–9
Iraqi refugees in, 39, 48–54
Persian Iraqi refugees in, 51–4
political system in, 42
possible U.S. war against, 39–41
repression in, 42–3
sharia in, 44
Shiite Iraqi refugees in, 39
student protests in, 42–3
unemployment rate in, 43
see also Iran-Iraq War
Iran-Iraq War, 30, 38, 48–9, 51–4,
        68, 69, 333
    chemical weapons used in, 36
    as instigated by U.S., 49
    suicide volunteers in, 46–7
Iraq, 40–1, 47, 54
    ancient culture of, 20
    anthem meeting in, 117–18
    British rule in, 112–13
    compared to Soviet Union, 365
    corruption in, 69–70
    cynicism in, 9, 28
    fear of Saddam in, 7, 8–9, 14–23,
        79
    Iran and, 38–9
    Kuwait invasion by, 106
    migrant workers in, 68
    military zones of, 162
    national anthem of, 117–18
    1920 anticolonial revolt in, 13,
        127–9, 410, 439
    1958 revolution in, 10
    1991 uprising in, 48, 49, 335–6
    offer of 'accelerated cooperation' of,
        155
    oil in, 9, 10, 103, 220, 439
    peace activists in, 89–91
    people of *see* Iraqi people
    relations with U.S. of, 362
    Shiite Muslims in, 38–9, 40
    state-run TV in, 71
    teaching of history in, 27–8
    UN sanctions on, 24, 89

U.S. policy toward, 25–6
U.S. soldiers captured in, 216
weapons of mass destruction of, 25, 33, 36
Iraq Daily, 26, 71, 110, 113, 272–3
Iraqi Air Defense Ministry, 148
Iraqi Airways, 65, 371
Iraqi Army, 276, 415
Iraqi Communist Party, 364, 402
Iraqi Embassy, DC., 391
Iraqi Embassy, London, 198–9
Iraqi Embassy, Vienna, 157–8
Iraqi Governing Council, 400, 409–11, 429, 437
Iraqi National Symphony Orchestra, 171
Iraqi Olympic Committee, 295–7
Iraqi people
  prewar passivity of, 142–3
  pride of, 7–8
  response to occupation of, 108–9
  view of U.S. politics of, 139
Iraqi Radio and Television Corporation, 70, 226, 233
Iraquian Former Political Prisoners Association, 403
Iraq Victims Compassion Campaign, 370
Iraq War (2003), 7, 8, 35, 56–7, 62–3, 90–1, 94
  alleged capture of pilots in, 208, 211–12
  Aziz's claims about, 219–21
  bombing patterns in, 222
  civilian casualties in, 204–6, 227, 250–4, 266–7, 269, 274, 276, 290–2
  coalition demands before, 137, 140
  competing battlefield claims in, 224
  defensive preparations in, 137
  first bombings in, 188, 189, 190–1
  initial troop movements in, 196
  Iraqi claims of victories in, 247–8

Iraqi strategy in, 227–8
  'shock and awe' tactics in, 200–1
  start of, 144–5
  timing of, 64
  U.S. occupation after, 108–9
  U.S. plane supposedly shot down in, 213–15
  U.S. preparations for, 64
Ishtar Sheraton, 70
Islamic Call, 56
Islamic foundations, 43
Islamic fundamentalism, 108, 121
Israel, 3, 13, 103, 158, 220, 437
Issam (driver), 373, 379
ITN network, 180

Jabbar, Jassim Obeid, 110
Jadiriyah palace complex, 98
Jaffar, Muhammad, 358–9
Jamaluddin, Ayad, 404–7, 440–2
James (Sudanese room cleaner), 287–8
Japan, 116
Jawad, Mr., 27
Jesus Christ, 47, 61
Jews, 62, 366, 437 *see also* anti-Semitism
jihad, 439
Jihad (driver), 143, 341, 382
jihadis, 239, 269–70, 295
  Palestinian, 309
Jordanian Embassy, 341, 411
journalists, 70, 84–6, 95–7, 116, 189, 266, 371
  arrests at border of, 174–5, 178
  arrests of, 225–6
  assaults on, 302
  blunder committed by, 74
  bribes given by, 72–3, 74
  bus tours of, 266, 280–1
  chemical weapons awareness training of, 35–7
  communication difficulties of, 96, 210–11
  deaths of, 288–93

journalists – *cont.*
  deportations of, 211
  embedded, 72
  exodus of, 162, 165–6
  guides assigned to, 14, 72–3
  as hostages, 100, 153, 165
  hotel restrictions on, 165–7
  hotel room frenzy of, 95–6, 97–8
  human shield pretense of, 98–9
  Iraqi, 71
  missing, 264–5
  possible use as human shields of, 167
  pressure to leave Iraq on, 152–3
  prewar influx of, 73
  regime's intentions toward, 168
  remaining in Baghdad, 179–80
  reported casualties among, 216
  restrictions on, 192, 210, 246,
    261, 440
  travel difficulties of, 136
  vulnerability of, 100
Jubour, Khalaf al-, 401–2
Jubour, Sheikh Ibrahim al-, 380,
  400–1
Jubouri, Amal, 388
Jubour tribe, 380–1, 400
Judah, Tim, 179
Jumeil, Salman Amoud, 255
Jumhuriyah Bridge, 281, 287, 293,
  302, 368

Kabul, 291, 369
Kadhimiyah mosque, 424, 433
Kala, 257
Kalthum, Um, 121
Kamal, Hussein, 334
  defection of, 159–60
Kamal, Saddam, 160, 334
Kaplow, Larry, 179, 239
Karbala, 342, 429
  Battle of, 115, 268, 269, 270
Karim (barber), 66–7, 259–60, 288,
  302, 371, 373
Karzai, Hamid, 124
Kelly, Kathy, 240, 246

Kenya, embassy bombing in, 85
Khadum (Mukhabarat official), 73–4,
  75, 260, 289, 391
Khairi, Samir, 140, 147, 154–5, 169,
  328, 338–9, 357–63, 366, 385,
  412, 445–7
Khalid (author's minder), 102, 107,
  113, 115–16, 150
Khameini, Ayatollah Ali, 39, 42, 55
Khandhari, 130
Khatami, Ayatollah Muhammad, 42,
  43
Khazraji, Nizar al-, 170–1
Khifa (translator), 295, 298–9, 304
Khoei, Abdel Majid al-, 406–7, 423,
  442
Khomeini, Ayatollah Ruhollah,
  42–3, 46, 55, 59, 405
Khorramshahr, 48
Khuzistan, 48–51
Kipling, Rudyard, 111
Kirkuk, 196, 324, 369
Korani, Sheikh Ali al-, 60–3
Kozyrev, Yuri, 179
Kufa, 429–31, 434
Kurds, 25, 38, 41, 57, 162, 258,
  369, 411
  peshmerga militia of 196
  poison gas attacks on, 170
Kut, 125, 137–8
  British cemetery in, 138–9
  siege of, 111, 125, 139, 268, 338
Kut War Cemetery, 138–9
Kuwait, 2, 24, 27, 31, 49, 64,
  106–7, 158, 193, 356, 391
Kuwait City, 339

Lathikia restaurant, 207, 283
Lawrence, T.E., 13, 112–13, 125,
  127, 128
Leachman, Gerard Evelyn, 13, 125–9,
  130, 131, 132, 133–6, 409
  assassination of, 128, 329
Lebanon, 407
Le May, Curtis, 93

Lenin, V.I., 365–7
Lenin's Embalmers, 365–7
  Light Armored Vehicles, 296, 300
Lion (Mukhabarat agent), 29, 31–2
Liu, Melinda, 174, 178
Lloyd, Terry, 216
looting, 294–9, 301–2, 307, 310–11,
    323, 339–40, 352, 367–8, 376,
    387
Los Angeles Times, 102, 179

McAllester, Matthew, 98–9, 200, 264
  disappearance of, 225, 239–40
McCoy, Brian, 310
McGeough, Paul, 97–8, 166, 169,
    173–4, 182, 186, 191–2, 207,
    209–10, 222, 224–5, 236–7,
    240, 248, 255, 260, 291, 295,
    329, 331, 368, 371
Machiavelli, Niccolò, 41
Madame Sabah, 219, 368
Mahdi *see* Twelfth Imam
Mahdi Army, 426–7, 430, 433
Majid, Ali Hassan al-, 162, 193
Mansour, 183–4, 274, 286, 308–9,
    340, 361, 403
Mansour Hotel, 70, 165, 166, 189
manteau, 44
Marcos, Maria, 284
Marines, U.S., 292–3, 296–7, 304,
    310, 358, 370–1
  First Division of, 423
marj'iya, 61
Marouf, Professor, 28
martyrdom, 247, 259
martyr's brigade, 161
masgouf, 122
Maude, Stanley, 110–11, 113,
    114–15, 136
Mazas, Jacques Féréol, 171
media
  allegations of Zionist control of, 77
  Defense Department warnings to,
    191–2
  see also journalists

Medical Union of Iraq, 344
Médicins du Monde, 250
Mehdi, Ra'ad Abdel Latif, 206
Mehrdad (translator), 49
Melia hotel chain, 70
Melia Mansour *see* Mansour Hotel
'Mesopotamia' (Kipling), 111
Mesopotamian Expeditionary Force,
    110
Meynell, Godfrey, 87, 89
Mill, John Stuart, 34
Miller, James, 99
Milo_evi_, Slobodan, 85
minders, 69, 72, 165, 190, 247, 261
Ministry of Culture and Islamic
    Guidance, Iranian, 39, 124, 386
Ministry of Justice, Iraqi, 303
Ministry of Oil, Iraqi, 294, 301
Ministry of Trade, Iraqi, 296, 298
Mohebian, Amir, 39–42
Mohsen, 73, 203, 289, 371, 389–90
money changers, 68–9, 234
Montazar, Abu, 298
Moore, Michael, 232
Moran, Paul, 216
mosques, 16–17
  Saddam's half-built, 190
  see also specific mosques
Mother of All Battles mosque, 408,
    435, 438
Mount Lebanon hotel, bombing of,
    418–20
MSNBC, 85
Muhammad, Prophet, 1, 2, 61, 407
Mujahedin-i-Khalq, 312
mujahideen, 55, 439
Mukhabarat, 9, 21, 23, 29, 70, 73,
    190, 192, 200, 208, 215, 235,
    321, 322, 328, 360–4, 369,
    391, 401–3
  prison of 321–2, 361
Mukhtar, Mokhaled, 18–19
Muntafiq clan, 1–2, 126, 127
Museum of Natural History, 374
Mushaqi, Khalil Salah al-, 255–7

Mushaqi tribe, 257
Muslih, Mouayed al-, 437
Muslim (author's minder), 131–3, 135, 137, 138, 165, 180–1
Mustafa, Salaar, 14, 16–17, 21, 72, 102, 208–9, 268–9, 275–6, 371
Mustansiriyah Medical College, 204
Mustansiriyah University, 375
Mutanabbi (Iraq poet), 334
Muyad, 231–2
Myanmar, 44
My Best Friend's Wedding, 154

Nabil (physical therapist), 223–4, 227, 236, 263, 314
Nabil restaurant, 163
Nachtwey, Jim, 85, 179, 192, 210
Nadhmi, Wamidh Omar, 105–8
Najaf, 59, 212, 220, 247, 269, 398, 406–7, 424, 430, 442
narghile (waterpipe) café, 67–8
Nasiriyah, 212, 213, 220, 224, 227
National Geographic Explorer, 85
nationalism, 121
National Museum, 339
National Post, 179
National Public Radio, 179
NBC, 162, 174, 178
Nebuchadnezzar, 20
Neda, 285–6
Nelson, Craig, 179
nerve gas, 36
New Islamic architecture, 11
Newsday, 98, 200
Newsweek, 174
New York, 356
New Yorker, 35, 97, 152, 167, 173, 179
New York Review of Books, 179
New York Times, 85, 173, 431, 435
9/11 attacks, 88
Nineveh, 20
no-fly zones, 25, 28, 116
North Gate War Cemetery, 113–15, 136
Nuri, Ali, 49–50

oil fires, 229, 249, 315
oil industry, 90–1
    in Iraq, 10, 103, 220, 439
    in Kuwait, 2, 24
O'Keefe, Ken, 87–9, 117
Olympic Hospital, 348–9
O'Malley, Heathcliff, 99, 165, 174
Omar, Rageh, 180
OPEC, 156
Operation Iraqi Freedom, 420
opium, 44
Oscar ceremony, Moore's antiwar speech at, 232
Ottoman Turks, 10, 103, 110–13, 126
Owja, 119, 361

Pagetti, Franco, 425, 429, 431–2
Pakistan, 407
palaces, 14–16, 351
    protection of, 15–16
    Saddam, 14–16, 201, 312–15
    see also specific palaces
Palestine, 62, 103
Palestine Hotel, 95, 98, 156, 165, 169, 170, 176, 177, 187, 188, 189–90, 192, 194, 203–4, 208, 237, 238, 270, 274, 293–4, 304, 310, 370–2, 417, 421, 427, 432–3, 440
    author's room in, 209–10
    French television crew's arrival at, 216
    jihadis staying at, 239
    as official press center, 246
    rocket attack on, 413
    room rates at, 166
    shelling of, 288–90
Palestine Meridien, 70
Pasquale, Paul, 289, 292, 309–10, 320
peace activists, 89–91
peaceniks, 190, 191, 238
'peacenik' visas, 181, 225
peace patrols, 240
Persian Iraqis, atrocities committed against, 51–4

Petit Soldat (film), 92
Philby, H. St. John, 127–8
Philby, Kim, 127
Planning Ministry, Iraqi, 190, 192, 287, 368
Pollack, Kenneth, 34–5
Powell, Colin, 110, 162, 345, 433
preemptive war, 87
Première Urgence, 310
Presidential Institute, Department of Research in, 360
press IDs, 246
Primakov, Yevgeny, 86
prisoner amnesty, 79–80
prisoner release, 3–7
    missing prisoners from, 79
propaganda, 25–8, 70
protests, 6–7, 79–80
Protsyuk, Taras, 289
psychological warfare officer, 395–6
public monuments, 11–14, 82
Pyramids food shop, 225, 236

Qaddafi, Muammar, 13
Qassem, Abdul Karim, 12, 199
Qatar, 64, 380, 382, 392, 412
Qom, 59–60
Queen's Gate Mews, 198
quzi sham, 68

Radio Monte Carlo, 170
Raed, Sheikh, 426–7, 434
Raining Planes, 91–2
RAI 3 television, 5
Ramadan, Taha Yassin, 247, 259
    press conference of, 212–13, 216
Ramadi, 174, 178, 180, 212, 257, 328, 378–9, 399, 439
Rather, Dan, 85–6, 226–7, 370
razaq, 120
Razaq, Abdul, 131–2, 133–5
Razuki, Haq Ismael, 241
Reagan, Ronald, 13
Red Crescent, 307, 321, 430, 435
    maternity hospital of, 267–8

Reed, Oliver, 135
refugees, 35, 51, 54
Regan, Pete, 299–300
Remnick, David, 173, 179
Republican Guard, 21, 103, 142, 182, 220, 226, 227, 271, 272, 276, 294
Republican Palace complex, 15–16, 95, 141, 207, 215, 249, 273, 293, 326, 367, 386, 402
    battle for, 277–88
Resalat, 39
Return to the Marshes, 157
Reuters, 288–9, 309
Revolutionary Command Council, 17
Romania, 10
Roy, Ruth Lee, 13
Rumsfeld, Donald, 110, 155, 233–4
running water, 238, 375, 378
Russia, 94, 110
Ruzicka, Marla, 369–70
Rwanda, 85

Saad (Burns's minder), 181–2, 265
Sabri, Naji, 117, 156, 175–6, 212, 391–2
    author's first meeting with, 156–8
    execution of brother of, 158
    transformation of, 156, 158
Sachet, Kamal, 350
Saddam Arts Center, 18, 352
Saddam Center for Fine Arts, 114
Saddam Center for Reconstructive Surgery, 76, 346
Saddam City, 294–9, 317–20, 342, 387, 406
    looting in, 294–8
Saddam Fedayeen, 227–8, 398, 402, 428
Saddam International Airport, 14, 373, 382, 383, 442
    battle of, 271, 272, 326
    U.S. capture of, 273, 274
Saddam Teaching Hospital, 29

Saddam Telecommunications Tower, 178, 190, 235

Sadoun, Abdul Mohsen al-, 8

Sadoun, Ajaimi al-, 127

Sadoun, Nasra al-, 26–7, 70–1

Sadoun, Nasser al-, 1–3, 7–8, 33, 88–9, 108, 126–7, 415

Sadoun, Tamara al-, 1–3, 416

Sadoun Pasha, Ibn, 126–7

Sadoun Street, 66, 177, 222–3, 240, 261, 280, 302, 312, 315, 427

Sadr, Imam Muhammed Bakr al-, 55–6, 60, 319, 342, 403

Sadr, Moqtada al-, 406–7, 423–32, 434, 438, 441–2

Sadr City, 319, 387, 406, 432–3

Safwan, 31

Sahaf, Muhammad Said al-, 74, 245–6, 269, 272, 274, 281–2
  press briefings of, 233–4, 270, 279–80

St. Andrews University, 106

Salaah, 371–2

Salaam Palace, 329, 351

Salahuddin the Conqueror, 20, 112

Salam (author's friend), 419, 425–6, 430–1, 435, 438–40

Saleh, Osama, 249–54, 290–1

Salih (translator), 408–9, 411

Salloum, Farouk, 117, 118–24, 156, 233, 385–8

Saman, Behlul, 32–3

Salman, Um, 285

Salman (hotel desk manager), 178, 195, 207

Saman, Moses, 98–100, 200, 264
  disappearance of, 225, 239–40

Samarra, 323

Samarrai, Muhammad, 301–2

Samawa, 220

Sami (author's minder), 255, 258
  diabetes of, 262–4

San Francisco Chronicle, 179

Sassanian empire, 111

satellite telephones, 73, 96, 174, 210, 211, 217
  Thuraya, 174–5, 192, 327, 340, 355, 382

satellite television, 71

satphones see satellite telephones

Saudi Arabia, 13, 26, 126

Sauds, 126

Sayaff, Abu, 232

scaremongering, 152

Scud missiles, 13

Seaforth Highlanders, 114

Sengupta, Kim, 174, 178, 180

Serwan restaurant, 268

Seven Pillars of Wisdom (Lawrence), 112–13

Shadid, Anthony, 179

Shah, Saira, 99

Shahbander, Samira, 334

Shakir, Behjet, 22–3

Shamzedin, Professor, 27–8

Sheraton Hotel, 235, 246, 248–9, 261, 270, 274, 286, 304, 316, 329, 370

Shiite Muslims, 25, 38–9, 41, 47, 54–5, 59, 60, 61, 162, 336, 342, 359, 380, 387, 404–6, 408, 410, 421, 424, 429, 432, 35, 447
  role of religious leadership among, 61–2

'shock and awe' bombing campaign, 104, 200–1

Shroud of Turin, 82

Simon, Joel, 179, 240

Sinak Bridge, 261, 281, 287, 302–3

Sistani, Grand Ayatollah Ali al-, 60, 341, 406, 430
  police surveillance of, 61

Six Days, Seven Nights, 155

Skull and Bones Society, 88

Sky television, 204

Sloan, Gordon, 87

Soheila (Bashir's sister), 326, 331, 338, 353–4, 357, 364, 379, 383

Soviet Union, 198
Special Republican Guard, 142, 162
Stalin, Joseph, 365
Stark, Freya, 109
Steele, Jonathan, 180
Steffa (American woman), 403–4
Straw, Jack, 137
suicide bomber, 216, 247, 272
suicide bombings, 411, 412
Sumerian dynasty, 20
Sunduz, 196, 224, 308, 309, 311, 344–5
Sunni Muslims, 38, 41, 57, 121, 376, 380, 387, 408, 435
Sunni Triangle, 376, 378
Supreme Council for Islamic Revolution in Iraq (SCIRI), 54, 55, 58, 403
    Bush administration talks with, 58
Swain, Jon, 85, 180
Sydney Morning Herald, 97
Syria, 386

Taiee, Ala al-, 421–2
Taiee, Diyah al-, 101, 188, 219, 262, 274
Taiee, Sabah al-, 65–70, 97–8, 100–2, 113, 116, 125, 129, 150–1, 162, 164–5, 171, 175–6, 182, 185, 190, 192–4, 207–8, 236, 260–2, 267–8, 274, 295, 302–4, 310–12, 315–16, 323, 325, 331, 340, 371–2, 373–4, 375, 382, 412, 414
    Al-Saah bombing and, 282–3, 286
    on American bombing, 203
    and American parachutist, 215–16
    brother's death and, 364, 368
    on coalition POWs, 212
    daughter's miscarriage and, 218
    family of, 187–8
    love of bright colors of, 209
    pride in Iraq of, 247–8
    in Saddam City, 317–20
    son's kidnapping and, 421–2

Taiee, Safaar al-, 188, 219, 262, 274
Taiee, Taher al-, 151, 364, 368
Taiee, Uday al-, 74–5, 181, 203, 207–8, 212, 216–17, 233, 265, 274–5, 283, 289, 388–91
    escape of, 370–1
    on missing journalists, 264–5
    and restrictions on journalists, 165, 192, 210, 217, 246–7, 255
Talabani, Jalal, 440
Taliban, 40, 369
Tanzania, embassy bombing in, 85
Taras, 309
Tawfik, Samir Khairi, 81
Taylor, Charles, 85
Tehran, 43, 45–7, 51
Telecinco, 289
telepathy, 159–60
telephones, 237–8
    satellite, 73, 96, 174, 210, 211, 217
terrorism, 34 see also War on Terror
Thawra, 387–8
Thesiger, Wilfred, 109, 157
Thomas, Lowell, 125
Threatening Storm, The: The Case for Invading Iraq (Pollack), 34
Thuraya satphones, 174–5, 192, 327, 340, 355, 382 see also satellite telephones
Tigris River, 11, 70, 95, 112, 261, 281, 313, 368, 373, 404
Tikrit, 112, 117, 119, 151, 162, 323, 329, 358, 365, 369, 387, 413
Tikriti, Barzan al-, 84, 328, 333, 352, 359–62, 365, 366, 386
Tomb of the Unknown Soldier (Baghdad), 11–12, 270
traffic policemen, 182, 373
Transport Ministry, Iraqi, 294–7
tribalism, 121
Triumph Leader Museum, 12–14, 125, 130, 329–30, 351
truck gardens, 234
Trudeau, Pierre, 179

Trudeau, Sasha, 179
tunnel network, 95
turah, 113, 116, 137, 176, 217, 221–2, 225, 229, 234
Turkey, 112
Turkish baths, 113
Turkish Embassy, 114
Turkomans, 57
Twelfth Imam, 47, 61

Um al-Marik (Mother of All Battles) gallery, 13
Um Asil, 52–4
Um Qasr, 196, 197, 220, 224, 227, 233, 446
Undheim, Stein, 34
Union Between the Leader and His People, The (Bashir), 83, 146, 341
United Nations, 108, 140, 162, 213, 345
   General Assembly, 356
   headquarters in Iraq, 411
   proposed war resolution of, 164
   sanctions regime of, 24, 26, 28, 158
   Security Council of, 94, 155
   weapons inspectors of, 116, 159
United States, 7–8, 9, 24–5, 26–7, 28, 36, 37–8, 42, 51, 62, 90–1, 116, 120, 137, 162, 164, 175, 198, 212–13, 219–20
   bombing Taliban by, 123–4
   entry into Baghdad of, 273–6, 277–306, 327, 367
   ignorance about Iraq of, 109, 120
   Iraq's relations with, 362
   lack of support for Iraq uprising of, 50
   policy toward Iraq of, 25–6
   standoff with Iraq of, 106
Ur, 20, 69
uranium, depleted, weapons tipped with, 29

U.S. embassy, in Afghanistan, 370

Vienna, 391
Vietnam War, 8, 90, 92
Virginia, 391
visa extensions, 73, 75
Vodjanikova, Alexandra, 86
Voices in the Wilderness, 89, 240
volunteer martyrs, 247, 259

Wag the Dog, 272
Wahhabite Muslims, 121
Waleed, Dr. see Abdulmajid, Waleed
Walid, 262
Walken, Christopher, 94
War on Terror, 25–6, 88, 90, 413
Washington, D.C., 382, 391
Washington Post, 173, 179
Wazaty, Hassan al-, 139
weapons of mass destruction, 25, 259, 440 see also biological weapons; chemical weapons
Wesley, Eric, 392–3, 399
Wilayat-al-Faquih, 61
Wild, Richard, 374
Wilhelm, Travis, 393–4, 398–9
women
   in Iran, 44
   Iraqis' view of, 384
World War I, 110, 128–9
   British invasion of Iraq in, 110–13, 196

Yarmuk Hospital, 271
yas, 138
Yassin, Sheikh Ahmed, 438
Young, Gavin, 157
Youth TV, 71

Zawa Park, 368
Zhirinovsky, Vladimir, 13
Zoba tribe, 128